THE BONDS OF MATRIMONY/
HSING-SHIH YIN-YÜAN CHUAN
(VOL. ONE),
A SEVENTEENTH-CENTURY CHINESE NOVEL

Translated by

Eve Alison Nyren

Chinese Studies
Volume 1

The Edwin Mellen Press
Lewiston/Queenston/Lampeter

895.13
P976h-T

Library of Congress Cataloging-in-Publication Data

P' u, Sung-ling, 1640-1715.
    [Hsing shih yin yüan. English]
    The bonds of matrimony = Hsing shih yin yuan chuan : a seventeenth
century Chinese novel / translated by Eve Alison Nyren.
        p.   cm.
    Includes bibliographical references.
    ISBN 0-7734-9033-7
    I. Nyren, Eve Alison, 1954- . II. Title.
PL2722.U2H813   1995
895.1'348--dc20   94-37609
                                                                           CIP

This is volume 1 in the continuing series
Chinese Studies
Volume 1 ISBN 0-7734-9033-7
ChS Series ISBN 0-88946-076-0

A CIP catalog record for this book is available from the British Library.

    The Edwin Mellen Press   The Edwin Mellen Press
            Box 450   Box 67
    Lewiston, New York   Queenston, Ontario
    USA 14092-0450   CANADA L0S 1L0

                    The Edwin Mellen Press, Ltd.
                      Lampeter, Dyfed, Wales
                    UNITED KINGDOM SA48 7DY

            Printed in the United States of America

96 -5102
ADA-3682

Contents

Acknowledgements vii

Translator's Note ix

Preface xiii

Chapter One 1
　Ch'ao Yüan encloses a hunting ground and goes shooting
　A fox spirit is shot dead with his arrow

Chapter Two 17
　Ch'ao Yüan falls ill in consequence of slaughtering a fox
　Dr. Yang practices slapdash quackery

Chapter Three 29
　An Old Pedant appears twice in Dreams
　Ch'ao Yüan wants only to flee to his Parents

Chapter Four 41
　Hermit T'ung bows and scrapes
　Chen ko fans lust and miscarries

Chapter Five 57
　A Magistrate bribes his way from Sub-prefecture to District
　An Actor uses his influence at the Civil Board

Chapter Six 71
　Chen ko possesses her servant
　Ch'ao Yüan buys a position in the capital

Chapter Seven 85
　The Old Mistress Accepts a whore for the love of her Son
　The Young Master Runs Away abandoning his Parents

Chapter Eight 99
　A fast-talking concubine seductively leads her master into error
　A benighted academician foolishly throws his wife aside

Chapter Nine 117
An Ordinary Wife has no recourse but Suicide
An Old Widower finds redress at Court

Chapter Ten 131
An Academician offers a Bribe
A Sub-prefectural Magistrate Accepts a Gift

Chapter Eleven 145
Ms. Chi's Spirit Appears and Speaks
A Cruel Official Sees ghosts and Grows boils

Chapter Twelve 159
Circuit Intendant Li goes on a tour of Inspection and Takes up a case
Judge Ch'u upholds the law and overturns a previous judgement

Chapter Thirteen 177
Judge Ch'u Completes the Committal
Intendant Li Passes Sentence

Chapter Fourteen 191
An idyll in jail
A birthday party on death row

Chapter Fifteen 203
A cruel man scorches the earth around his victims
A heartless fellow turns his face away from those in need

Chapter Sixteen 215
An Honorable Man must finish what he has begun
A wise mother can see where it will all end

Chapter Seventeen 229
A fevered man grows empty-hearted and sees a ghost
A venal official gives up his position and goes home

Chapter Eighteen 243
A rich and Influential Man makes a topsy-turvy marriage proposal
A young gentleman buries two at once in a double funeral

Chapter Nineteen 257
Ch'ao Yüan plots his way to another man's wife
Little Ya splits a pair of heads

Chapter Twenty 271
Ch'ao Yüan comes home in a dream
Magistrate Hsü uproots evil on the road

Selected Bibliography 289

Acknowledgements

This translation is intended for people who cannot easily read the Chinese original, not for sinologists who will form their judgements of the novel from original texts rather than any translation. I do not know if my many excellent teachers will approve of my translation, but it would not have been possible without all they taught me. In particular, I would like to thank the late Charles Lo, who taught me at Hunter College and Columbia University and to whom I owe my basic competency in Chinese language; Professor Hans Bielenstein at Columbia, who taught the one best language course I ever took; Professor C.T. Hsia at Columbia who encouraged me and decisively influenced my decision to specialize in literature rather than linguistics; and, most of all, Professor Andrew Plaks at Princeton. Three years of Professor Plaks' seminars immeasureably enriched my understanding of all fiction. It was in his seminar that I first read *Hsing-shih Yin-yüan chuan*, of which I here translate the first twenty chapters. and my reading of the novel is much influenced by that seminar. I owe special thanks to Professor Atsuhide Sakakura of Kwansei Gakuin University. Though at the time I had no affiliation with his university or other claim to his consideration, Professor Sakakura was always ready to share his expertise in Ming dynasty history and bureaucracy. Lastly, thanks are also due to Dr. Fan Pen Chen at SUNY/ Albany, for constructive comments on the first three chapters in particular.

Translator's Note

Hsing-shih Yin-yüan chuan 醒世姻緣傳, which I have translated as *The Bonds of Matrimony* (hereafter *Bonds*), is an anonymous seventeenth-century Chinese novel almost certainly written closely after the fall of the Ming dynasty to the Manchus. The author calls himself A Follower of the Western Chou. The Western Chou period (about 1100-771 B.C.) was considered to exemplify many Confucian virtues; therefore we can infer that the author identifies himself with those virtues. Indeed, it would be almost impossible for any seventeenth-century literate Chinese man not to, any more than a modern writer of fiction would be likely to be against freedom of speech.

This novel was out of print for many years, perhaps because it is very long (this volume comprises the first twenty chapters; there are 100 in all) and has an unusually large lexicon, which would have made printing expensive in pre-modern times. Another probable reason is that the novel was just one of many. The seventeenth century saw a great increase in the amount of fiction published, and in later centuries in China critical opinion grew less disposed to consider fiction as a genre worth thinking about seriously.

We have the late Hu Shih 胡適 to thank for the novel's rescue from oblivion. Hu Shih declared that the novel was written in the dialect of central Shantung, and that it must therefore be by P'u Sung-ling 蒲松齡, a writer of fiction from that area who would have been alive around the right time. Further reasons for this attribution were supposed resemblances in story lines between the vernacular *Bonds* and stories in the classical idiom by P'u. Since then most scholarly attention to the novel has focussed on whether it is or is not by P'u, a well-known author.

It would be difficult to prove that P'u did not write it, but he certainly was not the only literate man in his area in the seventeenth century, and the supposed similarities between P'u's stories and *Bonds* are not impressive. In *Bonds*, there is a putative karmic flamework in which a fox spirit and wronged wife wreak revenge; there are also shrews in P'u's stories, karmic revenge, and fox spirits. However, in the novel, the karmic framework appears to be used merely as a structural convenience; everything attributable to karma is more convincingly attributable to mundane causes, and the narrator is consistently scornful of those who believe in Buddhism or use superstition as an excuse for not taking their own destinies contructively in hand. A modern example of a novel that similarly uses a karmic framework only to debunk it is Yukio Mishima's *Sea of Fertility* tetralogy. Obviously there is no direct connection between *Bonds* and Mishima's work; I raise the latter simply as an example of how a karmic framework can be conveniently exploited by an author who does not believe in karma superstitiously. In P'u's stories, however, there is more emphasis on the relation of mysterious and strange things outside quotidian experience.

Shrewish wives are stock characters in fiction all over the world; their appearance in two works is hardly indicative of relation between the works. Finally, looking at P'u's stories and this novel, we must remember that, to outsiders, products of a culture all have a great similarity; we are all outsiders to the seventeenth century of China, and, given the disappearance of many fictional works from that time, are liable to mistake zeitgeist for more meaningful resemblance.

In any case, it is fortunate that Hu Shih made his rather over-confident claim to identify authorship of *Bonds*. Thanks largely to this, the novel has been reprinted in several editions and is now much more easily available for study. It is well worth study, since up to now most research in Ming-Ching dynasty Chinese novels has focused on several novels from the sixteenth and eighteenth centuries. (This is obviously an unsatisfactory state of affairs. Would anyone think of a history of any Western literature that entirely omitted the seventeenth century? Why should we be so much more slip-shod in approaching Chinese literature?) Here is a novel that helps fill in the gap, and it is, moreover, literarily excellent in many parts.

Among Chinese novels, there is a development from those based somewhat on historical materials to increasing subjective works. For instance, the sixteenth-century *Shui-hu Chuan* 水滸傳 has some historical basis for the band of men whose adventures it describes: slightly later, *Chin P'ing Mei* 金瓶梅 has as its point of departure an episode from *Shui-hu Chuan*. *Chin P'ing Mei* chronicles the decadence of one household as rather pointed analogy to political decadence: in the eighteenth century, *Hung Lou Meng* 紅樓夢 likewise describes the decadence of a family with political implications, but with much more emphasis on subjectivity than existed in the earlier *Chin P'ing Mei*. As these novels were all famous, we can presume some influence on later ones by earlier ones, but their progression also shows general tendencies in Chinese novels per se, and *Bonds* fits chronologically and technically between *Chin P'ing Mei* and *Hung Lou Meng*. It, too, depicts domestic chaos as emblematic of a decay in the way of the world at large. It is less obviously indebted to earlier novels or historical sources than in the case of sixteenth-century novels, and not yet as strongly individual in voice as novels of the eighteenth century.

This tendency to subjectivity has also been noted in western novels, of course. The similarity gives rise to speculation that it is in the nature of long stories or novels to become more and more inward in focus simply as a function of genre. However, one basic difference between Chinese fiction and western is that the European novel arose largely out of genres such as diaries, pseudo-diaries, and collections of letters, whereas Chinese novels seem much closer to Chinese historiography in genesis than to any such autobiographical roots. Perhaps the fact that Japanese fiction, like western fiction, began as pseudo-diaries, explains partly why Japanese fiction has been so much more popular with western readers than Chinese fiction has.

Overall, Chinese fiction in the past has been less subjective and more socially concerned than western fiction, but still it did move to more individual concerns and philosophical trends in seventeenth century China, and putting greater emphasis on problems of personal guilt may have accelerated this tendency. *Bonds* seen in this light is discussed by Andrew Plaks in his article "After the Fall," which is listed in the selected bibliography following this translation.

In China, there is a long tradition of the importance of factually and morally accurate historical reportage. The historian was charged with the important task of recording what happened both as lessons for the future and to damn the reputations of evil men in power. Add to this the Confucian idea of the family as microcosm of the state, and of the successful functioning of the civilized world as depending on the collective virtue of educated elite men, and it becomes obvious that a tale of a bad man's domestic disorder must have wider implications for society at large, and that the author considers writing about such a negative example must have educative value.

In the preface to this novel, the author mentions a man of the State of Ch'i whose wife and concubine brought him to his senses, and says that the moral of the story is that a good wife is a prerequisite for a good man. In the novel, there are two major stories, each with a man, his wife and his concubine as major characters. The wives and concubines abuse their husbands. Does this show that their husbands have been prevented from being good by having married badly?

The parable of the man of Ch'i is taken from *Mencius* 孟子. In the original story, which was well-known to all literate Chinese in imperial China, and probably to many less literate, the end of the story is not that the wife and concubine reform their husband. Rather, when the wife learns that her husband's conduct is shameful, she returns home and, with the concubine, laments bitterly on the miserable lord and master that is their lot. Mencius draws the moral that few men who have succeeded in material terms have not caused their wives such distress. The wife and concubine are thus not agents of their husband's lack of virtue, but the truest witnesses to it. In the Confucian world order, men were responsible for order in the empire and in their families; lack of such order meant something was wrong with the men.

With the author's use of this parable in mind, his conscious ironic alteration of it, and the fact that he wrote the novel anonymously near the time China's last native dynasty was replaced by the Manchus, largely due to Chinese corruption, the reader will see that this is a lament for the end of the civilized world, and a chronicle of how the venality of minor men led to such a sorry conclusion.

Preface

In the *Four Books*, Mencius has written that there are three ultimate pleasures for the cultivated man. Can you imagine what pleasure would surpass that felt by a man if out of the blue someone came to him with the offer he be emperor? Maybe you don't know the indescribable levels of spiritual and emotional delight to which these three pleasures reach.

The pleasure of being an emperor is nothing but outward splendor, evanescent as foam on water. It isn't in the same class with these three pleasures. No power is strong enough to coerce these three into your possession and no riches can buy them. A spiritual man or a saintly one, a moral man or a philosopher, any and all will end well with these three pleasures, but if he lacks them, a man can go ahead wasting his energy pursuing the Ultimate Way or Sage Virtue, or he can behave impeccably and refine himself into great purity, or he can plunge into his studies and achieve all sorts of things there, but still he will be wanting.

Emperors Yao and Shun of the age of the five emperors, Yü who founded the Hsia dynasty and T'ang, founder of the Shang, Dukes Wen and Wu of the Western Chou, and, carrying on the tradition, the sage teacher Confucious, were all men who achieved the highest wisdom and spirituality, yet not one of them ever tasted the great happiness brought by these three pleasures. Ruling the empire can't even be compared to them. So, you may well ask, what are these three pleasures?

The first is to have both parents alive, and brothers living free of rancor. Think about it: a baby is born thanks to its parents. The baby is like a tender shoot easier to crush than to raise. Every moment the baby's parents concentrate their hearts on the dangers of fierce winds or pelting rains to that tender sprout. How much heartache they spend on guarding this oblivious consciousness! When the baby cries in distress, its parents are tormented by worry. They wear themselves out consoling their child, and their kindness is truly as great as all heaven.

A newborn baby is powerless to pay back the bottomless debt of gratitude it owes its parents. In his struggling years, a young man will be hard put to afford even a cup of water. When he matures into wealth and position is the time for him to return his parents' kindness. But what if they don't wait for him? If either or both of his parents die before he has a chance to care for them lovingly in their old age, even if he's an emperor you tell me whether or not he'll be happy when he thinks of those parental spirits gone to the underworld!

Brothers are born of the same father and mother. The only difference between them is order of birth. They share the same blood and breath of life. Often they become unequal in wealth. Then they may become locked in mortal competition, killing that same breath of life in jealous conflict. Brothers follow the ways of the age, treacherous as those ways may be, like a man riding a tiger. They cut all restraints of honor and fly at eachother. Isn't that a fine disregard for conscience! If a man is at war with brothers, even though he has achieved the highest official rank and gets to hold the axes of Tung Shan, like the Duke of Chou, is his a pleasurable or a painful situation?

When both parents are alive and well and in their rightful places of honor at the head of the household, when brothers live in loving harmony at their parents' feet, the rich with their luster and the poor with their modesty, this is the pleasure of correct familial relations in the divine pattern. The lowly who enjoy this pleasure can look down on those with higher status who do not enjoy it, and uneducated men who possess it may rightfully pride themselves in front of sages. This is why we say that the first pleasure is that of having both parents alive and brothers living free of rancor.

The second is to be free of guilt before heaven and shame before men. Most people might think this isn't much compared with being an emperor, but think of how thunder and lightning start up at one false move from the emperor, and also anomalies of rain, sun, harvests, and eclipses. He looks aside and speaks of other things—but if I were such an emperor I'd be mortified when faced with Mencius' precepts. If you consider how shamed and guilty an emperor would always be feeling, you can see how hard it must be to bear despite his incomparable position. It is better to be an ordinary man who has only his shadow to consider when he walks his own way and only his pillow to consult when he goes to sleep. He has no maggoty nibblings at his heart or queasy flutterings in his stomach. He doesn't take advantage of others, prize wealth over honor, deceive himself or turn a blind eye to what he knows is right, and he is trustworthy and loyal. He is straight and just and everything about him is correct and bright. He isn't afraid of heaven and doesn't start at thunder. You can knock at his door as late as you like, and you'll find him sleeping peacefully and dreamlessly.

Think of Emperor Kao Tsu of the Han dynasty, who wilfully poisoned King Chao and cruclly murdered Lady Chi. When there was a solar eclipse it terrified him and he couldn't keep from exclaiming,

"Is this unnatural movement of heaven aimed at Me?"

It wasn't many months after that before he was dead.

Ch'in Kuei got as far as the position of Prime Minister in the Sung dynasty, and even the great general Yüeh Fei, with all his military triumphs, could not escape death at Ch'in Kuei's hands. But when Ch'in Kuei saw the mad priest he was so scared he wished he could sink into the earth. Considering all of this, you can see that being free of guilt before heaven and shame before men is indeed the second pleasure.

The third is to gather the talented men of the empire and educate them. What this means is that the cultured man takes very seriously the continuity of the teaching of eternal truths and doesn't bother much with ephemeral scholarly fads.

Even though the third pleasure has to cede primacy to the previous two, it's still ahead of ruling the empire. But I would urge here in my discussion one more pleasure that should be placed before all three of these. If this fourth is not included, even though your parents may be alive, their lives will be so miserable they'll wish they were dead. Even if all your brothers are getting along well at the moment, you will certainly be bitter enemies in the future and you won't be able to face heaven without guilt or men without shame, let alone teaching the talented men of the empire. Now, listen, what do you think could be this one thing so essential to the enjoyment of the three cardinal pleasures? What you need is a good wife.

When your parents are in their places at the head of the household, it won't be you who attends them all day, and the quality of their lives depends entirely on a dutiful daughter-in-law.

Chao Wu-niang was right when she was careful of her good name, so people came to her aid. Her example shows that you can only be sure of your parents' safety when you have a good wife.

Brothers go through many years together. How could they not have some misunderstandings? A good wife, in pillowtalk with her husband, doesn't goad her husband into quarrels; she gently counsels him back into harmony with others.

It's human nature for a man to be swayed by his wife, even though he won't listen to anyone else. She can fire him up with a few provoking references or melt icy anger with a soothing word or two. Sun Jung's wife was right when she said that outsiders are glad to be your friend when you're doing well, but it's your brothers you can count on in times of need. So isn't it true that brothers can't live free of rancor towards each other unless they have good wives?

When a man behaves as if there were nothing sacred and all principles had evaporated, he can fool other people, but not his wife. Even though that man of Ch'i managed at first to blind his wife, as effectively as if he'd put a pail over her head, to his begging leftovers from graveside offerings, she did finally suspect his stories of high society. One morning she got up and followed him, following the riddle of his behavior. If she weren't a good wife, why would she bother to care whether he were begging or not? A bad wife would only concern herself with whether he'd eaten or not and leave it at that. But this wife wept in the courtyard along with her husband's concubine. The two women lamented and accused him until he left off that sorry business.

Chung-tzu despised his brother for living a life of ease at the court's expense, without working for his keep. In contrast to his brother, Chung-tzu fled to Ling, where he made a living sewing shoes. If his wife had been a bad one, she would have despised poverty and a lowly position, and she would have nagged him about it every day all day. Then what chance would there have been of Chung-tzu's not sharing his brother's fat stipend and house in the city of K'ai, shaming himself before heaven and men, just like his brother Tai did?

It's really something how such an outstanding man happened to have such an outstanding wife. She sat by him, processing hemp while he sewed shoes. One day the king of Ch'i rode up in a four-horse chariot with gifts and a request that Chung-tzu become the Prime Minister of Ch'i. Chung-tzu had already turned the king down when Chung-tzu's wife came home with a load of firewood on her back. She saw a bunch of horses and servants in front of her door and asked what was going on. When she found out the king had been there, she was afraid he'd come back with more presents so she got her husband to flee with her by night into the mountains. Doesn't that show a man can be without guilt before heaven and shame before men only when he has a good wife? If a wife's a bad one today it'll be clothes she wants and tomorrow it will be jewelry, and there isn't enough firewood and we need to buy soy sauce and we're running out of oil, on and on, making such a racket your vision will blur from the clamour, you'll be distracted and your heart will grow sad. Even if you were as fond of studying as Yen Hui, you wouldn't have enough peace and quiet to sit down in your study to read, let alone teaching the talented men of the empire. Anything you had learned before would melt away with the days and months.

Lo Yang-tzu was worried there was no income for his home while he was off studying, so he came home to check on how things were. His wife was weaving when he came in, and when she saw him, she took a knife and sliced the cloth in two.

She said, "If you don't finish these studies, this loom won't work either!"

Stung, Lo-Yang-tzu studied hard, and went on to become a famous official. So isn't it true that you can't teach the talented men of the empire unless you first have a good wife?

The only problem is that good wives have always been few and far between. As we all know, a couple is predestined from their former incarnations, just as is the rise of a king or any great man. The old moonlight man ties together the feet of the intended with his red cord. Then, no matter whether you're at the opposite shores of the ocean or ends of heaven, no matter if you're as bitter enemies as the states of Wu and Y'üeh, never fear but you'll be drawn together.

According to this theory of karmic predestination, all couples should be well assorted and harmonious. Why, then, out of any ten couples are there eight or nine who aren't doing too well? Either one is cleverer than the other, or one is more attractive than the other, or the husband hates his wife, or she is cruel to him. He might abandon her and set a whore up in her place, or she might have an illicit lover behind his back. There are endless deviations from the ideal and countless hardships piled one on top of the other in these unhappy unions.

Truly,

> "Husband and wife began as two birds sharing the bough
> Now they've quarrelled they're like foreigners"

Reader, can you tell me how such a karmic twist of fate could possibly happen? It's all a matter of what people did in former lives and generations, obscurely fashioned in the dark, and minutely calculated by the star of reckoning.

If you see a wife who is a good housekeeper, dutiful to her parents-in-law, respectful to her husband, friendly to her sister-in-law, and orderly and thorough in all she does, then in her former life she was either her present husband's close friend, or his soulmate, or one who owed him a debt of gratitude. This is what we call a Good Marriage. The two spouses are full of good will for each other. She is chaste and he is wise. They are as happy together as fish in water, as close as lacquer on the wood.

Then there are the other ones. Maybe in a former life one of them took advantage of power to maltreat the weak, who could only swallow their words and taste bile. Maybe one of the present unfortunate marital partners practiced frauds in his former life and enriched himself at the expense or others, or caused others' deaths with his treacherous plots. His greatly wronged and resentful victims couldn't be revenged in that life so in this one they are paired off as the spouses of their enemies.

Can you imagine why it is so fitting for implacable enemies to be yoked together like this? Doesn't it seem that a little kindness could cancel out their resentments, instead of endless retribution like this? Maybe you haven't stopped to think how close a relation a marriage is. There are many things said and done between a pair joined by heaven, things that wouldn't pass even between yourself and your parents or brothers. Therefore a marriage is a closer relationship than any other, and there is no hatred stronger than that which can flourish in a marriage.

In the very rare case of an emperor like Chieh of the Hsia or Chou of the Shang, while he may be disposed to persecute people, if you won't take a government job, he won't be too likely to come after you. Also, in the rare case of parents like Ku Sou, even if they set you at hard labor fixing barns and digging wells all day, at night you can get away and hide. This is why when karmic enemies meet in any relation other than that of marriage, they can't isolate each other from the depraved crowds of society well enough to really get down to work and have fun punishing each other. Even if you find yourself the father, son, or brother of your predestined foe, you can't get any real satisfaction out of tormenting him. There's only marriage for that.

A wife and husband are like a boil and the neck it sits on.

If you excise the boil you'll die, and if you leave it you'll be in constant pain. During the day you have no escape, but the night's twice as bad. The government's laws don't reach into the marriage bed and your parents' authority is no help. Your brothers can't do a thing. Neighbors may raise futile criticism, but not one will come pull you apart if your wife is nagging you to death. Even if you're killing her with a beating, not a one of them will come and try to reason you out of it. If you treasure life, she'll do her best to murder you, and if you wish you were dead she'll keep you alive. She'll take a dull knife that hasn't been honed for a year and saw it back and forth on your neck and rain blows and abuse on you. Isn't that a much better revenge than sending a man to Yen-lo Wang's forest of sword trees, grinding stones and eighteen lower Hells?

Reader, why should I go on at such length about this matter of marriage? It's because of the story that follows, which took place in the Cheng-t'ung era of this dynasty. There was a couple whose enmity took form when one of them killed the other in a former life. The killer was reborn as a man, and his victim as his wife. This same man had mistreated his wife in his previous incarnation, and favored his concubine. In the next life, that wife became his concubine. Both wife and concubine in this new incarnation were experts at abusing their lord and master, and at defaming his name.

It might not be obvious at first that bad marriages are due to bad karma, as above, but if you want to know what lay at the root of this particular one,

I will tell you in detail how it all began.

> Take the husband from the wife and she loses her home
> Take the wife from the husband and he loses his ruler
> Forever intended and bound in the ether by a red cord
> Every step drawing them closer
> Until they form one
> Two hearts sharing one secret
> Nestled like mandarin ducks by night
> Dancing like phoenixes by day

> But for some unlucky men
> Passions rend apart the intertwining branches of their marriages
> All day storms rage
> The domestic hen chased out
> A wild fowl cherished
> His wife's dense grief grows thick in the inner chamber
> Her jealousy clashes with his anger
> She can sing sadly of abandonment
> She can buy the song of Chang-men to woo him back
> For all the good it will do.

> Then there is the domineering wife
> All eyes for the willows on the other side of the door
> He wakes up to the sound of her enraged bellows
> She ties his hands
> Vituperates his ancestors
> Viciously insults his family
> He clings to her as to a disease
> Fearing a scene if he doesn't
> In name a fine marriage—
> In fact he's met his match.

> Sleep with a tiger
> Lay your head down next to your assassin's
> Heaven won't have it otherwise
> All that's left is to meekly play your role

I have chosen plain language
To waken all the world

Another poem says, as the *Classic of Songs*:

On the island downriver
The lone bird cries, "Kuan Kuan"
How fine a match the empress Wen

You can't say it's just his mother
who sets a ruler on his course
The flowering of the Chou was more a wife's work
Spirits attuned as fish to water
In nuptial accord like mandarin ducks
A pair of phoenixs in glorious balance

The weeds of discord that sprout in marriages
Are the fruits of old sins
Wreaking their implacable vengeance.

Chapter One

Ch'ao Yüan encloses a hunting ground and goes shooting
A fox spirit is shot dead with his arrow

There's a poem that says:

Rich young men lean to splendor
They're elegantly amorous, profligate and wild
They know no limits
No literary phrases on their glib lips
Money's no object when they pick a whore
They're busy as ants gathering their friends
for dice and overdrinking
They roar at each other and charge out to
enclosed hunting fields
Their clothes are trimmed in mink
But also leopard fur for that martial look
They say nothing that isn't unclean
But they will someday hear their own defamation
They swagger around bullying elders with their vigor
Humiliating the good with their strength
They throw every prudent consideration aside
To go fishing for new erotic experience
Their day of doom, and their families', is nigh.

In the age of the sage kings, peacefulness filled the air like incense and a creature known as the ch'i lin was born. The male of the species was the ch'i, and the female the lin. When the ch'i lin walked, it chose a spot where there were no insects or plants before stepping forward. It wouldn't harm one blade of grass or any other plant, or a bug. Although the ch'i lin was a being emblematic of the sage kings it didn't consider itself an order of being exempt from the relations that tie all living creatures.

    Man is the informing spirit of the myriad creatures. Like them, he is born of nature, and he has the natural endowment of the breath of virtue. Heaven and earth are his parents and all beings his brothers. Heaven and earth wouldn't create a being by its nature traitor to the rest of creation. That is why a man who is sincere and whose divinity is not warped worries more about the other myriad living things in the world than about his personal achievements. No man who doesn't take great pains to see that each creature enjoys its rightful place has any right to claim the good heart of a sincerely humane man.

If a man doesn't believe animals share the same nature as his own, he'll set himself apart from other men as well. Such a man will never be great.

Among all the animals in the world, there are a few like tigers and wolves with evil dispositions we despise for eating humans, and there are rats that burrow through walls, penetrate rooms, and chew up people's clothes and books. There are also flies and mosquitos that bite people and ruin things. These creatures could be beaten dead right in front of merciful Kuan-yin without incurring any punishment. Aside from these, all others that fly, crawl, swim or walk are harmless to men. Why should men murder them? A man may think he's different in kind from them, but they're all born of nature alike.

Even leaving out of consideration stories like those of the bird presenting a jade bracelet to Yang Pao in gratitude, or dogs, tortoises and horses repaying debts of gratitude by helping their benefactors or giving them presents, a man who is blessed with the chance to live a cultured life in this world should naturally have compassion for animals' suffering. As he widens his compassion, he will move slowly from compassion for animals to compassion for his wife and children, and to caring for the common people.

If he goes the other way, and is hard-hearted to animals, soon he won't be satisfied with killing a lamb but must kill an ox. Then killing an ox won't satisfy him and he will have to kill a human. When even that isn't enough for him, gradually he will become like Duke Hsien of Ch'in and the emperors Ming and Su-tsung of the T'ang, and kill his own sons. If that were not true, why say "the cultured man should avoid the slaughterhouse?" He should avoid seeing or hearing the act of killing because it will numb his sensitivity to suffering. That is why it is imperative for parents and elder brothers to nourish and encourage a boy's native compassion. As he matures it will become an integral part of his nature and he will not act contrary to its dictates. His life will be long and his good fortune inexhaustible.

At the beginning of this story, there was a young man named Ch'ao Yüan. He lived in Wu-ch'eng in the province of Shantung. His father was named Ch'ao Ssu-hsiao, of local scholarly repute. Ch'ao Ssu-hsiao was never very successful at the state exams. He only passed the lowest level exam. They had just enough to get by, and their household was poor but respectable. At the age of thirty Ch'ao Ssu-hsiao became the father of Ch'ao Yüan. Because Yüan was an only son, his father cherished him inordinately. Eventually Ch'ao Yüan grew to the age of sixteen, and he'd turned into a red-lipped, pearly-toothed, clear-eyed youth with a handsome brow. Indeed he was:

white as powdered Ho-lang
fragrant as Hsun-ling.
Only, he wasn't too quick at his studies or terribly bright. Even so, this coarse bar of iron too could have been filed into delicate needle for the finest embroidery with instruction and refinement. However, his case was hopeless because his mother spoiled him with uncritical love and his father was even worse. In any ten days there must have been nine when Ch'ao Yüan didn't study, and that one day he did study, he was hardly settled before he had the maid going back and forth for tea, and a boy for snacks, and it wasn't late when he had someone come take him home. Even bumbling around like that he was so clever he could write out the beginning of the primer "shang-ta-jen-k'ung-yi-chi" all by himself, but later his horizons broadened and he grew even more extreme, flinging the *Thousand Character Classic* utterly out of his considerations.

All he did was bet on cards and drink, and catch birds and fish, hunt, and snare rabbits along with the rest of his good-for-nothing little friends. Mr. and Mrs. Ch'ao didn't see anything wrong with all that. Fortunately, the household of a man who'd only passed the lower exam had limited material resources and the Ch'aos couldn't support their son in unlimited profligacy. Their poverty restrained his volatile and excessive tendencies somewhat.

Ch'ao Ssu-hsiao sat for years for the second level exam, but he never passed. Finally he was allowed to go as a tribute student to Peking. That was close to the beginning of the dynasty, and there was a large pool of students to bear the costs of "flag-raising". Also, it was not as expensive then as it is now to go to the capital, so Ch'ao Ssu-hsiao had a little more financial leeway than modern degree candidates, and he had his son married to the daughter of retired scholar Chi. After Ch'ao Ssu-hsiao concluded his son's marriage he went to the capital for the palace exam. Right at that time there was a vacancy in the top administration of the Board of Rites, which was being temporarily managed by the vice-president of the board. This vice-president had formerly been the educational intendent of Shantung, and it was under his aegis that Ch'ao Ssu-hsiao had passed the first exam, and first on the list of students, too.

When the vice-president met Ch'ao Ssu-hsiao again now, they chatted a little, he commiserated with Ch'ao for former hard times with the higher exams and then said,

"Even though you haven't qualified for a government job yet by passing the second exam, you're not too old. You don't have the look of someone who'll end his days as a village school-teacher. Go ahead and have a crack at the palace exam. If you pass, your worries are over, and, even if you don't, there are special qualifying exams. You certainly won't do worse than anyone else. Besides that, I've been in the capital a few years and I can look after you."

Ch'ao Ssu-hsiao listened to him and did as he said.

In his second year in the capital, Ch'ao Ssu-hsiao gave up on ever passing the standard second level exam.

"My former examiner wants me to take it, and even if I don't pass, I'd better take advantage of his presence here and qualify for some position before he leaves for somewhere else. If I pass after he's gone, I'll probably get some kind of subordinate subprefectural job. All I'll get for all my studies is yessir and kowtow. It would be the death of me," he cogitated.

He told the vice-president what he was thinking. The vice president agreed entirely and sent him off to the Board of Civil Employment with an application and a test paper. The commissioner at the Board of Civil Employment just happened to have been examined under the vice-president in the vice-president's days as an educational intendent. It was only after the vice-president filled him in that Ch'ao Ssu-hsiao sat with the rest for a Board of Civil Employment exam.

The quote which was to be their theme "Having a populace and altars [what need is there to study mere books]" was familiar to Ch'ao Ssu-hsiao, and he had the confidence that came from being a tribute student marked for good employment, so he produced his answer and did so well that he landed himself a job as the magistrate of a sub-prefecture. Of course Ch'ao Ssu-hsio was very happy about it, and it increased the vicepresident's prestige as well.

Now Ch'ao Ssu-hsiao thought, "Even though I got the magistracy of a sub-prefecture, which sub-prefecture can make the difference between heaven and hell. I'd better find the vice-president, my old examiner, while he's still in town and get a good place. There's no point to waiting."

When the year was ended and the rolls of office posted, he was in luck. His vice-president had been promoted to president of the Board of Civil Employment and Ch'ao Ssu-hsiao didn't have to bother running around begging favors before he was presented with the position of magistrate of Hua-t'ing sub-prefecture. Hua-t'ing was in the Southern Metropolitan district, a famous, large sub-prefecture hard for even the holder of the second degree with a lot of economic clout to pull into his grasp and Ch'ao Ssu-hsiao got it without even breathing hard.

When the news came to his house, did any of his friends and relatives believe it? Hardly!

They all said, "Hua-t'ing's belonged to second degree holders for generations. How could a tribute student possibly get it?"

The messenger disturbed the neighborhood with his yells and screams, creating a furor until he got the 300 taels for bringing good news. Before two more days were out, everyone saw the official announcement and then they knew it was true. Ch'ao Ssu-hsiao hung the announcement with red and sent it over to the hall where he'd been examined, as an offering, but he had to write a note for 150 taels before they'd hang it up for him.

Back in Wu-ch'eng, when all the local sycophants heard that Ch'ao Ssu-hsiao had become a subprefectural magistrate, and at the choicest place in the empire, they all wished they could parade Ch'ao Yüan's balls around on their shoulders. They wanted to get between his cheeks and lick his anus. Those with little entreated him to become his servants and begged letters of introduction or recommendation, doing their best to throw themselves on the benevolence of someone luckier than themselves. Those of middling means wanted nothing better than to place their own lands and homes at Ch'ao Yüan's disposal, as his official residence. The credit shops and money lenders of the city prepared and sent imposing gifts.

The proprietor of a credit shop said, "Whenever you need some money, be sure to write me a request. We don't weigh our scales, and we'll throw in a few cash extra for you. If you find any inferior grade coins in our money, we'll replace them."

A moneylender said, Since your father has only just gotten a post, Sir, perhaps you won't have enough money at your fingertips?"

"We have 200 taels for you."

"We have 300 taels for you, just take it. We'll lower the interest as a gift to you. If you don't keep the money long, we wouldn't even consider charging interest at all."

Then there were those among his relatives, in-laws and friends who came forward, this one with thirty taels, that one with fifty.

Ch'ao Yüan was tempermentally predisposed to throwing money around, but as the son of a poor, aspiring scholar his taste for lavishness had been like military prowess that never got to the battlefield. When he thought now of how hard he used to have to work at getting one or two hundred cash out of the credit shops, and all the devious stratagems he had to employ to get a couple taels out of anyone, while now money came to his door all by itself and the senders didn't even want him to sign a contract saying he'd pay it back, it made him happier than anything ever had before. Any money sent him, he took, any more he needed he borrowed, and anybody who came to him he took in without bothering to check backgrounds. Before ten days were out he had several tens of attendants and several thousands of taels. He spent over 10,000 cash every day, and all of it borrowed from credit shops on I.O.U.'s. He used 250 taels to buy three fine horses, 300 for six pack mules. He rode back and forth buying silk gauze and fitting appointments for his living quarters. Money can even buy gods, and within a month Ch'ao Yüan was riding high as the King's son-inlaw in that dream-country of Huai-an.

Then Ch'ao Yüan sent Ch'ao Shu, a low-level servant who had been with the household for a long time, along with four of the new ones, with a thousand taels to be used by to Ch'ao Ssu-Hsiao.

Once Ch'ao Ssu-hsiao got his fine position, the capital debt lenders were always at his door. If only he'd put their money to use! They'd charge a mere ten percent, and their silver was the very purest, weighed generously!

Ch'ao Ssu-hsiao was new in his official post, and it was a very large sub-prefecture. He had to pay calls on the President of the Board of Civil Employment, and receive provincial officials so it wasn't long before he was borrowing money. Since there was a whole troupe of money lenders competing to supply his daily expenses, that was no problem.

As soon as Chao Shu got to the capital with the four other servants and 1,000 taels in hand, he plunged right into buying silks, having silver-trimmed belts hammered, calling tailors, getting cups inlaid, and having incense concocted, seals cut, winged hats and leather belts constructed, and court ceremonial robes made, a rainbow variety, all finished and ready. The following month, Ch'ao Ssu-Hsiao took a letter with him to the Mi-hsiang region in Tung-chiang where he bought three first-class Fukien official sedan chairs, for Ch'ao Ssu-hsiao, Madam Ch'ao, and Ch'ao Yüan. He also bought a second-class sedan chair for Ch'ao Yüan's wife, Ms. Chi. He bought curtains of felt and pongee for the sedan chairs, and when he had done all he'd been sent to do he went home. Everything was gorgeously ready for Ch'ao Yüan's arrival, which was filled with more pomp and splendour than there's any need to detail.

Now that Ch'ao Yüan had joined his parents at his father's new post, there was a new problem. How could such a lively, amorously inclined young man bear to be shut up in a boring old yamen all the time?

In contrast to Ch'ao Yüan, there was a Yamen staff member, named Hsing Ch'en, whose style was Kao-men. Hsing Kao-men was from Wei-chuan in Honan. Hsing was an interesting young man, holding the lower degree. His manner was easy without being over familiar, and always full of polite consideration towards anyone worth listening to, even impoverished book-worms. For the stupid people who blindly concentrated all their energies on getting rich, he had only scorn, even if they were related to royalty. However,

Ch'ao Y'uan considered himself a young gentleman, and Hsing Kao-men one of the underlings, to be treated with condescension.

When Hsing Kao-men later became a Board president, do you think he'd waste a moment noticing the likes of Ch'ao Yüan?

After lolling around the yamen for half a year, in a spurt of boredom Ch'ao Yüan got together a pile of money and went off to Su-chou where he bought some outlandish toys, had some clothes made that violated the sumptuary laws, bought some incongruous potted plants, rented a boat, hired a troupe of performers, and then came home with Ms. Chi. His old friends in Wu-ch'eng thought he was the same old Ch'ao Yüan and they figured they could part him from his money with confusing stories, or by making him sell things at a loss, or extorting presents out of him, so they all came out to meet him and soak up a little of his prosperity. Little did they know he had grown beyond them, and, although he forced himself to meet them, his glance was decidedly cool, not at all like his former easygoing self.

He sat in his chair facing north, looked down his nose, mouthed a few empty phrases in a Peking accent, and got up to bow them out before they were ready to go. When the group saw that this was how he intended to play it, and that they might as well beat a recalcitrant donkey as try to get anything out of him, they left. When the new servant saw his master's attitude, he knew enough to turn those men away if they should come again. Besides, Ch'ao Yüan had bought a great mansion from Board President Chi for 6,000 taels and was doing his best to have "an aristocrat's portal, inaccessible as the bottom of the sea", so how could his old buddies come knocking at his door?

While shedding his old friends could be considered the natural thing for a man who had suddenly risen in the world, the same could hardly be said for his wish to discard his wife, in favor of someone more in accord with his new wealth.

Ms. Chi's father had never made it into the official arena, but he was of an old family. She, while not very tall, was no midget, and although her beauty wasn't awesome, she wasn't despicable. Her face wasn't white as white jade, but it wasn't smudgy dark either. Further down, while her feet were not "three inch lotuses" they weren't big as carts.

Other people might think her ordinary, but when Ch'ao Yüan looked at her, he used to see a heavenly beauty, unparalleled in all the empire. Ms. Chi took advantage of his fondness for her by being capricious, so he grew to fear her. Now she was still the same old Ms. Chi but Ch'ao Yüan saw her with new eyes that slid with contempt over her yokel looks.

"How does a face like that deserve a household like mine!" he said.

He looked down on her father, old Chi, for being so poor he could hardly afford the clothes on his back.

"He should know better than to associate with people better off than himself."

In his heart, Ch'ao Yüan had crossed the borderline of disgust, and this began to show in the rude way he treated the Chis.

Ms. Chi didn't realize he had changed. Every move she made was full of arrogance, and she never opened her mouth unless it was to scold him or stirred her hand unless to hit him.

Ch'ao Yüan didn't answer back, but he glared at her furiously when she scolded him. When she hit him, he didn't hit back, but he didn't accept it meekly as his due, the way he had before. He began to fend her off with his hands or run away from her. Then gradually he did begin to answer back when she paused in scolding him, and he might put his foot out to trip her if she hit him. Eventually the two of them were yelling and each other and hitting each other and finally he was the one beating her up. He used to be afraid she'd hang herself if he made a wrong move, and she used to frivolously bar him from the bedroom.

These days, Ch'ao Yüan didn't worry about her hanging herself. He just wished she would, so he could make a good marriage with a beautiful girl from a prominent family. So what if she did hang herself or slit her throat. It wasn't as if that old father of hers would be able to do a thing about it. Reading the sutras for her funeral and seeing her out of this world wouldn't have bothered Ch'ao Yüan as much as it would have to pull one hair off his body.

As far as the bed-chamber went, he used to have no place to go except the bedroom he shared with her. If she wouldn't let him in, or once in wouldn't let him lie down to go to sleep, he was in a predicament. Now, however, he had several studies, with a gauze-curtained bed in each, and silk coverlets and bamboo matting on each bed. Each was enclosed with screens to keep in the warmth. Within the screens he kept glowing stoves and braziers, cotton stuffed quilts and duck feather feather-beds.

Also, there was a group of female entertainers who first came to the house to "sing the story of Catamite Lung Yang." They stayed on.

The question was no longer whether Ms. Chi would refuse him entrance to her bedroom. Even if she opened the doors up wide, sprinkled the floors with brine and hung the lintels with bamboo twigs like the palace ladies of King Wu did to attract his mount, it wouldn't have lured Ch'ao Yüan. So all Ms. Chi could do was wait for absolution. Her nerve shrank from day to day, while Ch'ao Yüan's heart was growing wilder.

Ch'ao Yüan would take a maid and then decide she was no good after two days, but every day he was in a fever for Chen ko, who sang principal female parts in the troupe. This Chen ko wasn't all that exceptional; she knew a few good tunes and she was a very lively entertainer. Ch'ao Yüan was completely taken with her and he sent a messenger to tell her "manager" he wanted her for his concubine no matter what it cost. He had the messenger say that Ms. Chi wasn't at all well and would probably die soon, and then he would elevate Chen ko to the position of wife. Despite the fact that Chen ko was all for it, she shamelessly played him for everything she could get.

"It took over 3,000 taels to get this troupe in shape and we still haven't earned even several hundred back. If you're going to take me, the only one trained for female principal parts, it's the same as if the whole troupe was gone. Why not take them all and reward them however you think?"

She sent him her reply, and then the go-between, his people and her attendants all got down to chiselling as much as they aould, until a deal was struck. Then, inevitably as wool grows on sheep, Ms. Chi was bought for 800 taels and became a member of the household.

Ms. Chi wasn't so cowed she was afraid to show her anger and say what she thought, but she was no match for her husband, who did as he pleased. Ms. Chi wasn't about to give in and welcome a concubine, and Chen ko didn't want to humble herself. Ch'ao Yüan may have had money and influence, but his home was a mess.

Following the suggestion of one of his hangers-on, Tung Chung-hsi, Ch'ao Yüan decided to maintain a separate establishment. He bought a new house, had clothes and jewelry made, servants hired and maids bought, and in no time it was shimmeringly complete for Chen ko, whom he put there.

A whole month passed that Ch'ao Yüan didn't go to Ms. Chi's house. She gradually began to run out of firewood and rice, which she had to go beg at Chen Ko's. She was like a mute downing gall, unable to express the bitterness of it.

One day, the sixth of the eleventh month, a good snow began to fall. Ch'ao Yüan had the cook set up three or four tables of wine and had a brazier lit in his pavilion of lingering spring. Once he had everything arranged he sent polite invitations to his rich friends to come and view the snow. They arrived slowly, and each took a seat. The girls in the troupe poured wine and pressed the guests to drink. They didn't sing that day.

All present exhibited a sly lascivious manner, and everything they said was offensive. There was no hiding the fact they were a bunch of nouveau-riche dirty bastards riding high.

There was fresh game on the table, which led them to talk aimlessly about,

"Lots of rabbits and pheasants around this year. Wolves and tigers all over the place. That's supposed to be a bad omen for the harvest."

"We all have horses and dogs and falcons. What do you say we go have an enclosed hunt and have some fun one day?"

One smart young man said, "If we're going to have a hunt, there's no place like brother Ch'ao's villa. First, there's plenty of level ground at the foot of the mountain there and lots of game; second, I like the idea of making him host us all!"

Ch'ao Yüan couldn't have thought up anything better himself. He pulled out an almanac and picked the fifteenth of the month as auspicious for hunting. They all agreed they should dress up a little and present a nice sight, and meet at the hour of the hare (6:00 a.m.) on the drilling grounds to start off together. They also discussed gathering sacrifices to the mountain spirits and to sanctify their pennants.

"Never mind that," Ch'ao Yüan said, "I'll take care of it."

That was all set then and they kept drinking until the fifth watch (4:00 a.m.) the next morning, when the snow came to a stop. Some went home and some stayed in Ch'ao Yüan's heated rooms with the girls. Ch'ao Yüan had drunk all night, and then got up to a little amorous activity with Chen ko, so he slept until the hour of the monkey (4:00 p.m.).

When he awoke, his friends who had stayed in the front rooms had all gone away. Ch'ao Yüan didn't wash or fix his hair. He had a couple of bowls of hot and sour soup, then sat a while. He got his lantern, and, although still feeling his hangover, went to bed again with Chen ko. In bed, he told her about how they were going to have an enclosed hunt on the fifteenth, starting out from the villa, and that he had to make some preparations. Chen ko questioned him closely.

Then she said, "If you're going to spend the day hunting, I want to go along and have some fun for a change."

"You're a woman—what would you be doing in a bunch of men? Besides, we'll be mounted and you're not going to be able to keep up in your sedan chair," he replied.

"You think there's one of them whose portrait I couldn't draw from memory? I've been with at least one out of ten of them so you can't imagine I'd worry about that crowd! And you'll be on horseback will you? I can tell you my riding's going to put you to shame! Didn't I used to dress up and gallop on over to perform at every funeral procession? Then, if I wasn't being "Chao-chün leaving camp" it was "Meng Jih-hung busts the thieves". What's different about riding at a hunt? I don't see what the matter is with you if you can't understand that much."

"You're right," he said, "It'll be even better with you along. Tomorrow find that dark-green sprinkle-embroidered coat and get it lined in vermilion plain damask by Tailor Chen. That'll look fine on horseback the day of the hunt."

Chen ko laughed. "My innocent little boy. Me, wear old clothes to a hunt? Like some old eunuch? I think I'd be better off with my golden quirt from the troupe's stage props, my pheasant head-dress, and python embroidered shoulderpiece. I'm going dressed as an opera warrior."

Ch'ao Yüan lay back on his pillow.

"Perfect, absolutely perfect," he said, "but why borrow the troupe's stuff? It's tarnished and disgustingly dirty.

"Let's get new things made—they'll come in handy some other time."

They engaged in some pillowside combat.

The next day, Ch'ao Yüan got up and then he was busy for several days, arranging things for the hunt. He wanted to be much better turned out than the other rich young men; it wouldn't do to look only as good as they. For Chen ko he had made a bright, new, red "flying fish" a narrow-sleeved 4-claw dragon design robe and a dark green embroidered shoulder-piece. For 36 taels he bought a mink lined cap and for seven silver cash he had a pair of wearable little riding shoes sewed in purple hemp lined with lambskin. He ordered a golden-yellow braided belt and bought her a double-bladed sword. He selected a black horse and had it trained, and also picked out six plump servants' wives, four robust housemaids and ten sturdy farmers' wives. He had a fox-lined cap made for each of these women, and a sky-blue padded outrider's jacket, a dull green plain cloth padded shoulder piece, and puce cloth riding shoes lined with leather. They were to have knives shoved in their belts, left and right. He also chose one husky woman and dressed her in proper military garb, planning to have her ride behind Chen ko as an attendant.

He also had his own clothes made up, and those of his servants and hangers-on, complete in every detail. He borrowed thirty horses from the military guardsman Liu Yu-chi, and got twenty-four horseback performers. As well as his own dogs and falcons, he borrowed four hunting dogs and three falcons, also from Guardsman Liu.

He dispatched men to the villa to slaughter two or three pigs and make three or four stones' flour milled, to eat on the day of the hunt. Around the hour of the hare on the morning of the fifteenth, those ten or so rich young men made their appearance, one after the other, at the drilling field. They, too, had worked hard on their appearance, and they all ended up looking bizarre.

Ch'ao Yüan arrived last. From the house, he had his troups array themselves. First there was a group of equestriennes in the front line, and behind them, Chen ko dressed up like a martial heroine on horseback. Then there was a thicket of flags and banners. Behind those were ten or twenty women forming the rear guard and the Ch'ao Yüan with his soldiers. They were all in step and their perfect formation never faltered. Although this was clearly a rustic entertainment, the scope rivalled Chou Ya-fu's splendidly disciplined camp.

When the others saw him, they all cheered. He dismounted and showed them Chen ko. In the past, they'd all been her dear friends but since she'd become such a fine, proper woman they couldn't let loose with their usual wisecracks. They exchanged a few constrained words and had some stirrup cups

Ch'ao Yüan was afraid the crowd would disturb the order of his crack mounts, so he had each group separate off to the side, let off the fireworks, and began the ride to the hunt. In no time they had arrived at the villa, at the border of the enclosed hunting ground.

Indeed,

Horses like leaping dragons, men sturdy as bears
Tiger troops with clustered flags rippling in the wind
led the way
Leopard tails decorating chariots behind
buoyantly competing for attention
Falcons on their gloves, dogs held by tethers
Men like Kuan-k'ou Erh-lang
Arrows feathered and bows snaking
All present vaunting themselves the like of
the three sworn brothers of the peach garden
Every household member, every guest,
old, young, tall, short, fat or timourously thin
Came out to stand in ranks and paste flattering grins on
Competed to crowd round their great man of the day
Every servant's wife and every other woman
dark, pale, fair, or ugly
On little feet or big clodhoppers
Pushed herself into the crowd
Competing for attention with her winsome smiles
Riding to the fore to meet the little lady

The great man in his dark padded jacket, raven
feather trim, and pale multi-colored fine-embroidered
"flying fish"
The little lady wore a padded jacket of ape's blood scarlet,
a delicate short "priest's robe" and overrobe
embroidered with four-clawed dragons.
He on a fine steed fleet as the wind
Iron Cudgel in hand
Brimming with martial dignity
She on a mount dazzling as the sun
two leather shields pendant
Fury radiating before her

When a heroic woman puts on war-gear
Unlike when Hsiao-chün went hunting
The cloud god doesn't dare stir up his vermillion clouds
to cloak her victims from her

When evil stars array for battle
They don't count on Han huan-hou cutting their bridges
or Hsin Han-p'ing twice targetting the bright sun

Crowds of wolves and violent tigers
Swift deer and dark foxes
Pipes blown, cymbals sounded, song filled the skies

But the peak of magnificence marks the turn down to sorrow
So what good is it all

They stirred up quite a few deer, pheasants, rabbits, badgers and wolves.
Everyone loosed falcons and dogs and put arrows to their bows. They shot and
bagged a lot of game.

In a cave on Mount Yung, an ancient vixen had lived a long time. She used
to change her shape and confuse people outside. Later she left the mountain
to go to a village of the Chou clan. There she called herself Hsien-ku, and
entranced a little farmer, so she hadn't had time to make mischief on Mount
Yung. She just looked in on her old place from time to time.

Sometimes she changed into a peerlessly beautiful girl, and others into a
decrepit old woman. It was in that guise people often ran into her.

On this particular day, she had just come back from Chou village, and was crossing the hunting ground. Why didn't she run back where she'd come from the minute she saw all those horses, falcons and dogs? She was sure of her powers and assumed her human shape would fool the dogs. Also, she had had an evil longing for Ch'ao Yüan for a long while in her heart. The fact that he had a Diamond Sutra in Sanskrit by the altar in his house kept scores of protective spirits around him there, so she'd never had a chance to get near him. Now, here he was out in the open, flaunting his depravity by taking his whore out hunting and totally disregarding the separation of male and female spheres. She'd never have a better chance than this.

So she changed into a beautiful girl not yet twenty years old, dressed all in white. She walked, not too fast and not too slow right in front of Ch'ao Yüan's horse. She hadn't walked more than a couple of steps before she turned around, gazed at him, and pulled his soul right out of his body.

Ch'ao Yüan thought, "I know every single person on this mountain, but I've never seen this stunner before. She can't be from any great house, because she doesn't have any attendants with her. She must be a new widow, all in mourning. This is one fine delicacy I'd better grab! I'll get her home and have her play "Two beauties" with Chen ko, O-huang on the left and Wü-ying on the right. Won't that be sexy!"

Her illusory bag of skin was all that was needed to fool his carnal eyes and he was wrapped in his plotting for her, but the more perceptive falcons and dogs knew her true form. The dogs bounded forward and the falcons tumbled through the air to the attack. The fox panicked and fell into her original shape. There wasn't any crevice of escape in the solid wall of hunting beasts around her. She fled under Ch'ao Yüan's horse, hoping he would save her, but Ch'ao Yüan was a man who liked killing. Not only was he not about to save her with tender compassion, he pulled his curved bow out, fit an arrow to its string, and pulled with his right arm while his left held the bow steady, aimed straight at the fox under his horse, and shot true. One wail, and the fox was thrown in the air with the force of the arrow striking home. A yellow dog rushed in from the side to grab her in his jaws. Before the eyes of all assembled there that day a thousand-year old demon met her sorry end.

She was pulled from the dog's jaws and tossed on the pile of game.

They called in their troupes, had the horses stabled, and went back to the villa to eat. Then the men returned triumphantly to town and went to Ch'ao Yüan's house. Chen ko returned separately with the women.

Back home in town, wine and snacks were served to all. They divided the game evenly, except that Ch'ao Yüan took the white fox. Everyone said good-night and left. Cha'ao Yüan saw them to the door, and he had just stepped over the threshold when he felt a blow full in his face and broke out in cold shakes. He thought he was just overtired, so he went to bed and slept.

But from that night, inexplicable things began slowly to take shape, as you will see in the next chapter.

Chapter Two

Ch'ao Yüan falls ill in consequence of slaughtering a fox
Dr. Yang Practices slapdash quackery

Don't presume on your brash strength
Don't be so sure your vitality won't ebb away unseen
Add cruelty and murder to your foibles
And not even the Doctor of Lu can cure you

As we were saying, after Ch'ao Yüan saw his guests off he felt his face whacked by some invisible assailant, his body was shaken with cold shivers, his hair stood on end and he did not feel at all well. He held up for a little while and gave his portion of the game, along with the fox, to his servants. Then he went to Chen ko's room and sat blankly in a chair with his head hanging.

Chen ko, back from her rowdy day, wanted to talk over every detail with him, but Ch'ao Yüan wouldn't put his oar in and barely answered her. She began to feel low herself then and asked,

"You were all smiles on the way back—how come you're so upset all of a sudden that you can't even open your mouth? You must have had a run-in with Yü Ming-wu again."

Chao Yüan didn't answer, just shook his head.

Chen ko tried again, " Really, what's the matter? Your face is almost gray as mud. I'll have the servants make a couple of bowls of hot and sour soup for that cold I see you caught on the road. Then you go sweat it out on the k'ang and I guarantee you'll be cured."

Ch'ao Yüan said, "Tell your maid to warm a jug of wine. I'll have a couple of large cupfuls and see how I feel."

The maid brought four plates of snacks to go with wine, warmed a jug of wine nice and hot, and put two pairs of long-stemmed, carved lacquer cups with silver inlay and two pairs of ivory chopsticks on the bedroom table. Ch'ao Yüan and Chen ko listlessly picked up their heads and downed a few huge cupfuls, then gave up on it. They called the maid to ready the k'ang and get out the quilts. Then the two of them got up on the k'ang to sleep.

Ch'ao Yüan kept waking up, and he mumbled constantly. He slept until the first watch (8:00 p.m.) when a fever flamed over his body and he cried out that his head hurt Then he lapsed into babbling incoherence.

Chen ko panicked. She called a maid to light the lamp and start a fire, woke up his old nurse, and got everyone in to watch over him. She also sent someone to go knock on Ms. Chi's door and ask Ms. Chi to come see what she could do.

A few days before, Ms. Chi had heard that Chen ko was going to dress up in her battle costume and buy new shoes and sash to go for an enclosed hunt at the villa, and with a pack of brutish men friends at that.

All Ms. Chi had to reply to that, forcedly, was, "Oh great. Going hunting. I suppose now we have this lady general Yang among us we don't have to worry about those rebellions that have been going on all year."

But in her heart she was saying, "I don't believe a word of it. These old women—they start talking about rain at the first puff of wind. Even though she was a whore, now she's a married woman, is it likely she'd put on her military costume and go out hunting with a gang of men? They're just saying that to get me angry, but I don't have the energy to bother with it. If she were really going out hunting I might as well keep a lover. Why shouldn't that shameless creep of a husband wear a cuckold's green turban as well as a spendthrift's cap?"

She treated the rumor of the hunt as so much wind and put it aside.

On the fifteenth of the month, Ms. Chi got up and was just sitting on her bed fixing her footbindings when she heard the whole house resounding with clamour. First she heard the forty drummers borrowed from the military camp and then she heard three shots.

"Whats's all the music and fireworks about," she asked.

Her woman said, "I told you, but you didn't believe me. It's Chen ko going off to the hunt."

Ms. Chi was silent a moment. Then she said, "How can that be? Have they left yet?"

The woman said, "They're getting ready now to set off."

"Let me get a look for myself at what's going on," said Ms. Chi.

She wrapped a cloth around her head, and put on a pair of brocade shoes bound in lambskin, a shortsleeved bodice and trousers, and went out. Just as she did, Ch'ao Yüan and Chen ko were mounting their horses. Ms. Chi got behind one of the leaves of the outer gate, so that her lower body was properly out of sight while her upper leaned toward the spectacle. She was furious and she was miserable.

All the neighboring women came out to see Ch'ao Yüan and Chen ko off. Some envied them, some criticized, and some poked fun. When they saw Ms. Chi at the gate they all came over to greet her.

She said, "I haven't done my hair or face yet, so don't be formal."

She invited them in for a cup of tea, but they declined her offer and stood outside gossiping desultorily about neighborhood matters.

There was one Mrs. Yu who said, "But Mrs. Ch'ao! Why didn't you go along for the outing, instead of sitting around bored in the house?"

"Oh, me with my ugly face and big feet, " said Ms. Chi , "I'm not fit to go hunting with a bunch of men. I'll just hide myself in the house and live out my bitter days without complaining."

Mrs. Kao, wife of the fourth Kao brother, said, "You do not have an ugly face or big feet, Aunty Chao, though you might be too heavy a load for the horse."

Mrs. Kao went on, "That husband doesn't have any sense; if he has to treat her with respect and flatter her, keep it at home! What kind of behaviour is this! He's really too much. All right, so she did used to dress up to act the part of Wang Chao-chun or Meng Jih-hung and get up on her horse with the other girls for a cortege, but can't he draw the line between priest and layman? Nevermind that he has the whole neighborhood talking, I don't think his father would like hearing about this at his official post."

Ms. Chi said, "It can't be helped if the neighbors want to laugh at us, and if my father-in-law knew he'd be so far from minding he'd say his son knows how to have a good time and put money to use, not like some stick in the muds.

There's a temple to the Goddess of fertility near my in-laws' house and my mother-in-law was planning with me to go some day when it wasn't too crowded to go pay our respects. Otherwise we'd be wasting the good luck of having the Goddess for a neighbor. When my husband heard of it, he didn't have a word to say a good son would think of. Like a fool he couldn't stop going on about how everyone at the temple rubs up against each other and makes eyes at each other, about men pinching your bottom and unravelling your footwrappings. He made his mother so furious she didn't know what to do, and we never did go to the temple. If I hadn't gotten so mad I slapped him I don't know what awful things he might have said to his mother."

Mrs. Kao asked, "Doesn't his father scold him when he offends his mother like that?"

Ms. Chi replied, "My father-in-law just about split his face in two laughing. He even said, 'you'd better not go, but since he's said it all I don't have to,'. That's how my father-in-law disciplines his son."

"Mrs. Kao said, "You certainly are nice to him. I won't lie to you; it's more than I could do to bear with a husband like that. I'd rather kill mine than let him humiliate me like that."

"Couldn't my mother-in-law have the nerve to say a word to him?" Ms.

Chi said, "No, she just got upset and went off with her eyes squeezed tight to go cry in some corner. I'm the only one who'll stand up to him, and there are times I've cursed him out or given him a slap or two."

Mrs. Kao said, "Since you're so good at giving him what-for I guess you must have what-forred him into Mr. Born-in-the-mill-room!"

They all asked, "How do you mean 'Mr.Born-in-the mill-room?

Old lady Yen spoke up, "My, don't you see? Mr.Born-in-the mill-room went hunting by the well and ran into his Ma Li San-niang. Now Mr. Ch'ao is out hunting with his little woman, so isnt it just the same?"

Everyone said, "We'd never have thought of that one! No wonder they all say Old Yen's the one who knows all the stories."

"You tell me to keep him in line, " Ms. Chi said, "But even though I haven't changed, is he the man he used to be? Even before he brought in that piece of his into our home, he'd already begun to be on his high and mighty with me. I've handed in my letter of surrender. How am I supposed to keep him in line?"

Mrs. Kao said, "Aunty Ch'ao, you're a smart person. You just listen to me. Stop getting yourself worked up and lay down the law, because if you don't, and if you let him go on in this insane way, your household will fall apart. If he scatters all his possessions and wears himself to death it's you who'll bear poverty and live in mourning after he's gone down the drain! You might as well be the frog arguing with the locust—you can't hop away and I can't fly.

In our house, when things are going along well, I won't say a word even if he takes my last clothes for her. Let him sleep a night or two with her, I won't make a quarrel about my position or sit around full of jealousy. But if my husband started parading around and mixing with some wild whore, that's what I wouldn't stand for."

"And what if he's already gotten mad and thrown you aside? Could you make him listen to you then?" Ms. Chi asked.

Old Yen said to Mrs. Kao, "Each man's a unique case. If he wants to be Kao with the demon head and toad's eyes, you be the tiger woman. If he wants to be King Wen, you just trot out the music and ritual, and if he's going to be King Chieh or King Chou of the Shang you pick up your spear and halberd. Then he doesn't dare show his claws. You can be the little dragonfly that undermined the magesty of the seven Dharmas and the eight idols, and conquer him as easily as Chung K'uei did the ghost in Emperor Ming's dream. You live right, show kindness and demand respect, and if he's as correct as your Kao it's only fitting. Now Ch'ao Yüan's like a raging demon. That Chen ko's been an actress and she knows how to sing to his tune. When she dresses up like Meng Jih-hung it's enough to cow any bandit! How can Madame Ch'ao, a mere weak woman like yourself, compete with them in their antics?"

Mrs. Kao said, "Dogs'! Sometimes a swan can beat a hawk. I have mine under my thumb."

Still talking, they took their leave of Ms. Chi and dispersed. Ms. Chi went back into her room and fell into thought. She couldn't help feeling infuriated at what she thought, so she screamed and stamped and had a good cry. She never did fix her hair, and eventually she heated the k'ang and went to sleep on it.

Halfway through the night she heard a pounding on the door.

In the past, a knock on her door at night wouldn't have caused her any alarm, since she was a woman with no stain on her conscience but her domineering behaviour to her husband. However, now that her husband had triumphed over her a few times, her female nature, just like the nature of a eunuched palace courtier, reverted to its native pusillanimity.

She thought, "Why would anyone be banging on the door so urgently? Some busybody must have told that bully I was at the door watching her leave with him, and talking to the neighbors. Now he wants to make something of it. What if I did go out and say a few words to the others? It's not half as bad as her making a spectacle of herself out hunting with that bunch of her 'friends'."

She unsheathed the knife she kept by her bed, and placed the knife in her sleeve, waiting to see what would happen. (If he comes in fighting I'll take the chance to stab him one-two through the head and then hang myself for reparation). Having thought it through and got her courage up, she called her maid and woman to open up the door and ask what was going on.

There was only a servant's wife outside, flustered, who said, "I don't know what's wrong with the young master! He doesn't feel well, and he's out of his head babbling. Madam, please hurry to him!"

Ms. Chi said, "What's he to me? He doesn't want me by him when he goes hunting, but he does when he's sick, does he? He was proud as an avenging spirit today, mounted up with Chen ko, full of himself. Is it likely he'd be sick this soon after? This is a plot of that shameless whore of his to make me come out so she can murder me! You tell him that if he won't treat me as a lawful wife deserves I consider I don't have a husband and whether he's really sick or just faking it I'm not about to go to his rooms in the middle of the night. If he wants to take care of me, there's always tomorrow. If she wants to chop me to pieces let him do it in broad daylight! If he's sick, he'll either get better, and then there's nothing more to be said, or he'll die and then let his parents go ask his whore for revenge, I really don't care."

The servant's wife repeated everything Ms. Chi had said, word for word, to Chen ko.

Chen ko said, "So that's how she-wants to be! Too bad if he gets better, and if he doesn't so what. It's a good thing I'm here. I can be counted on!"

Even though Chen ko sounded brave, she was worried in her heart. Ch'ao Yüan fell deeper into unconsciousness, and she didn't wait for the light of day before sending a servant to call Dr. Yang of Hsüan-p'u road.

Among all of Ch'ao Yüan's friends, Yü Ming-wu was the closest. He lived right across from the Ch'ao's. He was a clerk in the Bureau of Military Lands, and had a sizable establishment. He saw the servant Ch'ao Chu come back from Dr. Yang's and asked,

"Where are you going so early in the morning? And in such a rush?"

Ch'ao Chu said, "Ever since the Master saw you off last night, he felt like he'd been slapped in the face, and he got cold shivers. Then in the middle of the night, he got feverish and now he's unconscious, just babbling. I've been at Hsüan-p'u road to ask Dr. Yang to come treat him. The Doctor's still getting ready so I came back first alone."

Yu Ming-wu said, "He was just fine yesterday; how did he get sick all of a sudden?" Then Yu Ming-wu got a couple of other friends of Ch'ao Yüan's who had gone to the hunt and who lived nearby, to go over at sit at the Ch'ao's. Their names were Yin P'ing-yang and Yü Feng-chi. Just when they got there, Dr. Yang also arrived. They all greeted him politely, and told him how they had been out hunting the day before, come back here, and each gone home. They even told Dr. Yang about Ch'ao Yüan shooting the fox spirit. Dr. Yang took it all in.

This Dr. Yang was a well-known quack who was a steady customer for four-ingrediant soup, which he gave for toothache, and three-yellows powder, which he gave for stomach problems. His behaviour was not very exemplary, and his character even worse. He was a pushy man who insinuated himself into people's homes and then carried tales about other men's wives all over town, so most people kept a distance from him, but Ch'ao Yüan felt an affinity for him and always called him when a doctor was needed.

Dr. Yang thought to himself, "Ch'ao Yüan's just brought that fierce Chen ko into the house as his concubine. I myself have had the benefit of her instruction, and even though I took those pills and that powder, I still lost the battle. Luckily for me, I had a secret weapon and it was barely a draw even with that. Even though Ch'ao Yüan's young and strong, he can't possibly hold up with her besieging him day and night. I think he must be wrung dry. Then yesterday he went hunting, which must have been tiring, and at night I'm sure they had another misty session. No wonder he's beaten to a pulp. It's a good thing he's still young. I can guarantee he'll be up and around in no time if I give him some restorative soup."

Then he thought, "I heard he moved out of his wife's place and is living with Chen ko. If I go in there to examine his pulse, I'll bet Chen ko will come out to see me. On the other hand, with Yü Ming-wu and the others there, maybe she won't show herself. Or maybe she will, since they're all close friends and were out hunting together just yesterday. I don't think she'll bother hiding herself, but with all these people around, it won't be easy for me to let her know what I have on my mind." Dr. Yang was much too busy with these sneaky thoughts running up and down like a bucket on a rope through his mind to have his heart in finding the cause of Ch'ao Yüan's illness. Ch'ao Chu came out and said, "Please come in, Dr. Yang."

Yü Ming-wu and the others said, "We want to go, too."

"Nobody else is there, so there's no reason why not," Ch'ao Chu said.

They crossed the main hall, came to a corridor, went down the corridor and finally came to Ch'ao Yüan's room. This is what they saw:

Green balustrades carved in layers
Apes-blood scarlet drapes hanging round the door
A gold-lacquer writing table
Parrot green embroidered folded mats
A bed of dull wood against the north wall
Kingfisher blue quilts layered over brocades
A polished brick smokefree k'ang by the southern window
doubled felt over wicker frame
There lay the patient, eyes staring, mouth mumbling
Three maids stood by shuffling untidily,
their chatter buzzing
The brazier and animal shaped censers glowed red
emerald scrolls of smoke curled from the great stove
More outlandish decorations that I can say
More extravagant outlays than you can imagine

Ch'ao Chu led the way in, with Dr. Yang behind him. After Dr. Yang came Yü Ming-wu, Yin P'ing-yang, and Yü Feng-chi. Ch'ao Chu lifted up the soft bed-curtains, and together they stood by Ch'ao Yüan's pillow.

Yü Ming-wu was the first to open his mouth and say,"You were full of energy yesterday at the hunt. How could you get sick so suddenly? You must have caught cold when you took off your clothes."

Ch'ao Yüan didn't answer, just nodded his head.

Dr. Yang said "This isn't an external ailment. There's vacuous heat all around your face. It's a sickness caused by your kidneys drying up."

All five of them sat down by the bed. Dr. Yang inched his chair closer to the bed and asked an older maid with her hair in a bun to get him a book to steady Ch'ao Yüan's arm while he took the pulse. If the doctor had wanted some fine silver ingots, that wouldn't have been any problem, as there were some in Chen ko's chest of drawers, but, since his request was for a book, it caused some difficulty. The maid looked all over before she located one that lay beside Ch'ao Yüan's pillow. On its cover was written "Secret pleasures of a spring evening depicted".

Dr. Yang said, "If I put his arm on that his pulse will accelerate. Bring me a different book, maybe the Official Directory. The maid looked around some more and found another book under the pillow. This one was entitled "The Tale of Sir Ever-Ready". Fortunately, the doctor didn't open it to see what was inside, and he didn't know anything about Sir Ever-ready, so he placed the book on top of a stand, took Ch'ao Yüan's left arm out from under the quilt, and placed it on the book. The doctor put his head to one side and closed his eyes, giving a performance of "Doctor Taking Patient's Pulse" but for one thing he already had a preconceived notion of what was wrong, and for another he was busy speculating hard:

"Chen ko's really in the lap of luxury now. I wonder if she remembers old Yang?" he thought as he aimlessly poked around at Ch'ao Yüan's wrist for a while.

"As I said, not externally caused. A purely internal affliction," he said.

Yü Ming-wu asked, "It isn't serious, is it?"

Dr. Yang answered, "That's not the point. If some doctor misread his pulse and diagnosed an external ailment and made a prescription on that basis, you'd never be able to stanch the patient's sweat. I'm afraid I have to say nine out of ten patients in such a situation would die. However, I will give him the correct medication and after four or five doses of restorative soup with the addition of two fine medicines, ginseng and gastrodia elata orchid root powder, I guarantee he'll be up for New Year's to enjoy himself with us."

After he told them that, they all left. Ch'ao Chu took five taels and went with Dr. Yang for the medicine.

Dr. Yang said to Ch'ao Chu, as they walked along, "This illness has affected your master quite badly. He looks plump but he's hollow inside, just like a high wall with no foundation propped up by poles. I hear that these days he never goes to his wife's rooms, just lives with Chen ko. So that was their place I saw?"

Ch'ao Chu answered everything he was asked, got the medicine, went home and handed the medicine to Chen ko, saying, "The directions are written clearly on the package. He should take a dose now. Wait and see how it affects him, and then adjust the next dose accordingly."

Chen ko asked, "What else did the doctor say? Did he tell you anything about your master's illness?"

Ch'ao Chu said, "He told me the Master looks sturdy but is all empty inside, just like a wall rotted full of holes, and said 'tell your mistress to have some restraint and not wear him all out'."

Chen ko smiled briefly before yelling, "That stinking little donkey fart! Who needs his stinking gallowsbait's advice! How am I supposed to be wearing him out anyhow!"

Meanwhile they were cleaning out the medicine pan, cutting up fresh ginger, finding a few red dates and adding a tael and two cash' worth of ginseng to the dose. Once the medicine was cooked up it was sent to Ch'ao Yüan. By chance that crooked doctor had stumbled on the right remedy, or maybe it was just Dr. Yang's lucky day. Either way, once Ch'ao Yüan took the medicine, he slept quietly. As evening fell, they made up another dose, which he took. During the night he perspired a very little and stopped babbling. By midnight, his fever was almost half down, and by morning he had regained consciousness. Chen ko told him all about how he'd fainted and how she'd sent for Dr. Yang, how Dr. Yang had diagnosed his illness, and how Yü Ming-wu and the others had come to see him.

She squeezed a few tears out of her eyes and said, "Thank heavens you're better. If anything had happened to you, I might as well have died, too. If I was a little slow about killing myself, that wife of yours would be glad of the opportunity to do me in."

Ch'ao Yüan said, "You scare too easily! You know I'd be dead if it was up to her, so why did you even bother to go call her? If you don't believe me, go sneak a look—right now she'll be clacking away at her prayers and sutras."

Chen ko said, "Before you say any more, look into your heart. After all husband and wife are husband and wife. I know very well I'm just number two around here."

"My cock says you're my wife, not that Chi woman. Go have someone get Dr. Yang to come take another look at me and tell me if I should take more medicine or not."

She called Ch'ao Chu over to the bedroom window.

"Go call Dr. Yang to come look at your master again, and ask if he should take more or less medicine now. Tell the Doctor your master slept well after taking that medicine, most of his fever is gone and he's conscious now, not babbling. Take a horse and hurry back."

Ch'ao Chu went to Dr. Yang's house and told the Doctor all Chen ko had ordered him to. Dr. Yang smiled with such pleasure his eyes shone and his eyebrows lifted.

"All you need to cure any illness is the proper diagnosis. With the proper diagnosis, what need is there of more medicine? Only, since he's so weak and drained, he should take a few more doses just to build himself up. There's no need for me to make another visit for such a minor complaint. If I was anybody else, knowing how rich your master is, you can be sure there'd be a lot of money spent and no cure. Now I've cured Chen ko's fine husband for her, how do you think she'll express her thanks?"

Ch'ao Chu told him, "Yesterday I told her what you said about how she shouldn't wear out the master."

"And what did she have to say to that?"

"Nothing, except that you're a donkey fart and nobody needs your gallowsbait opinion."

They laughed and talked for a while. Dr. Yang got his horse and went back to the Ch'ao's house with Ch'ao Chu. He sat in the main hall until invited on in to Ch'ao Yüan's room.

When Ch'ao Yüan saw Dr. Yang, he said, "Sorry we put you to work last night! I was unconscious, but now I've taken that medicine I feel much better and my heart is settling down. "

Dr. Yang's face split in a wide grin and his traitor's eyes shone blandly, "You have nothing to fear in my hands."

He asked again for a book upon which to steady Ch'ao Yüan's wrist while taking his pulse. Once more the maid pulled out "Sir Ever-ready". When Ch'ao Yüan saw the book, he grabbed it and told the maid to go to the east room and get another one. She came back with one called "Ask not of others". The Doctor took Ch'ao Yüan's pulse.

"You're better than half cured. If you take one more dose I guarantee you'll be all better," the doctor said.

He said his goodbyes to Ch'ao Yüan and Ch'ao Chu led him out under the window of the east room. Chen ko poked a hole in the window paper and peeked out. When she saw Dr. Yang go by, she called out his childhood name, not too loud and not too soft.

"Little Leng-teng! You have a big mouth!"

Dr. Yang suppressed a smile and coughed. Ch'ao Chu sent a servant boy to accompany the doctor home and pick up more medicine. When the medicine arrived they cooked it as per directions. Ch'ao Yüan took it, and did in fact get much better.

Yu Ming-wu and the others in that group often came by to see Ch'ao Yüan, and sent an endless stream of delicacies like Mi-lo olives, crisp pears, smokey tangerines, and waterchestnuts, one following on the other. Ch'ao Yüan took a whole month to rest up. On the fifteenth day of the twelfth month he got up, washed his face and fixed his hair. He still felt rather tenuous and unsteady, probably because he wouldn't give up his carnal union with Chen ko, despite being ill. On this day, he kowtowed to heaven, and earth, made his offerings at the altar, and then went to the back apartments to see Ms. Chi.

"Hey, you—Chi!" he said, "I've been meaning to thank you for visiting me. I'm finally up from my sickbed so I came just to say thanks."

"Who do you think you're talking to?" she retorted, "Don't waste my time with your idiocy. Don't thank *me.*"

They exchanged a couple more phrases through the door, then Ch'ao Yüan went to the front rooms. It wasn't yet sunset, but he got into bed and went to sleep.

On the sixteenth, after he got up, he got out the game that was his portion from the hunt. He inventoried it, and saw that although a month had gone by the cold weather had kept the game fresh. He planned to send some of it for New Year's gifts. For a while, he looked at the white fox pelt. It was very thick and warm, and pure white. He called a servant to skin the fox and send the pelt to the tanner to be cured. He was going to have a saddle pad made out of it.

It was now close to the year-end festivities and Ch'ao Yüan was busy overseeing candle-making, cooking of delicacies and slaughter of pigs. Paper offerings to be burnt had to be bought, as did couplets to hang on the doors. New Year's incense had to be ordered, liquor brewed, rooms and courtyards swept out, lamps set up, painted charms for the lintels readied, and Dr. Yang paid, so, what with one thing and another, Ch'ao Yüan had no time to step outside. He calculated he might as well wait until New Year's to go out, since then he could take care of New Year's visits and visits thanking those who had been to see him during his convalescence all at once. The days at that time of the year are short, the nights long. Before he knew it, it was New Year's and chaotic revels until the third watch (2:00 a.m.). Now,

"New lintel charms have replaced the old, new firecrackers burst"

If you don't know what happened next, read on.

Chapter Three

An Old Pedant appears twice in Dreams
Ch'ao Yüan wants only to flee to his Parents

Fathers and mothers have no care but for their child
Worry for its safety always foremost in their minds
But look at the bleached skull
And say if it's worthwhile to slave like an ox for your sons

To continue, a servant of the Ch'aos', Li Ch'eng-ming, with the white fox-skin under his arm, was about to go out the door. He was going to send it to be cured and then made into a saddle blanket, a nice saddle blanket for Ch'ao Yüan to use on New Year's Day. However, Li hadn't walked ten paces out when a huge sparrow-hawk flew down from above at his face, and slapped him in his face with its right wing. He felt like he'd been slapped by a ghost's hand. The sparrow hawk grabbed the fox-skin in its claws and flew up into the clouds. Li Ch'eng-ming was temporarily stunned. He walked, mumbling, back inside. His face was colorless. Li told Ch'ao Yüan exactly how the sparrow-hawk had slapped him in the face and stolen the fox-pelt. Luckily for him, Ch'ao Yüan's house wasn't strictly run, so nobody gave him a hard time. They just said how it was such a shame, such a nice skin, and well, it's lost now.

On New Year's Eve, Ch'ao Yüan had some new clothes unfolded, had a clerk get calling cards ready, and ordered his horse curried. He had a few drinks, had the bed made up, and went to bed. He also saw out the few year with a last salute to Chen ko. Then he curled up and fell sound asleep.

There in front of him he saw an old, white-bearded man, seventy or eighty years old. The man had an ivory felt cloth around his head, and wore a moderately used plain belted robe of coarse cloth.

The old man said, "My little Yüan! It's me, your grandfather. Now you listen to me; here your father's provided you with a fine life, but you don't want to live becomingly. No, you have to get together a crowd of men and women for some 'hunt', making a laughingstock of yourself. That's not so important, but now you've really brought catastrophe on yourself. That fox spirit of Yung Shan had been perfecting her powers for a thousand years until she was in a state of total spiritual power. She ranked number four or five in the troops under T'ai Shan Yüan Chun. You should never have let evil thoughts take root in your heart! It was fate that you two should be attracted to each other, so that can't be helped, but when she looked to you for help, you shouldn't have shot her dead! It would have been enough to just not help her. Then, on top of killing her, you had her skinned and her pelt sent off to be cured. She's the one who smacked you in the face the other day when you were seeing your guests out. She's the sparrow-hawk that slapped Li Ch'eng-ming in the face. It's lucky for you that both you and your father are riding on rising fortunes now—the spirits at your door and hearth won't let that fox in. Just now I came to receive my New Year's offering from you, and she was on the mounting block holding her fox-skin. She told me all about the way you wronged her and she said if you hadn't let evil thoughts into your heart and seductive glances into your eyes, of course she'd have gone away! But you lured her right in front of you and then you killed her.

She said you'd be sure to go out tomorrow and when you do, she's going to have her revenge. But she won't have your life until your luck ebbs and your friends desert you. She also said that even if your wife, Ms. Chi, isn't a meek wife, she's a good woman. The reasons Chi acts the way she does is that in a former life she was your husband and you were her wife. You were an unloving, abusive wife, so in this life she's come to pay you back. Still, her only fault is a bad temper. Otherwise she's a good person, so she hasn't hurt your family's name or brought ruin on your household. Once she's paid out that debt of several years' unkindness, you two will part friends.

If you don't treat your wife with kindness now, than you'll be adding further mistreatment to what you already gave her in the previous life. I'm afraid rancor will pay rancor, and it will never end! If you persecute her to death, the burden of that crime, added to the crime of killing the fox will be too much.

Listen to your grandpa—don't go out tomorrow. Hide inside a couple of months. If you wait a few months, and then go to Peking, with your parents, you may be able to escape this calamity. When you leave the house, keep that carnelian-seal Diamond Sutra by you. The fox wants to let fire loose on your villa, but she couldn't get in to maneuver, because that sutra is here, keeping a lot of spirits watching over the place. You can see how afraid she is of the Diamond Sutra. She also didn't want to scare your wife, who was her senior in a city association three generations ago.

As the old man was getting ready to go, he tapped Chen ko hard on the head and said, "An who is this lascivious witch come to ruin all my children and grandchildren?"

With that, Ch'ao Yüan woke up and realized it was all a dream. Chen ko cried out from a nightmare, and woke up with a pain in her forehead. They heard the fourth quarter of the fifth watch (5:00 a.m.) being struck. Ch'ao Yüan began talking to Chen ko as he dressed.

"I shouldn't have shot that fox the other day. I just had a dream, and it was really weird! I'll tell you about it sometime."

In his heart, he was beginning to feel afraid. At first he wasn't going to go out that day.

Then he thought, "I'm all better, and if I don't go out for New Year's, won't I be bored to death? If I stay in, all my friends will come here, and I don't feel up to hosting another drinking party."

He thought it back and forth and decided to go out after all, and see what happened. He'd already washed up, and combed his hair, changed, burnt incense on the alter to the spirits of heaven and earth, and kowtowed to the ancestors when the east lightened.

Meanwhile, Chen ko was still suffering from a headache, in bed. She couldn't get up, and was racked with hot and cold spells.

Ch'ao Yüan said, "Since you have a headache, don't hurry yourself. I'm going to pay my New Year's respects at the temple, and then go to the yamen to leave my card. There will still be plenty of time after I get back from that for New Year's visits, and then we'll eat."

He put on a chestnut silk robe with a large arbutus design, set a mink hat (it had cost him fifty-five taels) on his head, and, with one servant carrying a red-gauze shaded lamp, another carrying his card-case, and three or four more servants tagging along empty-handed to clear the road before him and crowd along behind, strode out the door. He stepped up on the mounting block and was about to get on his horse when he fell, striking the side of his head on the block, as if pushed by somebody standing on the block. Fortunately, his hat was thick, so that all that happened was that a piece was torn off the hat and a lump the size of a peach raised on his head. The skin of his head wasn't broken. He was unable to move for several hours. They carried him home, took off his clothes, wrapped his head, and laid him in his bed across from Chen ko's. Then he began to believe his dream of the night before, and he mumbled to himself.

The day after New Year's, they had to call Dr. Yang again.

Dr. Yang came into the room and laughed, "Are you two dying of love? Here we have a beauty and a genius, shouldn't be any problem there!" He sat down and chatted a little.

Ch'ao Yüan told the doctor how he'd fallen on the block the previous day, and said, "Chen ko didn't fall asleep until the third watch and at the fifth watch she woke up from a nightmare, with a headache, and hot and cold spells. She didn't get up once all New Year's Day."

Dr. Yang answered, "I don't even need to take your pulses to know what's wrong with you two! I can guess most of it. You've been so busy getting ready for the New Year you exhausted yourselves. Up late every night, up early in the morning, and drinking, too, I'm sure," and, he whispered in Ch'ao Yüan's ear, "You two celebrated the end of the old year so hard you can't see straight or think clearly—no wonder you missed your step on the mounting block!" As he spoke, the doctor edged his chair closer to the bed and took Ch'ao Yüan's pulse.

"Exactly as I said."

He ordered a maid to pull a chair over by Chen ko's bed. The maid pulled aside one of the bed-curtains and caught it on a hook. Chen ko couldn't resist playing up the situation, and coyly covered her head with the quilt.

Dr. Yang said, "First put out your right hand. After he'd taken the pulse in her right hand, he told her to put out the left, and he took that pulse. When the maid turned away for a moment, the doctor twisted Chen ko's wrist sharply. She didn't dare cry out, so she had to take it in silence, but she pinched him back hard enought to raise a welt or two.

Dr. Yang pulled his chair back and said, "I see you're exhausted. And there's a bit of an external infection."

He called a servant to come with him to get medicine and said goodbye to Ch'ao Yüan. The servants led him out to the main room and gave him a big cup of tea. Ch'ao Yüan had given him a tael for the medicine, and delegated the servant Ch'ao Feng-shan to go with the doctor.

In a little while Ch'ao Feng-shan came back with the medicine. One of the women cleaned out two medicine cups and carefully cooked up the prescription, following the directions. Ch'ao Yüan's medicine was nothing but restorative soup, since all that was wrong with him was that he'd had a fall and wanted pampering. Chen ko's was a soup of angelica root. After she took it, she perspired, and her fever abated overnight, but her head ached more than ever.

Ch'ao Feng's wife said, "I'm going to look for an almanac of spiritual disturbances. Then we'll see what's wrong and cure her."

She sent someone off to the temple of the god Chen Wu, to ask the Taoist priest Ch'en there to lend his book. Then she looked up the thirtieth. The book said that the spirits of the hearth would be restive, and to present them with five strips of paper money, and with tea, liquor and cakes.

Ch'ao Yüan said, "It wasn't the thirtieth when she woke up with a headache. It was already New Year's morning. Look again."

For New Year's the book said, "You encounter familial wrath. Demons sit right in your household sanctum. Repent and pray."

Ch'ao Yüan suddenly remembered his grandfather's appearance in his dream, hitting Chen ko on the head and cursing her. It was right after that that she had awoken with her headache. "Encounter familial wrath" clearly referred to his grandfather's disapprobation.

Ch'ao Yüan ordered Mrs. Ch'ao Feng, "Don't wait for evening. Go right now to our household alter and pray to the spirit of my grandfather. Tell him if he'll let Chen ko be, she'll go herself and apologize."

Feng-shan's wife was a good talker. She went in front of the tablet of Ch'ao Yüan's grandfather on the family alter, knelt on one knee, kowtowed four times and supplicated the old man's spirit with the following prayer:

"Now we are in the New Year's season and we hope you will come to receive our offerings. Sir, you haven't been keeping a benevolent watch over us. Why stoop to our poor human level, and go making her head ache and giving her a fever? Even if she did offend you somehow, we'd expect you to be too big to dwell on the faults of beings lower than yourself. Please ignore her faults in kindness to your grandson. If you do her any harm, not a morsel will ever pass his lips again!"

She finished her prayer and went back to the bed-chamber. Strange to say, Chen ko's headache slowly subsided.

On the other hand, the left side of Ch'ao Yüan's face, and his eye, were swelling up worse and worse, becoming tight and painful. His whole left side was so sore he couldn't turn over. On the third day of the new year, he sent a man again to ask Dr. Yang for some medicine.

Dr. Yang had Chen ko on his mind, so he was glad of an excuse to say, "I'd better go have a look at him so I can adjust his dosage."

He had a horse readied and rode back with the servant. Then he sat in the main hall while the servant went in to say that the doctor had come himself and wanted to take Ch'ao Yüan's pulse. Ch'ao Yüan was dull and imperceptive enough to think it was just as natural as that iron pulls the compass needle for Dr. Yang to be so friendly that of course he didn't mind a bit taking the trouble to ride over himself. Ch'ao Yüan had the doctor shown in.

Chen ko was all better that day. She had fixed her hair and dressed herself in new clothes, head to toe, to pay her respects to the spirits, just before the doctor walked in. She modestly avoided him and went out the east door, but he did get a look at her.

After the doctor finished examining Ch'ao Yüan, and said goodbye to him, he walked out under the window from which Chen ko had called out to him on his last visit.

Through the hole she'd poked in the window last time, she said, "Little Leng-teng! Leave well enough alone, do you hear?"

Repressing a laugh, as before, the doctor pointed to a golden-furred little pekinese dog and said to the servant who was seeing him out, "What do you keep a strange little dog like this around for, waiting for a chance to bite people!"

Then he had his tea in the main hall, and there's no need here to go into the details of how much the medicine cost and how it was fetched.

Chen ko walked into the bed-room and said to Ch'ao Yüan, "You could tell a person if you're going to ask the doctor in. He just barged right in, and there I was, blinded by the light. I was just done with my morning obeisances and he got a look at me."

Ch'ao Yüan laughed at her, "So you mind him taking his powders and pills for you?"

Chen ko stared at him and yelled, "Where did you hear that filth?" Ch'ao Yüan laughed, "That's filth from the actor's pavilion at Ying P'ing-yang's studio." Chen ko had nothing to say to that so she just laughed and shut her mouth.

She called a maid to place a table in front of Ch'ao Yüan's bed so she could eat with him, and said, "You have a rest. I'm going in to the household sanctum to kowtow to your grandfather and thank him for having mercy on me the other day."

Ch'ao Yüan said, "That's right, you should do that. Take a few women with you."

Chen ko strode in to the household sanctum and walked in front of the tablet of Ch'ao Yüan's grandfather. She knelt down, but didn't even have time to kowtow when she looked up, screamed, and ran out. Her white gauze skirt-caught on the door frame and she fell in a pile with such force one of her high red shoes flew off her foot and landed three or four paces away. She was pale with fright and unable to say a word. The three or four women who had accompanied her were afaid to go pick up the shoe, but they raised Chen ko up and then burst into Ch'ao Yüan's room to tell him what had happened, giving him a scare,

Chen ko sat for a while before she could speak, and it was only then that she realized her shoe was missing. She called a little servant boy to look for it.

"I'd just kneeled down and I was going to kowtow and there was an old man about eighty years old, in a purple turban and jacket of rough brown cloth. He coughed and scared me so much I ran out the door. It felt like someone had me by my skirt and was trying to pull me back into the room, she told Ch'ao Yüan.

"That's my grandfather," said Ch'ao Yüan, "How come he's so active these days? The other night he came to me in a dream, and what he told me then was really frightening—saying I shouldn't go out for New Year's or I'd suffer revenge. On his way out he tapped you on the head and cursed you. You woke up screaming from a nightmare, and that's when you started to have that headache of yours. How come he keeps appearing all over like that? He told me a lot in that dream, and it's beginning to look like I'd better do as he said."

Immediately he sent servants to burn paper offerings to his grandfather, to apologize for his failings and ask for help.

Chen ko didn't fall ill again, but she was listless the whole New Year's season, and low-spirited. Even though Grandfather Ch'ao had appeared, Ch'ao Yüan's fortunes were subsiding and not even the old man's spirit could hold off Ch'ao Yüan's nemesis for long. So, in a few days when the swelling over his eye had gone down and his side was not as painful, so he could turn over, Ch'ao Yüan noticed the fine spring panorama outside. Presented with that view, he felt like a scabrous monk on a jewelled throne—all talk and no action.

While all this had been going on, Ms. Chi had been living lonesomely in her back suite, with a few of her own maids, and her woman. When New Year's came, she wasn't about to humble herself to Ch'ao Yüan and he didn't feel like sending her anything to celebrate the holiday with, so her rooms were truly bleak. Her maids and woman saw that Ch'ao Yüan's suite was full of leftovers. They went stamping and banging around with long, tearful faces, heaving huge sighs and grumbling.

"This is what we get for devoting our lives to serving her. Even beggars get a steamed bun and a coin at the end of the year, but with this limp thing as our mistress we have even less hope of a happy, long life than an eighty-year old woman going to be a bride would!"

One of them said, "It's your own fault if you didn't work at accumulating virtue in this life or before. Those people out front with Chen ko have obviously practiced virtue in a former life. We can't compare ourselves to them."

They howled their complaints like this at the top of their lungs, without bothering to worry that Ms. Chi might hear them. She pretended not to hear, but she felt angry and hurt.

That was how things stood when her father, and her brother, Chi Pa-la, came to call and wish her New Year's cheer on the seventh day of the new year. Old Chi walked back to her rooms, where he saw the cold stove with an empty pot on it, no firewood, and his daughter sitting there with tears in her eyes and pain on her face. The servants pursed their lips and looked meaningfully at each other, said little, and didn't bring out so much as an empty teacup for his refreshment.

Old Chi sighed long and hard, and said, "Who would have thought you'd be living like this while he enjoyed his riches? What are you waiting for? You still have clothes and jewelry—take some out and sell them so you can celebrate the New Year. Or maybe you're waiting to take out your unhappiness on your old father? Or for your brother to stand up for you?"

Ms. Chi laughed shortly.

"What proper wife has to go sell her clothes and jewels in order to eat?"

Old Chi stood up and said good-bye, and "Try to bear things. Maybe he'll come to his senses, and you'll have a good life yet."

As he spoke Old Chi, too, cried.

Ms. Chi said, "Don't you two worry about me. I'll bear all I can, and if it gets to be too much I'll either wait for my parents-in law to come back so I can tell them all about it, or I'll just die and make myself plain that way."

She saw them out after she'd finished speaking. Indeed, it is easier to adjust to respect after humiliation than the reverse. He had used to fear her like a living boddhisattva, who might crush him in the palm of her hand or dissolve him with her mouth. If she told him she was going to hit him, he wouldn't dare evade the blow. He lay down flat for it. If she began to scold him, he stood nailed to the spot and took it, rather than run the risk of infuriating her further by leaving before she had had her say. Now that he had revolted, he treated her more like a swaggering disobediant son treats his parents than anything else. Not only was he now devoid of the least speck of fear of her, he had hundreds of ways to show her his utter contempt. Even a statue of wood would have been annoyed by this treatment, so it's no wonder that she grew frantic.

When her father and brother were gone, Ms. Chi went back inside. She began to think about how mean Ch'ao Yüan was, and how unfeeling her servants were, and she couldn't help bursting into tears.

"Oh god of heaven! Lower your head and hear my prayer! Remember it doesn't reflect well on you if people see you letting everyone turn their backs on honor and forget all that's due to others! How can you let them mistreat a fine upright woman until she becomes a starving sinner in hell? And that stinking piece of his, wife to thousands, treated with as much respect as some living goddess! I burn good incense to you so you'll see I'm treated right, but you're just like all the others! You're on that thieving woman's side! But I know just what I have to do to foil their plots, and I'll do it, too! I will, I'll die and go to the yellow springs. I'll pull him in front of King Yen-lo, and then we'll see which is green and which is red, which white and which black!"

She cried until it hurt, and of course made a lot of noise.

Ch'ao Yüan turned his head to listen a while, then said, "Who's crying like that? Everything's supposed to be peaceful and happy to start off the new year right. What's going on in her stinking hole in the wall. Have someone go find out."

"No need for that," Chen ko replied, "I can tell you now she's gotten to the tantrum scene in the play "The Inconstant Husband Ch'iu Hu". I wasn't going to say anything, but now I may as well. When all is said and done, there's no getting around the fact that it's me who's the extra one around here. If you send me away, she'll be your wife and you'll be her husband, like before. It's all my fault that she's cursing you as bad as she can."

Obviously, this was said to incite Ch'ao Yüan to treat Ms. Chi with even greater coldness.

He said, "Nevermind. Let her curse away. They say 'one curse means ten years' sunny fortunes and ghosts and demons distanced from the door'."

He also sent a maid back and told her, "You say 'Here we are in the first month of the new year. It isn't very smart to make all this noise now, when the master hasn't even got up from his sickbed. There'll be plenty of time to curse him after he's dead.'"

The maid said all that to Ms. Chi, who screamed, "And I know where that came from, that stinking piece of his! She can do anything she pleases, but back here I might as well be in Hell. There's no New Year here.I'd better cry now while he's alive to hear me. If I wait until he's dead, people might think I'm crying because I miss him."

She tried to keep crying and kept up her noise as loud as she possibly could.

The maid went to Ch'ao Yüan and Chen ko, and repeated it all, word for word.

Ch'ao Yüan laughed a little. Chen ko's face flushed.

"I guess she's showing her love. 'A blow's as good as a kiss,'" she said. She narrowed her eyes and began to scold, "Don't just sit there looking silly. If you don't have a good lip, don't take up the flute."

"My little Chen ko," Ch'ao Yüan rejoined, "calm down, now. Remember that dream Grandfather sent us on New Year's, and how we have to depend on his protection and do as he said."

Chen ko snorted loudly and spit. "Like P'an Chin-lien said, a three-legged toad is something special, but you can have as many thousands of two-legged cunts as you want."

Ch'ao Yüan stayed in bed until the fourteenth of the month. His swelling was down, and much of the pain was gone. He was almost recovered.

He said to Chen ko, "It's time to put up the lanterns. I'm going to pull myself out of bed and oversee that. You tell some of the women to buy boxes of sweets. Then we can look at the lanterns and have some fireworks let off. If I don't get up soon, everyone will be saying how dull we've gotten."

Chen ko couldn't say enough in praise of this bad idea. Ch'ao Yüan made the effort to put on his clothes and stand up. Without washing his face or combing his hair, he put a cowl over his head. He still felt dizzy. The servants hung lanterns all over, and set out a small family-style set of drinking implements. He brought out two pots of plum blossom, and one of welcoming spring wine, which he put in the bedroom, for later drinking with Chen ko.

They enjoyed themselves with the lanterns and drinking for three nights straight. On the night of the sixteenth, under the brightly shining lanterns, he told Chen ko about an astrologer.

"He's over at Yü Ming-wu's now, waiting to come to me and be a member of our household, when I have time to see him. Tell someone to pack up an especially nice set of snack-boxes, along with two big jugs of wine, and a box of snacks and one of rainbow sweets, and give him all of it to celebrate the holiday."

Chen ko had a servant prepare all that, and said, "He's home at the right time, too. I was just wanting someone to tell my fortune. You should really get yours told, too, and see what directions are unlucky, so you can avoid a few ghosts!"

She gave the boxes of provisions to Ch'ao Chu as she teased. Ch'ao Yüan went out with Ch'ao Chu and told him in secret to take the boxes to Ms. Chi.

"You tell her 'Aunty Chen is sending these to the Mistress for the holiday.' After that, come back and say that you gave them to the astrologer at Yü Ming-wu's house. Don't tell Chen ko that you actually gave them to my wife."

"Yes, I understand," Ch'ao Chu said. He arranged the three boxes, picked up the jugs of wine, and brought them back to Ms. Chi, saying, "Aunty Chen's sending these—to the Mistress for passing the holiday."

Ms. Chi flushed right to ears and screamed, "That shameless tramp—it isn't enough she's stuck her head up against my sky and tracked all over my land and taken my man. Now she's giving me holiday goodies! That's about as likely as snot going up your nose instead of down, isn't it!"

Her woman councilled her, "She meant well, and now she'll be humiliated if you refuse her present."

Ms. Chi said, "I don't need your stinking opinion. If she isn't humiliated for herself, maybe you'll be humiliated for her, I suppose," and, to Ch'ao Chu, "You take that out of here right now or I'll really get mad!" She chased him out and slammed the inner door.

Ch'ao Chu took the boxes back to Ch'ao Yüan and said, "That astrologer has left the subprefecture, so there was nobody to accept these."

Ch'ao Yüan followed him out of the room and he told Ch'ao Yüan every word Ms. Chi had said. Ch'ao Yüan laughed but didn't say anything. Unknown to Ch'ao Yüan, a maid overheard their conversation and reported it to Chen ko. If Chen ko had never heard about it, the matter would have ended quietly, but she did hear it, anger spurted up from her heart while hatred galled her bitterly.

She flew headfirst into a temper, shrieking and yelling for a while incoherently, and then crying, "That shameless bastard! Whose side are you on anyway? If you care so much for your wife what am I doing here? If you want to go do your duty, you go right ahead. I don't have you tied to me with a rope, you don't have to bother with this song and dance. Send her a thousand boxes of sweets! A thousand steamed buns! You can even give me to her, for all I have to say in it! A very good story too, about that fortune teller or Taoist or whatever, just to give her a chance to curse me out with her foul mouth! I guess it's my sky over my head, and my land under my feet and the man I've been faithful to is my man. I never heard anything about your heaven or land or man!"

She spewed endless abuse. Ch'ao Yüan was as abashed as Jen Po Kao handing the Jade Gate Pass over to his former whipping boy, Pan Chungsheng, with an apology to the left and a self recrimination on the right.

He kept saying, "I only wanted you two to get along. You can't possibly think I care about her."

They quarreled noisily until the second watch (10 p.m.). No lanterns were lit or incense burnt. Everyone went to bed dressed. Ch'ao Yüan had just fallen asleep when he saw the same old man who had appeared in his dream on New Year's, now coming into the room with a walking stick in his hand. The old man used the stick to push one of Ch'ao Yüan's bed curtains aside and catch it on a hook.

"My grandson Ch'ao Yüan! You're going to regret ignoring an old man's words. You didn't do as I told you that day. You just had to go out. If I hadn't been there holding her back, she'd have killed you with that fall. Anyway, you're due another half year of life. The fox with her debt of revenge, is watching your every step and is as busy as ever doing no good. Your wife's getting some bad ideas, too. I'm going tomorrow, so if you don't rush to throw yourself on the protection of your parents up north, there won't be anyone here to help you out. It's so awful! When you go, be absolutely sure to have that Diamond Sutra with you. Don't forget."

He also lifted up the curtain from Chen ko's bed and had his stick raised to bring down right on her head, but he paused to say, "Contaminating everything around her! What vicious poison was in her heart today?" He pulled back his stick, "No, what good would it do? Just cause more trouble for my grandson."

Chen ko dreamed that she saw the same old man who had been ready to strike her with a stick at the family altar. Waking from her dream, she threw off her quilt, jumped off the k'ang and burrowed in under Ch'ao Yüan's covers.

"He scared me to death!" she cried.

Ch'ao Yüan also woke up with a shout.

"Don't go Grandfather! Stay here and help me!"

The two of them clung to each other so closely they formed one sweaty body, and told each other their dreams.

Ch'ao Yüan said, "Grandfather's sent me two dreams. It's very clear that if I don't do what he says, there's certain to be a catastrophe. Lets get everything ready as fast as we can and go to my father's official post. The only thing I don't understand is why my grandfather kept saying to go north, when my parents are in Hua-t'ing. From tomorrow on, I'm not going out at all. I'll send someone to the villa to get the Diamond Sutra, have the luggage packed, and pick a lucky day to head south.

Indeed,

> Ghosts and spirits can foretell the future
> Catastrophe makes itself evident as it nears.

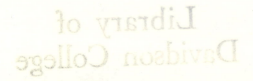

Chapter Four

Hermit T'ung bows and scrapes
Chen ko fans lust and miscarries

Ill-read but wearing a hermit's turban
Calling himself a recluse but always in and out
of the city
His mouth like a matchmaker's, his tongue always wagging
His attitude a concubine's, his posture always cringing
Telling stories about the enlightened, "his cronies",
Wildly claiming those in high places as "his relatives",
He lays his alchemy and fortune-telling before his patrons
He cheats them easily of much silver

The arts of the bedchamber are better left alone
Don't wager your life on women
Chen ko paid high for her wicked stimulants
She miscarried and almost died

After those two dreams and bouts of illness, Ch'ao Yüan was very subdued. Ms. Chi had never had any fault except her domineering behaviour, and Ch'ao Yüah had only grown to despise her after he became rich and went up in the world. The presence of Chen ko had also made him treat his wife even more like dirt than he had before, depriving her of her rightful place in the household. Now, in the cold morning light, Ch'ao Yüan thought over how his grandfather had upbraided him for his bad behaviour, and, despite himself, discovered a small residue of conscience in his heart. From then on he desisted a little in his haughty ways.

On the seventeenth of the month, he slept until the rest of the household was up and busy. Then he dragged himself out of bed, fixed his hair and closed up the celebrations by burning offerings at the family alter and having the lanterns packed away. After that he gambled for copper cash with Chen ko, who had Ch'ao Feng-shan, his wife, and the maid Hsiao Ying-ch'un standing behind her and advising her on strategy. Around noon Ch'ao Yüan and Chen ko ate,and the dishes were cleared away.

A small servant boy came in and said, "The gentleman from across the way, Mr. Yü, has come with a turbanned man I don't know to visit you, sir."

"Where does that man sound like he's from?" asked Ch'ao Yüan

"He's loud and screechy, like a northerner," answered the boy.

Ch'ao Yüan wondered, "Who could it be?"

Chen ko said, "It must be that astrologer you sent those snacks to the other day, come to thank you!"

Ch'ao Yüan laughed, and had a maid bring him a straight gown.

Chen ko advised him, "You'd better take off that gauze hat and put your cowl on, and say you're not better yet. If you sit around the house all dressed up, but don't go out to return people's calls, they'll be talking behind your back."

"You have something there", he agreed. He took off his gauze hat, put on his cowl, and a white fox-fur lined jacket. Then he went out to greet his guests.

He walked out to the middle gate and told a maid, "Tell the women to put together a box of snacks. These people may stay a while."

Having arranged that, he went out to the main hall and saw a man in a turban:

Swarthy faced as Chang Fei and dull-haired

Gowned in shining flecked satin

Shod in shoes ornamented with red thread

His vulgarity precedes him

Talk flows around him

The West wind causes the leaves of the t'ung tree to fall

But a good for nothing is ready for the cold winds.

Yü Ming-wu said to Ch'ao Yüan, "Here we are in the holiday season and you don't step outside your door. Are you watching over your flowers here at home?"

"Watching over my flowers! After that fall on the first of the year I've been laid up until now."

He invited them in.

The turbanned one said, "In this holiday season, do let me express my admiration and respect for you with a bow—no, no, don't get up, please."

Yü Ming-wu joined in, "This is brother T'ung of Ch'ing-chou. His given name is Ting-Yü. He's good with potions, and, having heard your reputation, came to pay his respects."

Ch'ao Yüan said, "So, a guest from afar, over a prefecture away. I must apologize for letting my trifling indisposition keep me from appearing properly dressed. I don't dare accept your greetings in this state."

T'ung Ting-Yü said, "Please don't worry yourself, just let me offer you a bow to express my deep appreciation for your indulgence in granting me this interview."

Ch'ao Yüan wouldn't let him, and they finally all inclined as equals. A little boy from Yü Ming-wu's household, who had been standing there with a visiting-box, came over. T'ung Ting-Yü opened the box and took out an old-fashioned folded visiting card.

Opened, the card read:

> Herewith included as gifts are
> One pack of white pills
> Two products of my maladroit brush, Two sashes
> Four aphrodisiacs
> Offered with respect. This insignificant T'ung of
> Ch'ing-chou hopes you will accept these tokens of
> his esteem.

T'ung unfolded the card and handed it to Ch'ao Yüan. Ch'ao Yüan scanned it and had a servant on the side take it. Then he joined his hands and bowed gratefully to T'ung Ting-Yü. He also ordered the gift put away. He and his guests now relaxed, sat down, and made social conversation for a while.

Then, T'ung Ting-Yü took the initiative, "Although I'm just a poor man, I have studied a little bit of this and that, and know a few exotic concoctions. Well, I was fortunate enough to be the beneficiary of such kindness from the elders in my district, and the young scholars, thanks to my little knowledge, that I can say in all truth that Board President Ch'ien of the Board of Civil Office, and Board Vice President Sun, head of the Censorate, Chang Nien-tung in the Provincial Bureau and Chi Ta-fu of the Han-lin Academy were all just like a father to me. But with all of them around me, there just wasn't enough of me to go around. Whenever I visited one of them, he'd keep me at his house for several days, so I couldn't help not getting around to everyone. Then when I did go see them, they'd say, 'You're getting so cold and profit-minded, now you're flying high you don't have time for us'. So then I never even got out of the gates of Ch'ing-chou city and really I'm just like that little frog at the bottom of the well who hadn't seen anything at all except the one patch of sky. Even so, everyone I met told me, 'In Wu-ch'eng there's a man named Ch'ao Yüan, the son of a provincial official, a good host and one who understands how to treat worthy men. He cares nothing for money but he values his friendships. If you go to him, he'll see you clothed well. He divides his possessions generously with his household, and such an attractive, masterful man, too' So I was thinking of you as if you were both my parents rolled into one, and I was resenting every hour I couldn't throw myself at your feet, but I was so bothered and busy with all those important people who wouldn't let me be, how could I get away to you?

"Well, then, Board President Ch'ien was appointed to head the Military Board and he begged ignorant me to go along with him, you would have thought his life depended on it. When the others heard about it, were they likely to let me go? They all said, 'If you go with Ch'ien we'll starve ourselves to death in sorrow. Don't tell us you'd be that cruel'. When Ch'ien heard how they were hanging on to me, he told them, 'You say you can't bear to give him up, but all you want is for him to mix you up few medicines you want right now, while I'm thinking of his future. Look at him! Is this a man destined to obscurity? Let me see what I can make of him. My being appointed to the Board of Military Affairs is a good chance—I won't have any trouble at all making him into a third-level commander, even a titled general.

"Also to tell the truth, he needed me to mix a few doses for him," Tung added softly, "so finally the others gave up."

Ch'ao Yüan observed that T'ung always called himself 'ignorant me' and Ch'ao Yüan 'sir'. T'ung spoke about all those important people in quite familiar terms, and yet seemed in awe of Ch'ao Yüan.

"Get some licquor ready in the back," Ch'ao Yüan told a servant.

The servant went to do so, and then Ch'ao Yüan asked, "So, now, has Ch'ien gone to his post?"

T'ung Ting-Yü replied, "He already went to the capital on the twelfth of the month last year. If ignorant me hadn't stopped by to see you, sir, I'd be gone with him. I'm really in luck today. I feel as if the sun had given me an audience."

He was so flattering that Ch'ao's heart itched for more. The liquor was served and they drank until the watch was sounded, when T'ung left.

Ch'ao Yüan saw him to the outer door and then stood rooted to the spot, saying, "Due to my slight indisposition I don't dare go out yet. Permit me to say good-bye from here."

T'ung Ting-Yü said his good-byes and crossed back over to Yü Ming-wu's, accompanied by Yü's servant-boy.

Ch'ao Yüan detained Yü Ming-wu, and said, "We haven't spoken in quite a while, and it's still early. Let me give you a few more drinks."

Yü Ming-wu said, "You haven't entirely recovered yet; we'd better make it another day."

As they stood by the outer door, Ch'ao Yüan asked Yü Ming-wu for more information about T'ung Ting-Yü's background.

Yü Ming-wu said, "I haven't known him very long myself. It was the singer Chao Ch'i-Yüan who told me that T'ung makes really top-notch medicines, and was on his way down-province to try for promotion. Actually, Chao Ch'i-Yüan hadn't known him that long, either, and it turned out he didn't have any regular place to stay. That's why I let him stay in my back pavilion."

Ch'ao Yüan said, "Well, he certainly is friendly as his type is supposed to be, and it sounds like he's done all that patron and client stuff. All that's left to complete the picture is for him to produce a few paintings. Have you seen any?"

Yü Ming-wu said, "He isn't much of a painter. He just does a few willows and apricot blossoms, and not too well."

Ch'ao Yüan asked what did T'ung want with him anyway?

"What does he want with you?" answered Yü, "When that kind of man comes to a new place, of course he's going to ask around about all the wealthy and prominent locals, expecially who likes to entertain and who keeps a small household. He picks out a few great houses, leaves his card there with some small gifts, and knows he won't lose anything by it."

Ch'ao Yüan asked, "I was wondering, how much should I pay him for those things he gave me?"

"How many packets of medicine was it?" asked Yü Ming-wu.

"I didn't look very closely. Four or six, maybe."

"He sells that medicine for five cash a dose. A whole catty of his white pills might be worth a tael, the two sashes would go for a tael and two cash, the paintings for a scant three taels. It's six taels altogether, and you already gave him a drink, so now if you pay him a scant two taels, you'll be even.

Ch'ao Yüan said, "He seems like he wouldn't even bother to notice two taels."

"Figure it out for yourself, then," said Yü Ming-wu, "And if you do overpay a little, it will just reflect well on your generosity."

Having finished their conversation, the two parted. Ch'ao Yüan went back into the house. Chen ko sat down after she'd greeted him.

"Did the astrologer give you a good fortune?"

Ch'ao Yüan laughed, "He didn't tell mine, but he did yours and he said you'd lose big in the end!"

Then he thoroughly examined T'ung's gifts. He picked up one of the four packets of aphrodisiac and held it in front of Chen ko.

"See this book of fortune? Four books for four seasons."

Chen ko tried to grab it, but Ch'ao Yüan said, "Why even bother for something worth less than a tael," and hid it in his sleeve.

"Bring some tea," he said, "and then we'll go to sleep. Enough yammering for now."

He had some tea, then went out to the closet in the back and took the aphrodisiac according to its instructions. Then he came back, sat a while, and finally got ready for bed and lay down.

There's no need to detail what passed on the pillows that night. The next morning they woke up at the hour of the dragon (8:00 a.m.) all smiles.

Ch'ao Yüan ordered food and drink prepared. He was going to invite T'ung Ting-Yü and Yü Ming-wu to drink in his Sun-ray pavilion. He sent a servant to invite them over for lunch.

Yü Ming-wu looked at T'ung Ting-Yü and said, "Old T'ung, your magic's working!"

T'ung said, "It always does unless they shut the door in my face and won't even try it."

They joked a little more, and went over to the Ch'aos'. They were led into a garden, laid out to the west of Ch'ao Yüan's main hall. In the north of the garden, facing south, was the Sun-ray pavilion. Towers, terraces, and rustic reed cottages were scattered about the garden, and it was altogether a fine, big place, but far beyond the meager landscaping abilities of the vulgarian Ch'ao Yüan, so the decorative elements were strewn around like junk in a shady antique shop. The three greeted each other. Ch'ao Yüan was a much more punctilious host than he had been the day before. Chen ko herself came out to observe the scenery, and the food was more lavish than it had been. Each of the three men at the table knew exactly what it was all about, so there was no need for explicitness.

At the first meeting they were getting acquainted, and at the second they were old friends. Ch'ao Yüan didn't put on his official's accent, as he had the day before, nor was T'ung as entirely obsequious as he had been. They unbent quite a bit as they drank. They stayed until the second watch (9:00 p.m.), when Ch'ao Yüan saw them out as far as the second door.

Yü Ming-wu was all set to go home, but first he whispered into Ch'ao Yüan's ear, "How was it?"

"As good as they say! I want more."

Yü Ming-wu said, "I was talking to him, and he said he plans to leave soon, so as to be able to help celebrate the eunuch T'ien's birthday on the second day of the second month."

Ch'ao Yüan said, "Tell him to give me all the medicine he has. He won't lose by it."

They gave each other parting salutations and said good-bye.

One day went by, and then on the second day T'ung sent a formal note announcing his departure, with a package of aphrodisiacs folded inside it. On the package he had written:

"Perishable. Use promptly."

Ch'ao Yüan took the packet and said, "We'll have a going away party for him tomorrow. The twenty-second is an auspicious day." He sent off someone with the invitation, and also invited Yü Ming-wu. When the day arrived they had their drinking party and dispersed. On the morning of the twenty-second, Ch'ao Yüan sent T'ung eight taels, five in payment and three as a farewell gift.

Chen ko said, "You're always wasting money, but when it comes to little things you're so calculating. You should give a little more to a man who's at all the best houses. Give him a little something for show. You can't count the five taels, they're payment, so that means you're only giving him three taels—how could he even lower himself to take it?"

Ch'ao Yüan said, "Yü Ming-wu said I could just give him a tael or two, so I've already doubled it."

Don't listen to him, " Chen ko said, "You can't go letting other people make your decisions for you. You could give T'ung ten times more and it wouldn't be too much. And just handing over money isn't nice, it's like paying for a service. Now, listen, wrap up six taels as thank-you money, get him a length of coarse gauze, a pair of shoes, a pair of damask socks, and ten gold fans, and then you'll have sent him off right."

Ch'ao Yüan laughed, "Your wish is my command! This is really telling fortunes for the great." He wrote a formal note and had it taken over to T'ung.

T'ung was more grateful than words could express, and Ch'ao Yüan's generosity reflected well on Yü Ming-wu as well. T'ung himself came over, full of thanks, before his departure.

"I will remember your kindness, and return."

Yü Ming-wu lingered at the door again, pointed at Ch'ao Yüan, and laughed, "I can see Chen ko's hand in this! You're usually generous enough but not this magnificently!"

Ch'ao Yüan replied, "That sort of person is like a matchmaker. If you don't part on good terms, they go all over saying awful things about you."

Yü Ming-wu said, "He was just hoping for a few taels. He really would never have expected all that."

Ch'ao Yüan invited Yü Ming-wu back in, but Yü said, I'll go back home to keep him company while he eats, and then send him off," and said good-bye to Ch'ao Yüan.

After that Ch'ao Yüan began to get ready for his own departure. He was going to have new curtains of oiled pongee made for the offical's second-class sedan chair he had had bought for his wife, and let Chen ko use it once the curtains had been fitted by a craftsman. He set the twenty-first day of the second month as the date they would leave. and paid three taels down to reserve twenty-four pack mules, which would cost him two and a half taels each to go from Wu-ch'eng to Hua-t'ing. He wrote a note to pay the remainder of their hire. Every day he was busy assigning overseeing duties. Clothes for all his attendants, and the disposal of his hunting trophies had all been taken care of previously.

By now, the first month of the year was over. Ch'ao Yüan picked an auspicious day to sent a man over to the Yung-shan villa to get the Diamond Sutra. Unexpectedly, on the fourth day of the second month, right after supper, several Yung-shan vilagers arrived in a panic at his house.

"Last night at the second watch (10:00 p.m.), we don't know how it started but a fire burnt down the villa and then went out by itself without burning anything else," they told him.

When Ch'ao Yüan heard that, he knew very well that it meant the fox was daring to show her hand now that the sutra was gone from the villa. He said how it was too bad! It was really a shame! Then he gave the villagers a hard time for a while before he went in and told Chen ko about it. He remembered what his grandfather had said in his dream, and he was really getting scared.

Indeed, "good luck never comes in pairs and bad luck never comes singly."

Chen ko hadn't had her menses since before the enclosed hunt, and, in fact, she was five months pregnant. When T'ung had presented them with those aphrodisiacs, they should have known that even if you have the tools at hand for heavy work, there are times it behooves one to stay with delicate embroidery. But she never took care, and shook loose her five-month pregnancy. She couldn't help being terrified when she heard that the villa had burned down. On the afternoon of the sixth day of the month she felt pain in her lower back, and slowly the pain intensified. She ached continuously until just before dawn on the seventh day, when she miscarried a girl.

Chen ko was nineteen years old at the time. It was her first pregnancy. She hemorrhaged and then fainted away. They waited for her to wake up, so they could clean and tend to her.

When Ch'ao Yüan saw her, he said, "I paid eight hundred taels for this worth-her-weight-in-silver lady. Can't leave her lying there like that!"

Quick as flame catches, he sent a servant for Doctor Yang to come look at her.

Dr. Yang may have had the title of a physician, but there was no medical expertise behind it. When had he ever looked at the medical classics of the Yellow Emperor and Wang Shu-ho? When he had to treat anything worse than a cold, he was just a blind man in a bell-tower. When a woman gives birth, she's on the border of life and death, and if she steps over it, she's dead, while if she pulls back, she'll live. That's no situation for a quack.

Outside the southern gate of the city there was a doctor who specialized in gynecology. His name was Dr. Hsiao. Despite his availability, Ch'ao Yüan sent for Dr. Yang instead. Dr. Yang himself should have given thought to the fact that there's hardly a hair's breadth between miscarriage and death, and that this was no time for him to try his luck.

However, Dr. Yang thought in his heart, "What's there to worry about? She's lost some blood, that's all. Some ten-fold restorative soup will build her up,and these days everything I do turns out well."

He often said to people, "I have my own way of doctoring people, and I don't mind telling you what it is. To cure the rich young fellows the main thing is to cut down on their food and lower the internal fire. To cure a woman, no matter what ails her, all you need is ten-fold restorative soup, and to cure a miserable poor man you need to cheer him up. This is the route to recovery, and the little detours on the way don't matter."

Since that was his philosophy of healing, even for Chen ko's miscarriage, all he prescribed was ten-fold restorative soup, along with a dose of the soup often given to settle pregnant women's stomachs, strengthened with a tael and a half's worth of ginseng.

In this case, not even Dr. Yang's good luck sufficed. Chen ko's noxious hemorrhage didn't stop. Her head ached and she had a persistent fever; her belly swelled up tight as a drum and she panted like an ox. His pretty-as-a-picture Chen ko was almost done in, and Ch'ao Yüan didn't know what to do. He was a wreck from dashing around, getting oracles on bamboo at the temple to Sung general Yüeh Fei, having astrologic and milfoil prognostications done, having a shamaness dance, and paying the bamboo-knocker to divine by bamboo and the mirror-diviner to divine by chanting and looking for the future in a mirror. He was busy reciting the Taoist Sutra of Preservation at the temple of the city god, offering vows to Buddha, vows to serve the god of north star for three years, and vows to fast for a lustrum. He even tried having medicine made with a piece of his own flesh as a charm.

It was a good thing that his neighbour, Yü Ming-wu saw the state he was in asked what was going on. Yü Ming-wu came over to visit him, and Ch'ao Yüan told him all about it.

Yü Ming-wu said, "Dr. Yang never did know anything about women's ailments. Dr. Hsiao Pei-Ch'uan at the southern gate is the one who knows about these things, and you made a mistake when you didn't call him. Get a horse ready right now and send someone to get him."

Then Yü Ming-wu looked up at the sky and reconsidered, "By now he may have gone and got himself drunk, though."

Ch'ao Yüan sent his servant Li Ch'eng-ming on a fast horse. Li was off like the wind.

This Dr. Hsiao could always put his finger on the exact cause of any ailment related to childbirth, and he cured ninety-nine out of a hundred of the women he treated. He had just one small problem, which was that before he went to see a patient he liked to have a drink, and after he'd had two drinks he didn't want to go out any more to see any patient. If he got as far as the patient's house, he wanted a drink there, which he enjoyed so much he didn't feel like standing up, going home, and making up medicine for the patient. On any day, if nobody had come to ask for him by the hour of the horse (noon), he took in his sign, closed up shop, went inside to pour himself a drink, and kept drinking until he was as soundly asleep as the legendary Chen Hsi-yi, who slept a hundred days at a time. He was as far gone from this world as Confucious dreaming of the Duke of Chou ever was. His bad habit often caused trouble to people. He was such a skilled doctor, but he never could regulate his own life.

On this day, it was drawing close to the end of the hour of the sheep (3:00) and he was still getting himself drunk. When Li Ch'eng-ming arrived at the doctor's, he found the door shut tight. Li dismounted and threw a pebble against the door, but only a balding maid came out.

"Go in and tell the Doctor that the gentleman Ch'ao Yüan requests him urgently, and that I have a fast horse here for him," Li said.

The maid said, "It's no good. He's dead drunk in bed, and there's no chance of him getting up again today."

"What do you mean," said Li, "I'm talking about life and death here! I could almost die I'm in such a hurry, and you sound awfully relaxed!"

The maid answered, "I'm not saying you're not in a hurry but once he's drunk he's just like a clod of earth. Even if you carried him out of here, what good would it do? He might come out first with some crazy answer to your questions, but then if you ask him any more it'll be like trying to call back the dead."

Li Ch'eng-ming said, "My good sister! Go in and have a look at him and see if you can't wake him up, if not, let me in and I'll ask him myself. Otherwise I'll hire four men and we'll carry him off, bed and all."

The maid said, "Wait a minute. I'm going to see what the mistress has to say."

She went in and told Dr. Hsiao's wife what Li Ch'eng-ming had said. Mrs. Hsiao went over to her husband and began shaking him. His eyes popped open and stared.

"The Ch'ao household wants you!"

Hsiao mumbled, "So what if bandit Ts'ao's gaunt in the well. Have someone get him out."

Louder, she said, "People want you to treat a patient!"

This time he answered, "If people want you to be fleet with cakes go ahead."

"You really kill me with that tune of yours," his wife said, and she told the maid, "go on outside and tell the gentleman's servant to come in and have a look for himself."

Li Ch'eng-ming came in.

"We have a very sick person who urgently needs the doctor—what's the meaning of this?" he demanded of Mrs. Hsiao while pushing and pulling the doctor who was like a sack of mud.

"You take your time waking him up," said Li, "while I go back home and tell them what's happening here, otherwise they'll be worried."

Mrs. Hsiao versified briefly, "He's drunk and dormant, begone—Tomorrow bring your request and money".

Ch'ao Yüan was waiting with his eyes peeled in hope of the sight of Dr. Hsiao. Li Ch'eng-ming, having failed resoundingly, came back to report how he'd found the doctor dead drunk.

"I was afraid you'd be unable to bear waiting with no news, so I came back first to let you know what was happening. I'm going back now, and I left someone waiting by the southern gate, so no matter when he does wake up, we'll know."

Li changed his mount and rushed off. When he got back to the Hsiaos', he knocked, tied his horse by the window, and was admitted.

Respectfully, he asked, "Is Dr. Hsiao awake yet?"

Mrs. Hsiao said, "No, he's busy talking to that Duke of Chou. Once the Duke leaves, you can ask anything you like. You'd better wait in the main room, sir. If you're tired, there's a bed inside, too. I'll have your horse taken to the donkey shed and given something to eat."

Having settled Li Ch'eng-ming, Mrs. Hsiao made him four dishes of drinking snacks, a plate of dried bean lees, a plate of pickled meat, and a pot of warmed wine. The maid who had opened the door for him originally left the food and wine on the table, brought in a little brazier, and placed a dish of eight cakes and a couple of bowls of gruel on the table, too. Li Ch'eng served himself, and he welcomed the food as much as Han Hsin welcomed the food a washerwoman gave him below the city wall. Due to Chen ko's illness, the Ch'ao household had been in such a turmoil that Li Ch'eng-ming hadn't had a chance to eat.

When he had finished eating, the maid cleared away the plates. Li Ch'eng-ming went back to the donkey shed, saw his horse fed, and came back in. The maid gave him a rug, a sheepskin comforter, and a pillow. He lay down on the bed, blew out the lamp, and fell asleep fully clothed. He was just going to have a little nap before he got Dr. Hsiao up and into the city, but it had been a long, tiring day for Li, and he was fast asleep as soon as he put his head down. The Duke of Chou ran straight into Li Ch'eng-ming, as he departed from Dr. Hsiao. By the fifth watch (4:00 a.m.), Dr. Hsiao was seeing out the Duke, who then held Li in conversation.

The doctor sneezed a couple of times and asked for a drink of cold water. His wife told him that Ch'ao Yüan had sent for him.

Dr. Hsiao said, "Hurry up and warm a pot of liquor to clear my head. After I've had a little, I'll go back to the city with that man and see the patient."

His wife said, "They have a sick person there and they're waiting for you as anxiously as Chen Kou watched the moon when he thought the moon goddess was in love with him, and you want a drink! Do you think there will be any time to spare once you've eaten something and woken up? You listen to me—don't bother with your hair, just put a cloth over your head and set out now, in the dark. Go right over to the Ch'aos', diagnose what's wrong with her, and bring some medicine with you."

Dr. Hsiao said, "Yes, you're right, but if I don't have a little sip how will I ever clear my head of this hangover?"

He got up while he spoke and even washed his face. He put a cloth over his head, and a sky-blue padded gown on, and went to wake up Li Ch'eng-ming. Li was now in the same state the doctor had been in before, and he only woke up after crying out incoherently a few times. They spoke, Dr. Hsiao had horses readied, and the doctor told his servant to get his medicine case. They arrived together at Ch'ao Yüan's and went in to announce themselves.

Meanwhile, Chen ko had spent the night with her stomach swollen as tight as a drum and she felt so oppressed she almost wished she were dead. Ch'ao was so excited he was hopping around like a baboon, running in and out. He rushed to invite the doctor in.

As Dr. Hsiao walked in, he said, "A fine house you have here. Hurry up and put on a pot of liquor for me. If I don't have a little sip I'll never get over this hangover."

"I'm getting it ready now!" said a servant.

The doctor went into Chen ko's room, took her pulse, and said, "There's nothing to fear. No problem seeing what's wrong. The secretions of the afterbirth are stopped up. Watch, she'll be half cured before I finish my drink.

Ch'ao Yüan said, "I'm depending absolutely on you. Of course you'll be well rewarded for your trouble."

They went back to the main hall. The doctor took out his case, mixed up a liquid medicine, and had the medicine sent back to be cooked up for eight minutes with a goblet of water. Then he took a pill as big as a round eye, and said it should be dissolved in warm yellow wine, and be washed down by the liquid medicine that had been cooked with water. Then he put his case away. Ch'ao Yüan presented him with two taels as the 'gratuity for opening his case'. Dr. Hsiao politely declined once, before he took it. Ch'ao Yüan also rewarded the servant who had brought the doctor, by giving the servant a hundred cash. Then they set out the licquor.

Dr. Hsiao said, "Sir, you go in and watch the patient take her medicine, and instruct the servants in looking after her. Me, I'm going to have a drink. I hope you don't expect me to stand on ceremony?"

Ch'ao Yüan said, "Please let me pour you a drink before I do as you say."

Ch'ao poured the doctor's first cup of wine, and drank one to keep him company.

The Doctor urged him to go in to Chen ko and said, "Sir, bring me a tea-cup. This little wine cup is such a bother."

Chao Yüan went back to Chen ko and asked a maid, "Have you cooked the medicine?"

"It's all ready," the maid said.

Ch'ao Yüan used a silver spoon to crush up the pill in wine, and then poured the hot liquid medicine over it.

Chen ko, her face swollen and purple, said, "I'm ready to burst and that doctor went and covered my head with the quilt so I could hardly breath. That gallowsbait stank of licquor, too-almost killed me with his slimy stink. I haven't got my breath back yet."

While she was talking, the medicine was prepared. Ch'ao Yüan brought it to the bedside, assisted Chen ko to a sitting position against the pillow, and poured the pill mixture and the medicine in her mouth. After she drank that she farted twice, and her stomach seemed less swollen. She was quiet for a while, then she burped twice and felt even less swollen and in much better spirits.

The doctor took a mouthful of wine, and said, "Sir, has she had her medicine yet? Once she does, she should fart a couple of times and burp a few times. Then the swelling will go down and she'll be more at ease."

A servant went to see, and reported back, "Like you said, she's beginning to feel less full."

Dr. Hsiao opened up his case, took out another pill and said, "Grind this up in warm wine, and have her wash it down with caramelized sugar and yellow wine. I'll have another drink and wait to see how the patient's doing.

Chen ko took this medicine, too, as directed, and in about half the time a meal takes she felt a sticky oozing down there. She touched herself, and her hand came away bloody. They told Dr. Hsiao about that right away.

The doctor was well on the way to being soused and said, "The dark blood will stop soon and fresh blood will begin to flow. Get a bucket ready."

Chen ko felt that the swelling of her stomach had greatly ameliorated, and she felt as though she had to urinate. She was helped over to the chamber-pot, and hemorrhaged four or five catties of blood. They helped her back to bed, where she passed out for a while. Her swelling was entirely gone, and when she woke up, she asked for a bowl of gruel. They told the doctor of her progress.

By now, Ch'ao Yüan had collected his wits. He went out front to thank the doctor.

"Elder Pei-ch'uan! You're not a great doctor—you're an immortal! That medicine worked like magic."

He accompanied the doctor in a few more drinks. They ate, and then the doctor took his leave, saying,

"After she's slept through the night, let's see how she's doing. You can send someone to me for more medicine. There's no need for me to come here again."

They called Li Ch'eng-ming to lead out the doctor's horse and see him off.

Mounted, the doctor joked with Li, "So now I've cured your eight-hundred-tael lady, I guess I deserve at least half that amount in thanks."

Li Ch'eng-ming said, "Why stop at eight hundred? If she's worth eight hundred taels, the master's worth eight thousand, and if she died, he'd never be able to go on without her. You've saved the entire household, not just one person."

Dr. Hsiao said, "I've been well paid today, so when you come tomorrow, you don't need to bring anymore money. Just bring a big bottle of wine. I like that wine of yours."

Li Ch'eng-ming said, "Never mind one bottle, you can have ten."

As they talked, he saw Dr. Hsiao home. Then he reported their conversation back to Ch'ao Yüan, including the doctor's request for wine. Chen ko wasn't on her feet yet, so Ch'ao Yüan was still worried. If you want to hear if she was up by the tenth of the month, read the next chapter.

Chapter Five

A Magistrate bribes his way from Sub-prefecture to District
An Actor uses his influence at the Civil Board

Don't think just because a man's a "scholar" he's erudite
Though he shows himself a fine Confucian in the light of day
Even a beggar brazen on his pile of dirt
Is superior to this fast-talking Yu-meng, risen by obscure
machinations
Squeezing taxes and extorting extra payment for "exchange-rate"
Levying redemption fees and every imaginable charge
Not for him the admonishments carved in stone cautioning
good official behaviour
Not for him the records of criminal prosecutions
All he can see is his enrichment and burgeoning prestige
Not his final calamity
He will twist reason and turn right and wrong upside-down
to suit his argument
People laugh at his pretensions
An actor is his great protector

As dawn crept over the sky on the ninth of the month, Chen ko's head stopped aching, her fever went down, the swelling in her stomach subsided and her after-birth secretions stopped. Her breakfast tasted good to her, and she was ninety percent better. Still, she had been living recklessly and now she had lost much blood, so she was exhausted.

Ch'ao Yüan sent Li Ch'eng-ming to Dr. Hsiao's for some more medicine. He also had Li take a tael in payment, along with an earthen jug of wine and five stones of polished rice to the doctor.

Dr. Hsiao didn't half mind the money and the rice, but what he really liked was the wine. He was as glad to see that as Ch'ao Yüan was to see Chen ko's recovery. He wouldn't take 'No' for an answer, but kept Li for a drink before money was exchanged, the medicine sealed up, and Li sent back home with it.

The next day was the tenth of the month. Early in the morning some conveyance agents brought twenty-four mules to Ch'ao Yüan's door.

The servant on duty at the door said, "We have a sick person here today. Can't you come back another day?"

The agents said, "In our line of work one day idle is one day's feed down the drain. Who's going to pay for that?"

The servant relayed that to Ch'ao Yüan.

He said, "The mistress isn't well, and she can't start out today. We'll have to give up the idea of leaving this month. I'll pick out an auspicious day for travelling next month. If they want to wait, they're welcome to. Otherwise, they can keep the down payment and go find other work. We'll hire somebody else when we're ready to go."

The servant returned with this message to the agents, who began screaming and yelling.

"This is our busiest season, the beginning of the year with a lot of people coming to hire our mules, but you reserved them ahead of time, so we didn't take any other work. If you send us away now, you're hurting our business and that's the truth! We go through so much feed every day that down-payment of yours won't even feed our mules for three days. You'd better compensate us for the rest of our time wasted!"

The agents were milling around half trying to break into the house and half trying to get Ch'ao Yüan to come out, when, fortunately, Yü Ming-wu came by to settle the dispute. He got them to accept the three taels' down-payment as compensation for the feed their mule would consume these few days, on condition that if they were rehired the three taels would not be deducted from their pay. He also called for a big bottle of wine to be warmed for the agents' consumption, and, finally, between threats and wheedling, he got them to leave.

Meanwhile, Magistrate Ch'ao in Hua-t'ing was putting all of his energy into currying favor with local Important People, as well as his superiors. At the same time, he treated farmers and mere holders of the first degree as if he had some grudge from a former life against them. As a result, he did not have good support from those below him. They all hated him because he took his responsibilities so lightly, and governed by bribery. In the sixth month of the previous year, he had passed his end-of-probation exam, and been officially confirmed. He made his rounds of the Boards and his recommendations were all in order.

In the ninth month, a troupe of actors from Soochow arrived unexpectedly with a letter of recommendation from Commissioner Chao who asked Magistrate Ch'ao to look after them.

The Magistrate read the letter and sent a man to see that the actors were put up at a temple. He ordered the yamen servants to rotate duties of keeping the actors in food and drink. The troupe rested for a couple of days, and on the third day the magistrate had a banquet, to which he invited the local Important People, and holders of the third degree, and Imperial Academy students, so they could enjoy these new entertainers. The magistrate also had a stage erected in the temple grounds, for a performance of the story of Mu-lien saving his impious mother from Hell, to be watched by all the common people. That went on for half a month before it was completed.

The invited guests left in order of precedence, each with an attendant entertainer. When the performance was over, each Important Person gave about ten taels, each family of the Academy students' gave thirty, the third-degree-holders gave eight, and other rich people donated five hundred. The six business offices of the yamen got together two hundred, so the total was over two thousand taels.

The first day of the tenth month was Madam Ch'ao's birthday, so the actors packed up and moved into the yamen to perform. When they saw Magistrate Ch'ao they thanked him over and over. He asked them for news of what was going on out there in the world. The rest of the actors gradually trickled away, but there was one female impersonator, Hu, and one player of men's parts, Liang, who kept standing there chatting away. Eventually the conversation arrived at the fact that Magistrate Ch'ao had passed probation and was eligible for promotion.

Magistrate Ch'ao said, "The way the world goes these days, if you don't have a connection somewhere, even if you're as good as Lung Chu or Huang Pa, the Board of Civil Employment won't promote you for free. The stiffer the emperor's laws get, the more the Board goes for money. Luckily, here in Hua-t'ing, I'm in charge of a large population, and each day I rack up another day's worth of prestigious experience, but, all the same, it's up to the Board whether or not I get my promotion soon."

Liang said, "But, Sir, now you've passed probation, if you don't look after your own interests by going to the Board and seeing to it you get a good promotion, what are you going to do if somebody else schemes for this place? Then you'll have to go off to some remote, second-rate place or be 'promoted' to some terrible district that has nothing but problems. If you want to get on top of this, I have a very good connection, and it won't cost you much. I guarantee it'll go the way you want. I'm so grateful for your generosity that I'd like to pay you back this way."

Magistrate Ch'ao asked happily, "Who's your connection?"

"It's going to be as easy as pulling something out of a purse. All you need to to is send two of your trusted servants with me, and be a little patient. I guarantee I'll have good news for you by the second month of next year."

The Magistrate said, "Let's talk about this some more tomorrow after my wife's birthday is over. What you say makes a lot of sense; if I just leave things to fall out as they will and end up with some awful place, then what will I do?"

They agreed on that, and the next day Magistrate Ch'ao called Liang to a bare little room.

Liang told him, "There are a lot of important people in the capital who remember me with kindness, and I know quite a few at the Board of Civil Employment. I won't have any trouble going to them. If you don't think that's sure enough, I have one place I can go to that's solid as a cannon, and faster, too, but the only condition for that one, Sir, is that you let me go about it in my own way. You just concern yourself with results, not means. And tell those two you'll be sending them only there to fetch and carry, not to hang around asking questions and getting in my way."

Smiling, Magistrate Ch'ao asked, "So, who is this influential person you're talking about?"

"Chief Eunuch Wang Chen. If I ask there, there isn't the slightest doubt."

Thunderstruck, Magistrate Ch'ao said, "I wouldn't presume! How could I dare bother Chief Eunuch Wang Chen with my requests?"

Liang replied, "That's why I told you to just sit back and let me take care of things my own way."

"How much do you need?" asked Magistrate Ch'ao.

"First, you decide where you want to work. Then I estimate the price."

Ch'ao said, "Even though I've made a good name for myself, got four or five commendations, and finished probation, I'm afraid it would be too much to try for a really top position. Working on a Board's nice, but the emperor's very smart, and he keeps an eye on things, so that makes a commissioner's life hard. Outside of the Boards of Civil Office and Rites, which one is worth thinking of? Officials at the Board of Military Affairs always have to go running around to remote passes to take care of Essen's raids, and then, there's the Board of Punishments. It's true a lot of prisons have been going up lately, so that's a very lively area , but what you have to think of at the Board of Punishments is how easy it is for officials there to be stripped of rank and flogged for the slightest little thing. That leaves only the Boards of Works and Revenue, but lately jobs there are more trouble than they're worth. I don't feel lucky enought to try there. So, if a Board job is out, that leaves being a sub-magistrate at a prefecture. But those shabby yamens are so poor and one aggravation after another, I don't know. I guess after all there's nothing for it but to be a Department Magistrate. When you come right down to it, there's nothing like being a top-level official. Then you can do things the way you want."

"That's all very true, sir, but which Department were you thinking of?" asked Liang.

Magistrate Ch'ao said, "I can't go too far out. I'm a northerner, and I don't like to go far from home. Then, too, I'm getting older. T'ai-ts'ang, Kao-Yu and Nan-t'ung are all good departments, and close, too. But they're too big. Getting on as I am, I don't have the energy to take care of such a large place. Besides, lately there's been a lot of problems about people getting convicted for not coming up to quota, very hard to pass promotion there. After that, there's the Northern T'ung-chou District and Tao Tz'u in Honan. They're not too far from my Shantung. I'd really like the Northern T'ung-chou District. It's only forty li from Peking, and right on the water route from my Shantung. It's like being an official in Peking, first in line for blanket commendations and to pass probation. When you go to the capital, see if you can get that for me. That one would do very well."

They set the sixteenth of the twelfth month as an auspicious date for travel, and chose Ch'ao Shu and Ch'ao Feng to be the two servants to go with Hu. Ch'ao Shu and Ch'ao Feng had a thousand taels, as well as two hundred taels' travelling expenses. They hired mules and prepared to arrive in Peking, by the overland route, before the Lantern Festival.

Hu thought to himself, "Of course it's only right we should pay Magistrate Ch'ao back for his hospitality, but we ought to get something out of it too. A thousand taels isn't enough to do this right, either. It's a good thing Liang told him to his face to let us take care of it our own way. After I get to the capital, I'll keep my eyes open to see what we can do with this."

With the wind for dinner and rain their pillow, they travelled for twenty-eight days. They entered the Shun-ch'eng gate of Peking on the fourteenth day of the first month, arranged to stop at a little temple beside the waterway, and left their bags there.

The Chief Eunuch Wang Chen was originally Sub-director of Studies in Wen-an sub-prefecture. At the end of his probation, he was found wanting and the Yung-lo emperor had him castrated in punishment. Then Wang Chen entered the palace as a teacher to the women there. When the Cheng-t'ung emperor came to the throne, Wang Chen rose to his position of Chief Eunuch in charge of palace affairs, and also held the title of Grand Secretary. His power was almost as great as the emperor's. The members of the cabinet all left their visiting cards, and the ministers of the six boards knelt in his presence. When Wang Chen left the capital, officials had to kneel by the side of the road, and when he stopped to rest, local officials had to change into work clothes and get busy in the kitchen fixing his dinner.

When Wang Chen had been a Sub-director of Studies, there were two actors who were friendly to him. When he came to power, these two found their places, too. They became a regular part of his retinue. Eventually they became the teachers of the palace actors. Wang Chen was very fond of them. Later still, they became commanders of the secret police. They were so rich that gold, silver and gems were like shit to them.

These two were the way Liang and Hu had access to Wang Chen. One, Commander Su, was Hu's maternal grandfather. The other, Commander Liu, was Liang's uncle once removed.

On the evening that Hu and Liang arrived in Peking, Hu took a man with him to carry a basket with a ham in it, and also baskets of dried bamboo shoots, Hu Ch'iu tea, and salted fish, to his grandfather's house. They were announced and went in. Commander Su was very glad to see Hu. Hu's grandmother had been dead for quite a while, so the household now consisted of only three or four concubines, who all came out to greet Hu. He told Commander Su the details of Magistrate Ch'ao's aspirations. Commander Su nodded his head. He had food brought, and a study readied for Hu to stay in, but since Hu had left Ch'ao Shu and Ch'ao Feng at the temple, and, after all, they had the thousand taels, he demurred and said he'd go back to the temple to stay with them.

Commander Su said, "It doesn't make any sense to stay in a temple when your grandfather's house is right here for you. Have them brought here and moved in."

Hu ate, and, as evening fell, took two household servants and went to retrieve the luggage from the temple.

Ch'ao Shu and Ch'ao Feng said, "But the temple's clean and we're close to the kitchen and the heat here, so let's just stay here. Or else you can go stay at your grandfather's and we'll stay here—that's the easiest thing."

But the two servants didn't pay any attention to them. They packed up, called for two horses, put the luggage on the horses and took it away. Since they had the thousand taels in the luggage, Cha'ao Shu and Ch'ao Feng ran after as if their lives depended on keeping that luggage in sight.

Hu told them, "Let the servants go ahead with the luggage. We can take our time catching up."

On that day, the fourteenth of the first month, people were just beginning to try out their lanterns, and it was a peaceful scene with the lanterns under the clear moonlight. The three of them looked as they walked. Ch'ao Shu and Ch'ao Feng had assumed that Hu's grandfather was an ordinary Peking householder. When they arrived at his house, though, they saw three lofty tiered gates and a massive, black-lacquered, double-leaved main door. On the right leaf hung a rose colored seal-printed announcement of the occupant's status in the secret police. On both sides there hung New Year's talismans, and over it all, a couplet in cinnabar:

The Lord's benevolence deep as the sea
The servitor's scrupulousness weighty as a mountain

while over the lintel there was a small sign reading: "No loitering, disturbance, card-playing or gambling permitted. Offenders will be prosecuted."

"Why did he bring us here?" wondered Ch'ao Shu and Ch'ao Feng. But then they decided his grandfather must be a clerk or other functionary in the house, whose family was allowed to live there.

As they approached, a crowd of people stood waiting to serve them, and when they reached the door one asked, "What took you so long, sir? Your luggage arrived long before and the Master's tired of waiting. They went in the main gate, and Ch'ao Shu whispered in Su's ear, "Whose house is this? We can't just go in."

Hu said, "It's my grandfather's"

Ch'ao Feng whispered softly, "What kind of man is your grandfather, living in such a big house, with all these servants around the door?"

Hu said, "He's just a military governer in the secret police, that's all. The reason he has a servant or two is that he's the commander of the southern brigade."

As he spoke, they went through the inner door and he had the man on duty there show Ch'ao Feng and Ch'ao Shu to a small western room to relax. The room was brilliantly lit and too gorgeous for words.

Ch'ao Chu and Ch'ao Feng had some tea. Then they looked at each other's amazed faces and decided they had better go pay their repects to Commander Su before they relaxed and started talking about everything. Hu despatched a servant to Commander Su. After quite a while, the servant returned with a message from the commander, saying that as it was late now, they could see each other in the morning. For now the man on duty could keep them compnay, and Hu should come to him.

Hu said, "You two relax. I'm going to see him."

The two of them thought, "And we imagined he was just an actor playing women's roles! Who would have guessed he had this kind of background? We used to call him 'little Hu' and make fun of him and he never let on at all." They ate and went to bed.

The next morning, Hu had put on a straight belted robe of chrysanthremum-green floating silk gauze, a black velvet plain square cap with a purplish mink hat over it, red shoes and white socks. He walked into the study, and when Ch'ao Shu and Ch'ao Feng saw him, they didn't recognize him at first. Then they took a second look and saw it was Hu, and came forward disclaiming any qualification for connection with such a person. Hu opened up the luggage and took out a letter from Liang to Liang's uncle, Commander Liu, containing the request for Magistrate Ch'ao. Hu planned to take this over to Commander Liu's, along with the bamboo shoots and fish which he would have someone from Commander Liu's household carry. He told Ch'ao Shu and Ch'ao Feng to come along. Ch'ao Shu had expected Liang's uncle to be an ordinary man, and, since Liang had always been mentioning his uncle in Peking who would be glad to extend his hospitality, Ch'ao Shu thought it would be a good idea to go see this uncle. When he got to that door, it was the same scene as had been enacted at Commander Su's, all over again.

The group from Commander Su's reached the inner door, and Hu walked right in without waiting to be announced. He looked back at Ch'ao Shu and Ch'ao Feng shuffling around irresolutely at the threshold, not daring to come in.

"Come in and sit down," he told them.

"Maybe the two of us will stay out here. This is close to the lantern market — we'll go walk around there and then wait for you back at Commander Su's," they said as they as they edged out.

Now, Commander Liu was Commander Su's nephew so he was Hu's uncle twice removed, and Hu was Liang's cousin. When they did anything, it was all in the family. It had been Liang who had done the talking at first, and he had wanted to come to the capital to take care of the request to the commanders, but he worried that if he left, there wouldn't be any actor to play his roles, so the show couldn't go on. On the other hand, although Hu was the principal actor of female roles, there were other actors who knew those roles, so Liang asked Hu to go to Peking. After all, both of the intimates of Wang Chen were relatives of Hu as well as Liang, so Hu alone should be able to take care of things. On this particular day, Commander Liu was not at home. Hu went in to see Commander Liu's wife, his own aunt twice removed. She kept him to a meal, and when Commander Liu came home, Hu was there to meet him. Hu told him why he had come.

After Hu left Commander Liu, he went back to Commander Su's house. That night they banqueted and watched the festive lantern displays. Also, Ch'ao Shu and Ch'ao Feng had come back from the lantern festival, and they wanted to pay their respects to Commander Su.

Commander Su ordered them to come in. He wore a plain cap of nun's velvet, and a felt robe, very sober and dignified. He motioned them from the threshold to come directly in front of him. Ch'ao Shu couldn't get any farther than the threshold, where he kneeled and kowtowed four times.

"Master Hu just said that we'd come to the capital. He never told us about your house, Sir, so our master didn't prepare gifts to thank you—we hope you'll forgive us," Ch'ao Shu said

Commander Su said, "Master Hu has depended on you to carry everything on the road, so I hope you'll be kind enough to overlook any small remissness in my hospitality. There are many places to amuse yourselves in the capital and many things worth seeing. For now, why not go back to your room and enjoy the lanterns?"

He ordered one of the men on duty to take a bunch of firecrackers and accompany Ch'ao Shu and Ch'ao Feng in drinking.

On the sixteenth, after breakfast, Commander Liu came to Commander Su's house to repay Hu's call. Commander Su was taking a day off for the lantern festival, so he was unoccupied at home and kept Commander Liu to celebrate the holiday with him. It was passed splendidly. Over their banquet, they began to talk about how Magistrate Ch'ao was hoping that the two of them would raise him to the position of Magistrate of Northern T'ung-Chou District.

Commander Liu asked Hu, "What did he give you for us?"

"Just a thousand."

"That opening is worth five thousand," said Commander Liu, "Tell him to give us a thousand more, and we'll see what we can do, for your sake, at a discount of three thousand. If he doesn't like that he can try someone else."

Once he had said that, they didn't refer to the matter again.

Ten days or so later, Ch'ao Shu saw Hu, whom he no longer caled "Little Hu" but, resoundingly, "Master Hu", and said, "Master Hu! We've been here over half a month and haven't made any progress. We haven't used that money, either. What's going on?"

"What do you expect to be going on? He won't be promoted for another two and a half months. Why not just relax and enjoy yourself? You have free room and board here."

Ch'ao Feng said, "But we hate to inconvenience Commander Su with our presence for nothing."

Hu told him, "If Commander Su is willing to let you inconvenience him, you should be glad to do so for a year or so."

One day, at about suppertime on the tenth day of the second month, Commander Liu came to visit Commander Su. He was shown into the inner study and served. Hu was nowhere in sight.

Liu spoke, "How are you planning to take care of that business for nephew Hu?"

Commander Su said, "He expects a top-level District Magistracy for a thousand taels. It just isn't possible."

Commander Liu said, "But we have to consider that we're doing it for Hu. We two old men should do our best for him. Tell him to get another thousand taels and tomorrow it'll be more than half done. We two can split the two thousand taels, and give some to our nephews—that's only fitting for us to do, as an uncle and grandfather. Then we'll tell them to give up that acting and come to the capital so we can set them up in good careers. Something like deputy magistrates, maybe. That's a low position, but ts better than dressing up as officials in a play."

Commander Su said, "Or, we can wait until the thirteenth when we go to celebrate Wang Chen's birthday. We can both go talk it over with him. I don't think there will be any problem then!"

"But we still need that other thousand, " cautioned Commander Liu, "and I don't know when or if he'll come up with it."

Commander Su said, "Don't worry about that. The man's only human. How could he possibly resist paying two thousand for a post worth four or five thousand? Tomorrow I'm going to ask to see his two men and explain it to them, face to face."

Commander Su treated Commander Liu to food and drink, and they agreed that on the thirteenth, Wang Chen's birthday, they would take the occasion to put Magistrate Ch'ao's case before Wang. The next day, when Commander Su came home from the Yamen, he went to his rooms, changed out of his official clothes and had Ch'ao Shu and Ch'ao Feng called. Ch'ao Shu kowtowed twice and then stood waiting in a subservient attitude, his hands hanging.

Commander Su said, "I'm sorry to have neglected you during your stay. I hope you have not been too bored. That job your master wants is one people can't ordinarily get, even for four or five thousand taels, so how does he expect to have it for a thousand? Commander Liu and I have been able, by exerting our considerable personal influence, to have the price set at two thousand taels. You'll get it at only a third of what most people would pay."

Ch'ao Feng had, before entering the Ch'ao household, been a yamen servant, and he was sharp.

He offered, "When we came, our master did tell us that he wouldn't usually dare try for this sort of place, and that if he could have a chance at it, of course the few insignificant things we brought would not be enough. Now, sir, that you have told us to double the amount, it is very inexpensive and we have nothing to say except that our master will come to thank you and Commander Liu personally. But, we have a thousand taels here now, so why don't you take it now, to pass along, while we send a man back to get the rest? When we came, we didn't have many people in our party, and it isn't safe travelling so close to the New Year's holiday, so we didn't bring too much money with us.

Commander Su said, "You don't need to get the money right off I can put up some of my own, as long as he pays it back soon. The problem is that there's already somebody in that job, and when I looked into it, I found he hadn't finished his three year probationary period. What am I supposed to do about him? That's what's going to take some doing."

Ch'ao Shu and Ch'ao Feng ran back to their room, and got the twenty sealed packages that contained one thousand taels in all, and all of it they handed over to Commander Su.

On the thirteenth, Wang Chen's birthday, Commanders Liu and Su each prepared some rare and bizarre objects as gifts and arranged to go together to the birthday party. But when they got there, there were crowds of people, a whole landscape of mountains and seas composed of people pressed tight who wouldn't make way for the two commanders. Within, the three Secretaries, the six Board Presidents, the Nine Ministers, and the twenty-four Palace Ministers were gathered to celebrate. Su and Liu fought their way through the crowd to the distant door, with assistance of beaters armed with large bamboos. The Commanders dismounted at the main gate, and the doorman didn't announce them, just opened the door wide for them to go in. In they walked, wearing their red crepe official robes embroidered with Ch'i-lin designs, snow-white carved jade belts, and trailing the ribbons of their seals of office from their hands. They finally reached Wang Chen's outer chamber.

A chamberlain went in to announce, "Commaders Su and Liu."

Wang Chen said, "Show them in."

Then he said to the commanders, "I see you got all dressed up just to come kowtow to me. Go ahead and kowtow, then, but it would be easier if you'd come naked than it is in all that finery."

Commanders Su and Liu knelt down, kowtowed eight times and then recited, "We wish you nine thousand years of life and all four seasons of every year safe and peaceful."

When they stood up, they didn't wait to salute him in the normal manner, but ran back to get his presents, which they hastened to place in front of Wang Chen. Commander Su had given him a translucent jade box with a tiny gnarled jade peach tree inside. There were ten or so blossoms on the tree, all very life-like. If you looked very closely, you could see that the blossoms were carved in rubies. Commader Liu's present was also a kind of jade box but his had a plum tree inside. It's flowers were made of pearls. The gifts pleased Wang Chen.

He said, "You two are really smart! Where did you ever find these things to show your filial respects?"

Then he told a servant, "Put them away. Box them up and keep them clean. It's going to be the emperor's birthday soon. I'm going to present him with these."

Looking at the two commanders, he said, "All right. You've kowtowed and you've given me your presents. Go get your packets and then we'll have some fun."

The two commanders went to the room they were to share, took off their court clothes and changed into small caps and short houseclothes. They saw servants sweeping floors, hanging paintings and lanterns, festooning the walls, setting up screens and curtains, placing drum and gong stands, arranging tables and cushions and drapes around the tables. Everything was perfect, down to the last detail. Wang Chen came in for breakfast and took the seat of honor. All the civil and military officials took turns wishing him happy birthday. As one went back to his seat, another was getting up.

Commanders Su and Liu stayed at the palace that night. The next morning they got up and found the household busy cleaning up after the party. Wang Chen had his breakfast, changed, and came to their room.

The two commanders scrambled to kowtow and to ask him, "We hope his lordship was not exhausted by his hospitality yesterday?"

Wang Chen said, "I do feel just a little tired out."

He talked idly for a little with them, and watched the servants cleaning up. When the two commanders saw that he was getting ready to leave and return to his chambers, they came forward, and this time they didn't kneal. They stood and made their request.

Commander Su said, "These two unworthy servants have a request to make of your lordship!"

Wang Chen giggled and said, "Let's hear it."

They said, "Your two unworthy servants have a little villa in Hua-t'ing sub-prefecture and the magistrate there, Ch'ao Ssu-hsiao, has taken very good care of us out of deference to your Lordship. He's finished probation and been there about four years. He begs to be promoted and we entreat your lordship to drop a note to the Board of Civil Office."

Wang Chen said, "Where does he want to be promoted to?"

They told him, "He hopes to be promoted to the district level and to be near your Lordship so he may pay his filial respects to your Lordship every day. He honors your Lordship as a father."

Wang Chen said, "Why don't you go talk to the Board yourselves for a little thing like that? Why do you need a note from me? But all right, you can have your note saying what you like. Forget about having me adopting him, though. What do I need with the bastard? I don't want him walking around with my insignia any more than an army needs old ladies in the ranks."

The two commanders knelt and thanked him. Wang Chen had a servant bring him a note and her private seal, with which he stamped the note. The two commanders had a trusted man on duty take Wang Chen's personal note to the chambers of the Great Hall of the Board of Civil Office, where they also went to explain the details.

The official at the Board did just as the imperially phrased note ordered, and promoted the current magistrate of the T'ung-chou District to the sub-prefect of Lin T'ao-fu. Then he put Ch'ao Ssu-hsiao in the T'ung-chou District job, and it was all faster than a paper lantern catching fire. Ch'ao Shu and Ch'ao Feng could hardly contain their happiness at the news. They kowtowed to Commander Su, who then sent a couple of his men to accompany them to Commander Liu's, where they kowtowed again. They packed their bags and took the letter Commander Liu had given them for Liang. Commander Su kept Hu, so he was unable to go back with them. He also wrote a letter to Magistrate Ch'ao, telling exactly how it had gone, and telling him to come at once and take up his new responsibilities. He wrote, too, that the Ning-hsia area had frequent border problems these days with Essen, and that T'ung-chou was of strategic importance. Then he wrote about the second thousand taels, which his grandfather had lent for the time being, but which Magistrate Ch'ao should now entrust to Liang, who would bring it to Peking.

Ch'ao Shu and Ch'ao Feng turned home, full of victory's song and the clash of triumph's cymbals. Read the next chapter to see what happened then.

Chapter Six

Chen ko possesses her servant
Ch'ao Yüan buys a position in the capital

Now you're rich
Don't abandon the wife who shared your poverty
She was there for you in hard times
What use is a creature of kingfisher pins and pearls?
All you need for hunger is home fare
All you need for the cold is plain cloth
Stop coveting the lovely courtesan
She'll be gone the moment you look aside
Flown away
No homebody she
(To the tune "Near the River")

The fool wants a wild gamehen
Its feathers are so fine
But it always looks for its chance to escape
It won't eat from your hand

The domestic hen is heavy and slow
She stays with you until old age
She doesn't lie abed
She's up at the fifth watch to announce the dawn
The gamehen's feathers are beautiful as fresh flowers
Her fascination has always threated homes
The domestic hen is up at dawn
Then she spins flax hidden in her room

When Ch'ao Shu and Ch'ao Feng received the good news, they packed up their bags and settled their bills in the capital with the last fifty taels left out of their two hundred taels' travelling expenses. They said goodbye to Commander Su, reserved some mules, got together some porters, and went south.

Meanwhile, the twenty-ninth of the second month was the festival of the white-gowned boddhisattva's birthday. Chen ko was beginning to feel better, and she had shoes, candles, incense, and paper offerings prepared, which she planned to have Ch'ao Chu's wife take to the temple as offerings. She herself was just getting ready to go out for the festival when there was a commotion at the door. Ch'ao Yüan was just finished combing his hair. They were both startled by the noise.

A servant came in and told them, "It's those same seven or eight men who came last time with the good news of your father's job. This time they're here to congratulate him on being promoted to magistrate of the district of T'ung-chou."

Ch'ao Yüan was overjoyed, and thought, "No wonder Grandfather told me in two dreams to go north to my parents. I thought that since they were south of here there was no reason to go north, but of course Grandfather knew all along."

Ch'ao Yüan went out to see the well wishers and sent off a servant to buy eight rolls of red crepe silk to share his felicity with the bearers of good news, who he then sent to relax in the eastern study. The next day he had a drinking party for them and gave them a hundred taels of good-luck money. They all complained that it wasn't enough, so he added another fifty taels, which satisfied them. Then they left. All of his dearest friends were visiting in continual rotation with their congratulations. However, Ch'ao Yüan still didn't dare step outside his gate to see them off when they left.

Now, Ch'ao Ssu-hsiao had already heard the good news ten days before Ch'ao Shu and Ch'ao Feng arrived. When they came with the written notification, he looked it over and then sent them off to rest in a temple. He was generous with all who gathered to congratulate him, and they all left satisfied. He piled up his paperwork to be handed over to the next incumbent of Hua-t'ing, reserved two official barges, and picked the first day of the fourth month for his departure. He planned to go straight to T'ung-chou without stopping at his home town. He did also give the thousand taels more requested to Liang, whom he told to bid the rest of the troupe goodbye and accompany him on the large to Peking.

On the day Magistrate Ch'ao set out, there were a few Important People and holders of the third degree gathered to send him off, and it was passably impressive. The students and farmers of Hua-t'ing hated Magistrate Ch'ao as a verminous snake and they couldn't wait for him to be gone so they could exorcise the last traces of his baleful presence by sprinkling vinegar. Those farmers were not about to go through any ritual of "taking his old shoes as a souvenir of his kind administration". The Important People were surprised at this, and felt Magistrate Ch'ao had not been unusually cruel as a magistrate, so this reluctance on the farmers' and students' part must be due to a lamentable erosion of tradition in Hua-t'ing.

"We'll write some congratulatory poems, have our boys write their classmate's names on them, and have the teachers put them up. Then we'll have a pavilion put up, find a pair of shoes, and get our tenants to dress up as farmers to do the shoe ceremony," the Important People decided.

They planned it all out, and when the day came, sent off Magistrate Ch'ao boisterously. They got the populace of the city to buy the three sacrifices to wish him luck. In the crowd gathered there, some performed Taoist blessings, some burnt blank payer offerings, some sprinkled vinegar in with sutras, and all grew increasingly festive after he'd gone.

Magistrate Ch'ao had good weather for his journey. Before the fifth day of the fifth month, the Dragon-boat festival, he reached Chi-ning, where the barge was docked. He was going to disembark there to buy twenty or thirty catties of rouge to distribute as gifts when he arrived at his new job, and he also wanted to despatch servants to take his good news back home.

That night, Magistrate Ch'ao had just fallen asleep when he saw his father come aboard and say, "Your son Yüan has been up to some terrible mischief lately. He took it into his head to take his whore out hunting and then he killed a fox spirit! She tried to revenge herself twice, but both times I protected him and he wasn't killed. I'm afraid the luck you two have been enjoying has just about run out, so he won't be able to escape her much longer. You'd better make him go with you to your new job. For one thing, that will get him out of the fox spirit's way, and, for another, no evil spirit would dare follow him into our great capital."

Magistrate Ch'ao awoke and realized he had been dreaming. He woke his wife up, too.

She said, "I was just talking with your father when you woke me up."

The two of them told their dreams to each other, and they matched exactly. They were struck with the strangeness of their identical dreams.

In the morning, magistrate Ch'ao sent a letter to Ch'ao Yüan, saying that he hadn't wanted to waste precious time by going home in Wu-ch'eng, where of course people would be so glad to see him he'd have a hard time getting away, so he was just going to stop off briefly at the family graves to report his promotion by burning a memorial about it to the ancestors, and then continue on to his new job, as Wu-ch'eng was on the water route. He also wrote Ch'ao Yüan how Grandfather Ch'ao had come in a dream which was very strange "and your mother had the exact same dream. Pack up your bags and come join me at my new post with your wife. Once there you'll have plenty of chances to make a name for yourself, so don't miss this opportunity."

So far, Ch'ao Yüan had managed to keep his rascal of a father completely in the dark about his abandonment of his wife and purchase of Chen ko for eight hundred taels. Even though servants went between the two households frequently, they were with Ch'ao Yüan most of the time, so who among them would dare speak up to the Old Master. Now his father had sent a letter telling him to bring Ms. Chi to Peking. How would he get out of it this time?

Ch'ao Yüan had the bedding packed up, hired eight sedanchair carriers, took his Diamond Sutra in his hand, and got into the large sedan chair he'd bought previously. With six or seven servants accompanying him, he headed upriver. He travelled for two or three days, and then he met his parents' boat. They caught up on each other's news. He told his parents that Ms. Chi had been unable to travel because she had recently suffered a miscarriage. He and his parents should go ahead and she would join them later. Ch'ao Yüan and his parents rode the barge for a few days, until they arrived at Wu-ch'eng. There they paid their respects to the ancestors, and burned some paper offerings. Only then did Ch'ao Yüan tell Magisrate Ch'ao that the Yung-shan villa had burned to the ground, and a large amount of grain and other things in it, too. The magistrate spared a sigh or two over it, and then he and Madame Ch'ao went on by boat, going north. Ch'ao Yüan went with them a short way, to see them off, and said that he and his wife, Ms. Chi, would come along by either the land or the water route, once she felt better.

Then Ch'ao Yüan went home and said to Chen ko, "Dad was really happy to hear you'd joined our family, and he wants you to come along to his new post. I told him you were still recovering from your miscarriage and you'd be along as soon as you felt better."

At the end of the fifth month, after the worst of the summer heat was over, Ch'ao Yüan picked the seventh day of the seventh month as the day they would begin their journey over the land route. He reserved mules and sedan chair carriers and had the luggage packed up, all ready. On the fifth day of the seventh month, Ms. Chi went into the front courtyard with four or five of her servants and dragged the sedan chair her father-inlaw had bought her back to her own courtyad.

"My father-in-law bought this for me and I'd like to see that cheap bag of bones of a slave girl try to sit in it! If anyone has anything to say about that I'm going to smash this to a powder and then I'll take care of her."

A servant told Ch'ao Yüan about this. Chen ko was so mad her eyes bulged out and for once she was at a loss for words.

Ch'ao Yüan said, "Let her make a scene! We don't need that sedan chair for our trip. I happen to feel like buying another one, and one ten thousand times better, too."

In fact he did but a magnificent sedan chair, for 28 taels, from the household of an Important Person. That satisfied Chen ko.

Ch'ao Yüan had someone tell Ms. Chi, "I just bought a sedan chair for fifty taels. It's very nice. Come have a look at it."

Ms. Chi spat at the messenger, "Take a look at it! I don't care if you spent five thousand taels; I'm not about to waste my energy walking over there to see it. As long as you don't touch my sedan chair it doesn't matter to me if you spend fifty thousand taels."

She was so abusive the servant woman ran away to be out of range.

On the seventh day of the seventh month, they were all set to go and the servants had been thoroughly instructed on how to run the household in Ch'ao Yüan's absence.

Ch'ao Yüan and Chen ko set off northwards. They travelled uneventfully, progressing north by day, and resting at night. However, when they reached Peking, Ch'ao Yüan didn't bring Chen ko with him to his father's post. He wanted to talk his parents around before he introduced her to them, so he rented a fairsized house by the Sha-kuo gate, where he installed Chen ko with her household things. Her female servants and Ch'ao Chu all stayed there with her. Ch'ao Yüan stayed with her a few days before he took a few servants and went on by himself to his parents.

He told them, "Ms. Chi still hasn't recovered from her miscarriage. I was afraid you'd be worried, so I came on ahead."

Madame Ch'ao blamed him for that, and said, "Your house is right on the river, so why didn't you put her on a boat and bring her straight on to the yamen here? Why ever did you leave her home instead of bringing her along? Who but her husband should be looking after her? You've cerainly grown hardhearted! Besides, we have very good doctors in Peking, they'd have taken good care of her,"

She couldn't get over Ch'ao Yüan's behaviour and wanted to write to Ms. Chi's family to have them bring Ms. Chi on to Peking. Ch'ao Yüan managed to dissuade her for the time being. On the twenty-fourth day of the seventh month, he told his parents there was going to be a market at the temple of the city god.

"I'm going to go have a look at it and buy a few things. I'll be back in a few days."

They gave him their permission and sixty or seventy taels.

When they suggested sending along a couple of yamen runners, Ch'ao Yüan said, "With all my servants, what do I want with yamen runners?"

He took eight servants and went back to the house by Sha-kuo gate, where he stayed over with Chen ko."

To her he said, "It's a good thing you didn't go. That yamen's a fleabag so small there's no place to park your butt to piss or shit. After a few days in a little box like that we'd be crawling the walls. It's lucky for you I thought to go ahead by myself; if you'd been along, once you went in, you'd have to stay in, by yamen rules. Then I'd feel sorry for you, my little Chen ko."

She believed him. On the twenty-fifth, he took a purse of silver taels and went to the market at the temple of the city god, where he bought some unnecessary things before he went back to Chen ko's, where he stayed another seven or eight days. Then he returned to the yamen in T'ung-chou.

Meanwhile, Ch'ao Chu was at the house by the Sha-kuo gate. Ch'ao Chu was not a servant by birth. He had been a doorkeeper, and he had soldiered. He was about twenty-five years old, a dark, chubby fellow, and he had only been with the household since Ch'ao Ssu-hsiao's first government job, at which time he had come with the recommendation of a friend. Ch'ao Yüan was pleased with his cleverness and let him take care of everything. Ch'ao Chu was in charge of calling prostitutes and engaging actors, taking care of money and managing the flow of gifts. When Chen ko used to be an actress, Ch'ao Chu was always hanging around her trading wisecracks, and it was Ch'ao Chu who had carried through the negotiation of her purchase. You could say they were as close as a box and its lid. Stupid Ch'ao Yüan put this same Ch'ao Chu in charge of a household of women, and Ch'ao Chu's wife couldn't have been any closer to Chen ko if they'd shared two nostrils between the three of them.

The clothes of Ch'ao Chu and his wife gradually grew fancier. They made sure nobody talked about irregular goings-on in the master's bedroom, but in any case that dull master might as well have been blind and deaf. They didn't spend too much energy hiding the state of things from him, but he never did catch on. Ch'ao Chu had a gorgeous green hat with gold trim made for Ch'ao Yüan "in recognition of your great generosity". Ch'ao Yüan wore it happily, never connecting it to the proverbial green cuckold's hat. But although Ch'ao Yüan had achieved a cuckold's hat, what he wanted was an official's hat, so Ch'ao Chu's beautifully expressed gratitude did not get the full measure of appreciation it was due. Ch'ao Yüan told his father he wanted to have the rules "relaxed" so he could be admitted into the imperial academy. Accordingly, his father presented a petition that an exception be made for Ch'ao Yüan, and bent over backward to see that Ch'ao Yüan got into the academy as an extraordinary student, and to get the rules relaxed so Ch'ao Yüan could take a place in the official roster. Ch'ao Ssu-hsiao managed it so well he even saved

twenty or thirty taels and the thing was done for under three hundred. He found
an offical from home to help out, and they were able to have the background
investigation annulled in this case. An auspicious day was picked for Ch'ao
Yüan to enter the academy. Ch'ao Yüan presented himself to the head official
of the imperial academy, and the other officals, from the registrar down. From
then on, he took his place with the others, in full scholar's trim—a high browed
confucian cap, a round third-degree holder's collar, a sky blue cord in hand
and white-soled black shoes on his feet. However:

> Never read a book in his life
> His intellect untroubled by the written word
> Even he feels somethnng wrong
> Entering that hall in his sober blue robe
> As soon as he comes in
> Confucious and Mencius take their leave
> Who is he anyway?
> What is he doing here?

Every day, with the excuse that he was going to the academy to study,
Ch'ao Yüan went into Peking to see Chen ko. All his expenses were paid by
the T'ung-chou yamen. Recently, he had also gotten friendly with a slut who
lived near the academy. He paid her for his pleasure and said he was sleeping
over at the school, studying late, when he was really at that slut's place.
Fortunately, Chen ko was not left too inconsolably lonely. If he was going to
"study overnight" she would, too, so she didn't bother about what he was up
to. He was staying at the new girl's house until the twentieth day of the twelfth
month.

Chao Ssu-hsiao said, "Even elementary schools have off for New
Year's—what are you doing there in Peking?"

Ch'ao Yüan said, "You go home to Wu-ch'eng first. Now that I'm here,
I may as well go to the temple on the twenty-fifth before I join you."

Chao Ssu-hsiao did as his son suggested.

After that, what Ch'ao Yüan really did was to set up Chen ko's place for
New Year's. He made sure every detail, from head to toe and from mouth to
belly was complete. He bought four large, snow-white pearls at the temple
market, and also some jade hairpins and things like that for Chen ko. He
bought some embroidered outfits and a length of bright red wan-shou court
brocade as well.

That day there were two marvelous "living treasures" for sale at the
temple market. There was such a crowd of people around them that the price
was hidden from Ch'ao Yüan's sight. Ch'ao Yüan had a servant push the other

people aside so he could get a good look. He saw a large, square, gold-lacquered cage with a tiny red lacquer stand inside of it. On the stand was a miniature copy of the Heart Sutra written in gilt on celadon green paper. Alongside the stand was a dark gray lotus-pillow, and on the pillow was a bright red persian cat. The cat had eaten well, and lay purring in front of the sutra.

The man selling the cat said, "This cat is from the house of the Tathagata Buddha, in India. The Tathagata Buddha got mad at him because he broke the rules of Buddha by killing a rat who was stealing oil from a lamp. The Buddha first decided the cat should pay with his life, but, fortunately, the six guardians, the four Boddhisattvas, and the eighteen lohans all kept begging for clemency. So the Buddha let him live, but condemned him to life as a domestic animal among humans, and had him sent here by way of a westerner bringing tribute to our glorious empire in the middle of the world. The Buddha won't take him back for fifty years. If you listen carefully, you'll hear that he isn't just purring—he's chanting that sutra as clear as can be. He says 'Kuan-yin saves all from suffering' and he's begging mother Kuan-yin to take him back to heaven."

Ch'ao Yüan bent to listen, and it really did sound as if the cat were chanting the sutra.

"That's amazing," he said, "A bright red cat is strange enough, but he chants sutras too. Where is that westerner who brought him? I'd like to see him and ask him all the details."

The merchant said, "After he presented his tribute, he didn't want to wait around to sell the cat. I gave him two hundred and fifty taels to leave the cat with me, and he went back to his own country."

That surprised Ch'ao Yüan who exclaimed, "Why did you pay so much? What good is this cat to you?"

The merchant replied, "Listen to the gentleman will you What good is it to me? Why should I pay two or three hundred taels for this cat instead of thirty or forty for some other fine cat? It goes without saying this cat catches rats. Rats won't come within ten li of him! They go so far away you'll never see a trace of them again. This cat takes away the exterminator's business. When this cat comes to a neighborhood, the exterminator there goes so hungry his breath stinks and his teeth turn yellow. Never mind that, any household that keeps this buddha-cat has a whole crowd of benevolent spirits and celestial generals watching over it. I don't care what type of demons are plaguing you—monkey or fox spirits, it doesn't make any difference, the minute this cat comes, they're dead as sure as if he were General Chang T'ien-shih. Why, just the other day a girl in a household near the Han-lin academy was so bewitched by a fox-spirit she was about to die. They called in a couple of priests from the imperial alter, but it didn't do any good. She was ready to die a miserable death. Then they hung up a charm drawn by the hand of Chang T'ien-shih himself, and when it got dark that charm suddenly crashed like thunder. Everybody said the spirit was caught by the charm. Wouldn't you think so? But the charm was moving and then, when someone went close to it, it spoke.

It said, "That fox spirit is sitting at the door, but I'm holding it in."

The next morning, I came here to market with the cat, and I walked past that house. Wasn't there a crowd standing around? So I stopped to ask what was going on, and who would have thought it—that fox spirit didn't know this cat was outside. It dashed out, but at the sight of the cat it cried out, took its original fox-shape and died on the spot. I took that fox skin and made it into a collar to protect me from the spirits. See? Here it is, I'm wearing it."

The audience hung on his every word through the whole long account.

One said,"You must be joking. Your story doesn't hang together unless General Chang's charm didn't work!"

The cat-seller's face tightened stubbornly, "What do you mean, a joke? The house is right there. Those people are servants in the Han-lin Academy and they'll tell you the exact same thing.

When Ch'ao Yüan heard that the cat was useful in getting rid of spirits, and particularly foxes, he was of more than half a mind to buy it.

He said, "Well, you've talked long enough, but let's get to the point. How much do you want? I'll buy it."

The cat-seller said, "Would you listen to him! Would I waste my breath talking about this if I wasn't trying to sell? I owe a lot of money due at the end of the year and I expect to pay it all by selling this cat. When I bought it, I hope you don't think I had two hundred and fifty taels of my own money. I had to borrow half that before I could buy him. If I don't sell this fellow in a hurry, the people I borrowed money from are going to be asking for it back and it won't be easy for me to scrape together a few taels to satisfy them. I was originally going to ask three hundred taels, but I'll discount the price by ten taels and ask two hundred and ninety."

Ch'ao Yüan said, "That's the stupidest thing I ever heard! Impossible! I'll give you twenty nine taels of first-quality silver, weighed fair and generously. You can take it or leave it. The cat-seller said, "My good sir! Even someone from Soochow would pay me at least half what I spent, but you're only willing to pay one tenth."

Ch'ao Yüan said, "I'll give you three more. That brings it up to thirty-two taels. Will you sell?"

The cat-seller said, "I'm just desperate for money now the year is ending! If I could get through the year-end somehow I could keep this cat and exorcise demons for people. Then I'd earn more than I'd know what to do with."

When Ch'ao Yüan heard the word "exorcise" he wasn't about to give up. He increased hls offer to thirty-five, then thirty-eight taels, forty and then forty-five, but the merchant wouldn't sell. At that point, the cat-seller's collaborator decided there was danger Ch'ao Yüan might lose his temper, or the bystanders might interfere, so, by dint of tortuous cajolery, he got both parties to accept a price of fifty taels.

Ch'ao Yüan drew a silver ingot out of his purse and gave it to the cat-seller, who said, "Even though this is fine silver, how can I be sure it's worth a whole fifty taels? Let's go find a money shop to weigh it."

His collaborator said, "Maybe you're a fool, but would a fine, sincere gentleman like this fool you? What if it is off by one or two taels? Nobody else is getting anything by it."

So one man took his new cat, and the other took his ingot, and they parted mutually satisfied.

As the seller was about to go, he turned back and knelt on the ground, kowtowed to the cat, and said, "Lord Buddha! If this poor disciple weren't so hard up, he'd never leave you."

Ch'ao Yüan was about to go when he saw a man selling a parrot.

The man called, "Sir, please come back over here. Have a look at my parrot, just take a look! I'm in a tight spot, too, with the year ending, and I've got to pay my bills."

Ch'ao Yüan stood still and looked, then said, "I've already got parrots. I won't buy it."

The man siad, "Parrot, the gentleman won't buy you. You'd better ask him yourself. I don't have any more money left to buy you food."

The parrot flapped its wings and said, "If you don't buy, who'll buy?"

It sounded as human as could be. Ch'ao Yüan was so excited he almost started jumping around like a monkey.

"It's true what they say! You haven't seen anything until you've see the two capitals! Who'd ever think such marvels could be?" he cried, and asked, "How much do you want?"

The man said, "This one isn't like the cat, worth a lot of money because it can exorcise demons. I'm only asking to be paid for the time I spent teaching it. How much can I ask for, since all the parrot can be is a messenger in some rich man's house? If you really like it, give me a little more, otherwise give me a little less. I'm just a parrot teacher. Every six months I teach a bunch of them, but only three of four turn out. I'll be content with thirty taels. Then you can take it home and enjoy it."

Ch'ao Yüan said, "I'll give you twelve."

The man wouldn't sell.

Ch'ao Yüan began to walk away and the man ran after him, holding a few lentils he'd been feeding the bird.

"If you go without lettlng me sell him to you, he'll die of starvation."

The parrot kept crying, "If you don't buy, who'll buy?"

Ch'ao Yüan looked back at the seller and said, "You sure are a pest. I'll add two taels, and you won't lose anything by it."

He opened his purse and drew out two packages of money, one of ten taels and one of five taels. He gave the money to the parrot-seller.

The parrot seller opened the packages and said, "Fifteen taels is not quite enough, but never mind. I can see you're an impatient man. Go ahead and take him, then," and he handed over the parrot.

Ch'ao Yüan mounted his horse, and he and his servants on their mules were gone like a puff of smoke from the market.

When Ch'ao Yüan got home to Chen ko he was just like a foreigner bring tribute to the emperor's court. Chen ko ignored his two treasures but she couldn't get enough of the clothes, silks, pearls and jades he had bought.

Ch'ao Yüan said, "You little country girl, fooling around with those pearls when I have two miracles here."

Chen ko said, "That stupid cat? And that parrot? Living miracles? Dog's miracles!"

"My country girl! How many 'stupid cats' or parrots that can talk like this one did you have back home?"

"Hmph. What's so·special about them?"

Chao Yüan told her, "I know you can't bear not to have the last word, but look at this cat! Isn't it worth fifteen or sixteen catties?"

"What's so special about it? Peking is full of cats big as dogs and dogs small as cats."

"Even if we do have lots of parrots, can any of them talk like this one?"

Chen ko asked, "How come he doesn't have anything to say now?"

Ch'ao Yüan told the parrot, "Parrot, say something to the lady and I'll give you a lentil."

"If you don't buy who'll buy!" the parrot said.

"He's got that right," said Chen ko.

Ch'ao Yüan said, "Parrot, say something else and I'll give you a lentil."

"If you won't buy, who'll buy?"

Chen ko laughed and said, "You've been had, my silly boy. Try again and see if he has anything else to say."

Ch'ao Yüan exclaimed, "Parrot look—a cat!"

"If you don't buy, who'll buy?"

"You idiot, what did you buy a thing like that for? You could have used the same money to buy me some melon seeds to eat at New Year's. You've lost a few cash there!"

"What 'few cash'? I bought this parrot for fifteen taels," he said.

Chen ko snorted, "Fifteen taels! So you must be planning on selling it for fifty! No, really, how much did you pay for it?"

He told her, "I really did pay fifteeen taels for it."

"Hmph. Idiot!"

She stopped scolding him then, but asked, "How much did you pay for the cat?"

"This cat cost me one pure ingot," he told her.

"I don't know what's wrong with you gentlemen," she said.

"Don't tell me there's anything fake about this cat," he said, "do we have another that's bright red? Or one that can chant sutras?"

Chen ko said, "Bright red. What about green and blue and purple ones? Anyhow, they're just dyed. It isn't like they were born that way."

"You may be the lady who always has to be right but don't be so ready to talk about what you don't know! Spit on your finger and see if the color rubs off."

"Of course not, " she said, "madder doesn't run."

"You're not making any sense. How can you dye a living animal?"

"Why not? Do old guys drop dead when they dye their hair black? You know that white persian cat of mine—didn't that used to be red?"

"So why is it white now?"

"He shed in the spring and turned white."

That silenced Ch'ao Yüan for a while.

Then he looked at Ch'ao Chu and said, "Now we'll show her."

To Chen ko he said, "So if it couldn't chant sutras, you wouldn't think there was anything special about it?"

"Have it chant one then."

Ch'ao Yüan rubbed the cat's neck. It closed its eyes blissfully and began to purr.

Delighted, Ch'an Yüan said, "Listen to that! Listen to that! He really is chanting about the 'Boddhisattva Kuan-yin Boddhisattva Kuan-yin"'.

"This isn't even funny," Chen ko said, "What cat can't chant that one? You, maid, bring in my tortoise-shell cat."

The maid did. Chen ko rubbed the cat under its chin, and that cat, too, closed its eyes and began to chant about Boddhisattva Kuan-yin.

"Listen to that. If that cat of yours is worth fifty taels, my tortoise shell must be worth sixty. All cats purr like this. That sutra's no sutra. It's idots like you that keep all the cheats in Peking from starving."

Ch'ao Yüan sulked a while, and Ch'ao Chu, crestfallen, made himself scarce.

Finally Ch'ao Yüan said, "At least I didn't use my own money. I borrowed on Dad's credit. The cat's supposed to be a good mouser, so we'll keep it for mice."

He called a maid to bring some lentils for the parrot.

At the sight of her, the parrot flew up and cried, "If you don't buy, who'll buy?"

Chen ko said, "Talking up a storm now aren't you?"

They also had the maid take the stand and sutra out of the cat's cage and put in a dish of food, of which the cat ate only half.

Indeed,

"Every avaricious man deserves sons to spend his ill-
gotten gains"

Read on to hear what happened next.

Chapter Seven

The Old Mistress Accepts a whore for the love of her Son
The Young Master Runs Away abandoning his Parents

How long it is since we parted
How long the road between us now
All our friends have fallen into decrepitude
If we were to meet again
We would need to be led by the hand
But don't dwell on it

At night we cannot know what the morning will bring
at any moment a despatch may arrive
The smoke and pounding drums of war eddy
Then we hear the officials have left their posts
Which of them is loyal?
Like the larcenous nightjar, enjoying others' nests
They wing in a tumult over the wilderness
Abandoning family
—To the tune "Incense procession to Buddha"

Ch'ao Yüan and Chen ko rioted away some time until a maid brought in a low table with dinner, which she placed on the hot k'ang.

They were in the middle of eating when a second maid ran in, flushed with tears, saying, "There are a whole lot of rats crawling into the red cat's cage, taking its food!"

Ch'ao Yüan said, "Don't be silly. So what's the cat doing, then?"

"Nothing," said the maid, "Just lying there with its eyes closed."

Chen ko said, "The Buddha cat doesn't bother with rats right under its nose, but rats a thousand li off are as good as dead, I guess," and, laughing, "I fell for the same thing the first time I heard it. Last year when I visited the imperial relative Chiangs, I saw that white cat of mine come running out into the sunlight, but then it was blood-red, the strangest thing you ever saw. Mrs Chiang said 'haven't you ever seen a red cat before?' and she tried to fool me into believing it was from a foreign country, but I wasn't about to believe her. Later I asked one of her women, Aunty Chou, about it.

That Aunty Chou told me, The Mrs. is having you on! It's dyed. If you don't believe me go take a look at the pavilion out back and tell me if you don't see a whole crowd of them, twelve or thirteen, red, green, blue, white, purple. They look as pretty as anything in the sunlight.'

I said, 'Aunty Chou, give me a red one just for fun!'

She said, 'Wait until the master comes out. I'll ask him to give you one.'

Just as she was talking to me, Imperial Relative Chiang came out, so she asked him, 'Chen ko wants you to give her a red cat, Sir.'

He said, 'You think a red cat's such a cheap thing I should give her one? Give something away worth one or two thousand taels? Let her perform ten thousand plays for me and then we'll see.'

So I said, 'All right, never mind, I'll just buy two cash' worth of hair dye and a white cat and dye it myself."

He looked at Aunty Chou and said, 'You told her?'

"She kept at me until I had to,' she replied, then looked at me and said, 'If you want to have one, thank the master for it.'

I kowtowed to him and took a red one home with me. Mrs. Chiang saw me going out with it and asked me what I had there, was I running off with one of her cats? I told her the master had given it to me, and took it on out. Then I had a porter take it home. Weren't people amazed at it! But three or four months later it shed and turned back into an ordinary white cat.

At the beginning of the next year I saw Imperial Relative Chiang again, and he actually asked me, 'How's that red cat of mine you took?'

I told him, 'I exchanged it for a white one.'

Come to that, I've had a parrot experience, too. I bought a young one at a flower shop for three taels and hung it in my room.

Every day whenever a guest came that parrot heard the phrase, 'Maid, bring water. The gentleman needs to wash his hands.'

After hearing that day in and day out the parrot began to repeat 'Maid, bring some water. The gentleman needs to wash his hands.'

Liu Hai-chai thought it was the funniest thing he ever heard, and he kept after me, wanting me to give him that parrot, but I wasn't about to.

He said, 'I'll trade my black donkey for it.'

'That and what else?' I asked.

"I'll throw in a bolt of raw silk.'

So I exchanged the parrot for that. He took the parrot home and hung it in his room.

That day his wife's brother came for a visit and the parrot started screaming, 'Maid, bring water, the gentleman wants to wash his hands.' His wife was so embarrassed she turned completely red, but the more she yelled at the parrot to stop the more it went on.

When Liu Hai-chai came home, his wife said, 'Quick! Go hang that parrot's cage somewhere far away! Disgusting!'

Liu had a servant go hang it in the guest room. That day it was his turn to host a meeting, and whenever someone came in the room the parrot screamed its sentence, making them all laugh. Then Liu sent it back to me, and he wanted his donkey back but he said to keep the silk. I told him I'd already sold that donkey and I didn't give it back to him.

"What happened to the parrot?" asked Ch'ao Yüan.

Chen ko told him, "One day I was out and nobody brought it in for the night, so it froze stiff.

Yang Ku-yüe said, 'It's still warm. Let me take it home and see if I can cure it.'

He heated up a cup of hot ginger soup and poured it down the parrot's throat, wrapped the parrot in an old handkerchief, and left it on the k'ang. By the time the sun was going down, he saw the handkerchief moving a little. He opened it up and found the parrot coming to. After that, he kept it for several months, but it died of some medicine he'd cooked up."

While talking, they had finished dinner and pushed the plates aside.

Meanwhile, Ch'ao Ssu-hsiao was expecting his son back on the twenty-sixth, but the twenty-seventh came and there was still no sign of Ch'ao Yüan.

Magistrate Ch'ao said to his wife, "I wonder what Yüan's up to in Peking. Here we are at the twenty-seventh and he's still not back. I hope he hasn't got himself swindled, that would be no laughing matter."

Madam Ch'ao heaved a sigh and said, "Don't worry about anyone swindling him. I heard a rumor—it seems he's taken an actress as his concubine and ignores his wife completely these days, so Ms. Chi's just about dying of frustration. I hear he brought that actress of his along, but he didn't want us to know about her, so he's keeping her in Peking."

"Who told you that?" asked Chao Ssu-hsiao.

His wife answered, "Who'd dare tell me straight out? I overheard the servants talking and put two and two together."

"So that's what's going on, is it?" said Ch'ao Ssu-hsiao, "But, no, I can't believe it. Ms. Chi's nobody to get on the wrong side of. She wouldn't let him do anything like that."

"That's a fine way to talk!" said his wife, "'The crueler the emperor, the less people can do about it, but if the people are wicked, even the emperor can't do a thing'".

Ch'ao Ssu-Hsiao said, "If that really is how it is, let's invite them to the yamen and get it over with. What's the point of making him stay outside?"

His wife said, "It's up to you, but Ms. Chi's going to blame us for this."

"Who cares about that?" he asked, "Get a room ready and send for them."

The next day he sent Ch'ao Feng with a letter and a hundred taels with a letter, and told him to be quick.

The letter read:

As the year ends, our only son is far from us, and we wish we had him here with us to sweeten the sunset of our days.

The year has almost run its course, yet you remain there. We have heard that when you arrived, you brought a 'side chamber'. Why did you not tell us? Why did you take up residence outside? In so doing you gave yourself much trouble. Today we send a man to welcome you both to our home. We shall not reprimand you. Fearing you may have some additional expenses, we enclose one hundred taels. Send Ch'ao Feng back with any message you may have.

—To Yüan from his father

Ch'ao Feng took the letter and went into Peking mounted on a yamen horse. He found Ch'ao Yüan's lodgings, and, as the door happened to be open, went right in. As he entered, he ran into Chen ko. She was wearing a dark green gauze jacket, a sky-blue bodice, and bright red satin trousers with no skirt over them and she was playing kick-ball in the courtyard with Mrs. Ch'ao Chu. When she saw Ch'ao Feng she flew back into the house. Ch'ao Yüan was at that moment just coming out of the house. Ch'ao feng kowtowed to him. Ch'ao Yüan said, "I was just about to go back to the Yamen. What are you doing here?" Ch'ao Feng replied, "Since you'd been gone so long, the old master sent me to get you, and also Chen ko."

"How did he find out about Chen ko?" hissed Ch'ao Yüan, 'Who told them?"

Ch'ao Feng said, "I wouldn't know how they found out, but this morning they sent me here to tell you to come back, and said for me to go back first if you had any message. I have a letter here from the old master, and two envelopes of money, too," which he gave Ch'ao Yüan. Ch'ao Yüan opened the letter and skimmed it to get the basic message. He wasn't entirely pleased. He ordered food and drink to be brought to Ch'ao Feng, so Feng could hurry back with his reply. He figured he'd need to pack and rent servants and horses to go back to T'ung-chou with Chen ko. After Ch'ao Feng had eaten, Ch'ao Yüan gave him three hundred cash and a letter to take back to Ch'ao Ssu-hsiao. It read:

Your son Ch'ao Yüan submits this letter in humble apology for his inhuman behaviour. How could I bear to tell you of my transgressions? Since you write of your forgiveness, I'll bring my "little wife" so that she may kowtow to you. There's only one other thing, which is that I don't want to stay in the back room. Please have the eastern study swept and cleaned fast. I have received your hundred taels.

—from your son Yüan

That evening, around when the lamps were being lit, Ch'ao Feng set off for the yamen. He answered the parents' questions, "The young master will come tomorrow with his new lady, and he wants the eastern study readied." Madam Ch'ao said, Did you see her?" Ch'ao Feng said, "When I went in she was playing kickball, wearing trousers, with Ch'ao Chu's wife. She ran inside when she saw me." "What kind of a person did she look like?" Madam Ch'ao asked. Ch'ao Feng told her, "You have seen her yourself Madam, she's that Chen ko who was the main actress of female parts in the girls' acting troupe."

"There were about a dozen women in that troupe. I don't know which one you mean."

Ch'ao Feng said, "That day they performed for your birthday and you saw them off, wasn't she Hung Niang? Then they did skits, and she was Chen Shao-ch'ang in the Jade Hairpin, wasn't she? You even said she sang particularly well and you gave her two handkerchiefs and three taels more than the others, though she didn't thank you for them."

"Oh! So that's her? A nice girl," said Madam Ch'ao.

When Ch'ao Ssu-hsiao heard who it was, he said, "Oh no! She's the one?"

"It's all right if she is, " said Madam Ch'ao, "A nice, lively girl. You must have seen her act, too."

"No I did not see her, " said Ch'ao Ssu-hsiao, "But I did hear about her. Don't you know who we're talking about here? Isn't she the one who had a new degree-holder die right on top of her? The one who treasurer Fan was keeping when his wife hung herself, and the whole thing was hushed up? I hope you know she's not likely to know her place. What do we want with her?"

"Things will work out once the two of them come home," said Madam Ch'ao.

"How do you expect a half day in our household is going to change her habits of a life-time?" Ch'ao Ssu-hsiao asked.

"She's a pretty, clever girl. What are you so worried about?"

"What do we need her charades and cleverness and airs for? She's more than a match for Yüan and his wife, she'll have them both at her beck and call."

He then said, "Have the eastern study readied for them."

The whole night was occupied with preparations for the couple's arrival, with workmen called to past up window paper, fix the ceiling, and ready the k'ang. Their work went on until the sunset of the following day.

Meanwhile, after Ch'ao Yüan saw his father's letter, he was busy with packing for his return to the yamen, with Chen ko. Chen ko took her time with her preparations, and showed no desire to get started. Ch'ao Chu dragged his feet, too, and, behind Ch'ao Yüan's back he told Chen ko she shouldn't go.

To Ch'ao Yüan he said, "Since that Yamen's such a little flea-bag it won't be livable with all these people crammed in. There'll hardly be room to sit down and eat. In my opinion, Sir, it would be a better idea for you to go back alone now, and come here again at the lantern festival."

Ch'ao Yüan said, "If I said it was so small, that was only because I wanted to fool Chen ko. There's plenty of space in the yamen! The only thing worth worrying about is how we'll use all that space in the eastern study suite. There aren't so many of us, so if we don't feel like eating in one room, we can go eat in another one."

Ch'ao Chu persisted, "But you're still at the academy, Sir. If we all go to the yamen you'll be lonely when you come to Peking. Once Chen ko moves into the yamen, they won't let her come and go as she pleases, you know."

Chen ko said, "He's right. You go on by yourself. I'm not going."

"What are you saying?" said Ch'ao Yüan, "This is New Year's and my parents are welcoming us with open arms. We should go pay our respects. They've sent for us and even given us travelling money. What excuse do we have for not going? We are going to go and pass the lantern festival with them. After that, there will be plenty of time to think about coming back here. I won't give this house back to its owner. We'll lock it up with all our things inside and have someone watch it for us."

Even though Chen ko and Ch'ao Chu weren't too happy with that, they didn't dare say anything else against it. The next day was the twenty-ninth. Ch'ao Yüan and Chen ko got into their large sedan chair and went to the T'ung-chou yamen, along with a number of horses and mules.

They entered the Yamen and Chen ko descended from the sedan chair. Wearing a bright red narrow-sleeved robe and a white damask embroidered skirt, with kingfisher pins all over her head, she walked into the central courtyard. There, in the center of the courtyard, sat old Mr. and Mrs. Ch'ao. Ch'ao went forward first to greet them. Then Chen ko went to make her eight obeisances and present her mother-in-law with a hollow pillow.

Chao Ssu-hsiao took a look at her:

> Her face luscious as a peach
> Her bearing lissome as a willow
> Her movements alert and quick

Her splendid tiny lotus feet glimpsed fleetingly
Though not, perhaps, quite Pao Ni descended from heaven,
She was every inch Hsi-tzu who so beguiled the king of Wu
While not quite quite Tan Chi
She was the equal of Tung Cho's fair nemesis Tiao Ch'an
If you don't believe me
Open your eyes and take a good look

When the elder Ch'ao's saw this pushy "little wife" wriggling around in front of them, they frowned, grew gloomy, and sighed in displeasure. When she had finished her greetings, they gave her two taels and sent her back to the eastern study. Chen ko was very annoyed that her parents-in-law didn't show more enthusiasm for her.

On the second day of the new year, Ch'ao Yüan wanted to go into Peking for the annual reopening of the academy, and to pay New Year's calls on the teachers there, and on Commanders Liu and Su. The actors Liang and Hu had taken up their respective official posts and, bearing Ch'ao Yüan a fraternal friendship, wanted him to visit them first. Ch'ao Yüan had horses and men readied and went to his house in Peking. Once he arrived there, he found it desolate without Chen ko's noisy presence. There wasn't even a maid there. He felt very lonely. He told Ch'ao Chu to go and get a couple of women he knew, living across from the academy, to keep him company for a few days. Then Ch'ao Yüan spent the holidays carousing outside, and, as before, it was Ch'ao Chu who kept an eye on the house.

On the tenth, Ch'ao Yüan bought presents, had two outfits made, and also a set of bracelets for four taels, sealed up eight taels, and sent off the two women.

Then he went back to T'ung-chou, where he hung his lanterns, set off his firecrackers, and passed the lantern festival with Chen ko. He planned to attend the academy once the second day of the second month had passed, and also to go on a pleasure trip around Hsi-shan. This time he picked the nineteenth day of the second month as the date he would return to Peking, which he did, and, as before, he had the two women from near the academy come stay with him.

This carefree existence was cut short when the city was mobilized in reaction to the increasing severity of Essen's depredations on the northern frontier. There were conscriptions, requisitions, fortifications, spy alerts, munitions, and curfews. The barricades went up, troops crowded the streets, and it was all very martial and impressive. The city gates closed early at night and opened late in the morning.

Wang Chen had been a teacher before becoming a eunuch, and he had sons and grandsons. He now egged the emperor on for all he was worth to go into battle personally. What Wang Chen had in mind was enfeoffment of his progeny as lords, which reward he expected for the brilliant idea of advising the emperor to go to battle, where the emperor's great charisma would repel Essen.

Ch'ao Yüan didn't know anything about Wang Chen and the emperor, and when he saw how things were in Peking, he not only couldn't spare a thought for his sovereign, he didn't bother to worry about his parents. The words "loyalty" and "duty" were not in his vocabulary. He was so scared by what he saw in the streets that he soiled his pants, ran back to his rented house, sent the two women away, packed a few essentials and bribed a gatekeeper to let him out of the city. Fast as the wind, he got to T'ung-chou and the yamen door. There, huffing and puffing so he was every bit as inarticulate as Ts'ao Ts'ao at the banquet informing on Yen Liang, he meant to communicate to his parents that he wanted to abandon them, grab some money, and run away with Chen ko.

Ch'ao Ssu-hsiao said, "If things are that bad, don't bother about your position at the academy. Write up a letter of resignation right now, and if they won't let you go, then let them call you a criminal but go anyway, and come back here."

Actually, Ch'ao Yüan didn't want to stay with his parents, who he feared might keep him locked up in the city, and he didn't want to give up his position in the academy, either. After all, the whole alarm might blow over, and afterwards he would want that position. What he really wanted was to go back to Peking with Chen ko, and sit out the crisis on the sidelines, without bothering himself about his parents' safety, only he couldn't quite say that outright.

Ch'ao Ssu-hsiao said, "Like they say, of the thirty-six strategies, running away's the best. Even if Essen doesn't get this far, I don't want to go risking my neck. Anyway, I can get out of it for a few thousand taels. Even if it means I have to spend some time meditating at the Board of Punishments, that's better than getting my head split by Essen. Let's all pack up and go home to Wu ch'eng."

Ch'ao Yüan agreed that was a good idea. Ch'ao Ssu-hsiao called a man to write his resignation letter, and went to find his secretary, Hsing Kao-men, who he wanted to insert an elegant petition in the letter. Magistrate Ch'ao found Hsing Kao-men playing wei-chi with a man known as hermit Yüan.

As soon as the hermit and Hsing saw Ch'ao Ssu-hsiao, they stopped playing and began to discuss Essen's raids and the rumor that the emperor was going to go personally to the battlefront.

Hsing Kao-men said, "The portents are very unfavorable, and the emperor must not make a move. I suppose the Board of Astronomy will petition him not to, and the other officials will all speak out against it, so he won't go after all."

Ch'ao Ssu-hsiao said, "But Wang Chen is pushing so strongly for it. I don't think the emperor will be able to hang back."

"Well, what heaven determines will be no matter what we do," said Hsing.

"I've been troubled by the recurrence of an old chronic health problem of mine, " said Ch'ao Ssu-hsaio, "And I'm afraid I may die of it, so I've decided to hand in my resignation and go home. I've already ordered the basic form letter written, but it still needs a nice expression of my regrets—could I ask you for a draft? It can't wait; I'm planning to leave tomorrow,"

Hsing smiled faintly and quoted Mencius," 'And if I go, who will stand by the king?' When I look at the stars what I see there is that this is not an auspicious time for the emperor to drive out to war. That's what we should worry about. T'ung-chou is right in the center of the astrological configurations, so it's as firm as a rock. Why hand in your resignation? If you don't put your shoulder to the wheel in this time of crisis, you'll be criticised. Listen to me, Sir, and calm down. When I panic, you'll still have plenty of time to get away."

Ch'ao Ssu-hsiao couldn't have been less interested in Hsing's opinions than he was, but those opinions meant that Hsing would not write the finish of his resignation letter. Instead, Ch'ao Ssu-hsiao got his son to write a final section, which consisted of ineptly phrased amorality. Ch'ao Ssu-hsiao submitted this, without saying anything else on the matter to Hsing. After he submitted his resignation, all the relevant authorities duly signed off on it, with no special message. There was only one exception, a man named Chi, in the Office of the Passes. Chi was from Yünnan and had entered government service with the third, highest degree. He endorsed the resignation but appended the following rude note:

I do not believe I have had the pleasure of meeting you since your promotion from Hua-t'ing to T'ung-chou. How peculiar that you never previously mentioned any indisposition, but now suddenly claim to be ill. Where are you planning to go, I wonder. Now that inexpressible hardships loom on the horizon of the empire and thieves have entered our courtyard, can it be that you see fit to exaggerate some minor little problem as an excuse to run away from danger? If so, what sort of conduct is this? You may expect to be exposed. Do not underestimate the weight of an accusation from this office.

When Hsing saw that Ch'ao Ssu-hsiao didn't mention resignation any more, he thought the magistrate had given up the idea. After Ch'ao Ssu-hsiao did in fact try to resign, and received the warm words above, he halted progress on his resignation and decided-to send Ch'ao Yüan and Chen ko home without him. Once day, Ch'ao Yüan was sitting around, talking to Hermit Yüan and Hsing Kao-men, when the bamboo clappers announcing an urgent message out of yamen office hours sounded, and a missive from a military circuit magistrate was handed over. Opened, it was on snow-white official paper with turquoise borders, coal-black formal black writing, and red seal and heading.

This is what Ch'ao Ssu-hsiao read:

An examination of the administration of T'ung-chou and related tribute rice, military fields, and courier service is hereby accorded by the assistant commissioner of the Shantung Investigative Office, so as to find evidence for reprimanding the incumbent magistrate for using facetious pretexts to escape his duty, and to encourage and warn him of the importance of attention to his offical duties. On the eighth day of the third month we received imperial instructions to inspect the Northern Metropolitan Area and to put the border areas in order. Concurrently we have received Commissioner Chi's warrant stating the above accusation.

These are days when a ruler must be grieved and his servitors shamed, days when we should rush at cockcrow to annhilate the enemy. Yet the magistrate of T'ung-chou, Ch'ao Ssu-hsiao, bolts like a horse at the sight of food or an ant at the scent of ordure. How dare he have the audacity to connive at boldly making a pretext of illness to request resignation? He is liable at this point to heavy punishment, and is hereby further admonished to take this warrant seriously, put his jurisdiction in order as directed, become eager and energetic, discard all erroneous thoughts, devote himself to the defense of the city and be very careful he makes no further mistakes. This office would prefer to congratulate new merit and let past error be forgotten, but if the magistrate does not correct his errors, we have no choice but to investigate and memorialize. Take our sincere admonition to heart and recall we are now seeing "the beacons of Kan Ch'uan lit" and must all fulfill our duties as statesmen. If you persist in wilful negligeance, you will be impeached.

The sight of the above lines affected Ch'ao Ssu-hsiao the same way as a bowl of ice water thrown on his head would have. He was reduced to a speechless, quivering jelly. This was when Hsing found out that Ch'ao Ssu-hsiao had clandestinely submitted a request to be allowed to resign, totally disregarding Hsing's advice. Now Magistrate Ch'ao was as ashamed of himself as the King of Ch'i felt in front of Mencius after an ill-judged invasion of a neighboring state. He could have taken anything else, but this warrant had his heart trembling like a bucket on a rope with worry.

Once one thing goes wrong, more misfortune will generally follow. Ch'ao Ssu-hsiao had just gotten everything ready for Ch'ao Yüan to depart. Luggage, sedan chairs and horses were all set and they had picked the thirty-sixth as the day Ch'ao Yüan would leave with Chen ko. Suddenly, two minor Hua-t'ing functionaries turned up. One was Sung Ch'i-jen, the younger brother of Treasurer Sung, and the other was Ts'ao Hsi-chien, brother of Ts'ao the yamen runner.

They came to the door and said, "We've come with some news."

Ch'ao Ssu-hsiao wondered what it could be, and let them in.

They greeted him and said, "Cabinet Minister and hononary Hanlin scholar Chiang Yüan has come to Hua-t'ing with Chen Yü, the Marquis of P'ing-chiang, on an imperially commissioned tour of inspection. The common people have risen in thousands. Treasurer Sung, Runner Ts'ao, your private secretary Sun Shang and caretaker Ch'ao Shu have all been accused. Chiang Yüan ratified the accusations and referred them to the Chiang-su intendent, then the case came back to Chen Yü in his capacity as special prosecutor. Treasurer Sung and Runner Ts'ao have both been thrown in jail and interrogated every five days, and Sun Shang and Ch'ao Shu can't hold out much longer, either. If an order comes down to investigate who was in charge there won't be any way we can keep a lid on it."

The words fell on Ch'ao Ssu-hsiao's ears like snow being dumped on top of frost in his belly.

He asked, "Didn't any of the local Important People speak up for me?"

Sung Ch'i-jen said, "All he common people are mobbing together over this. They have the Important People terrorized, saying things like 'if you Important People didn't give us such a hard time, we could have worked things out. If you interfere with our complaints now, we'll take it all the way to the top and have it out!' So all the Important People care about now is covering up for themselves. How can you expect them to stick their necks out for you?"

Ch'ao Ssu-hsiao asked, "Did any of the lower degree-holders say a good word for me?"

Sung Ch'i-jen said, "At first they'd written up their own accusations and were ready to present them to Chiang Yüan, but luckily, just in time, two young gentleman, Yü and Chang, talked them out of it by saying, 'we are scholars, after all, and we have to be careful of our reputations. It isn't done to inform on one's superiors, and it won't reflect well on us if the accusation goes through. If it doesn't, even worse. Officials look at us with their predecessor's eyes, and then our new superiors won't even treat us like human beings. Besides, the common people have already filed their accusations, so let's let it be.'

The rest of the lower degree-holders said, 'This is just anger in a public cause. How can you two expect to dam it with your selfish considerations?'

Master Yü said, 'All we're saying is how it is—what's selfish about that? And if you want to talk about just anger for this member of the public, I'd like you to remember Magistrate Ch'ao took away my land and gave it to someone else. He made me give him all the silver I had buried there, and then one day while I was out he took my wife! Are you talking to me about just anger? Our friend Master Chang here had his wife raped by a bastard who they were only going to fine fifty taels but then he bribed the magistrate and the next thing you know the accused was in dire straits of poverty and they turned it around and fined Chang! At least it was cut down to twenty taels. In such a bad year I don't think Chang could have come up with the other thirty taels even if he went out and sold himself.'

Master Chang said, 'There's no need to bring that up, but since you have, I can tell you it really hurts still, in my heart.'

After that, the other degree holders decided that after all, Yü and Chang were good fellows, and what they said was true, so they decided to give up on making their own accusations."

Ch'ao Ssu-hsiao said, "Which Master Yü and Master Chang were they?"

Sung Chi-jen said, "You can hardly say their stories were ordinary. Don't tell me you'd forgotten?"

Ch'ao Ssu-hsiao said, "To tell you the truth, back in Hua-t'ing there was a lot of that sort of thing, so I can't place them right off. Anyway, what are you two doing here now?"

Sung Ch'i-jen said, "We want to ask you for a letter of extenuation, Sir. We know better than to try for pardons for our brothers, Treasurer Sung and Runner Ts'ao, and they wouldn't be able to go on living in Hua-t'ing even if they were pardoned now, so it would be best all around if they were conscripted to satisfy people's anger. Once they're out or sight, things will quiet down. We just hope the interrogators don't extort too heavy bribes from them, or flog them too much. Maybe a letter could get Sun Shang and Ch'ao Shu off."

Ch'ao Ssu-hsiao frowned and didn't say anything.

Ch'ao Yüan said, "What's all the fuss? Even if the sky falls the four Chin-kang pick it up again. Have a rest and something to eat and then we'll talk it over."

They sent Ts'ao and Sung off for refreshment.

Ch'ao Ssu-hsiao said, "I don't know what to tell them? What if Chiang Yüan has already submitted the case officially for further adjudication? Even if he doesn't, if Treasurer Sung and Runner Ts'ao are conscripted, they'll be called to the Military Board, and we're so close here rumors could easily damage me."

Ch'ao Yüan said, "Relax! Nothing could be easier. Leave it to me."

Then Ch'ao Yüan had his packmules readied. He sent Ch'ao Chu off to Peking to tell Hu and Liang he had something urgent to discuss with them. Ch'ao Chu hurtled off into the night, and Ch'ao Yüan sat waiting for the chance to talk to Hu and Liang, which now took precedence over his own departure.

Indeed, though fortunate winds fill your sails, at any moment furious rains may rout you.

If you want to know whether Ch'ao Yüan was able to leave T'ung-chou on the sixteenth as planned, continue reading the next chapter.

Chapter Eight

A fast-talking concubine seductively leads her master into error
A benighted academician foolishly throws his wife aside

At 14 she became your wife
Timorously she greeted her new parents
Though her home was a humble scholar's
Yours was the family of a poor aspirant
Now you've gone up in the world
Things are quite different
Nothing but jade and pearls will you wear
Always you have gifts for your betters
Before your steps turn to the temple
Always your spoon is ready when you enter the kitchen
You liked her well enough
when she was in the bloom of youth
Who could have foreseen how times would change
That you would betray your first love
She is still your wife by every right
But your heart is no husbandly heart
Money counts for much with you, feeling for little
She withers without your affection
And while she was never a great beauty
She's no hag now
All because of your fickleness
Contention has grown
Maggots only enter wood that's rotten
Only the susceptible man can be enchanted
Now the homely dove is driven out
Her mournful cries falling on desolation
While youth is fleeting
Some bonds are not meant to be lightly broken
Will the blue heavens answer her pleas?
Will the white-hot sun hear her cries?
All beauties should have mirrors
To reflect their black hearts

When Ch'ao Chu reached Peking, he asked all over and was looking for Hu, until evening, when he found Hu. At that time, the curfew was very strict, so Ch'ao Chu stayed with Hu overnight.

Wang Chen kept on urging the emperor to take personally to the field of battle, and none of the civil or military officials could prevent it with their loyal remonstrances. By the time the emperor had reached T'u Mu, the news was already bad, but there was still time to flee, hide behind the fortifications and save the situation that way. Wang Chen wouldn't allow it, because if they had retreated quickly a mere thousand of his own chariots would have been left behind and lost. The enemy swarmed over the emperor and his forces like ants, and millions of arrows flew. Thank heavens that the emperor was preserved and the arrows fell like rain on the ground in front of him. Essen thought it was very strange, and went forward to see what was going on. It was only then that Essen realized that the emperor had come in person to the battlefield. The sacred dragon was caught out of his element, and the ant-like troops of Essen crowded around and took him. The civil and military officials in his retinue were all killed, and Wang Chen along with Commanders Su and Liu were among them. Now that Wang Chen was dead, the hatred everyone had felt for him all along was loosed and every relative of his was in mortal danger. Hu and Liang were keeping as quiet as hibernating bugs.

Hu and Ch'ao Chu both slept until around the fifth watch (4:00 a.m.). Then Hu got up and blacked his face with ashes. Since Ch'ao Chu had been to the Commanders' houses so frequently, he disguised himself too, before they went to find Liang's hiding place.

When he found Liang, Ch'ao Chu told Liang that Ch'ao Yüan had sent him to the capital especially to bring Liang and Hu out, as he had something to discuss with them.

Liang, unable to stay in the capital, had just been thinking of taking refuge with Ch'ao Yüan, so this was very convenient for him. Liang changed into tattered clothes and a battered hat, gathered a few small things, and left the city on Ch'ao Chu's mule. Outside the city, he hired a donkey of his own and was in T'ung-chou in time for breakfast.

Ch'ao Ssu-hsiao was startled to see the bedraggled condition of the two actors, and only understood after they had told him about the situation. He sent them in to wash up and change into more usual clothes. Then they greeted him formally and all sat down to eat. Ch'ao Ssu-hsiao told them what was going on in Hua-t'ing, and how he had been hoping for a letter of exoneration from the Commanders Su and Liu. He hadn't known that they were dead, and now that he did, he was at a loss.

Liang said, "What's the problem? Right now, Hsü T'ing of the Han-lin Academy is the man to know at court, and Hsü loves Hu like one of his own. If Hu writes you a note, and you take it along with a present personally to Hsü there isn't anything you can't get done."

Ch'ao Ssu-hsiao was ecstatic. They ate, Hu wrote the note, and Ch'ao Yüan took it. He readied thirty gold taels and eight large pearls, and departed speedily for Peking.

The next day, Ch'ao Yüan went to Hsu T'ing's door and gave the gatekeeper ten taels. The gatekeeper was so pleased with that he pulled the latch open faster than a run away horse gallops, and was all obsequious 'do please come in Sir to see the Master'.

Hsü T'ing opened up the package of money, took the pearls, and kept Ch'ao Yüan a while while he wrote two letters which he then sealed up. One was for Chiang Yüan and one was for the penal court at Hua-t'ing. He wrote that while Treasurer Sung and Runner Ts'ao shouldn't be pardoned, they were exempt from torture while being examined and made to confess, and they shouldn't be expected to pay too heavily. Secretary Sun and Ch'ao Shu were to be given new identities and legal action on their cases ceased. Then Hsü T'ing gave Ch'ao Yüan a length of white silk, a real gold fan, a privately printed collection of writings, and a bolt of light scarlet standard cloth.

It was the twelfth day of the third month when Ch'ao Yüan got those letters, and there happened to be a fine moon. He left by night and arrived in T'ung-chou by the third watch (midnight). He used his own key to open the city gate there and went into the yamen. Liang and Hu were already sound asleep. Ch'ao Yüan went to his father's bedroom, and, sitting on his father's bed, told him how it had all gone. Ch'ao Ssu-hsiao was glad he'd reaped such a profit with his gifts.

Since Hu and Liang had connections, the Ch'aos had treated them as honored guests. Ch'ao Ssu-hsiao nicknamed Liang "An-Szu" and Hu "Prince's dear". Since they swore brotherhood with Ch'ao Yüan, Ch'ao Ssu-hsiao called them "my worthy nephews", too, and all the servants addressed them as Master Hu and Master Liang. Madame Ch'ao and Chen ko treated them like members of the family, and did not hide from them they way the did from outsiders.

This all changed with the news of Wang Chen and Commanders Su and Liu's deaths, and of the inquisition of Wang Chen's relatives and followers. The Ch'aos suddenly cooled to Hu and Liang. While the actors claimed to be Hsü T'ing's friends, that was not at all clear-cut. It was true that Ch'ao Yüan's meeting with Hsü had gone exactly as Hu had said it would, though, and Hu and Liang were always casually mentioning how many friends of the commanders were left, and how many prominent court servitors would want to raise Hu and Liang to high positions soon. The Ch'aos decided to let Hu and Liang stay on a while at the yamen and wait to see which way the wind blew in Peking.

On the morning of the thirtieth, the Ch'aos gave Sung and Ts'ao of Huat'ing six taels of travelling money and Hsü T'ing's letter, and told them to deliver the letters to the authorities. After breakfast, Ts'ao and Sung left.

On the fifteenth day of the next month, Ch'ao Ssu-hsiao set up a banquet at the yamen to send off Ch'ao Yüan, at which a number of useful gifts were gathered for him to barter later.

Madame Ch'ao called Ch'ao Chu and Mrs. Ch'ao Chu to her and instructed them, "You two go back and tell Ms. Chi, now that my son has a concubine, she'll just have to accept it as one of those things. She should have made it clear at the beginning that she wouldn't stand for it—then he would have had to give in. It's her fault for letting him do as he pleased. Even if he wanted a concubine, he could have picked a girl from a nice family—how could he choose an actress? It's disgusting the way she goes making eyes at everyone! But now it's done, the rice is cooked and no matter what a person's feelings may be it's better to be a little broad-minded and stop fussing over every little thing! With patience, all things come right."

Here are fifty taels in broken silver for sewing, and two pearls and two gold taels, a bolt of raw silk gauze, one of gold cloth, one of blue satin and one of pink plain pongee, two skirts and two catties of cotton, which you are to take and give to Ms. Chi. When I see her, I'll check to make sure she received every last thing, and if there's the slightest thing missing, you two will account for it. You needn't go show off to your mistress Chen ko with this information, either."

Ch'ao Chu and his wife assented roundly, took the gifts for Ms. Chi and left.

On the next morning, the sixteenth, Ch'ao Yüan and Chen ko, along with some of their male and female attendants, said goodbye to the elder Ch'aos and took their leaves of Hsing Kang-men, Hermit Yüan, and Hu and Liang.Then Ch'ao Yüan got into his sedan chair with Chen ko and the procession got underway.

Indeed:

> A man of Yang-chou
> Travelling in style
> Leaving a trail of cash
> A lovely girl beside him

It was rather hard on Ch'ao Ssu-hsiao and Madam Ch'ao to be left forlorn and lonesome, but Ch'ao Yüan was content. He had money at hand, a woman who suited him at his side, he rode in a sedan chair the size of a room, and he was followed by all the motley crew of his man servants and plump, juicy maids. The weather was growing mild with incipient spring, and all on the road was prosperity and ease. He felt pretty good.

However, when happiness reaches its apex, it gives birth to grief. When everything is going smoothly, that's the signal that something will go wrong soon. That's how life is.

Ch'ao Yüan wended his way and when he reached Te-chou, it was still early. Some clouds began to seep unctuously over the sky from the northeast, and a dense rain quickly grew in force. He had to find a reasonably comfortable hostel to rest. By the time he had found one and had his lunch, the rain was pouring. People say that spring rain is as precious as cooking oil, but these rains were an embarrassment of riches, going on ceaselessly for two days. Ch'ao Yüan had a man go out to buy dinner and wine, and then he amused himself with Chen ko.

Now, Ch'ao Chu's wife was a wood-pecker incarnate. When she opened her mouth, a tongue a bit longer than her whole body began to show itself. She was also a Baron P'i of Wu incarnate, who knew through much experience how to impress her betters with her eagerness on their behalves. Fortunately, the punishment that was destined her in this life was to be like a broken steamer, always spewing hot air to little effect.

There wasn't anything to do while the rain went on outside, and she took up every word Ch'ao Yüan or Chen ko spoke. That wouldn't have done any harm, but when she felt her mouth lying idle, she couldn't keep herself from telling Ch'ao Yüan and Chen ko everything Madam Ch'ao had said. Ch'ao Yüan made a face at her, but do you think she caught on and shut up? If she had quoted Madame Ch'ao verbatim that would have been quite enough of a feat, but she wanted to flush the snakes out of the grass, and she even added things Madame Ch'ao had not said.

"Madame Ch'ao told us to tell Ms. Chi 'If someone sent a rotten piece of goods like that Chen ko and had her kneel in all her brazenness on the street, offering her to us for free, I'd be afraid she'd pollute our door and beat her off with a pole! Why spend eight hundred taels on a worthless woman like that? I almost feel like calling her out in front of me, tearing her clothes off, cutting all her hair off, beating her till she's a dying pulp and then calling a beggar to take some loose change for taking her away. However, I can't do that here at the yamen, so Ms. Chi, don't be angry, but wait until I come home. Then we'll take care of things."'

The reader can imagine that an actress is used to all kinds of humiliations. She can bear having her hair pulled, her eyes scratched out, and her nose bitten off. She gets used to being called a whore and being walked all over a hundred different ways. But now Chen ko was getting fat on Ch'ao Yüan, so it wasn't likely she'd stand still for this abuse.

She promptly pulled apart her hairdo, wailed to heaven, cursed the earth, rolled around and beat her head on the floor, in a colossal tantrum. All the women in the neighborhood, and all the neighbors stood around looking at her. Waiters and wine shop boys stopped their work and came to have a look. She considerately announced the plot of the story so nobody had to take the trouble of asking what it was all about. Ch'ao Yüan and Ch'ao Chu were both angry at Mrs. Ch'ao Chu, and even she was beginning to be afraid of what she'd done.

Chen ko cried and screamed her fill for half the night. The next morning the rain stopped, and she grumbled and shouted as they finished their trip. When they arrived, some of the maids and servants who had accompanied them did go back to say hello to Ms. Chi. Ch'ao Chu told Ms. Chi what Madame Ch'ao had ordered him to, and he enumerated and handed over every item Madam Ch'ao had entrusted him with for Ms. Chi. Ms. Chi asked if her mother-in-law was well, and then cried and exhorted heaven and earth a while when she saw the gifts for her. After she'd done that she took the gifts into her room.

The next day, Chen ko asked Ch'ao Chu for the gifts Madam Ch'ao had sent to Ms. Chi.

Ch'ao Chu told her, "They were already given to Ms. Chi yesterday."

Even though Chen ko had a few things to say to Ch'ao Chu about that, she didn't want to really quarrel with him. It was Ch'ao Yüan at whom she directed her blazing eyes and bloody curses. Even though Ch'ao Yüan was blindly in love with her, even he felt it was too much.

"What do you have to make such a big deal of this for?" he asked, "I didn't have anything to do with it! What's the point of going on about it like that if my mother did send her a few presents?"

Chen ko said, "It isn't the presents I mind! It just makes me mad. There I was kowtowing left and right to them, and all they did back was throw me two taels. And you put such sleazy cheap gauze on the windows all the servants saw, too! I guess I have plenty of everything for the asking, so I don't need her damned things, I just want to scatter every tael of hers, bash her her over the head with them and burn it all."

Ch'ao Yüan said, "'Madame Chiang asks for so little'—It doesn't matter whether or not you feel like throwing around my mother's presents to her, just watch out for her father and brother. They love to go around spreading stories! And even my mother can say things like Mrs. Ch'ao Chu told you, when she's worried for me. She just lives for me. Don't be fooled by that gentle face of hers—admit you're outclassed."

He left her with that to think about, and slowly her fury ebbed. You can see that if a husband stands up and lays down the law , no matter how evil the wife or shrewish the concubine, she'll back down. Even that fierce piece of goods, Chen ko, faced with a modicum of resolve on Ch'ao Yüan's part, would give up her tantrum and come to terms.

Meanwhile, in Lu-ch'eng subprefecture, there was a man named Liu Yu-hsi. His mother had a maid named Ch'ing-mei, aged sixteen. Ch'ing-mei became ill from dry consumption, a disease that kills ten out of eleven of those it strikes, in seven months if it's fast, or eight months if it's slow. Madame Liu tried everything to have Ch'ing-mei cured. Ch'ing-mei herself took a vow to become a nun if she recovered. Indeed, if you're not fatally ill, medicine will cure you, and if you're ready to be enlightened, Buddha will receive you. One day an itinerant doctor took refuge from the rain inside the Lius' doorway. The doorkeeper passed the time of day with him and happened to mention that there was a serious case of consumption in the house.

The doctor said, "There are two varieties of this illness. One is in the nature of nervous exhaustion, with a great loss of vigor and blood, and that's just like a dry well; you can pour all you like into it and it won't help. The other kind is due to a blockage of vital energy obstructing the blood's pulse. Once the blockage is removed, the patient naturally gets better. So not all types are incurable."

The doorman told the doctor about Ch'ing-mei's case.

The doctor said, "Let me have a look at her. I won't prescribe anything unless I see that she's curable."

The doorman went in and told Madame Liu who called Ch'ing-mei to go to the door and let the doctor have a look at her.

Still standing, the doctor took Ch'ing-mei's hand and felt her pulse. He saw that although she was sallow she was emaciated and spectral.

Then he said, "This isn't a serious case. One dose will cure her."

From inside, Madame Liu said, "Since she's an orphan, if you can cure her I'll have her make you a robe or purple-flower plain cloth and a gauze hat, and a pair of shoes and socks—and do you have a wife? If so I'll have Ch'ing-mei make her a set of clothes in plain cloth, too, and recognize the two of you as her parents . . ."

The doctor's face blossomed into smile at that. Madame Liu gave him two hundred taels sealed up as a gratuity "for opening your medicine case".

The doctor said, "How can I accept payment if she's going to be my daughter?"

Madame Liu said, "It's just a trifle, just to pay you for opening your case, so please accept it."

Then he did accept it, and took out a packet of pills the size of green soybeans. He counted out seven pills and had Ch'ing-mei take them that night with red-flower peach-kernal soup. As he was being entertained in a small reception-room, the soup was being heated for Ch'ing-mei, and she drank it. After about as long as it takes to drink a cup of hot tea, Ch'ing-mei's stomach began to ache more and more painfully. Shortly after it became unbearable, she urinated two or three catties of black, smelly urine and then a small bloodclot. They told the doctor.

. He said, "She's cured! If she avoids cold drinks and things like onions or garlic, and takes ten doses of restorative soup from a reputable pharmacist, she'll be as strong as ever in no time."

After that, Ch'ing-mei's face slowly lost it's sallowness, and she grew more robust by the end of the month. Madame Liu had gotten together the promised clothes and shoes and called Ch'ingmei to take the clothes and recognize the doctor and his wife as her parents. But Ch'ing-mei had vowed to become a nun if she was cured, and now she nagged Madame Liu every day to let her make good on her vow.

Madame Liu said, "Do you think it's so easy to be a nun? You haven't done it, so all you see is the advantages. Once you become a nun, you'll see all that's wrong with it, but it will be too late then for regrets. What you should to is to recuperate thoroughly, then marry and live a normal life."

There was a great deal of sense in what Madame Liu said, but Ch'ing-mei had her mind made up.

She said, "When I look in the mirror, I can see I'm no perfect beauty, so I won't be likely to become a gentleman's cherished wife or favorite concubine. Even if I did get to become an aristocrat's concubine, everything would depend on how much he favored me or not, and how kind his wife was. Between the husband and wife, I could be in as tight a spot as the Monkey King trapped under the T'ai-hang mountain, with no Kuan-yin in sight to rescue me. Even though Kuan-yin did let him out from under the mountain, she put that gold fillet on his head that his master could torture him with if he acted up. No, I don't want to waste any more time thinking about being a concubine.

"After concubines come prostitutes. Being a prostitute is pretty worthwhile. You get to wear the most beautiful clothes and cute make-up. Every day you get to flirt with different gentlemen, every day something new. You can linger with the ones you like, as for the others, it's easy enough to take the starch out of them. The only thing I don't like about the idea of being a prostitute is that if you turn down a customer, the procurer beats you, or if you see him but he loses interest, she beats you. When you go on call, you have to kowtow to the lady of the house like you were pounding garlic with your head and she still won't be glad to see you, acting like you came to steal her husband away. So after all it isn't so great to be a prostitute.

If those two choices are ruled out, what's left is to be the wife of some servant or farmer. Then he'll keep you in line.

You never get to go out if you're married, and even if you see a man you like you won't get your fill of him. In any case, if you value your life you have to stick to your husband and hope he holds you at night. I thought it over and I can't see how that's any better than being a nun. For women like that to feel superior is like a bat feeling superior to a Ch'i-lin because the Ch'i-lin doesn't have wings, and superior to a phoenix because the phoenix doesn't have fur! I'd rather be free to do as I please, like the censors are.

As a nun, every year all the young priests with strong backs will be my bridegrooms. I can go through them all and then start again. If one isn't satisfactory, I can change him for one better able to stand use—but I can keep them all on stand-by. That's what being a nun is about. Only, then you have to shave your head, and a lot of men say it's a bad business to go with a nun, so they're ready to stride right over that bald head.

"But if I become a Taoist nun, I can keep a nice head of black hair, and when I take off my turban at night I'll have my pick of young gentleman, old masters, scholars, and messengers. Then, if I go to somebody's house, no matter what princess or milady lives there and no matter if she's jealous or not, the minute she sees a Taoist nun she feels friendly all over. Then she invites you to have tea, to eat, to come sit by her on the k'ang. She invites you to stay a few days, and when you go, she sends you off cash, taels, new clothes, new turban, and new stockings. She gives you pennants and coverlets for the shrine, and food, it's a better party than even the warden of Wu-hsien gives! And then, the ladies pay you for procurement. That's what it is to be a Taoist nun. But if Madame's mind is set on preventing me from becoming a nun, I'll have to to something else instead."

All the servants asked, "Then what else would you do?"

"If I can't be a nun, I guess I'll die and get it over with."

The servants were buzzing away with that, and they repeated it all faithfully to Madame Liu.

She said, "I'll do as the silly girls wants and let her be a nun. But I don't see why she's so desperate to have priests, and I am quite sure the nuns I have in have no use for priests, either."

The servants told her, "Ask Ch'ing-mei about that, and she'll tell you there aren't any nuns who don't find them useful."

Madame Liu said, "That's really too much! Too much! The girl's insane. Now she's slandering women devoted to Buddha. It's a sin! Hurry and make her up a robe and turban and take her to the White Garment temple to be a disciple of the master there."

She took out an almanac and saw that the eighth day of the fourth month was lucky, the day for bathing the Buddha. The household was busy getting everything ready for Ch'ing-mei's ordination, and on the day Madame Liu herself put Ch'ing-mei in the sedan chair which took her to the temple. A more senior male disciple there was named Mei Ch'ao, with the same character for 'mei' as Ch'ing-mei, so her name was changed to Hai-hui.

Once Hai-hui arrived at the temple, she promptly reduced the master first to illness and then to death. After that, she and the two male disciples lived on at the temple. Hai-hui thus had no master, but she followed her vocation of being a nun. She was at the Grand Secretary's palace one day and a minister's another. She went everwhere she pleased, and all the ladies received her as warmly as she had predicted they would. Even without any other entrée, the Liu family connection would have sufficed to make her welcome anywhere in the world. Nouveau-riche families like the Ch'aos of course welcomed her. Even Ms. Chi's family, while they had fallen out of well-to-do society, was old enough to merit Hai-hui's attentions. As they say, "When a rich family becomes poor, they still wear damask for three years."

Hai-hui had been a frequent guest at the Chis' for about a year, and sometimes, when Chao Yüan wasn't at home, she went to see Ms. Chi for a change. There she might cheat Ms. Chi out of the odd piece of clothing or indulge in pointless talk but she didn't practice any special immorality.

A while later, a buddhist nun from Ching-chou, named Kuo, about twenty years old, came to stay at Hai-hui's White Garment temple. The Nun Kuo was plump and fair, a four-square woman. People said she had been a prostitute. All of Hai-hui's ladies took with alacrity to the Nun Kuo, and she was a frequent sight at Ms. Chi's, like Hai-hui.

How could anyone claim these were good women or that they did anything worthwhile? But this bald Nun Kuo was smart, at least. She made eyes at everyone, and set her sails to catch whatever wind might blow. As soon as she arrived in a house, she looked to see if the lady there had any depraved inclination, and, if so, used all sorts of arts to lead that lady further into depravity. If she saw that the lady of the house was a proper woman, she became full of sincerity and clothed herself in a parody of the opinions of those great Confucian scholars, the Ch'eng brothers of Honan. Then she would talk about "making the heart correct and the mind sincere" and the appalling falling away from the way of the ancient kings. She could converse about Confucious' advice to Yen-hui to reserve all five senses for proper objects, and her auditors were full of praise for her. The wicked ones and even the highly virtuous all said she was a true pattern for them all and she would surely be elevated into living buddhahood any day now.

Ms. Chi had only the one fault of being overbearing. Even though the fox spirit Ch'ao Yüan killed had been associated with Ms. Chi in a former life, Ms. Chi hadn't the slightest aptitude for foxy seductive wiles. Given her nature, Ch'ao Yüan never worried about her chastity. Even though the Nun Kuo was a frequent visitor, no lascivious innuendo ever nested in Ms. Chi's heart.

Things had been going on like this when Chen ko was enraged by Mrs. Ch'ao Chu's report of Madame Ch'ao's insults. From then on, Chen ko was as poised for action as a cook with a pile of beans looking for a pot.

On the sixth day of the sixth month, they had strung rope in the courtyard and Chen ko was hanging clothes to air when she caught a glimpse of a couple of people coming out of Ms. Chi's rooms. It was Hai-hui, with the Nun Kuo behind her.

Chen ko cried out in alarm, "Some fine officials! Some proper home! Some well-born high-lady! With a Taoist priest all turbanned up and a fat, fair Buddhist priest coming and going in broad daylight! I may not have much of a background, and I may have been an actress and I may have kept some men. Maybe I did accept customers, but even I wouldn't have those two! Like a fat bull's snout and a bald donkey! Even if I was ten thousand years without a man I wouldn't want them!" She yelled on and on.

Ch'ao Yüan was just napping in the Western Cool Pavilion. He heard a commotion, and crawled out of bed, disheveled and staring. He half-slipped on his shoes and went out to ask what had happened.

Chen ko was beginning to repeat herself, but she was nowhere near done. She pointed right at Ch'ao Yüan's face.

"I'd like to see that mother of your's here now to get a good look at her nice, well-brought-up daughter-in-law! If I did anything like that your mother really would strip me and shave my head and give me to the beggars! Do you expect me to shut up and take this?"

"Ch'ao Yüan asked, "Are you sure? How could there be priests wandering around here in the middle of the day?"

"Just look at the foolish bastard!" said Chen ko, "It wasn't just me who saw it—all these maids and servants were here with me sunning the clothes,—so there isn't one of them who didn't see it!"

Ch'ao Yüan asked them all about it. Some closed their mouths tight and didn't make a sound.

Some said, "That's right, they were there all right."

Others said, "What priests? That was Ch'ing-mei from the Lius'."

Ch'ao Yüan said, "That little Ch'ing-mei did become a nun, and she's quite impressive,looks like a priest. But who's the Buddhist?"

He was answered, "We don't know, but since it's somebody who goes around with Ch'ing-mei, it must be a nun."

Chen ko said, "Huh! Would you let a 'nun' like that in your house?"

Ch'ao Yüan said, "All, right, all right. Ch'ing-mei's always helping people get up to no good, and she might have brought a priest disguised as a nun. Hurry and bring me the door-keeper so I can ask him about it."

That day it was Ch'ü Chiu-chou's duty on the door,

Ch'ao Yüan asked him, "Did you,see a Taoist and a Buddhist Priest go in?"

He replied, "What priests? That was the Lius' Ch'ing-mei and a nun. They went in to see the mistress about lunchtime, and they've just left. Would I let them in if they were men?"

Ch'ao Yüan said, "Look, I know the Taoist was Ch'ing-mei, but who's the Buddhist? I guess you must know all the bald women in town, so which was it?"

Ch'ü Chiu-chou thought a minute and said, "I don't know her. Never saw her before."

Chen ko spat out at Ch'ü Chiu-chou, "If you don't know 'her' how can you say it's a her?"

Ch'ü Chiu-chou said, "What priest would be so white and plump?"

Chen ko said, "I guess there wouldn't be any point in a skinny dark one."

Ch'ao Yüan jumped up.

"That's enough!" he said, "I won't stand having those bastards make a fool of me! Bring old Chi and his son here."

In a little while, Old Chi, and his son, Ms. Chi's brother, arrived. They had been fetched on the pretext that Ms. Chi wanted to talk to them. Ch'ao

Yüan said, "It wasn't your daughter who asked you here, it was me, and I have something to tell you."

Old Chi asked, "To tell me? What could you have to tell me? You don't mean my daughter's shamed you with another man or anything?"

"What else would I have to say to you?" Ch'ao Yüan replied, "And you knew it, too."

Then he went on to tell Old Chi about Ch'ing-mei bringing in a fair, fat priest at lunchtime in front of everyone.

"If she wanted to cheat the way most women do, well, it happens all the time and I could pretend not to smell anything rotten, but your daughter had to go and do a thing like this! I may have taken a prostitute into my home, but I did it right and she's my concubine now, and a fine, upright one—the perfect example of a person who ignores all improper sights, sounds, and thoughts. You wouldn't see her sleeping around on me! But your well brought-up daughter, who I married, dares do this. I brought you here to tell you that, and that I'll see you in court. Now go take her away with you, and I don't want to hear a thing out of you."

Smiling genially, Old Chi said, "Master Ch'ao! Hold on a minute. Don't say such hard things; it's difficult to take words back. Ch'ing-mei and the Buddhist Nun Kuo from Ching-chou left our nephew's house a little while ago, walking east. The Nun Kuo had on a dark green gauze gown and was shod in blue. Now, wasn't that who you saw? You're not going to tell me she's got both tails, a pair of balls as well as a cunt, are you?

She's welcome at all the great houses around here. I hope you don't expect me to believe that Ch'ing-mei's been clandestinely introducing priests into all of them? Now you've had your say and tossed a tile up in the air, it's going to fall somewhere. If you want to take anything back, you'd better do it in a hurry. What did my little girl ever do to you? You haven't given her any new clothes in the past two or three years, and she's eating off her dowry. If you want to take me in front of a judge to lay blame, the pleasure will be mine."

His son, Chi Pa-la, exclaimed, "Dad, can't you see, his conscience is dead. He's figured out how to get exactly what he wants and if you stand in the way, he'll scheme high and low and send her back dead if not alive. Let him divorce her if he wants to. We can afford to feed her. Let her stay home with us and wait. Ch'ao Ssu-hsiao and Madame Ch'ao will come home one of these days, and then we can lodge a formal complaint. What's the point of trying to say who is in the right here. You want to go in front of a judge? These days, how many judges are like Judge Pao—all Ch'ao Yüan has to do is send some money express with a letter and lies will suddenly become true.

If a father and son go to court, the son's as good as dead, but in this case it's us who'll be dead.

Master Ch'ao! Do whatever you like. If you want to divorce my sister, write out the declaration of divorce, and then I'll go home and get her room ready and take her home. What's so hard about that? You rich people say 'court' every time you open your mouths. Don't you know we little people get so scared when we hear that word we pee vinegar?"

Old Chi said, "Come on, We'll go back to ask your sister about this."

They went to the back rooms together. The front chambers had been a vortex of chaos, but Ms. Chi seemed to be dreaming. She didn't know anything about it. When Old Chi and her brother told her, she was so mad she could have died on the spot. She shut her mouth and ground her teeth and almost did.

After a bit, she opened her mouth and said, "Yes of course! I keep a priest. Why not, if he's going to have a whore? And if he saw my priest, he should have caught him. Why did he let the 'priest' walk off? If there's no priest, don't say I'm keeping one. Never mind one priest. If I want ten I can have them and he can just watch and get himself mad. Tell him to write that divorce declaration, and I'll be off. I swear, if I have the slightest regret at leaving you can feel free to say I was a bad wife. You two go on home now. Come back early tomorrow and we'll talk."

Old Chi and his son left. When they walked out the main gate they met Yü Ming-wu from across the way and the court employee Yang T'ai-hsüan, who were standing in the door way, trying to decide if they wanted to go buy plums or not.

Yü and Yang greeted Old Chi and his son politely and said, "Uncle Chi! We see you so rarely. You must have been to see Brother Ch'ao today?"

Old Chi was panting with fury and he told them the long and the short of it."

"Now he's writing the declaration of divorce, and he plans to divorce my girl! I'm going home to get her room ready so I can welcome her home."

Yü Ming-wu said, "This is as silly as believing in ghosts! Priests? I was just seeing out a guest and Hai-hui and the Nun Kuo came out from over there. They walked over to greet me and ask how I was.

"I said to them, 'Hai-hui, you don't have to worry, since you have all of your hair, but the Nun Kuo's bald so she'd better watch out for the sun,' and I invited them in out of the sun for lunch. They're inside now eating. Why should Brother Ch'ao believe every tall tale he hears?"

Yang T'ai-hsüan added, "Our magistrate doesn't like Master Ch'ao too much."

"Why's that?" asked Yü Ming-wu.

Yang told him, "When a young man is chosen for the imperial academy out of school he should present his card, but one chosen or scholarly achievements should present a six-folded card. Yesterday, Master Ch'ao went calling with the wrong kind of card, and gave it to the magistrate. The magistrate pushed it aside and didn't say anything. He didn't get any presents either."

Just as he was talking, they saw Ms. Chi come screaming out onto the street with her hair flying and a dagger in her hand. She wore an old blue robe with an under-robe of yellow raw silk, and a skirt of soft white gauze.

Standing in front of the main gate she yelled, "Come out, you shameless bastard, and you, whore! Let's have it out on the street. We may be new around here, and maybe the neighbors don't know the background of all this, but ever since you bastard took your whore off to the capital about a year ago now, I think it would be pretty hard to fool the neighbors if I was keeping a priest! Now Hai-hui and the Nun Kuo come to see me and you say I'm having priests in broad daylight! You called my Dad and brother and now you're writing up a divorce declaration!

Listen everybody! Is there any home where Hai-hui and the Nun Kuo are not welcome? Do you mean to say all those women are receiving priests? I don't care how it looks, I want to tell it all, to all the neighbors and every passerby! When I die I want you all to go to court as witnesses for my poor Dad and brother! You damned bastard! If you saw priests coming into my room, you come out here and tell it to the whole street! Then feel free to kill me or divorce me. If you're in the right, don't hide in there!

"I'm not going to fight for my life with that whore—she isn't worth it. I just want to have it out with you, bastard, and I'll stake my life on that."

She was even going to run on down the street, but Ch'ü Chiu-chou, who had been watching the door, knelt down and raised both hands in front of her. He kowtowed and begged her to refrain.

Chen ko shut her door tight as an iron pail and didn't even breathe loudly.

Ch'ao Yüan flitted to the door and called, "Ch'ü Chiu-chou, hold your mistress back. Don't let her onto the street."

The passersby who saw a young woman having a tantrum in the door of an Important Family thought it must be an outsider the resident there had mistreated, come to air her complaints. They stopped to have a look. Some knew it was Ch'ao Yüan's wife, and a crowd gathered.

Yü Ming-wu said, "It won't do any good to try to go talk her out of this. Old Chi, you and your son had better go take her back inside. What kind of family are you, anyway? What kind of behavior is this?"

Old Chi said, "It's gotten to the point where neither of them will give in. What good would it do for me to try to talk her over now?"

Hai-hui and the Nun Kuo had finished eating inside Yü Ming-wu's house, when they heard what was going on. They squeezed their behinds out of there fast as a puff of smoke.

Yü Ming-wu rushed over to Mrs. Kao's house to tell her, "The Ch'aos across the street are having a brawl. She's run out on the street—it really looks awful. We men can't say a thing to her. Mrs. Kao, could you go talk to her? Nobody else can."

Mrs. Kao said, "I wanted to go see everything from the start but I had two silk cocoons on my hands, so I couldn't."

She pulled on a skirt of raw silk, walked across the street and greeted Ms. Chi. No matter how mad Ms. Chi was, she had to have the civility to return Mrs. Kao's greeting.

Mrs. Kao heaved a sigh and said, "My good Mrs. Ch'ao! If we women don't look after our reputations, who'll listen to us? You can discipline your husband all you like inside the house, and nobody will say a thing, but if you, the wife of an Important Person, with a lovely house, don't think he's paying attention to your yelling inside and you come running out to yell on the street—well, men have dog fur on their faces—you think you're going to shame him? We women have to think of our reputations! Listen to me. If you have something to say, say it in your house. I'll have those two apologize to you. I'll have them kowtow a hundred times, and if they stop at ninety-nine, my name's not Kao!

My good Aunty Ch'ao, listen to what I'm telling you. Go inside now. On a big street like this, there are always officials going back and forth. If one sees a crowd like this, he'll stop to ask what's going on. That official won't have seen what a hard time those two have given you—he'll just see you having a tantrum on the street. Officials stick together, and you won't come out ahead. They might even start an investigation and involve your father and brother—worse and worse for your reputation!"

Ms. Chi heard that, and no matter how fierce she'd been sounding, she did feel just a little bit in the wrong for making a fuss in the street. Mrs. Kao's blandishments suited her actual desire to get out of the situation, so she let Mrs. Kao press her back inside, where she told Mrs. Kao the whole story, start to finish.

Mrs. Kao said, "Make him account for himself, but, inside the house. We women shouldn't stoop to their level," and, softly, in Ms. Chi's ear, "and stop that yelling on the street, now."

Mrs. Kao got up, said good-bye and "Try to bear it! I'm going."

Ms. Chi was quiescent the rest of the evening, putting off the reckoning until the following morning.

Chapter Nine

An Ordinary Wife has no recourse but Suicide
An Old Widower finds redress at Court

Two types of people bring downfall to home and state
The home falls to concubines and favorites
The state crumbles before eunuchs
New friends divide old with their wiles
Strangers break up homes with a few little words
False tales might as well be true
When duty, goodness, flesh and blood
all turn to dust
Done to death and no regrets
Let the bystanders laugh until their jaws crack

Mrs. Kao talked Ms. Chi back into the house and with sweet words and sharp talked her out of her tantrum.

Ch'ao Yüan knew in his heart that there had been no priest. He knew that Chen ko had been conjuring up fake spectres and catching at the air. However, he didn't dare say anything that would put Chen ko in the wrong, and, also, now he had Ms. Chi where he wanted her he could divorce her on this pretext. With Ms. Chi out of the house, one of the goads to Chen ko's temper would be gone. That would make Chen ko happy, and then he could raise her to the position of his wife. He hadn't counted on old Chi and Chi Pa-la coming so fluently to Ms. Chi's defense.

Ms. Chi had a temper and couldn't be expected to stand for this injustice. Ch'ao Yüan had made the msitake of trying to split a rock with an iron spear and had ended up with his spear broken in two. Even though it looked as if he'd failed in his attempt to discredit her, was Ms. Chi content to be generous and let bygones be bygones? No, she was plotting how to peel off Chen ko's hide and reduce Chen ko to a bloody pulp. She was willling to pit her life against his in her quarrel with her husband.

However, she thought, "How could a mere weak women like me kill him? Even if I did succeed in it, it isn't any good for a woman to kill her husband, and if I did kill him but then failed in killing myself—I couldn't bear how people would treat me! But how else can I clear my name of his accusations that I keep priests?"

She thought it over and over and finally concluded, "I'm no match for him in a fight to the death. Why bother to go on like this? Even if I wait for my mother-in-law to come back, I don't suppose she'll protect me from the storm! No, after all, I'd be better off dead."

She was ninety-nine and then some percent decided when Old Mr. Chi and Chi Pa-la came to see her.

When they arrived at the front gate, Old Chi first sent in a message to Ch'ao Yüan asking, "Did you write that declaration of divorce? I'm here to take my innocent girl home."

Ch'ao Yüan evasively claimed to be sick in bed from all the stress of the quarrel and said he'd talk to them when he felt better.

Old Chi said, "We'd better get it over with. It won't stop with priests—next you'll be claiming she keeps actors." With that he went back to see Ms. Chi.

Ms. Chi asked her father, "Dad, is it true what Mrs. Kao told me, that you and Pa-la were across the street with Yü Mingwu when I came out screaming?"

Old Chi said, "Wasn't I just, standing there talking about all this when out you came."

Ms. Chi asked, "What did Yü Ming-wu have to say?"

Old Chi replied, "Just after they left you, Hai-hui and the Nun Kuo ran into Yü Ming-wu, who was seeing some guests off. He asked them 'aren't you afraid of drying up under this wicked sun?' and he invited them to rest inside where it was cool. When you came out and stirred up such a fracas, those two were inside his house eating lunch."

Ms. Chi brought out a small package from an inside room.

"Here are fifty taels, two gold taels, and two pearls. My mother-in-law gave them all to me. Dad, you take these home and keep them for me until I come back home myself. These thirty taels of broken silver are what I've saved in the past few years, and this here is some jewelry I never wear—two bracelets, two pearl tiaras, and two gold hair ornaments—brother, you take these home for me. Take this length of blue satin and have a tailor sew it up quickly into a long sleeved robe for me, and have a half-coat made of this pink gauze. Have my sister-in-law make me some underthings with this floss, and keep the catty of floss that will be left over. Tomorrow, as soon as the clothes are made up, send them to me so I can go home dressed properly.

Old Chi asked, "Why do you want winter clothes like that now in the middle of the summer?"

"What's it to you?" She asked, "Don't ask such irritating questions. If you're going to hang around here telling me what to do, instead of getting those clothes made up for me, I guess I would be better off taking my case to court! I'm going to put a few other things of mine in a chest. Send a servant tomorrow to take the chest home. It's important to get those clothes made—I won't keep you to dinner."

She sent off her father and brother, and put everything in her room in order, just as if she really were planning to go home. She also took out a lot of clothes and gave them one by one to her maids and women.

One woman said, "Ma'am, it's silly to divide up all of your things like this. When the master said he was going to divorce you, he was just letting his mouth run away with him! You're his lawful wife, and he married you in a proper ceremony in front of his parents. How can he divorce you while his parents are absent? Ma'am, you shouldn't go home."

Ms. Chi said, "So according to you, I should wait until he drives me away with a stick?"

"Who would dare do that?" the woman said.

Ms. Chi also had them take some loose change from her bed and distribute it among the servants.

She said, "This is for you to remember me by."

Her maids said, "If you do go home for a while, you'd better lock up this room and take us with you to serve you there. It isn't as if there would be anything left for us to do here."

Ms. Chi said, "Of course you'll go, too, even if you don't come with me."

By now it was about eight in the morning, and nobody had sent them firewood for breakfast. With her own hands, Ms. Chi broke a couple of panels off her new sedan chair, heated up a pot and made breakfast.

One of the servants said, "What a shame! Wouldn't it be better to burn the old sedan chair and use the new one to travel in?"

Ms. Chi told her, "I'm going to be divorced and I won't be a member of the Ch'ao family any more. How can I use their sedan chair then?"

Ch'ao Yüan had found out that Ms. Chi was all packed up and ready to go home to her father. That fit in with his plans, but he didn't know when she would leave. In the morning of the eighth day of the sixth month, old Chi and Chi Pa-la had the clothes ready, and they took the clothes to Ms. Chi, in a package. They also had a few men go to pick up her trunk. Ms. Chi had only a cloth bundle left.

She said, "I decided this old furniture isn't worth more than a few cash and if I take it people will accuse me of being a thief, so who wants their things anyway."

"You're absolutely right," said Old Chi.

Ms. Chi said, "I haven't finished packing up, so I guess I'd better go back tomorrow, but you two don't have to come. The weather is hot, so I'll want to get into the house quickly. We can talk afterwards. If you have any use for the things I gave you yesterday, go ahead and use them. Don't sell them to give me money."

Old Chi said, "Listen to her talk! Aren't you being a little short-sighted? You'd better reconsider. Never mind that I'm no match for him, with his wealth and position. Even if I were, it isn't as if you could make him pay with his life. Listen to what I'm telling you."

For a while he tried to argue her out of her resolve to go through with the divorce.

They used wood from the new sedan chair to cook lunch.

Close to evening, Ms. Chi took a bath, lit some incense, and bound her hair up tight. She put many hair ornaments in her hair, and rings on her fingers. She wrapped her footbindings neatly. She put on new cinnabar-pink silk trousers with a moon-white damask under-garment next to her skin, then a sky blue short jacket with a cinnabar pink pongee jacket over it, a moon-white great robe and over it all her new blue satin wide-sleeved robe. Then she used a needle and thread to sew together all the layers of her clothes, so there wasn't the tiniest opening anywhere. She placed one gold and one silver piece in her mouth. Then she took a peach-red phoenix sash. Very quietly, she opened her door, walked out to the door of Ch'ao Yüan's rooms and hung herself on his door frame.

It all took less time that two cups of hot tea.

Etheral steps on air, the shade of a girl on a swing.

While Ms. Chi found her death outside the door, inside Ch'ao Yüan was telling Chen ko his calculations.

"Now she's gotten herself in a mess! If I go ahead and say 'no I won't divorce her,' she's the one who'll lose face, so now she wants to go home to her father. Once she's gone, we'll rent those rooms of hers back there to someone else. We'll get three or four taels out of that, and we'll be rid of her, too."

They called a maid to open the door so the woman who made breakfast could do so. The maid opened the door, screamed and fell to the floor, silent.

"What are you screaming for, silly?" asked Ch'ao Yüan.

He had to ask several times before the maid got up off of the floor.

Still panicked, she said, "When I opened the door there was a woman hanging there on the door staring at me!"

"Did you recognize her?"

"I was scared to death when I saw her. How could I notice who she was?"

Ch'ao Yüan jumped up out of bed, pulled on his trousers, slipped on shoes and ran outside, saying, "Oh no! It's that Chi woman from the back. She's gone and hung herself!"

When he got to the door, he found he was right. He put his hand to her mouth. No breath lingered there, and she was as cold as ice. Then he was beside himself and began screaming for servants to come and let her down and take her inside to her rooms. The servants crowded around and were about to take her down.

Only the servant Li Ch'eng-ming had his wits about him, and said, "Don't let her down yet. Go call Old Mr. Chi and his son to come and see for themselves. Otherwise they'll say she was perfectly fine yesterday and why should she go kill herself today? They'll say we murdered her and then no matter what you say it'll be hard to defend yourself. Call the Chis right now and send Aunty Chen off to hide somewhere. If she's here when the women come in looking for her she'll have to stand their abuse.

All of Chen ko's haughty airs had disappeared into limbo.

She put her hair up simply, wore a plain old gown and an old moon-white skirt, and old shoes. Two servant women took her over to Yü Ming-wu's, knocked on the door, and sent her in.

Old Chi had had a hard time going to sleep. He lay down to sleep at the fourth watch (about two a.m.) but his heart kept palpitating and his muscles twitching until the fifth watch, when he finally closed his eyes, only to see his daughter wearing her new clothes and with a red sash around her neck.

She walked up to him and said, "Dad! I've died. Don't let that whore get away with it."

Old Chi broke out in a cold sweat and woke with a start.

Then his son was under his window shouting, "Dad, hurry up! I'm sure my sister's dead, I had a bad dream."

The dream he told Old Chi matched Old Chi's dream exactly. Father and son cried out a lament or two, and then got ready to go out. By then somebody from the Ch'ao household was banging on their door calling:

"Old Mr. Chi and young Master Chi, please come out!"

Old Chi replied, "Just now your mistress came home to us in her blue gown with a red sash around her neck. I'm ready."

Quick as fire he finished his preparations and ran over to the Ch'aos', with his son. When they got there, they saw Ms. Chi dangling from the door-frame. Father and son began howling with a total loss of constraint.

Old Chi grabbed hold of Ch'ao Yüan and banged his head. Ch'ao Yüan had lost his usual arrogance and was all kowtow and apologies.

He kept repeating, "Please think of my Dad. We're still all family."

Old Chi went inside looking for Chen ko. He flew into an awful temper when he didn't find her. Of course, by now, Ch'ao Yüan was reduced to a trembling lump of snot. None of that pack of servants and witchy maids dared step forward to restrain Old Chi, either.

Chi Pa-la said, "Dad, get a hold of yourself. My sister's dead and if you don't calm down, we'll offend our relatives here. I don't care about Ch'ao Yüan, but think of old Mr. and Mrs. Ch'ao. What good is this going to do?"

Old Chi thought of how his daughter had said that she would want to get into the house quickly, because of the heat, and that they could talk afterwards, and he knew his son, too, was thinking of the meaning that had been hidden in her words. He let his hands fall to his sides and stopped smashing things.

Chi Pa-la said, "Brother-in-law, you have to be the one to hold her while I cut her down. Then take her inside and lay her down."

"Where should I put her?" asked Ch'ao Yüan, "In her room?"

Chi Pa-la said, "Brother-in-law, you don't mean to say you are not the eldest son in your family? It won't do to have the funeral of the eldest son's wife leave from some back rooms. Open up your main hall and have it cleaned right now. Then call some maids to carry her in there."

They did so, and there she lay.

Chi Pa-la said, "Do you have coffin-wood in the house?"

Ch'ao Yüan said, "Yes, but I don't know if it's good enough."

"Do I have to tell you," said Chi Pa-la, "If it's good enough, use it. Otherwise, consider that you were husband and wife and send someone out to buy new wood."

Ch'ao Yüan said, "Please take a few men to Wei's by the Southern Gate and pick out some you find satisfactory."

Just as he was speaking, some carpenters who had heard the news showed up, and they went to the lumber shop with Chi Pa-la. There was one set of coffin wood there for eighty taels, one for a hundred seventy taels, and one for three hundred.

Chi Pa-la said, "My sister was the daughter of a poor man but the wife of a rich one. She deserves the best."

He argued the price of the three hundred tael set down to two hundred and twenty taels. Out of that, the proprietor of the lumber shop gave Chi Pa-la thirty taels in gratitude for introducing this piece of business, so in all the proprietor only got a hundred and sixty taels.

They hired about ten men and all of them carried back the wood, some with pieces balanced on their shoulders and some in pairs carrying the large pieces between them. They got back to Ch'ao Yüan's house and there began a flurry of actvity building the coffin.

Ch'ao Yüan saw that Chi Pa-la knew exactly what he was doing, so he left everything up to Chi Pa-la. He didn't mind paying two hundred and twenty taels for the coffin wood, and would gladly have paid a thousand.

By the afternoon, the coffin was ready and the inside was sealed with resin.

The corpse of the wronged woman had not begun to decay. Although she had died by hanging, her tongue didn't stick out and her eyes didn't pop out. In fact, death had removed the ferocity from her expression, and she looked calmly benevolent.

Material wealth may have evaded Old Chi, but he was of a good family. He still had three or four nephews who had passed their first exams, and a good number of men of note in his clan. There must have been over two hundred people from the Chi family who came to view Ms. Chi's body, as she lay in the main hall with white damask curtains around her and incense burning to her spirit, everything as it should be.

Chi Pa-la knelt and asked for the ancestors' indulgence.

Then he stood up and said, "My little sister's found her last home. Let's take this place apart."

The men outside tossed Ch'ao Yüan in the air. Some mauled him, and some pulled his hair. Others broke up his furniture and levelled rooms. They made a very satisfying mess out of the vinegar, rice and wheat in the kitchen.

A gang of women with bamboo flogs and poles, and even whips, searched the front and back of the house, under the beds and under the woodpile. Since they couldn't find Chen ko to beat up, they destroyed her bedroom, smashing every last thing there.

They made Ch'ao Yüan kneel down facing all the Chis and write confession.

He wrote:

I, Ch'ao Yüan have taken a prostitute, Chen ko as my Concubine and did believe her slanders of my wife. I habitually mistreated my lawful wife, Ms. Chi. I did not give her food or clothes, but locked her in a desolate room where I often insulted her. On the sixth day of the month, Chen ko slandered Ms. Chi with having Taoist and Buddhist priests in, when in fact it was the Taoist nun Hai-hui and the Buddhist Nun Kuo who had visited Ms. Chi. Chen ko incited me to divorce Ms. Chi. Ms. Chi could not bear the injustice and on the same night at an undetermined hour hung herself with a red sash on Chen ko's door frame. Today, I throw myself on my father-in-law's mercy, beg him to think of our familial relation, and to not take this case to court. I wish to give Ms. Chi a grand funeral and will spare no expense in it,

—written by Ch'ao Yüan on the eighth day of the sixth month.

He gave the crowd what he had written for them to read, and then gave it to Old Chi to keep. Chi Pa-la said, "We may as well let him stand up. We need him to help send off my sister. I'll take my time settling accounts with him later."

Wine was served and they invited Yü Ming-wu to drink with them. Yü Ming-wu said, "Uncle Chi, listen to me for just a minute. I know how hard it must be for you to see your dear girl dead. And of course Brother Ch'ao has behaved very badly, but now that she has died, your girl will be buried in his family's grave-plot. Besides, remember how close you've always been with old Uncle Ch'ao? Closer than brothers! For the sake of Old Ch'ao, just have Ch'ao Yüan do everything he can to make it up by giving your girl a fine funeral. Stop beating and cursing him."

Old Chi said, "My good brother Yü! I wouldn't have brought up my brother-in-law Old Ch'ao, but since you have mentioned that vicious, greedy hyena, I have to say I never saw anything like him. When he was a starving lower degree holder, I was a rich and prominent man. I won't bother to bring up how well I was doing in those days, but let's just say that brother-in-law of mine, before he got his government position, was fed by my family's rice, clothed in my family's cotton, and he drank wine made from our lees and ate New Year's buns made out of our flour. He lived under a roof thatched with our straw. He took, we gave, and that was how it was. Year after year he accepted all we gave just like a court accepts tribute. Then he was accepted at the Academy as a special student and took our girl into his family. Even though I'd fallen in the world and was no longer a rich man, I did all I could to give her a dowry. It was at least five or six hundred gold taels' worth. I had only four hundred mou of land left, and, fearing her dowry was too small, I gave her one quarter of that.

Later, Old Ch'ao went off to the capital for his exams and he needed travelling money. Poor as I am, I sold a pearl tiara of my wife's and gave every penny of that to him. Then he sold off twenty mou of the land I'd given my girl, for another forty taels, before he went. He waited almost a year for that special exam, and in the meanwhile every morsel that passed his family's lips came out of that land of my girl's!

Now he's an Important Person and he has all the money he wants. If his son was heartless enough to despise my daughter as not beautiful enough for his new estate, that Old Man Ch'ao was heartless enough to despise us all for being poor, as if to know us might blemish his reputation! He found new friends. Ever since he went to Hua-ting, about five years now, I haven't received one little note the size of my palm or one cash' worth of a present from him."

Yü Ming-wu said, "Listening to you, I can hardly believe what I'm hearing! Uncle Ch'ao wouldn't have behaved that badly."

Old Chi told him, "My good brother Yü! I'm not making up wild stories about him just because of my daughter's death. Let all my family here, and all of his, too, listen to me and if anything I say is untrue then I'm a beggar! His viciousness wasn't felt by me alone. What about all his other old friends here? What debt of gratitude did he ever pay? Yüan Wan-li was renovating his own house, and Ch'ao Yüan sent over twenty big planks of pine. A rich family is likely to have extra wood, so why not just give it for free? But Ch'ao Yüan kept at Yüan Wan-li to buy it, and finally Yüan said, 'if you'll take the price I'm offering, I'll take your wood, but if you don't like my price, I don't need your wood.' He gave Ch'ao Yüan forty taels, which he accepted. Now, the other day, Yüan Wan-li died and Ch'ao Yüan pulled his widow and little seven or eight year-old child into court claiming the market value of the wood, five or six taels a plank."

Yü Ming-wu said, "Brother Ch'ao didn't get anything out of that. The judge made him look very bad. Old Ch'ao didn't know anything about it, it was all Ch'ao Yüan's doing."

Old Chi said, "Whether he knew about that or not, I'll tell you about something he certainly did know about. A few years ago, he offended the Han-lin scholar Hsin, by refusing him temporary grooms from the yamen as he passed through, and they even had a tussle and his tally fell in the water. Hsin was in the process of sending up an official accusation, but Cheng Po-lung, from around here, who was a military courier in the capital at the time heard about it and hushed it up for us for eight hundred taels. He heard about the matter from another courier and said, 'It's a good thing you told me about this. Throwing the tally of an enfeoffed prince into the water is no laughing matter. We'd better pay to have this taken care of.' Then Cheng Po-lung took every silver wine vessal and trinket in his house, and all his wife's and daughter's jewelry and sold it off. He got eight hundred taels and used it to hush things up. Old Ch'ao did pay him back, little by little, but he never took one particle of interest. Later Cheng Po-lung was promoted and borrowed eight hundred taels from Old Ch'ao, for two notes of four hundred taels each. Old Ch'ao took his notes, but never gave him the money. A year later, Old Ch'ao tried to make Cheng pay that money he'd never even borrowed, and Cheng had to write a warrant and swear on it at a temple before Old Ch'ao Ssu-hsiao would let him off.

You know how expensive things are in the city. These past past few years whenever somebody went into the capital on an errand Cheng Po-lung would put them up, and once they were there, they'd stay two or three months. Ch'ao Yüan himself was there a few times. They'd all sit around Cheng Po-lung's house eating full-course meals, and if they wanted anything, all they had to do was dash off a note the size of my palm and he'd get it for them. The other day, Cheng Po-lung came home here and Ch'ao Yüan didn't even greet him. Ch'ao Yüan didn't give him one sip of water to drink.

When Ch'ao Yüan was at the academy, he caught typhoid and that Huang Ming-an, from here, was by his side day and night, watching over him like a father for forty days. Later Huang went to see him in T'ung-chou, and all Ch'ao Yüan did was to give him two taels and chase him out after giving him one meal. Huang was so mad he got sick."

Old Chi wasn't finished talking, but everyone else got up to leave. The Chis beat up Ch'ao Yüan again and hit him so hard he couldn't get up to put the funeral streamers on the door.

Chen ko was in hiding at Yü Ming-wu's house. She didn't dare go out of doors even early in the morning, or late at night, for fear of the Chis. Fortunately, Yü Ming-wu was an old friend, so she wasn't lonesome. Yü Ming-wu's wife had gone to their country place to look after the harvest, so Yü Ming-wu found Chen ko's presence convenient.

Old Chi talked it over with the other members of his clan, and decided to take it to court.

They told him, "Do whatever you think best. If you think you can win, go ahead. If you don't think so, then be realistic. If it were winter, we could wait before encoffining her, and that would give us time to put our case. But think of the time of year! We have no choice but to put her in her coffin now."

His relatives who held degrees told him, "How can you say that? He thinks he can treat us as if we weren't human beings. He forced a girl to kill herself. If we don't speak up, people are going to laugh so hard at us they'll swallow their teeth. After all, we did marry her to him, and if we don't do something about this, everyone will blame us. This is no time for cautious deliberations. Present the deposition tomorrow. That confession he wrote is our evidence."

Old Chi asked, "Where should we make this deposition of ours?"

They told him, "Cases involving loss of life have to be decided at the subprefectural level. Where do you think? The yamen, of course. And in the petition you had better say that Chen ko forced her into hanging herself. Don't say that she was beaten to death. It would be embarrassing if they investigated and found out that that wasn't true."

They discussed it some more and then left.

From there, Old Chi and his son didn't go home, but straight to the door of the sub-prefectural yamen. They found Sun Yeh-chi, the deposition writer, gave him two coins and had him write their deposition.

Here is what he wrote:

Petitioner Chi Tou, aged fifty-nine, of this sub-prefecture, reporting the oppression to death of a wife by a concubine. Tou's daughter, Ms. Chi, being married at a tender age to Ch'ao Yüan, had a harmonious marriage. Unfortunately, Ch'ao Yüan became rich and an Academy atudent. He despised Ms. Chi's appearance and for eight hundred taels bought an actress of principal female roles, Chen ko, as a concubine. He kept Tou's daughter in a solitary room with no food or clothes. He sometimes made pretexts to beat her. On the sixth day of this month, Chen ko mendaciously asserted that Tou's daughter had improper relations with Buddhist and Taoist priests. She based her tale on the sight of the Taoist nun, Hai-hui, and Buddhist Nun Kuo leaving the house. Chen ko incited Ch'ao Yüan to beat Tou's daughter and divorce her, so Tou's daughter hung herself on the door frame.

Tou is pained by the death of his innocent daughter and presents this deposition as a cry for justice!

Accused: Ch'ao Yüan. Chen ko, Hsiao Mei-hung, Hsiao Hsing-hua, Hsiao Liu-ch'ing, Hsiao T'ao-hung, Hsiao Hsia-ching, Ms. Chao, Ms. Yang.

Witnesses: Hai hui, Nun kuo, Yü Ming-wu, Mrs. Kao

On the tenth day of the sixth month, they waited for the sub-prefectural magistrate to preside. Old Chi went forward with the deposition. His name was taken, and the deposition put aside to be read. On the eleventh, the deposition was endorsed and two couriers, Wu Hsiao-Ch'uan and Shao Tz'u-hu were sent to gather the accused. The two first saw Old Chi and Chi Pa-la, and then went on to the Ch'aos.

The servant at the door saw they were from the sub-prefectural court and didn't dare show any lack of respect. He invited them in to sit, and then sent the message to Ch'ao Yüan that the two couriers had arrived.

Ch'ao Yüan, despite his aches and pains from the beatings, put on a white mourning turban and a robe of raw silk gauze to greet them. The messengers took out their warrant, and then they all sat down to drink. Over the drinks and snacks, they told him about how the situation stood.

"It's true she hanged herself and died. You can't argue with that. But that doesn't mean you have to pay with your life. The magistrate hasn't had time to give the case his attention, and it will be up to him which way this goes. Get ready for tomorrow. Tomorrow you'd better present your own deposition."

With that, they took their leave. Ch'ao Yüan took out two taels and said they should take the two taels as a tiny present to pay for their donkeys for the rest of their round. He told them that tomorrow, after the deposition was presented, he hoped to be able to ask their advice about something else. At first they demurred, so he called their groom to come take the money. Immediately after they left, he asked Yü Ming-wu over to discuss the problem. He also sent a servant to bring the deposition writer Sung Chin-wu. When Sung came, Ch'ao Yüan explained it all to him, gave him five taels and kept him for dinner.

Sung Chin-wu wrote:

Plaintiff Academy Student Ch'ao Yüan, son of Ch'ao Ssu-hsiao, the current magistrate of T'ung-chou, lodges a complaint of blackmail. Unfortunately Ch'ao Yüan took the wicked daughter of Chi Tou as his wife. This wife had a perverse disposition. She rebelled and turned her back on familial norms on countless occasions. One time, upon minor provocation, she took a knife in her hand and tried to murder Yüan. Yüan hid and she had a tantrum in the street. Yü Ming-wu and others restrained her, and she hung herself in shame at her own behaviour.

Chi Tou and his son Chi Pa-la have combined with over two hundred people to swarm over Ch'ao Yüan's house, beating Yüan almost to death, smashing the house and its contents to dust, and plundering clothes and jewelry. They wish moreover to swindle money out of him, so they have concocted their foul deposition. This plaint is a call for justice!

Accused: Chi Tou, Chi Pa-la, the Chi clan of two-hundred-plus people.
Witness: Yü Ming-wu

On the twelfth, this was sent to the Wu-ch'eng sub-prefectural yamen for endorsement. Again warrants were made and the couriers sent out.

Even though Ch'ao Yüan was rich and powerful, in this instance he was isolated. All those men who usually hung around with him were just a pack of feckless rich boys. Not one of them was serious or well-informed. As for as all his other "close friends", but he and his father had managed to alienate them all with arrogance. Which one of them would want to come forward and help him now?

Indeed, he was bereft of kith and kin.

Old Chi may have been poor, but he still had standing in his clan. Look at what happened on the day of Ms. Chi's encoffinment. No less than two hundred people turned out to support Old Chi.

So Ch'ao Yüan was quite worried, but there's a saying that sums up his way of thinking:

"When a lawsuit big as the heavens is dumped on you, you can buy it for as much money as it takes to fill heaven, so why worry?"

Only, while men's hearts may indeed reason thus, heaven might not. See the next chapter to find out how it ended.

Chapter Ten

An Academician offers a Bribe
A Sub-prefectural Magistrate Accepts a Gift

When an official combines the three attributes
of talent, scholarship, and wisdom
Lives irreproachably and virtuously
and ever hones his understanding of self, others and the world
He is a gentleman.

But we see:
Bending of laws
Acceptance of bribes
Brash disregard of wrongs
Benighted principles
Public discourse turned on its head
Right and wrong smashed in a heap
Humankind treated as despicable outsiders
unworthy to associate with the "thicket of scholars"
we see plundering of the robes of office
befouling of the fragrance of books

Hatred of these injustices pierces common men to their hearts
Mental pain wracks their heads

How can these officials live on
When they have piled wickedness on burgeoning evil?
There is no limit they won't go to
expressing their contempt of the common people
They ram through their arbitrary actions
They are licentious, thieving, lying hypocrites
Full of their power, relying on their wealth
They give free rein to their wrongful ways
Complete in every evil
Transgressing every rule

They cherish concubines
Make illicit assignations
Then, when a wife is pushed to suicide
And one of these men finds himself accused of murder
He intrigues and bribes
Pulling others deeper into dishonorable dealings

But the net of heaven in woven fine
Virtues and vices are all caught in it
and bring their own reward—
What a saisfying sight!

In the Chi family there was one Chi San. He was a dispicable man who was always thinking of money, and he was old Chi's senior in the Chi clan. All the others in the clan disliked him, but they were afraid to cross him. When Ch'ao Yüan found out that Old Chi had filed his claim, Ch'ao Yüan thought it would be a good idea to get Chi San on his own side. As evening fell, Ch'ao Yüan sealed up two taels which he told Ch'ao Chu to carry in his sleeve to Chi San. Ch'ao Yüan hoped that Chi San would help patch up the quarrel.

Ch'ao Yüan also sent a hundred taels to Old Chi in reimbursement for Ms. Chi's dowry, and he even sent Chi Pa-la twenty taels to buy back the land that had come as part of Ms. Chi's dowry, including the twenty mous that had been sold off.

Contrary to Ch'ao Yüan's expectation, Chi San arrogantly took the line, "If you want to patch things up, go do it yourself. Even though it is true that the sight of money to me is like the sight of blood to a fly, I'm not about to sell my own granddaughter in the clan. I'm not afraid of evil men, but I am of wronged ghosts!"

After saying a few more words in the same tenor, he sauntered back indoors, and Ch'ao Chu brought back his words to Ch'ao Yüan. Now Ch'ao Yüan saw that it wouldn't be so easy to stifle the case. He knew he couldn't hide out any longer from his parents, so he sent Li Ch'eng-ming by night to tell Old Mr. and Madam Ch'ao in T'ung-chou what was going on. He wanted his father to write a letter begging clemency, right off before the case was already lost and his own position entirely discredited.

Ch'ao Yüan also sent out invitations and set up a banquet for the two court messengers who had come with the warrant. He gave each of them forty taels, and a tael each to their young grooms, five taels each to their assistants, and in this way he bought their complaisance. Further correspondence on his case was thus delayed until his father's letter should arrive.

On the second day of the seventh month, Ch'ao Ssu-hsiao wrote a letter and had Ch'ao Feng and Li Ch'eng-ming take it and try to bribe the case away. The next morning, Ch'ao Feng and Li Ch'eng-ming arrived in front of the sub-prefectural yamen and found an unsalaried official prognosticator to take their letter in. The prognosticator knew they had come on a matter of life and death, and held out for six taels before he would take the letter.

When the magistrate opened the letter, he flew into a tempestuous fury. He shouted for the prognosticator who had brought in the letter to be beaten a hard fifteen strokes. He shouted to have the two court messengers, Wu Hsiao Ch'uan and Shao tz'u-hu, summoned. When Wu and Shao heard the summons, they didn't dare go in person and sent a couple of outside messengers go to take his message. The magistrate wasn't having any of that, and shouted for the messengers to be beaten, too.

The magistrate said, "This is a case of murder! The petition was presented twenty days ago and the criminal is still left at large so he can try to evade punishment by using his connections! How much did he give you two scoundrels, that you brazenly make a plaything of the law?"

The two messengers were now entirely concerned with their own problems and proceeded to stretch the truth in their own favor.

"Academician Ch'ao was severly injured when the members of the Chi clan beat him. To this day, he hasn't been able to get out of bed. Besides, the woman who died is well-known for her lying ways, and Yü Ming-wu is going to be a witness to that. That's why we delayed in presenting the documents. We'd never dare take bribes!"

The magistrate said, "Spare them a beating this time. The documents are to be presented and the case heard tomorrow. If these two obstruct justice again, they shall be beaten to death."

He knew just when to relent.

The messengers Wu and Shao flew off to tell Ch'ao Yüan about their interview with the magistrate. Ch'ao Yüan had already heard about the prognosticator's beating and that Wu and Shao were to be beaten. He was just wondering what if anything he could do to save the situation when Wu and Shao arrived.

They said, "Master Ch'ao, have you heard what happened?" It looks like those couple of taels you gave us were the price of our lives! If we're beaten to death, even people you paid off will be gone and can't help you. You'd better think of something fast or this case is going to run away with you!"

Ch'ao Yüan said, "She hanged herself, and anyway she's in her coffin now. What can they find out with an investigation? Besides, I guess I can expect a little consideration, as is due to my position."

Shao said, "Well, of course. I suppose if you weren't going to be given special consideration maybe that prognosticator wouldn't have had the benefit of a whole fifteen strokes!"

Ch'ao Yüan said, "All right, all right, I know you're worried. What do you suggest I do?"

Wu said, "I don't guess Old Chi's going to be able to find any way around us two."

"How do we do it?" asked Ch'ao Yüan.

Wu said, "It'll take at least a thousand taels."

They talked it back and forth and agreed on amounts of money to be distributed up the official ladder and settled on seven hundred taels with which the messengers departed. They agreed to come back in the evening to let Ch'ao Yüan know how it had gone. The two messengers went back to Wu Hsiao-ch'uan's home, where they wrote the following submission:

The two messengers Wu Sheng-tao and Shao Ch'iang-jen petition the honorable magistrate re the hearing of academician Ch'ao Yüan et. al....

On the top: they wrote "Seventh Month" and on the bottom the day, and in between, where the location of the hearing should be shown, they wrote "five hundred" in tiny characters. In those days, this was the clandestine way, currently in favor, of signalling that a bribe was offered at the Wu-ch'eng yamen. If an official wanted to accept it, he'd write his endorsement in thick, red ink over the small characters and send it along, and by their own mysterious means, the bribers would find a way to send the sum offered into the inner chambers of the yamen. If the official scorned the sum as too small, he would toss the paper aside, and since it had disappeared, the briber would of course understand why and come up with a more satisfactory offer.

On that day, the messengers sent it in, and it came back endorsed with a date written in thick red ink over the "five hundred" but there was also appended the following note:

"In addition, prepare sixty gold taels and have that ready to pay for expenses to be incurred in repairs of the city temple."

The two messengers brought this to Ch'ao Yüan, who had no choice but assent. Ch'ao Yüan sent out all over to money shops to get the gold taels and the other seven hundred. They managed to gather the requisite sum, which of course could not be short by a fraction of one cash. After it had been gathered, Ch'ao Yüan had the two messengers present it. The two hundred taels he gave them was used fifty taels each to intermediaries at the yamen, ten taels each to the outside messengers, one tael each to the grooms, and the remainder for Wu and Shao to split between themselves.

The next morning, principals and witnesses were summoned, petitions presented and warrants produced. When the watchman's rattle sounded the second watch (nine a.m.) all concerned were in attendance at the sub-prefectural office. Ch'ao Yüan had brought along ten or twenty strings of cash which he had Wu and Shao distribute up and down the line at the yamen. The Chis, as plaintiffs, spent some money too, but it didn't compare. Ch'ao Yüan had saturated the yamen, inside and out, with his money, so none of the yamen officials treated him as a criminal. They acted as if he were some well-respected gentleman come to pay his respects to the magistrate.

He was politely shown into a guest reception room, where he sat down on a high-backed chair. A crowd of his servants swarmed protectively around him. The two messengers led the Chao household women back to a little pavilion behind the reception rooms and the Ch'ing-i hall. Back there, the yamen servants began bringing them a ceaseless round of melons and snacks, while the old man who looked after the reception rooms poured tea. It was quite a social whirl.

All waited a while while the magistrate took his seat in the main hall. The gate-keepers sounded their clappers, the treasury-servants banged their drums opening court, the middle gates were opened and Ch'ao Yüan and his motley retinue knelt down by the second gate. From above, Yü Ming-wu's name was called forward. One of the two messengers scurried forward to say, Yü Ming-wu is a clerk at the bureau of Military Colonies and is now at work."

Then Mrs. Kao was called. This is how she looked:

> Hair loose and tangled as weeds
> Complexion like a warty gourd
> A skirt of heavy blue linen
> and dark jacket of plain cloth
> Her kerchief a knot of loose threads
> Her leggings half rags
> Full of manly fervor she knelt on the platform
> Resonantly she called for heavenly justice
> If that magistrate weren't so greedy
> Wouldn't she have seen that academician get his just rewards!

The magistrate began, "Now, Mrs. Kao, you had better tell the truth. If you are partial in your testimony my finger-screws are most unforgiving!"

Mrs. Kao said, "Your honor shouldn't talk like that to a woman of respectable family. Why should you put finger-screws on me?"

"I will if I have to, and I don't care how respectable you may be."

"I hope you don't mean that might can move right. After all 'not all eight guardian deities can budge the word right'."

"Yes, I've heard that one," the magistrate said, "but you just concern yourself with telling the truth. Why would I put finger-screws on you? Well, just tell me now, how did Ms. Chi die. Go ahead."

Mrs. Kao said, "I don't know how she died, but I did go over to see her and talk her out of making a scene a day or so before."

"Tell me about that 'scene'."

"I live across the way from the Ch'aos. They're Important People, and I never did visit them much, because I don't care to visit where I have to bow down in front of people. But last year, in the eleventh month, Ms. Chi came out to the main gate to see Master Ch'ao go off for an enclosed hunt. I met her then, and she came out to chat with the neighborhood women. We all talked for a while and then went home. Then this past sixth month, on the sixth day, I was at home in trousers and busy with some silk cocoons, when I heard screaming out on the street. I asked the children what was happening and they told me, 'it's the wife of that gentleman across the way. She was working herself up and yelling at everyone in the middle of the street.' I said what a shame it was she had to go and exhibit private failings to the whole world. A fine gentleman's wife, young too, but she never stopped to consider what people would say. Whatever did she mean by it? I wanted so badly to go see it, but my hands were full so I couldn't go out right that minute. A little later my neighbour Yü Ming-wu came over and said, 'Mrs. Ch'ao across the street is in a temper. She's run out on the street to make a scene. What kind of behaviour is that? We men don't dare go talk her out of it. Mrs. Kao, you go talk her back inside. Nobody else can.'"

Mrs. Kao paused in her narrative, "It's a long story. I have heavy linen pants on and the weight is killing me. Can't I please stand up while I tell you the rest, instead of kneeling?"

The magistrate said, "You may stand. Stand over there to the side and continue."

Mrs. Kao went on, "Since you say to continue, I'd wanted to go out from the beginning of it but my hands were full. So then I pulled a skirt over my trousers, still talking to Yü Ming-wu, and then went outside. There was a crowd of people on the street, packed so close they could have been sewn together. It wasn't easy getting through them, but I pulled with one hand and pushed with the other until I finally got to the Chaos' door. There she was, a knife in her hand! She was shouting she'd like 'pit her life against that shameless whore's".

The magistrate said, "Who did she mean by 'a shameless whore'?"

Mrs. Kao said, "The prostitute Mr. Ch'ao took as his concubine."

The magistrate asked, "Where did she used to perform?"

"Your honor, it isn't as if you ever had a drink with her or saw her perform."

"Nonsense, of course not. Go on, Mrs. Ch'ao was cursing and what else?"

Mrs. Kao said, "I got myself in front of her and said; 'Aunty Ch'ao, we women can't grab the top perch! You sound fine and loud, but do you realy think it'll get your husband on his knees begging forgiveness? You shouldn't have come running out on the street—is that a womanly way to behave? Hurry up and go inside. If you have something to say, say it in there.' She wanted to keep telling me all her troubles but I said, 'I won't listen to you out here. I'll hear you out inside.' She repeated how 'that whore was inciting him to divorce her' and I said, 'Hurry inside! If you keep throwing a tantrum in the street, then you will be giving him grounds for divorce!' As I talked to her I pushed her inside."

The magistrate asked, "Where was Chen ko at the time?"

Mrs. Kao said, "With all the uproar never mind Chen ko hen ko, she hid herself."

"Where were Ch'ao Yüan and the others?"

"Master Ch'ao Yüan was hiding behind the second door, watching."

"And what did he say when he saw this?"

Mrs. Kao said, "Master Ch'ao watched and told the servants to 'restrain Mistress Chi and don't let her out yelling on the street'. He didn't say anything else."

"So according to your testimony, Ms. Chi was screaming on the street while Ch'ao Yüan hid quietly behind the door, and Chen ko was also hiding somewhere. It sounds like they were both terrified of her. Why was she so dissatisfied she had to hang herself, then?"

Mrs. Kao said, "How foolish can you be, your honor? Imagine if somebody had wronged you—taken your money, treated you cruelly? Wouldn't you be at your wits' end? And do you think whoever wronged you would be willing to face you?"

The magistrate laughed shortly and said, "Nonsense. Did you go in with her or not?"

Mrs. Kao said, "I pulled her inside. It was the first time I was ever in their house. She asked me to sit down and I asked her what did they do to make her so furious, and for her to tell me all about it and get it off her chest. She said, there was a Taoist nun with a full head of hair, named Hai-hui. Hai-hui used to be a maid in the household of one of her relatives, but left to become a nun. Then there was also a Buddhist nun named Kuo, from Ching-chou. The two of them had spent the morning with Ms. Chi and had passed Chen ko as they went out the gate."

The magistrate asked, "Didn't Chen ko and Ms. Chi live together?"

Mrs. Kao said, "They had separate residences—you in yours and me in mine. Chen ko lived in the front and Ms. Chi lived in the back."

"And where did Ch'ao Yüan live?"

"It would have been all right if he'd lived both places, but he never went to the back. He lived entirely with Chen ko in the front."

"Tell me again. How did the nuns happen to be going out of the door while Chen ko was there?"

"Chen ko just happened to see them, and she started yelling that Hai-hui was a Taoist priest and the Nun Kuo a Buddhist priest. She slandered Ms. Chi with keeping priests as lovers in broad daylight. Master Ch'ao should have said right out he wouldn't hear a word of it, but not only did he listen, his ears grew legs to run after Chen ko's words! He called his wife's father and brother and wanted to divorce her. What a humiliation for her! Where was this lover she was supposedly keeping? Can you wonder she was upset?"

The magistrate said, "Maybe they were priests dressed as nuns. It happens."

Mrs. Kao said, "You needn't worry abou that, your honor. Hai-hui used to be called Hsiao Ch'ing-mei, and she was a maid in Liu Yu-hsi's household. Everyone knows the Nun Kuo from Ching-chou, too. Hasn't she been to our house, for that matter?"

The magistrate said, "She doesn't dare come to my house. What time did Ms. Chi hang herself?"

Mrs. Kao said, "I left her after I tried to talk some sense into her. I don't know how she died."

The magistrate asked, "Did Ms. Chi say anything to you about suicide?"

"She didn't say she would try to kill herself, only that she would pit her life against Ch'ao Yüan and Chen ko."

The magistrate said, "I see. Stand aside."

Then he called the others forward.

He asked the Nun Kuo, "Where are you from?"

She answered, "Ching-chou."

"Why did you come here?"

"Board Secretary Kao of Ching-chou's wife gave me a letter of introduction to the household of the imperial relative Chiangs', so I could spend the summer there. In the autumn I planned to make a pilgrimage to the peak of Mount T'ai."

"How come a plump woman like you doesn't have any bosom I can see sticking out?"

The Nun Kuo pulled her outer robe down and showed her two big breasts. She pulled up her inner robe to give him a good look. Hai-hui was all ready to take off her clothes, too.

"Nevermind," the magistrate said, "I have heard of you, Ch'ing-mei. Nun Kuo, since you came here to enjoy the Chiangs' hospitallty, you should have stayed quietly at their house instead of wandering around breaking up families and causing a woman's death! For that, each of you nuns should be beaten a hundred strokes. However, I will suspend the punishment, and further interrogation of you, for twenty stones of grain fine each."

The nuns said, "We religious folk live by begging and hardly get enough to eat. How can we come up with that much? We can't do it even if we wear ourselves to the bone begging."

The magistrate said, "Foolish scoundrels! I'm giving you a very good deal. You can tell people this when you go begging and I can't imagine how much you'll get from them."

The two nuns didn't protest any more.

Then the magistrate called Ch'ao Yüan.

"You are a member of an official's family, and an academician! What are you doing, fooling around with prostitutes, instead of living soberly? You have even driven your wife to suicide, and as I look into it, I begin to believe that both you and Chen ko should pay with your lives."

Ch'ao Yüan said, "My wife was the most domineering woman in the whole sub-prefecture! Her father and brother egged her on, too, so how would I ever dare mistreat her?"

The magistrate said, "She couldn't prevent you from taking a prostitute as your concubine, so how much of a domineering wife could she have been? You two have committed crime actively and by negligence. You will be stripped of official status. This case need not go before the Board. You will pay a fine of one hundred taels to be used for repairing the Confucian temple. Chen ko is excused from appearing in court and will pay a fine of thirty taels, which will be donated to relief funds."

Then the magistrate called forward the maids Mei-hung, Hsing-hua, Liu-ch'ing, Hung-t'ao and Hsia-ching. He also called forward the womanservants

Chao and Yang.

He asked them, "What is your relation to Ch'ao Yüan?"

Mrs. Chao replied, "We take care of the house."

The magistrate said, "I can't absolve the seven of you. You were all there, and you didn't say a thing to prevent your mistress from hanging herself. Bring forward seven finger screws."

The court servants on either side sang out, "Yes, sir!" and ran forward with seven sets of fingerscrews.

Then the magistrate said, "On second thought, I will absolve you. You can each pay a fine of five taels to be donated to relief funds."

Then he called out for Old Chi and Chi Pa-la, and said, "You two scoundrels are really despicable! After you daughter got married, instead of counselling her to be a good wife, you incited her to be a shrew. How shall I put it? It isn't that uncommon for men to take concubines, or to take prostitutes as concubines. That's no reason for a wife to go tearing out on the street to throw a tantrum with a knife in her hand. You clearly caused her death, and you took advantage of the situation to swindle money out of her husband."

As he spoke he was rumaging for his tube of bamboo tallies so he could assign the number of strokes the elder and younger Chis would be beaten.

Old Chi said, "Your honor, you must investigate this thoroughly and find the truth. You don't mean to say you're going to go by Ch'ao Yüan's word alone, and ignore what everyone else says? Ch'ao Yüan may belong to an official's family, and I myself may not have been fit to serve, but am I not the son of an official, too? You'll find my relatives at every level of officialdom in this city.

When a person's daughter is going to be married, a person likes to see her able to rely on her husband, and hopes she can live in harmony with her in-laws forever. Why would I incite her to the contrary?

Who said it was uncommon for men to take concubines? But there has to be a distinction maintained, between the wife's position and others'. You can't put the concubine in the wife's place—that's like wearing shoes on your head and a hat on your feet! While his concubine lived surrounded in luxury and dining on choice delicacies, he left his wife in a desolate room naked and hungry. At New Year's he didn't even send her one crust of a steamed bun. She was half-dead already. Then, instead of relenting, he was going to cut her off entirely, lending an ear to that whore's ridiculous accusations of an affair with priests.

Your honor, what decent wife would stand for being called an adulteress? Interrogate those nuns again, and if there was any priest around, then Ms. Chi was guilty and deserved to die and even if she did the crime is all on her side. Then I'll die without a murmur. But if the result of the interrogation shows there was no priest, Taoist or Buddhist, and that whore stabbed a woman to death with her sharp tongue, then, your honor, it's the same as a conspiracy to murder. Then if your honor does not call Chen ko into court, every married woman of good family will live in fear for her own good name."

The magistrate said, "You say she was a prisoner in a desolate room. What's your proof of that? If he never gave her any food or clothing, how did your daughter live these past few years?"

Old Chi said, "The new home he bought for six thousand taels used to be the residence of a Board President and consisted of eight compounds. He and Chen ko lived in the second compound, and Ms. Chi and her servants in the seventh. If there hadn't been a well in back, she wouldn't even have had water to drink. When Ms. Chi was married, the little dowry we gave her was no less than six-hundred-odd taels and I also gave her a hundred mou of land, considering that her mother had already died. All she ate and wore came out of that dowry, and when Old Ch'ao went to the capital, he sold off twenty mou of her land."

"You lying old beggar!" said the magistrate.

Old Chi continued, "Don't go by current appearances alone. I was rich before I became poor. He was poor before he became rich. How does that make me a beggar?"

Mrs. Kao had been standing all this time on the east side of the court.

Now she came forward and said, "What he's saying is true—even though he's poor, he's from a good family. Doesn't everybody in this city, high and low, know him?"

"Get that woman out of here!" cried the magistrate.

The court servants were about to take her out, but Mrs. Kao said, "I'll leave! Who wants to stay in this hot room anyway? You're the one who summoned me with your black ink and red seals to come. Now you want to throw me out! Damn thief! Gallowsbait!"

She kept cursing him out garrulously as she made her way out.

The magistrate didn't miss a beat, and continued, "Chi Pa-la, for now I will suspend your beating and your court interrogation. You and your father will each be fined four great papers."

Reader, what is a great paper? It's that soft red bordered paper which is both a notice of money to be paid in redemption of a crime, and also a method of calculating the amount of money due in silver. At that time, each great paper meant six silver taels, so the elder and younger Chis together owed forty-eight taels.

A further thirteen taels or so would be added as various fees.

Calmly, Old Chi petitioned, "Who should present the great papers for me?"

"You present them yourself."

Old Chi said, "That will come to around sixty taels. Thre's no way I can squeeze that much money out. Even if I cut off my flesh and sell it, I don't think I can get sixty taels for it. I can't go around begging like the nuns. Who'd give me anything if I did?"

The magistrate scowled and said, "Call Ch'ao Yüan."

Then, "Ch'ao Yüan, that piece of land was originally part of Ms. Chi's dowry. Now that she is dead, give the land back to Old Mr. Chi so he can sell it."

Ch'ao Yüan said, "Your gracious honor mustn't listen to his lying petitions. If he were so poor he could hardly eat, where would he get a piece of land that size for his daughter's dowry? Anyway, the land was planted in her name but my family owned it before."

"Since what year?" asked Old Chi, "How much did your family pay for it and where's the deed? Who witnessed it?"

At that, Ch'ao Yüan was silent and gave up trying to argue the point.

The magistrate said, "Since you've already sold twenty mou of the land, we'll let that be, but return the rest to Old Chi."

Penalties had been apportioned and court was adjourned. Some said the magistrate had conducted the hearing very well, and some were full of righteous anger at the travesty of justice, while others cursed. That's how it always is, so there's no point in describing exactly what people said.

The presiding clerk immediately wrote out a notice "Ch'ao Yüan et. al. excused from further testimony. Fines attached."

Then the clerk wrote out a warrant:

WIFE OPPRESSED UNTO DEATH BY CONCUBINE

Ch'ao Yüan to be fined one hundred taels to be used for repairing the Confucian Temple. Hai-hui to be fined twenty stones of grain or ten taels; the Nun kuo to be fined twenty stones of grain or ten taels. Each of the maids Mei-hung, Hsing-hua, Hung-t'ao, Liu-ch'ing, Hsia-ching, Ms. Chao and Ms. Yang to be fined five taels, altogether thirty-five taels to be contributed to relief funds. Chen ko to be fined thirty taels, also to go to relief funds. Chi Tou to be fined four great papers each worth six taels; Chi Pa-la fined four great papers, each worth six taels, altogether forty-eight taels. Mrs. Kao to be fined ten stones of grain or five taels. Moreover, Ch'ao Yüan will return eighty mou of land to Chi Tou. Ms. Chi is to be interred with fitting ceremony by Ch'ao

Yüan. This is entrusted to the messengers Wu Sheng and Shao Ch'iangjen, to be delivered by the eleventh of the tenth month, paid.

The two messengers were entrusted with the warrant and sternly instructed to deliver it to all concerned. The Magistrate also took a piece of papar and wrote out a judicial note:

It is adjudged that Ch'ao Yüan, having married Ms. Chi in his youth, did take the prostitute Chen ko as his concubine later in life. Though it is well-known that "beauties give rise to jealous feuds and a new woman in the palace means rivalry" Ch'ao Yüan did not take care to handle the situation well, with the end result that the concubine is alive and well, but the wife is dead. Mei-hung and the other maids stood aside while their mistress died. The nuns Hai-hui and Kuo caused agitation in people's homes. Chi Tou and Chi Pa-la were not able to instill correct principles of wifely conduct in Ms. Chi, so she finally hung herself. Mrs. Kao did not conduct herself with the meekness becoming to a woman, and schemed to give false testimony. All the above offenders have been questioned in court as per the law. The year has been one of drought, and aspects unfavorable, so chastisement has been lightly apportioned, further investigation declared unneccesary, the case rests, and all attendent documents are hereby deposited.

The departmental clerk stacked, stamped, and shelved the documents.

Now that the case was over, Ch'ao Yüan conducted himself with 10,000 times more arrogance than before. As soon as he got home from court, he called Chen ko back from across the way and brought her home. Although Yü Ming-wu had claimed work as an excuse to avoid appearing in court, he was resting at home, and saw Chen ko home himself. Ch'ao Yüan came out to the door to greet them. He thanked Yü Ming-wu for his trouble, but Yü Ming-wu, for his part, did not congratulate Ch'ao Yüan on his court success. They talked a little about the court case and decided to inter Ms. Chi after the harvest.

The next day, the two messengers came to see Ch'ao Yüan. He was full of thanks for their valuable advice, which had helped him come out of the case well. He treated them to the best his house had to offer. They agreed to go the yamen on the eleventh with the penalty money. Of course he paid not only his own hundred taels' penalty, but also Chen ko's thirty and the maids' thirty-five taels, and Mrs. Kao's five.

Ch'ao Yüan said, "I don't mind about the others, but paying that five taels for Mrs. Kao really sticks in my throat. She just had to have her say, and I don't know how long she would have gone on if the judge hadn't had her thrown out."

One of the messengers said, "She yelled and screamed when I showed her the warrant."

Ch'ao Yüan said, "Well, I say it isn't worth getting her mad at us. Wasn't the magistrate himself a little afraid of her? Any other woman he would have had in the finger-screws until he'd tortured her heart out!"

The messenger said, "Master Ch'ao, You've sized it up very well. The magistrate saw she's a bad one, and he wants you to pay for her."

Then they asked him when he was planning on turning the land over to Old Chi, so Old Chi could pay his fines.

Ch'ao Yüan said, "It's much too early for me to turn it over. If I did, he'd be in fine shape after he sold half of it to pay his fines. I'm depending on you two to give him a hard time. That will make me feel good."

The messengers said, "But if we don't turn the land over to him and get his receipt, how can we have the papers back to the magistrate on time?"

Ch'ao Yüan said, "It's only a matter of ten days or so. I'm not planning to torment him for months."

Then the messengers left.

As a general rule, no advantage should ever be carried to the point where one's adversary in driven to desperation. You should always leave him a little room to maneuver. Then you can chase him and he can run, and finally he'll run away. Then you can relax. If all routes ahead and behind are blocked, never mind a man even a dog will turn and take the offensive.

Actually, If Ch'ao Yüan had quickly ceded those eighty mou of land to Old Chi so Old Chi could pay his fines, and if the messengers had not been intent on harassing Old Chi, maybe Old Chi's ire would have subsided and he would have been resigned to his bitter cup.

Final victory is ever elusive, a sudden reversal always possible.

To see what happened next, read the next chapter.

Chapter Eleven

Ms. Chi's Spirit Appears and Speaks
A Cruel Official Sees Ghosts and Grows boils

Don't say there are no ghosts
They've been with us since long ago
Ghosts are not ethereal beings
They're right here beside us
Ghosts wax and wane with the state of your conscience
If your heart bears examination
No ghost will come knocking
But if you say what you shouldn't
Your heart will recoil in shame
Then the ghosts will rise in attack
Since we know ghosts are our own hearts' creations
We can see how calamities are due rewards
A person who stores up virtue
will find the future lucky
One who acts wickedly will be surprised
by swift disaster
When ghosts have you by the neck
and spirits have your hands tied
It's only your own wrongs coming back to you
I ask you all—Isn't "karma" fearful?

Chen ko hid in Yü Ming-wu's house for over a month. When she came home, the case was won and Ms. Chi was gone.

While Ms. Chi had been alive, even if she were as powerless as the later Chou kings, Chen ko had been like the wilful feudal lords of that period, who never did quite dare throw off the yoke. With Ms. Chi dead, Chen ko was a bee with no queen to command her. Every other word she said was a curse about "ghost" this or "demon" that. She scolded the housekeepers and beat the maids. The old procuress who had sold her into the household came and went as freely as a relative, and everyone called her the old lady. If Ch'ao Yüan offended Chen ko in the slightest particular, Chen ko would let loose her temper until it seemed her tantrum would never end. Chen ko was ten times fiercer than Ms. Chi had been in the early years of her marriage. When Ms. Chi had wanted to go to a temple and burn incense with her mother-in-law,

Ch'ao Yüan had spoken up against it, and prevented her from going. These days, if Chen ko wanted to go gambling, she got a bunch of friends together and did, and if she wanted to go to Wan-hsien mountain, she did. If she felt like going to the royal temple, she rushed off in her sedan-chair, just as she wished. Nobody held her back. She also went frequently to see the old procuress.

There was a relative of the Ch'aos, named K'ung. He was a holder of the highest degree. Someone in his household died, but Ch'ao Yüan did not plan to have anyone from his own household pay a condolence call, as Ms. Chi was dead and his household had no mistress, and thus nobody whose proper role it would be to pay condolence calls on people of the K'ungs' status. All by herself, Chen ko decided to go. She thought a condolence call would be a fine time to show off her many jewelled hairpins and brocade clothes. Ch'ao Yüan didn't say no, so she had the large sedan-chair readied, and picked out some maids and women to accompany her. Her beautiful attire and many attendants created a stir in her wake.

When they all arrived at the K'ung household, she was carried in her sedan-chair through the second door, and then got out of it. The doormen struck their drums twice and Mrs. K'ung hurried out to meet the guests. When she saw it was Chen ko, she stopped dead in her tracks. Chen ko walked forward and paid her respects to the tablet of the deceased. Mrs. K'ung apathetically forced out a 'thank you' and an invitation to drink a cup of tea.

"When I heard Mrs. Ch'ao was here, I wondered, oh, did Ch'ao Yüan remarry? But it was only you after all. I really must speak to him and see that he gets properly married, since you have not been raised to the status of a wife. Then you can all live in a proper home," Mrs. K'ung said.

While Mrs. K'ung spoke, the drums were beaten again, in announcement of more guests come on a condolence call.

Mrs. K'ung had a message taken to the doormen, "Take a good look and be sure it isn't another 'Mrs. Ch'ao'."

Despite that message, she rushed out front to meet these new guests. They paid their respects to the deceased, and she thanked them with great courtesy, not at all the way she had received Chen ko. She invited the new guests in for tea. They were the wife and daughter-in-law of courtier Su. Their clothes weren't half as splendid as Chen ko's, and they had only two attendants, not her magnificent train. When they saw Chen ko, they bowed in greeting.

"And whose wife is this lady? She looks familiar, but we can't place her."

Mrs. K'ung said, "She ought to look familiar. This is Ch'ao Yüan's woman."

"Oh," said Mrs. Su the elder, "She's so changed I didn't recognize her."

Mrs. Su was a mature lady, not as impulsive and heedless as Mrs. K'ung, so she greeted Chen ko properly. Then they all took their seats, after the usual polite insistence to each other to take the seat of honor. Chen ko's face was as colorful as a garden in the third month, livid, scarlet, and green in splotches. She said she had to leave.

Mrs. Su said, "Surely you haven't taken offense at something I said? Must you leave so soon?"

Chen ko said, "We're busy at home now, maybe I can see you some other day."

Mrs. K'ung didn't bother to see her out.

It was Mrs. Su who said, "Oh, hadn't you better see her out?"

Mrs. K'ung said, "There's no need for that when I have other guests still here."

She had an old woman who did odd jobs around the house "see out Mistress Ch'ao".

After Chen ko was gone, Mrs. Su said, "She's even prettier than before! I really didn't recognize her. So I guess she's become his wife?"

Mrs. K'ung said, "No, and I feel like telling that relative of ours, Ch'ao Yüan, 'why don't you marry a proper wife and have her pay calls on other families—keep Chen ko as a plaything, if that's what you like, but don't let her go around displaying herself like that'. And I'm going to have to speak to that doorman—announcing her as Mrs. Ch'ao, so I thought Ch'ao Yüan had gotten remarried. I was so excited I dashed out in hurry, and it was only her after all. I didn't give her the time of day."

Mrs. Su said, "The doorman saw that big sedan chair of hers, and all her attendants. How could he know? When anybody comes to our door, regardless of her position, I treat her with the same courtesy. It reflects on our household as much as on the guest's reputation."

Chen ko had been clothed like a goddess, confusing the members of the K'ung household as to how she should be received, and the result of her inappropriate finery was mud on her face. She scurried home, sallow and tigerish with fury, pouting until she looked worse than Ms. Chi ever did. She pulled down her hair and ripped off her clothes, sighing and looking thoroughly unhappy.

Ch'ao Yüan didn't know what was bothering her, and he obsequiously asked.

She said, "Can't you see I don't feel well? Why do you keep talking at me? The way everyone looks down at a concubine, I'd be better off in my old line of work."

So Chen ko was hopping mad.

Li Ch'eng-ming's wife unwisely asked Ch'ao Chu's wife to come measure rice out for dinner, but Mrs. Ch'ao Chu had been around and wasn't about to stand for any insult, nor was she afraid af quarrels. She was the kind of person who would plunge her hand straight into a beehive to get some honey.

"It sounds like you're telling me, not asking me, " she said.

At that point, Li Ch'eng-ming's wife should have backed down, but she decided to escalate the quarrel by taking the measuring cup and basket and sitting smack in front of Chen ko, measuring out the rice herself, and full of grievance.

Chen ko's eyes almost leaped out of her skull. She began to scowl. She wished she could roll ten thousand curses into one little phrase the potency of which would melt Li Ch'eng-ming's wife into a bloody pulp with no time wasted.

"You dog-stinking, donkey-stinking cunt with ten thousand men up you! I've heard you calling me 'Aunty Chen! Aunty Hen! I'll aunty your chen. You'd better start calling me 'mistress' or take your stinking mouth far away. Damn slavey. How many 'Aunty Chen's' do we have here, hmm? When that good for nothing piece of a Ms. Chi was around you could call me anything you liked but she's dead now and I'm still hearing 'aunty, aunty' coming out of you. If the damned whores in this house don't even respect me, how do you think those old women outside are going to act? Like that piece at the K'ungs' with all her talk! You'd better be careful or I'll curse you so hard all your ancestors will fall out of heaven! If you think there's going to be any new mistress over me, or concubine below, you can think again. From now on, you'd better not call me 'aunty' and I won't have that piece of his around either. Call the servants to move her coffin into the back room and bring me her funeral drapes. I need some rags for my period."

She called for a man to carry out Ms. Chi's coffin.

Ch'ao Yüan said, "Wait a minute. We can't do that. Old Chi and his son have stirred things up into a mess already, and they say they're going to appeal the court decision at the circuit court. I wouldn't care even if he was going to memorialize at court, but I am afraid of that circuit magistrate. If Old Chi appeals there, do you think I can hush it up with money again? Do you think anyone in the circuit court cares about my position? That circuit magistrate is a real Judge Pao!"

Chen ko, "Don't bother me with your hot air. So it was me who killed that little piece was it? Drag her out and examine the body, and if there's a wound on her anywhere, I'll pay with my life. If there isn't, I'll toss her bones on the fire and throw the ashes out."

Chen ko slapped herself on the face, hard several times.

In a changed voice she said, "Cheap whore! Whose bones are you going to toss on the fire? Whose ashes do you plan to throw out? Damned cheating whore—you'll get what you deserve. I'm letting you bring it on yourself while I stand by. Shameless whore, so you think you can have my coffin removed, my bones burnt, and my drapes for your rags?"

She slapped herself against the mouth again, resoundingly. Her mouth swelled up and turned purple.

Ch'ao Chu's wife said, "Oh no, it's the mistress come back, speaking through her. Listen—isn't it the mistress' voice? We'd better go kneel down to her."

Chen ko continued, "She scolds you for calling her 'aunty Chen' but you'll call her that and nothing else. She'll kneel to me, or else you will, and give her face fifty slaps. Count them!"

In fact, Chen ko did walk down the room, knelt correctly, and began counting while she slapped herself. By the time she had finished, her face was as inflamed as a baboons's behind.

Then Chen ko said, "Pull the whore's hair!"

She started pulling her hair out in big clumps.

The maids all knelt down on the ground, kowtowing and begging for mercy.

Chen ko said, "You miserable, cheating slaves. How dare you beg me for mercy to her? Remember King Yen Lo is in Hell, and take care of your own accounts, instead of worrying about other people!"

The maids banged their heads against the floor like pestles and said, "Mistress! When you were alive, maybe you couldn't see into our hearts, but now that you're dead and a spirit, you must know whose conscience is clean and whose isn't. Since you've gone, there isn't one of us who hasn't grieved your wrongs, and none of us would cheat you."

Chen ko said, "So you want to argue! What has happened to my two little maids since they fell into your hands? You all eat hot noodles and give them thin gruel to eat. How come Li Ch'eng-ming's wife gave my head-dress to her son to play kick-ball with? You've all been doing just as that whore said, and you never set out as much as a bowl of watery rice for my spirit. Slaves and your leaders—all cheating me in your vicious hearts. Tear off her clothes!"

Chen ko tore off her clothes, exposing her upper body. Her white flesh gleamed and her two breasts stared. Ch'ao Yüan sat there watching, scared into shaking paralysis.

Chen ko said, "Whore! As if you had any shame! Peel off those pants."

All the maids kowtowed madly.

"We beg you, Mistress, to let her leave her trousers on. You don't really want to see her naked kneeling in front of you, do you?"

The maids looked at Ch'ao Yüan and said, "Master, why don't you do something? Come over here and kneel to the mistress! We all have to speak up for her."

Chen ko was about to take off her trousers, but said to herself, "All right. The whore can keep her pants on."

Ch'ao Yüan knelt down like a post stuck in the ground and said, "I should never have listened that day to what other people said. But when I found out the whole story, I was willing to let bygones be bygones. It was you who wouldn't let well enough alone but had to go kill yourself. I spent two or three hundred taels on wood for your coffin, and bought the best silk for your funeral drapes. You're going to have a fine funeral."

Chen ko said, "I don't need your silk, and in any case she plans to use it for her rags. If she wants to curse out everyone here at home, thats all right, but how can you sit there and listen when she starts calling Mrs. K'ung this piece and that piece? You pushed me into my death, and my death still hasn't been paid for. Then you plotted against my Dad and brother. If it weren't for the constant vigilance of Grandfather Chi Hui's ghost, what would have prevented that judge you bribed from beating them to death?"

Ch'ao Yüan kowtowed again and said, "Now you're a higher being, so why stoop to our level? Aren't you supposed to be above all this? Please leave Chen ko alone. I'll have ten days of sutras recited for you and I'll even use two hundred taels to buy you an outer coffin, lined in mortared masonry, and then I'll give that land back to your father. If I dare go back on my word, you can possess me."

Chen ko said, "Why would I want to possess you? You'll meet your match soon enough. Your luck is running out. Why should I bother with you?"

Ch'ao Yüan told her, "We had some good times when we were married, too. Why don't you stop arguing like any old live person and start giving me your spiritual protection? Then I'll burn you some incense and light burnt offerings to you."

Chen ko said, "Hurry and burn some paper money and pour a libation in my room. Even if he is the worst cheat in the world, I don't need to stoop to his level. Someone else is going to take care of him."

The servants burned a large number of paper ingots to her ghost, and then burnt more incense and spirit-money in front of her coffin. From that day on, they punctiliously laid out two meals a day for her ghost, and Ch'ao Yüan didn't dare plot any more aganst Old Mr. Chi and Chi Pa-la.

After the spirit ceased speaking, Chen ko closed her mouth and fell headlong on the floor, as if she'd had a fit. Her face was as ugly as the red-faced Taoist deity General Wen. The servants carried her to bed and covered her up without clothing her. She went to sleep for a while.

As evening came, Chen ko recovered consciousness. Her whole body ached as if she had been tied up for a month and beaten a thousand strokes. Her face was unbearably swollen and painful. She did not remember anything that had happened that day. The others told her every detail.

She asked for a mirror, and what she saw there scared her.

Even though she was no longer possessed, she felt confused and dizzy, as if she were floating in the clouds. A servant was sent out to Dr. Yang's for a dose of soul-settling soup, which she drank down, but the next day she still wasn't herself.

Meanwhile, all the defendants in the court case had paid their fines on time. Even the two nuns had done as the magistrate said and gone begging door to door in order to pay. The ladies of the great houses donated a steady stream of three taels here and five taels there. Each nun was able to present her ten taels as well as the charge of two taels and five cash to compensate the cost to the governemnt of casting standard silver money out of miscellaneous coins, but still had thirty taels left over. They prayed vigorously to Buddha for the magistrate's long life. However, Old Chi and Chi Pa-la still had to come up with a total of sixty taels before the matter could be closed. Even though Ms. Chi had given them some silver, they weren't about to use it. They wanted Ch'ao Yüan to cede them the eighty mou of land so they could sell it and pay their fines that way.

Ch'ao Yüan said, "The magistrate told me to cede the land, but he didn't say anything about what's growing on it. Right now there are black and yellow beans waiting to be harvested on that land. I'll hand it over in the tenth month, which is early enough."

The two messengers, Shao and Wu, who had received their instructions from Ch'ao Yüan, began tormenting the Chis cruelly for the money. A thousand mouths couldn't tell all the evil of those two government servants. One day they went to the Chis', but neither Old Chi nor his son was in. Wu Hsiao-Ch'üan dragged out Chi Pa-la's wife to be publicly beaten as an example.

Just as he was dragging her off, Chi Pa-la came home and put a stop to it.

Chi Pa-la said to him, "Even if Ch'ao Yüan's paid up, those two nuns can't have. You don't mean to say that my father and I are the only ones who still owe our fines, do you?"

With an angry flourish, Wu pulled a little booklet out of his leggings. He opened it up and showed a record of payment received from each person named, including the two nuns, except the Chis.

He held that out in front of Chi Pa-la and said, "If you two weren't the only ones, why would I be pushing this hard for payment? After all, when all's said and done, aren't you all related?"

He put the booklet away as he spoke, but what he didn't realize was that instead of being securely placed in his leggings, it had fallen on the ground. Chi Pa-la loosed his own sash, stepped forward, and let the skirt of his robe fall over the booklet. Then he gathered up his robe and, surreptitiuosly, the booklet. Wu Hsiao-Ch'üan was still obliviously singing his tune and putting on his act. They agreed he would come back in three days for the money, and if they still couldn't pay, then he could take some family member for a public beating.

Chi Pa-la saw Wu Hsiao-Ch'üan out. Then he went back to his own room and opened the little booklet. There were over a hundred warrants inside, some for arrests and others for settlements. There was also one paper with the title "Hearing of Academician Ch'ao Yüan et. al." with a large red-ink endorsement and appended note "in addition, prepare sixty taels and have that ready to pay for expenses to be incurred in repairs of the city temple."

Chi Pa-la wondered what that was doing there. Then he thought of how the other day, when he went to change some money at a money shop, Ch'ao Chu was also there changing money. When Ch'ao Chu had seen Chi Pa-la come up he had said to the money changer 'talk to you later, but get the money ready'. Chi Pa-la had asked what Ch'ao Chu was doing there, and the money changer had told him just changing a few taels, but as they hadn't been able to agree on a rate would probably come back later.

Chi Pa-la had asked, "What did he want to change the money for?"

The money-changer had replied, "How should I know what he plans to do with the money? But he's searching the whole city for gold and says he need no less than fifty or sixty taels of it, and he needs it fast. Who knows what he's up to?"

Chi Pa-la thought on, "Those two sons-of-bitches! They've trampled on me long enough. With this piece of paper in my hand, I can make life unpleasant for them."

He also considered, "Wu's even worse than Shao. Once he realizes I picked this up, he'll certainly come back for it, and if I don't give it to him, he's sure to force his way in and search for it. Then if he finds it, he'll accuse me of theft of his official papers, and it will all turn against me."

He looked around him for a safe place. Then he pulled a brick out from under the bed, hollowed out a hole in the brick, placed the brick back in place, and laid the bed back over it. There was no visible change.

Just when he had finished hiding the booklet, along came Shao with two outside messengers, Wu's wife and daughters-in-law, and his married daughters. They all came blazing in and Wu ran headlong into Chi Pa-la, leaving them both stunned.

Wu said, "You pretended you were just picking your robe up, but you put your hand into the tear in my leggings and pulled out my book of warrants. You'd better give it back to me!"

Right off, Wu directed the women he'd brought along to search Chi Pa-la's wife and the bedroom. They didn't leave any corner undisturbed. Outside, they searched Chi Pa-la, but did they find the slightest trace of that warrant book?

Chi Pa-la said, "If this isn't just like seeing ghosts in broad daylight! If you find it, I'll die right here on top of you, but since it isn't here for you to find, how dare you bring a crowd of people in to search, violating my home and even poking around my wife?"

He took a bronze face basin, turned it upside-down on the street and began to bang on it, shouting, "Here's the court messeuger Wu Hsiao-Ch'üan come with a crowd of women to plunder an honest man's house in braod daylight!"

The neighbors on both sides of his house, and all the passers-by gathered and made a dense crowd. Chi Pa-la told them each and every one of his grievances. The bystanders criticized the court messengers as as bad as a living Yen Lo descended to plague people, and then they dispersed for the most part. Only twenty or thirty stayed. These people told Chi Pa-la to open the door so they could go in. Inside there were twelve or thirteen women searching and wrecking the house.

None of the bystanders was courageous enough to say "you shouldn't bring those people here to invadc a man's home with their searching, even his bedroom and his wife." All they did was to cringingly suggest the search might perhaps stop now.

Wu searched the whole outside of the house thoroughly, stopping just short of digging up the ground. There wasn't anywhere inside Chi Pa-la's wife's trousers, on her chest, between her legs or even under that piece of cloth the women didn't search. Behind the bed, under the mats, inside chests and trunks and vanity boxes, even her bed-slippers and personal wipe were turned inside out, but no booklet was found. This made Wu Hsiao-Ch'üan look foolish, and it didn't seem as if anything else would happen for now, so everyone dispersed.

Chi Pa-la said, "Don't think you can come to a man's house and insult him just because you work for the yamen! Even if you were the magistrate himself, I'd take you to court for this!"

Wu and Shao could see it wouldn't do them any good to persist, so they left after a little more invective.

Now Chi Pa-la said to himself, "Even so, unless I present some money, my story won't be found convincing."

Just about then, the Ching-t'ai emperor had taken the throne and proclaimed an amnesty, and the greater part of officaldom received honorary titles. Pearls were in great demand, and as valuable as ginseng. Chi Pa-la took two pearl tiaras his sister had left and took them to a used-goods shop to sell them. The shopkeeper, Chen, was unexpectedly avid for them and wanted them right away, and even after he'd talked the price down by twenty or thirty taels, Chi Pa-la got seventy-six taels for them. He took this to the yamen. The messengers' rooms were silent and empty, so he went back and found a man named Chang who was sitting on his turn watching over the treasury. Chi called out to him, and said he had come to pay his fines.

Chang said, "We need the messenger with the original warrant, so he can note on it that you paid. Since he isn't here with the warrant, I could take your payment, but you wouldn't have any proof that you paid."

Chi Pa-la left him and went further into the desolate and quiet yamen. Passing through the door of the Rites Office, he saw a man with a document on heavy yellow memorial paper in one hand and keys in the other, opening a door. This happened to be Chi Pa-la's cousin Fang Ch'ien-shan. He worked in the Rites Office, so he invited Chi Pa-la in and asked what he was doing there.

Chi Pa-la replied, "I've brought the money to pay my fines."

Fang Ch'ien-shan asked, "Have you paid yet?"

Chi Pa-la said, "No, the treasury official didn't have the warrant, so I didn't."

Fang Ch'ien-shan suggested, "Why don't you just hang onto your money for a few days? Right now the magistrate has a huge boil on his back, and he's terribly sick. Yesterday he had a famous surgeon named Yen from his own prefecture come in, and the surgeon said it was divine retribution, so unless he prayed for forgiveness, no medicine would do any good. Then the surgeon walked out, and nobody tried to keep him, but he did mention that the boil is going to rot out the magistrate's insides within ten days. I went right to the temple of the city god and had a Taoist priest write up a prayer to be burnt. I sent the prayer into the yamen and now we're supposed to have a seven-day vigil praying for the magistrate's health and long life."

"I hadn't heard anything about that," said Chi Pa-la, "When did he get sick?"

Fang Ch'ien-shan said, "You don't mean you didn't know! The day he heard your case, he began to feel a little uncomfortable, but he still held court three or four more days. By the fourth or fifth day, he couldn't move. The day he was hearing your case, I was sure you and Uncle Chi would get at least twenty-five strokes each, but when he grabbed hold of his tallies, and then Uncle Chi stood up for himself, there wasn't any beating after all for you two. That really surprised people. But there was a reason for that. When he put out his hand for the tallies, he saw a man in a red jacket with a long beard who grabbed his hand and stopped him. Later, when he went back to the yamen, that spirit in the red jacket kept appearing. The magistrate had sacrifices of pork and mutton made, but the spirit was as active as ever, and hit him on the back. The minute the spirit hit him, the magistrate got a bitter taste in his mouth, felt hot all over, and grew a boil the size of a bowl on his back. He said the spirit had a beard over two feet long and a black mole on his left cheekbone. His household servants leaked the story—he's been trying to cover it up and keep outsiders from hearing about it."

Chi Pa-la said, "From what you say, that spirit's my grandfather! My grandfather ahd a gorgeous full beard at least two feet long, floating like a spirit's even when he was alive. He had a black mole on his left cheekbone. But I wonder why Granddad's so active? How do you know we were going to be beaten that day?"

Fang Ch'ien-shan said, "You don't mean to say you don't even know that much? That day I'd just gone over to the message box. I was waiting there for some papers to come through. There was a gentleman waiting there. He took a look at me, and I don't know who he mistook me for, but he called me over and gave mc a note. It was from Wu and Shao and it said that Ch'ao Yüan et. al. had arrived and were to be heard. Usually once this sort of note is passed in, it means there's going to be some kind of arrangement made. I held it up to the light, and there under the date were the characters 'five hundred'. The red endorsement beside it said to prepapre another sixty taels in gold to fix up the temple idols. That means the magistrate thought five hundred taels wasn't enough, and he wanted sixty gold taels more. The rest of the day, the Ch'aos were out changing money to get all the gold in the city. It was such a to-do there can't be anyone who didn't hear about it."

Young Mr. Chi said, "What happened to the note?"

Fang Ch'ien-shan said, "Just as I was going out, I ran into Wu and gave it to him. Since the magistrate got his fat bribe, it isn't likely he wasn't going to beat you, is it? that day Ch'ao Yüan was putting money in the hands of the court servants, too, telling them to hit hard. If it weren't for your grandfather's spirit watching over you, even if you hadn't died you'd have had one layer less of skin."

Chi Pa-la said, "My dear cousin! If you knew all that, why didn't you tell me anything? Then I could have been ready. Wouldn't it have been the cousinly thing to do?"

Fang Ch'ien-shan said, "Cousin, there are a lot of things you don't know. You didn't even know that this cousin of yours worked in the Rites Office. If I hadn't called out to you, you still wouldn't know it! And where was I supposed to find you to tell you?"

Chi Pa-la said, "Wu Hsiao-Ch'üan and Shao Tz'u-hu haven't been to my house causing trouble in the past three or four days. Do you know why not?"

Fang Ch'ien-shan said, "How would they dare show themselve? All those yamen servants who were going around oppressing people are keeping quiet now because they're afraid their victims will take their revenge and tear them apart."

Fang was just warming to his theme when three orders on white paper were sent out from the yamen's inner office. One was an order to go to all the lumber shops and get the best cypress boards. One was to buy two hundred lengths each of two kinds of white cloth, and to buy ten lengths of white silk damask while the last required expeditious approval by the Rites Office for building a Taoist ceremonial area. Once the ceremonial area was built, officials and their families would lead sacrifices and libations and burn incense on the first day. The next day local Important People would do the same, the third day would be the turn of all the school teachers and students, the fifth the turn of the secretaries and clerks of the six offices in the yamen, the sixth the city households and the seventh farmers from outlying areas.

All went as instructed, and on the seventh day, there were at least two or three thousand country people, thanks to a temporarily acting granaries official who was hoping for a permanent appointment. He got everyone to come by sending yamen servants with warrants to drag out all who would, and beat up the rest. These yamen servants also amassed quite a few taels, which they split among themsleves, giving five or six taels that were left over to the Taoist priests to buy food with.

When Chi Pa-la returned home, he recounted to Old Chi everything Fang Ch'ien-shan had told him. It was only then that Old Chi understood all the ins and outs of the matter. Together, he and his son bought some paper ingots and prepared a sacrifice of food to thank Chi Hui, who was Old Chi's father and Chi Pa-la's grandfather, for his covert protection.

Wu and Shao never came again to insult them in their home. Moreover, the Chis kept their money, based on Fang Ch'ien-shan's advice, and after a few days in fact there came an announcement that the magistrate, loving and virtuous father and mother to the people of Wu-ch'eng, had succumbed just as Dr. Yen had said he would. The boil had spread until there was a rotten patch the size of a basin on his back and all of his internal organs flowed out of it. There was no way to prepare him decorously for his funeral. They had to skin a sheep, use the skin to plug up his back and sew him together before they could get him into his coffin. After the thirty-fifth day and a great number of religious services, the new incumbent took his place and the coffin home.

The old magistrate's home was in Soochow. Just as his funeral procession reached the Shui-p'ing prefecture, it ran into Essen, Essen's troupes, and the captive Cheng-t'ung emperor. Essen's men took all their pack animals and everything of the slightest worth they had been carrying. Luckily, they all hid quickly so they weren't killed, and the magistrate of Lu-ling was a relation. They left the coffin above ground and took refuge at an inn there in the city, waiting for Essen to leave, and preparing their baggage for Soochow.

Indeed:

> One bad man will be worn down by another
> The thief be plundered in his pillage
> It's easy to see divine reckonings are
> stronger than men's plans
> Everything is like the old man who kept his son
> by losing his horse
> Blessings and evil in intertwined disguise

Chapter Twelve

Circuit Intendant Li goes on a tour of Inspection and takes up a case
Judge Ch'u upholds the law and overturns a previous judgement

When peace rules
The country flourishes
Heaven and earth unsullied
Weather in its seasons
Timely rain in good measure
Miasmas lifted

Then civil officials are incorrupt
Martial officials fiery
And so,
Government servants are not greedy
and the common people little afflicted
Evil men are driven out
The virtuous raised high
Scholars vie in refining their knowledge
Court servants speak out against abuses
Bribes are stopped
Scrambling for positions halted
Laxness blocked
Opportunism dealt with severely
Bad men are driven back where they came from
Good men are feted
Domineering ways are cut short
Tyranny is shaved down
Each man is at ease as in a tower gazing
over spring vistas
Pitfalls for the commen man obliterated
Such officials are to be praised!

The man who rules this world
is the life of his subjects
Gladly fulfilling the charge of the Yellow Emperor
Realizing the teachings of Confucious and Mencius

The tablet on Mount Hsien to Yang Hu
raised by the grateful inhabitants of Hsien-yang
The Eulogy of the wild pear
sung in grateful remembrance to Duke Chao of Chou
Each shows virtuous government writ large
Proclaim it to heaven
And pray to the spirits
That the virtue of such men be rewarded
Their descendents numerous
Their power decisive in rule
and continued by their sons
Never ending this millenium!

Now, the Cheng-t'ung emperor had always been a ruler of transcendant virtue. No labor in the cause of a peaceful empire was too great for him. Working to that end, he often ate his meals late and was up dressing before dawn. Outside in the provinces he had such men as the provincial governor Yu Chung-hsiao, in his palace he was surrounded by men as fine as the three Yangs, and he had a saintly empress beside him. This was a felicitous combination hardly to be met with once in a thousand years. Even so, the evil machinations of the eunuch Wang Chen, who usurped power and oppressed officials up and down the line, were stronger. Was there any official who didn't have a slave's expression and a servant's bent knee before Wang Chen? Morale sank into the ground. But also, it is true that the men who let themselves be ground down were not the firm and resolute type. They were like wax spears covered in silver foil. It can't be denied that such a spear is pretty, but the minute it runs into anything, it collapses. Look, however, at the diamond drill. Despite its small size, it cleanly pierces anything before it, no matter how hard the object may be.

At that time, in the Tung-ch'ang district of Shantung, there was a circuit intendant on the Lin-ch'ing district circuit. His rank was that of senior assistant at the office of provincial judiciary, and his name was Li Chun-chih. He came from Mou subprefecture in Honan, and had received the highest degree. As soon as he came to the post of prefectural magistrate, he felt a paternal concern for all the good plain people he saw, and a collegial respect for any aspiring scholars who walked the straight and narrow. However, when it came to depraved pretenders to scholarship, or perverse commoners, he showed no leniancy.

He could listen all day with delight to the conversation of an Important

Person who worked for the public good, and who was a diligent uprooter of public harms and promoter of the public weal. But, if some hangers-on of an Important Person went around flaunting influence, causing incidents, and acting maliciously, don't imagine Magistrate Li would avert his eyes and let it pass "out of consideration of the man's position".

When he received a petition, he considered it without prejudice. All he cared about was whether or not the petitioner had right on his side. If so, the petition would be granted, and if not, the petitioner would be prosecuted to the full extent of the law. Even those he prosecuted had no grounds for complaint. He didn't care if a complaint came in after the statute of limitations had expired, and he didn't stick at small formalities. As soon as a charge came, he endorsed it. As soon as he endorsed it, he wrote his note on it and handed it over to the plaintiff to hold, not bothering with bureaucratic delays. Some plaintiffs were willing to settle out of court and there wasn't even any need to surrender the complaint and send people back and forth. Other plaintiffs were determined to have it out, and have their days in court. Their cases were judged in order, no matter if it were the morning or the evening session, no matter if they had handed in every last scrap of paperwork and had it duly entered in the court record, and no matter where they were at the time—yamen, city office, or banquet. Cases that could be solved by some good advice were. If a defendent was extremely ingenious in his explanations, he was just beaten moderately and let off for the time being, with no fines or confession required.

In contrast to magistrate Li's lenience in court was his stringency in regard to finances. He was very clear on the point that every tael of land-tax sent to the capital had to have a three percent surcharge for smelting into standard coin, and the surcharge was paid locally for local officals' use.

He said, "An official has to be able to eat and to entertain his official guests, and he needs access to funds for this, but as to using your money myself to buy land or build houses, you can rest assured I will never engage in such robbery. On the other hand, if you expect me to sell my own land or pawn my possessions to keep the local government running, you can rest assured I won't do that either! I'm no Ch'en Chung-tzu."

He was very frugal in buying the clothing and food for the yamen, so that, far from needing to plunder the financial resources of the subprefecture, he had enough money left over from the three-percent surcharge on land taxes remitted to the capital to buy grain and store it. Then, when a bad harvest year came, the poor were able to borrow grain from his government office.

In that subprefecture, private individuals charged ten percent interest on grain lent, while the government only charged five percent. Since in fact some people never did pay, the net interest was more like three percent. After another two or three years, the granaries would be bursting again, so every month, some grain was issued from the granaries to relieve the most miserable, to feed convicts, and to help the poor celebrate their marriages and funerals.

The beauty of his government didn't stop there. Even if I grew a hundred mouths, I couldn't tell you all of it, but I'm afraid you may be worried I've forgotten about the story at hand to go on about this.

Obviously, it would have benefited and given lustre to the imperial government to let a wise magistrate like this take great responsibility, but would the usurpers of power let him have a first rate position? No more than a bunch of Buddhist priests would let a layman be one of them!

Just given that he held the highest degree and that he was honest, he should have been promoted to a managerial position at the Board of Rites, and then promoted to be Senior Secretary. Given his scholarly attainments, he should have been given an Education Commissionarship. He would have been fine as an Education Commissioner. But no, they wouldn't. All he got was the job of Circuit Intendant, and after five years of service there, he still hadn't been accorded a local councillorship. All he got was the rank of Senior Assistant.

Intendant Li was stationed at Lin-ch'ing, and because it was a market town, there were all kinds of slippery rascals there. In Lin-ch'ing the general feeling was that "Heaven is distant and the emperor is far". People had no respect for anything. Bandits roamed at will, and there wasn't one single day that passed without influential people bullying the weak.

Life was hard for good men in Lin-ch'ing, but, from the day Intendant Li put on his robe with its emblem of the mythical Ch'ai beast that sees good an evil at a glance, fastened his belt of fine silver, picked up his seal and put on his stern expression they had a man even beyond compare with Chang Kang of the Eastern Han or Wen Tsao of the T'ang. He was just like the legendary Judge Pao.

Intendant Li sent out proclamations earnestly councilling all to reform their ways. He only followed up cases involving murder or other truly villainous behaviour. All other miscellaneous cases on the docket, dated before his intendancy, were closed without further investigation. Once he had taken office, of any ten arrogant men who tried to oppress others, nine were caught in Intendant Li's net, and the one who got away was not guilty of anything major.

At irregular intervals, Intendant Li would put on his turban, mount a donkey, and, accompanied by two men, make an inspection round of the eighteen districts for which he was responsible. Since he was liable to pop up at any time, none of the officials in those eighteen districts dared be too blatantly lawless. The magistrate of Wu-ch'eng, however, had presumed on his own position, and abuses in Wu-ch'eng grew worse daily. Intendant Li's attention became more and more focussed on this magistrate. On the day that Intendant Li heard the Magistrate of Wu-ch'eng had died, his first thought was to prevent that magistrate's hoard of underlings from getting away with their ill-gotten gains, and he went straight to the Wu-ch'eng yamen, unannounced, accompanied by twenty or thirty soldiers. Once he arrived, he did not go into the chambers but straight to the main hall, where he had the drums beaten thrice calling all personnel in. He waited for the employees of the six offices to trickle slowly in. He called the roll once. Then he had those with whom he had no business that day go stand on the east side, and those he meant to speak to he had stand on the west side. Some didn't show up at all, but he let it pass if they hadn't committed any other offense. Anyone he meant to speak to who did not show up he immediately had arrrested by the soldiers in his entourage, and beaten forty or fifty strokes, depending on the nature of their offenses.

The two messengers, Wu Hsiao-ch'üan and Shao Tz'u-hu, hid themselves well, but the intendant's net was finely woven and nobody was about to risk his neck for the likes of Wu and Shao. In no time, he had them hauled in in front of him. They each got fifty strokes and were handed over to the jailer to be locked up until their hearing. Before their hearing they were to be treated impartially, neither abused nor granted special leniency.

The intendant gave a lecture to those standing on the east side and then let them go. Only then did he go back into the chambers, where he wrote a proclamation as follows:

We are now mobilized to extirpate tigerish yamen officials and thereby to give vent to complaints of injustices of the common people. Be it known that the officials of Wu-ch'eng sub-prefecture have been avaricious and peccant. They have committed crimes of staggering magnitude and have abused the common people, whose just resentment is deep. The pain of all spirits that have observed this must be extreme. The incumbent circuit intendant has commenced the investigation and had already informed the provincial judge and magistrate. The former Wu-ch'eng magistrates's unspeakable conduct had brought its own reward, and Heaven has struck him down. It is our duty to eradicate the rabble that continues to fan the flames of evil under cover of that wolf's prestige, even as he lies dead. We have begun arrests. All who have tasted the bitter poison of this yamen's oppression will now come forward and lay their reports before us. Dead ashes cannot rekindle, and the caged tiger will never again turn upon you. Do not neglect this opportunity to obtain redress. Such neglect will cause you regret for the rest of your life. Be cognizant of this and act accordingly.

At least a hundred complaints welled up in response. Chi Pa-la, for one, wrote up a form. It was taken in and laid on a table. He walked into court to wait for his name to be called.

Intendant Li read Chi Pa-la's complaint, which was as follows:

Plaintiff Chi Chi-tz'u, aged thirty-five, of Wu-ch'eng subprefecture in Tung-ch'ang prefecture, reporting a murder. My younger sister was married at a tender age to Ch'ao Yüan. Ch'ao Yüan listened to the slanders of my sister by his concubine, Chen ko. Their calumny oppressed my sister into suicide by hanging. The voracious messengers Wu and Shao took over seven hundred taels in silver and sixty gold taels as bribes in payment for making sure Chen ko was not called into court, so my sister's life has not been avenged. This is proven by a note endorsed in red by the magistrate of Wu-ch'eng. I implore the Intendant to personally undertake this investigation, and have it heard by judge Ch'u so that justice may be done.

Accused: Chen ko, Ch'ao Yüan, Hsia-ch'ing, Wu Sheng-tao, Shao Tz'u-hu, Liu-ch'ing

Witnesses: Mrs. Kao, Hai-hui, the Nun Kuo.

After Intendant Li read this he asked, "To whom were the seven hundred silver and sixty gold taels paid?"

Chi Pa-la answered, "I do not know to whom, but I have the note endorsed by the magistrate in red as evidence. He handed that up.

The Intendant said, "Where is the evidence for the seven hundred taels?"

Chi Pa-la told him, "Look under the date in red ink."

The intendant held it up to the light and saw the two characters reading "five hundred". He muttered to himself a little.

Then he nodded at Chi Pa-la and asked, "Why does your deposition say 'seven hundred'?"

Chi Pa-la said, "The five hundred had already been paid. The other two hundred was for the messengers Wu and Shao."

The intendant sighed a couple of times and said, "How can this be? Your sister must have been guilty of adultery, or else she would have had no reason to hang herself."

Chi Pa-la replied, "If my sister were guilty of that, even death wouldn't atone for it. Why would Ch'ao have to pay such a fat bribe! The witnesses I've asked to have called are Hai-hui, a Taoist nun, and the Nun Kuo, a Buddhist nun. They frequently visited my sister. Chen ko insulted my sister by saying the two nuns were both priests, and that my sister was having an adulterous affair with them. Chen ko incited Ch'ao Yüan to persecute my sister to death."

Intendant Li told Chi Pa-la to wait in the criminal courtroom. The next day he returned Chi Pa-la's complaint with his endorsement. Then Chi Pa-la gave it to the criminal court judge Ch'u.

Judge Ch'u was from Szechuan. He had recently received the highest degree. He was young and uncompromising, a good official and altogether a suitable helper for Intendant Li. Once Judge Ch'u read the deposition and asked a few questions much the same as the intendant had, he said that Chi Pa-la could now leave the matter in his, Judge Ch'u's, hands.

Then Judge Ch'u sent a man to round up the accused in Wu-ch'eng. He made it a special point that Chen ko would appear in court, as she was named among the accused, not one of whom could be exempted. At the time, the new magistrate of Wu-ch'eng had not yet arrived to take up his duties, so they relied on the treasurer who was temporarily acting magistrate.

When the sub-prefectural yamen servants arrived at Ch'ao Yüan's house, they didn't announce that they had come to arrest him. They tricked him by saying that the Chis had paid their fines and were now looking for Ch'ao, who had been hiding in his house, in order to pay him what was due. Three or four sturdy women and five or six male messengers strode into the house. Ch'ao Yüan was startled.

The women charged tigerishly into the back and knew right away that the pretty one in expensive clothes must be Chen ko. They grabbed her and pushed her out. Ever since that day when Ms. Chi's ghost had possessed her, Chen ko had been very depressed and mopey. Now, this surprise scared her witless. Even the maids were scared out of their minds.

Ch'ao Yüan said, "Tell me exactly what this is all about!"

The first two men said, "Judge Ch'u, acting on a complaint forwarded by Intendant Li, requests the honor of your and your lady's presence. Since you are such a recluse here in your home, what else could we do? We had no choice but to invite you in this manner. We, as government servants, must do as we are told, so please don't blame us. We wouldn't dare lay a finger on your lady, so we asked our wives to come and attend to her."

Chen ko didn't have any idea what was happening, but she did figure out it must be something like the first court case, so she wasn't very worried. Ch'ao Yüan, however, heard it was am accusation from the circuit intendant, and officially authorized by that odd criminal justice, Ch'u.

In his heart Ch'ao Yüan thought, "This isn't any good at all. No matter what a case is about, it's nothing to worry about when you can take care of it with money. But those two high-and-mighty types won't take money, don't care about connections and aren't even satisfied with taking your life. They try to make life so awful you'd rather be dead."

Thinking still, he had his servants lay out food and drink in the back, so he could wine and dine the messengers. Their wives kept Chen ko company in her room. A messenger in the western room took out a warrant for the two maids Liu-ch'ing and Hsia-ch'ing and insisted Ch'ao Yüan produce them.

Ch'ao Yüan said, "They're our servants and they live here. I guess they'll come along once we do."

The court servant said, "Judge Ch'u is very strict. We don't dare take time to eat. We'd better get started so we can present your documents tomorrow in morning court."

Ch'ao Yüan said, "If we have to go to court, you don't expect us to leave without packing, do you? And what about money for expenses? I don't suppose you feel like carrying our cooking pots, do you?"

The messenger said, "Well, then, please have your servants pack quickly, and, whatever Judge Ch'u's way of doing things may be, I wonder if you think we're above accepting a coin or two?"

As he spoke, six or seven more yamen servants came in with Mrs. Kao, Hai-hui and the Nun Kuo.

Mrs. Kao opened the door and called out, "By my Granddad! And all my ancestors! Haven't you got me in a fine mess! That's what I get for living next door to Important People."

Ch'ao Yüan said, "Mrs. Kao, I personally will make up every offense you receive, and I'll do it so you'll be plenty satisfied. What can I say to keep you from getting all upset? I'm going to see that these two gentlemen don't lose out either.

Mrs. Kao said, "We don't even have a new magistrate yet, so the case must be being judged in the fourth court. I'll go over there early and get my part in it over with. I have to come back home to make sure my grain's threshed properly."

One of the yamen servants said, "It would be nice for you if it was the fourth court, but this is coming from the circuit intendant, forwarded to the criminal court. We have quite a ways to go."

Mrs. Kao said, "Oh, no, I can't do that. I only came with you because I thought we'd be going as far as the fourth court, but this is going to be over a hundred and ten li round-trip!"

She walked right out, and the servants chased after her.

Ch'ao Yüan said, "Let me go ask her to come back. Don't bother running after her."

He went after her and said, "My good Mrs. Kao! You're not acting like yourself! This whole case depends on you. What's a mere hundred and ten li trip? If you want to ride, I have plenty of horses and donkeys. I'll pick out a nice gentle one for you, and have a servant lead it. If you're afraid of riding, we have sedan chairs just sitting there, going to waste. Chen ko will have to take one anyway. And I have women to take care of you on the way. I'll send a man over to your fields with a few strings of cash to pay your threshers. Besides, I'll give you two rolls of flossy pongee, ten rolls of plain cloth, and thirty taels, right now."

Who would have thought Mrs. Kao would ever change her mind? But "Wine flushes the face and money moves the heart". Ch'ao Yüan softened up that steely Mrs. Kao drib by drab with his servile unction, until she said, "If you give me all that, I will go, but I'll say the same things I did the other day. If you think you can make me tell a different story, you're going to be disappointed."

Ch'ao Yüan said, "After all, we're all telling the truth. It isn't as though anyone beat her to death, is it?"

After all his efforts succeeded, and Mrs. Kao was talked back in, wine was served and everyone sat down to eat. Ch'ao Yüan sent some men over to the villa to get some mounts and donkey carts ready for Chen ko, Mrs. Kao, and the other women. They also readied food and luggage and so forth, and went across the way to ask Yü Ming-wu to keep an eye on the house in Ch'ao Yuan's absence. Ch'ao Yüan went into the back to see to the luggage and travelling money, and to ready his gratuities for various yamen servants. The servants each got thirty taels, and the four women they had brought got four taels each. The two messengers from the criminal court received eighty taels personally from Ch'ao Yüan. Mrs. Kao, Hai-hui, and the Nun Kuo each got five taels, fifteen in all. He sent each and every one of the things he had promised Mrs. Kao over to her house. Ch'ao Yüan asked Yü Ming-wu to try talking to the court mesengers about letting Chen ko off from her court appearance, and offered to pay an additional hundred taels for that, but they said:

"Good Sir Yüan! If it were just between you and us, don't you know we'd be only too happy? Not to mention how well Master Ch'ao has treated us, and with what generous hospitality. And wouldn't we both be happy to split that hundred taels and end up fifty taels richer each? But Judge Ch'u wants her, and even if we got ourselves convicted to execution for obstruction of justice, he'd have her in court in the end. You'd better just tell her to come along. As you can imagine, we'll do our best for her, since Master Ch'ao has been so kind."

By now, everyone had been talking so long it was evening. Ch'ao Yüan had his servants lay out bedding for the yamen servants and messengers to sleep on.

The yamen messengers weren't willing to trust Chen ko in a room by herself, so she slept with the yamen servants' wives.

Ch'ao Yüan had a younger sister who had married into an Important family surnamed Yin. They were very rich, but once old Mr. Yin died, the younger generation managed to waste all the wealth he had accumulated, and soon the house was bare. Ch'ao Yüan took advantage of his brother-in-law's bankruptcy by buying up what property was left, for a very small sum and after a very great deal of haggling, and thus he finished their impoverishment. He had been very mean to his sister ever since she had fallen on hard times. However, now he had to go far off to court and he needed a caretaker for his house, so he called his sister over.

The next day, the party got underway, and two servants were sent on ahead to find comfortable lodgings. The group travelled a ways, then had lunch and fed the horses and donkeys. Then they travelled some more and reached the city just as the shadows were growing long. The yamen servants Wu and Shao had let themselves in and joined the group. Ch'ao Yüan treated them with the same generosity he had the others.

The next day, they all had breakfast and changed their clothes, and Ch'ao Yüan got his deposition ready. Two pages came, with the announcement that "the court has sounded the second watch and your presence is desired."

Before long, Judge Ch'u took his seat in court. Ch'ao Yüan went in with his entourage to present his deposition. The yamen servants who had been sent to get Ch'ao Yüan and the others handed in their paperwork, and, when the roll was called, nobody was missing.

When the judge got to Chen ko's name, the court clerk sang out, "Chen ko!"

Chen ko came forward.

Chen ko was:

> The floating song of a bamboo flute
> The lingering echo of distant chimes
> The pliant willow bending to the wind
> Turned out as beautifully as Ts'ui-ying
> The bashful flower bedewed

Radiant as if playing the part of Cho Wen-chün's
graceful ghost
Black scarf over her hibiscus face
White lotus-root arms peeking out of her kingfisher-blue
sleeves
She was what you want at first sight
Was the judge used to such visions of loveliness?
Would he just as soon roast a crane,
Just as soon burn a lute for firewood?

Judge Ch'u took a look at her and ordered her to be present for questioning in the evening session. Then Ch'ao Yüan and the rest of his group went back to their lodgings. Ch'ao Yüan did not neglect to give the two court messengers who had come to Wu-ch'eng for him some silver to distribute among the yamen underlings. Even though those two took a large cut for themselves, they passed around enough silver to satisfy the others. Thus, though Ch'ao Yüan was not at home in Wu-ch'eng now, when it came his turn to be questioned, there were so many people fawning on him he didn't lose face by being called into court.

In the evening session, Judge Ch'u called for the first case.

It was a case where a person had been hung to death, and the plaintiff was asking for the reversal of an earlier decision. What had happened was that a fair, plump widow of around fifty years of age had been having an affair with a younger man in his thirties. She gave him everything of value the family possessed, but she still feared he would leave her because she was so much older than he. She tried to get her daughter-in-law in bed with her lover, but the daughter-in-law was a girl of good family.

The daughter-in-law thought how if she obeyed her mother-in-law, she would disgrace herself, but if she didn't obey her mother-in-law would persecute her, and concluded she would be better off dead. Her own family was useless and merely bore the tragedy in silence, but the neighbours couldn't stand still and watch such a thing happen, so they took it to court. The case went up to the sub-prefectural level, where the magistrate managed to burn the original complaint beneath myriad petty-fogging questions and penalties. Intendant Li, on one of his incognito rounds, found out about it and referred the matter to the criminal court, instructing that all concerned be questioned with particular severity, until any secrets thay had squirreled away under their skulls came out. The licentious mother-in-law was beaten forty strokes with paired bamboos, and was given a session with the presses and two hundred strokes with poles. Once the court was through with her, she was dragged out. The next case was Ch'ao Yüan's. The judge didn't call for the plaintiff, or for evidence. He started right off with Ch'ao Yüan, "what was Ms. Chi's relation to you?"

"She was this student's wife."

"What is Chen ko's relation to you?"

"She is this student's concubine."

"What is her family?"

"The Shihs."

"Does she appear to be of good family?"

"I won't lie to your honor. She was a whore."

"How did Ms. Chi die?"

"She hung herself."

"Why did she hang herself?"

"She hung herself because last year, when I went to join my father at his official post, where I stayed for a year and four months, I took my concubine instead of her."

"Why did you go with your concubine, and not your wife?"

"My wife was sick, so she didn't come."

"If your wife was ill, why didn't you leave your concubine to tend to her?"

"Because my father sent a servant to fetch us, so I had no choice but to go, and take my concubine."

"What kind of father would send for his son's concubine, and not his wife! Go on."

"After I left, a Taoist nun, Hai-hui, and the Buddhist Nun Kuo visited my wife frequently. After I had come home with my concubine, on the sixth day of the sixth month, the two nuns were coming out of my wife's apartments. My concubine caught a glimpse of them, mistook them for priests and said what a nerve they had running around like that in broad daylight. I made the mistake of believing it, and then of course I had to speak to my wife about it. She got all upset, and, before I knew what was happening she had hung herself."

Judge Ch'u asked, "What was she upset about if they were not priests? Why was it that your concubine did not observe them entering, only leaving, and that she then thought they were priests?"

"Ms. Chi lived in apartments in the back."

"And you?"

"I lived in the front."

Judge Ch'u called the maid Hsia-ching up and asked her, "What did you call Chen ko?"

"I called her 'Aunty'."

"What did this 'aunty' say when she saw the 'priests'?"

"Nothing much. Just that she'd seen a Taoist and a Buddhist priest coming out."

"What did your master say?"

"What do you mean, my master?"

"What do you call Ch'ao Yüan?"

"I call him 'Sir'."

"What did 'Sir' say, then?"

"He didn't say much. Just how did priests dare come in here."

"Did you call Ms. Chi 'Mistress'?"

"Yes, I called her 'Mistress'."

"What did your mistress say?"

"My mistress took a knife in her hand and wanted to fight Sir to death. She was outside cursing something awful."

Judge Ch'u asked, "Could you give me an example?"

"Like, 'cheap shameless whore! What did I ever do to you for you to push me to death like this.'"

"When she was cursing, where were Ch'ao Yüan and Chen ko ?"

"Sir was hiding inside the inner door, looking out, and Aunty was hiding in the house with the door closed tight."

"Where did your mistress hang herself?"

"On the door to their room."

Then Judge Ch'u called forward the maid Liu-ch'ing, and asked her similar questions. She answered in roughly the same way as Hsia-ching had.

But then the judge asked, "Why don't you tell me all the ways Chen ko tortured your mistress, other than her fabrication of the story about the priests? Nothing you've said agrees with what Hsia-ching told me. Bring in the presses!"

The servants on either side called for the presses, and the torturer brought a big press forward, which he dropped with a clang right in front of the podium.

Hastily, Liu-ch'ing said, "I'll tell you everything! Just don't press me!"

"Hold the presses, " said Judge Ch'u, "And we shall hear what you have to tell us. But if you tell one more lie, on the presses will go."

She said, "On that day—the sixth of the sixth month—in the morning, Aunty Chen called us out to air the clothes, just when Ch'ing-mei was leading a nun out of the mistress' rooms in back."

"Who is this Ch'ing-mei? If there were two nuns, why are you only talking about one?"

"Isn't Ch'ing-mei one, too?"

"What sort of name for a nun is that?"

"That was her name before, before she became a nun."

"In whose house did this Ch'ing-mei serve?"

"Mistress Liu's house, by the East Gate."

Then Judge Ch'u called Ch'ao Yüan forward and asked, "Which nun was Ch'ing-mei?"

"That would be Hai-hui," said Ch'ao Yüan

"Retire," said the judge, "Continue, Liu-ch'ing."

"Ch'ing-mei was walking in front and that nun was behind her. When Chen ko saw them, she began to yell something awful about 'Some fine official's house! Some proper home! Some well-born young lady! With a Taoist priest turbanned up and a fat Buddhist priest coming and going in broad daylight! I may not have much of a background, and I have been an actress and I may have kept some men. Maybe I did accept customers, but even I wouldn't have those two! Like a fat bull's snout and a bald donkey! Even if I was ten thousand years without a man, I wouldn't want them!'

While she was screaming, Sir came out and she pointed at his face and bastard this and god-damned no-good that. She even said, 'I'd like that mother of yours here now to get a good look at her nice, well-brought-up daughter-in-law!' Sir asked 'Are you sure? How could any priests be wandering around here in the middle of the day?' Aunty Chen said, 'Just look at the foolish bastard. There isn't one of all these maids with me who didn't see it!' Sir called the doorman and asked when he'd let the priests in. The doorman said, 'What priests? That was the Lius' Ch'ing-mei and another nun.' Sir asked who was the other nun and did he know her. The doorman said he didn't know her. Sir asked 'If you didn't know her, how do you know she's really a nun?' The doorman said he didn't guess Hai-hui would be running around with a priest. Sir said, 'Hai-hui doesn't like anything better than pimping,' and he bet she'd brought a priest into Ms. Chi's rooms. Then he jumped up and said, 'Enough. I'm not going to take these bastards' making a fool of me. Bring Old Chi here. I'm going to divorce her!' After a while Old Mr. Chi and his son came in, and I can't say what they said because I didn't hear it. A little while later Old Mr. Chi and young Mr. Chi came out from the mistress' rooms, and a little while after that the mistress came out on the street yelling and screaming with a knife in her hand."

The judge asked, "What was she yelling and screaming?"

"Shameless whore . . . bastard . . . those nuns didn't come at my invitation, and they were in your house too, after all! Who doesn't know them? You say I'm keeping priests in broad daylight but even if I really did, you wouldn't have much right to say anything about it! And now you've called my Dad and brother so you can divorce me and send me back home! Bastard! Whore! I want you to come out here now, and have it out with you in front of the neighbours! Let's clear this up, and then I'll take my divorce and go."

Judge Ch'u asked, "Where was Ch'ao Yüan while she was saying this?"

"Behind the inner door listening."

"Wher was Chen ko?"

"Hidden inside with the door shut tight."

"Under what circumstances did your mistress cease screaming?"

"Mrs. Kao from across the way talked her back inside. A day passed, and then, I don't know how, she hung herself on their door. When Hsia-ching went to open the door first thing in the morning she was scared to death. She didn't come to herself for half a day."

The judge ordered her, "Go over to the side."

Then he called Mrs. Kao forward.

Mrs. Kao walked in front of the judge and bowed. The court servants clamoured at her to kneel. Then she was asked about what had happened, and everything she said was the same as she had before in the earlier hearing at the sub-prefectural level.

Judge Ch'u called Hai-hui and the Nun Kuo and asked them, "When did you last go to see Ms. Chi?"

They replied, "The sixth day of the sixth month."

Ch'ing-mei said, "Her family was related to mine, and I often visited."

"Did Chen ko know you?"

"Of course she did!"

"Is this Nun Kuo a relative, too?"

"No, she came from Ching-chou a year ago."

Next, the judge called Ch'ao Yüan, and asked him, "Do you know thesc two nuns?"

"Only Hai-hui, not the Nun Kuo."

"Since you admit you know Hai-hui, how could you be so easily led to believe that the nun with her was a priest? Even if you didn't know the Nun Kuo, how could you let your concubine lead you into taking action to divorce your wife?"

"When I heard a priest had been to see my wife, I was so upset! But then I found out it was a nun, so decided to let it be. My wife was always bad-tempered, and she was the one who wouldn't let well enough alone but had to go hang herself."

"That may well be, " said Judge Ch'u, "Yet you, knowing her to be easily angered, insulted her vilely in the hope she would kill herself. It was a good plan, but it was murder. You and Chen ko will pay for Ms. Chi's life."

Chen ko was called forward, and Judge Ch'u asked her, "Did you really see a Taoist and a Buddhist priest come out of Ms. Chi's rooms that day?"

She replied, "I saw a tall, manly figure in a turban and a straight robe, and a big fair, fat bald one, walking across the front. At first I mistook them for priests, but later I found out they were nuns."

The judge said, "Since you knew you were mistaken, why did you then say 'some fine official's house! Some proper home, some well-born young lady?' and also, 'with a Taoist priest all turbanned up and a fat, fair Buddhist priest coming and going in broad daylight'? You said yourself that you had been an actress, didn't have a good background, and used to take customers, but wouldn't have anything to do with priests, and you cursed Ch'ao Yüan as a 'bastard and a god-damned no-good'. At the same time as you maliciously insisted on the mistress' putative adultery, you incited the master. It wasn't your hand that held the knife, but without a doubt it was you who plotted against her and robbed her of her life!"

Chen ko replied, "I just said a few things like that! Who'd expect him to go calling Old Mr. Chi and Chi Pa-la and demanding a divorce? And who'd expect her to go hanging herself? When she was outside yelling and screaming, I shut the door tight, and didn't even show my face, so I don't see what that has to do with me."

Judge Ch'u asked, "It looked as if you had proof for your assertion that two priests had come out of her rooms, so how could Ch'ao Yüan not believe you? What you said had a semblance of truth, and he took it as such, so she had no choice but death. As for your staying behind closed doors while she went out on the street with her complaints, that was merely the same as a poisoner staying out of the way while his victim succumbs. What need had you then of further injuring her?

Once posisoned, the victim is sure to die, and thus it is you who must pay for her life. With ten thoussand mouths I could still not voice sufficient recrimination for your deeds."

Judge Ch'u called Chi Ts'e forward and said, "I have ordered that Chen ko pay for your sister's life. In your accusation, you state that you have evidence from the brush of the magistrate showing that the court messengers Wu and Shao took bribes."

Chi Pa-la handed over the original warrant with the record of the fines. Judge Ch'u looked at it and said, "But accused and accusers are not differentiated here, from each other or from witnesses! Did everyone pay?"

Chi Pa-la replied, "Yes, all, you can see the stamp."

The judge asked, "Who is Chi Tu?"

"My father."

"And why is your own fine still unpaid?"

"Some land went to Ch'ao Yüan as part of my sister's dowry, and now the land was to be returned to us. We planned to sell that in order to pay our fines, but Ch'ao Yüan wouldn't cede the land, and the messengers Wu and Shao didn't press him to cede it. They purposely harrassed us for payment, knocking at our door with their insults and even tried to drag us out for public beatings."

Judge Ch'u looked again at the red-ink endorsement by the magistrate of Wu-ch'eng.

"And what does this annotation about changing money mean?"

"Under the red-ink date are the characters for 'five hundred'. You can see it if you hold the paper up to the light. The magistrate thought five hundred was too little, so he demanded sixty gold taels more."

Judge Ch'u said, "Your complaint mentions seven hundred taels; this says five hundred. Where is your proof for the other two hundred?"

"The five hundred taels were paid to the magistrate. The two hundred went to the messengers Wu and Shao, so aren't recorded on the note."

Judge Ch'u said, "Yes, I don't suppose they would have done all that work for nothing, would they?"

Chi Pa-la continued, "Wu came trying to get money out of me. He said that all the others had paid, so only my father and I had outstanding fines. He pulled out the papers to show me, and then put them away, but they fell out of a hole in his leggings. I snatched the papers and I got this booklet, too."

He showed the booklet to the judge. Inside it there were records of forty or fifty fines, adding up to at least ten thousand taels.

The judge nodded and sighed, "With such thieves in local office, it's no wonder people are bone poor and bandits swarming all over."

He placed the booklet in front of him and kept it there when he called the two messengers Wu and Shao. They were pulled forward.

The judge said, "Did you hand over the money? Where are the seven hundred taels?"

"Money? Seven hundred taels?"

The judge had the booklet shown to them.

"Which of you two wrote this?"

They opened their eyes wide and looked at each other.

They had no answer to that, and kowtowed.

The judge asked, "Never mind the five hundred taels shown under the date, how much did you keep of the other two hundred?"

They said, "There wasn't any other two hundred."

He asked, "Did the circuit intendant have your legs whipped the other day?"

"He beat us fifty strokes, "they said, "but not our legs."

"Well then, your legs could use a session with the press. Bring out the poles."

The two men were placed in the presses, and then the judge said, "and beat them, too."

They were beaten two hundred strokes.

Then the sentences of all the defendants were read.

Chen ko was convicted to death by strangling, Ch'ao Yüan to penal servitude and hard labor, Wu and Shao to penal servitude, and the two nuns were fined.

Then the judge said, "Ch'ao Yüan and Chen ko deserve a good beating and pressing, but I'll leave that to the Circuit Intendant."

They were led off to jail.

Ch'ao Yüan and Chen ko thus exemplified:

> What you do catches up with you
> Sooner or later you get your due
> Nor can you evade the mirror of your malefactions.

Chapter Thirteen

Judge Ch'u Completes the Committal
Intendant Li Passes Sentence

To start a home, get two ploughs
To break a home, get two wives
Even if the second is a good woman
It will never do
If she's a whore—even worse.
Read now this record of the bonds of matrimony
And the marvellous and ingenious workings
of calamity
Let it educate all to the dangers of rascality
By the sight of its accounts falling due

Ch'ao Yüan and all the rest were escorted down into the prison. When Chen ko heard she would have to forfeit her life for her crime, she finally realized this pot was made of iron. She hung on Ch'ao Yüan and sobbed madly. Ch'ao Yüan snivelled, too.

Mrs. Kao said, "You should have thought of this before! It's a little late for tears now!"

The two court servants said, "Even though that's Judge Ch'u's sentence, it still has to go to the circuit intendant, and then it has to be heard thrice, so you can't tell now how it will turn out. Crying like you are! When the final sentence is passed, then it'll be time to cry."

Chen ko's sobs lessened, but she quavered, "Ch'ao Yüan, you've got to save me! Don't worry about your money now!"

Ch'ao Yüan asked the court servants to go get the criminal court secretary. The criminal court secretary would now write up the case for the next step in the prosecution. Ch'ao Yüan gave him fifty taels, and asked him to make the crime sound a little less serious, so that it would be easier to ameliorate the sentence later. The secretary took the money and said he would do as Ch'ao Yüan said.

The two messengers Wu and Shao had their legs pressed until they snapped, and they both bellowed like stuck pigs.

The next day, the criminal court secretary had written up the rough draft of the committal, and he gave it to Ch'ao Yüan first. The secretary had softened the wording in all the important places, and Ch'ao Yüan suggested a couple more improvements. Then the secretary wrote a fair copy, which was sent in to the judge. When Judge Ch'u looked at it, he could see as clear as day that a bribe had been taken, but he didn't follow that up. Instead, he just had the secretary rewrite the committal again, so that it represented the truth. Then Judge Ch'u appended his own notes and sent it off the same day.

The committal read:

One Ms. Shih, or Chen ko, aged nineteen years, of the Wu-Ch'ao subprefecture in Ho-chien prefecture of the Northern Metropolitan District: Record of her youth and familial affiliation lost, as she was sold by her parents for an unknown sum to the unregistered entertainment house of Shih-liang as a prostitute. She began to take customers in the fifth year of the Cheng-t'ung reign, and also began training as a principal singer of female parts. In the second month of the following year, Shih-liang took her and others to Lin-yi in P'u-chou to do business, and then to Wu-ch'eng, where they settled.

Ch'ao Yüan, currently an Academy student, became her particular lover, as, after beginning relations with her, he became more and more attached to her. The two desired to marry. They settled their arrangements without a go-between. Ch'ao Yüan used eight hundred taels to buy her as a concubine. After that, had Chen ko stayed in her place, Ch'ao Yüan could have treated his wife and his concubine as would have been proper, but Chen ko enticed him with her lascivious charms and exacted his submission so that he did not make his residence with his legal wife, Ms. Chi, but with Chen ko. Ms. Chi has now been oppressed unto death by Chen ko. Ch'ao Yüan was also at fault for listening to Chen ko's incitements, and, at her incitements, abandoning his wife to a bare room, where she lived alone.

Ms. Chi's family had given one hundred mou of land as part of her dowry. She hired men to plant this land, and it was the only source of her food and clothing for several years. Ch'ao Yüan never concerned himself with her use of the land.

Hai-hui, a Taoist nun, and the Buddhist Nun Kuo, were both at fault for visiting Ms. Chi indiscriminately. When Chen ko coincidentally saw them coming out of Ms. Chi's rooms, Chen ko was at fault for broadcasting slanders. She said, for example, 'some fine officials' house! Some well-born young lady! With a Taoist priest all turbanned up and a fat, fair Buddhist priest coming and going in broad daylight! I may not have much of a background, and I did keep a few men and I did accept customers but even I only accepted nice-looking ones—those two are like a bull's snout and a bald donkey! Even if I was ten thousand years without a man, I wouldn't have them.' She also cursed Ch'ao Yüan as a bastard and a god-damned no-good, with the intent of goading him. In evidence of this, we have the testimony of the maid Ch'ing-mei. As Ch'ao Yüan had already ascertained the true nature of events, he should have silenced Chen ko, but instead he took opportunistic advantage of the situation by using Chen ko's accusations as a pretext to call Chi Tu, Ms. Chi's father, and Chi Ch'i-tzu, her brother, to his home to demand a divorce and make her father and brother take her home. Chi Tu replied that Hai-hui and the Nun Kuo were frequent vistors at the homes of all the ladies in town, and were nuns, not priests, as everyone knew. Also, Chi Tu said 'if you insist on a divorce on your traitorous grounds, we have nothing to gain in standing against you. Let us go home to get her room ready, and then we will come back to take her home. We will wait for when you father, Ch'ao Ssu-hsiao comes home, and see if he will talk reason.' After that Chi Tu and Chi Ch'i-tzu went to the back rooms to tell Ms. Chi the situation. Ms. Chi could not stomach the insult. After she saw her father and brother out, she took a knife in her hand and ran out in front of the house screaming. Chen ko feared Ms. Chi would look for satisfaction for her grievances, and hid inside. Ms. Chi thereupon ran out of the inner gate screaming 'It's not enough that you've tied the man so tight to you I haven't seen his face for two or three years! Now you find me such an offensive sight you have to concoct a plot to get me out of the way! Those two nuns don't belong to me—they've been to see you, too! Who is there, high or low, in this town, who doesn't know them? You shameless whore, slandering me with having priests in broad daylight, calling my father and brother to come and take me away. Come out here, you shameless whore! Let's have it out in front of everyone! If they weren't nuns, but priests, never mind getting me divorced—I'll lay my head down in front of you so you can slice it off! But if it's your shameless whore's plan to destroy me my knife is here for both of you and I'll pit my life against yours.'

The neighbour Mrs. Kao, saw Ms. Chi screaming on the street and brought Ms. Chi back inside the house. Mrs. Kao's testimony shows that on the seventh day of the same month, Ms. Chi's father and brother came to see Ms. Chi, but Ms. Chi said her preparations were not complete and that she would go home on the eighth. They went home. On the night of the seventh, Ms. Chi, at an unspecified hour, made her way surreptitiously to Chen ko's door and hung herself with a sash there. The testimony of Hsia-ching *et al* shows that Chi Tu, Chi Ch'i-tzu and others of the Chi family took down Ms. Chi's body and encoffined her the same day.

Chi Tu could not stomach the pain that had been caused his daughter, so he accused Chen ko in the sub-prefectural court. The late sub-prefectural magistrate, and the court messengers Wu and Shao went to arrest Chen ko. Wu and Shao are at fault for having accepted two hundred taels from Ch'ao Yüan. They divided this money between themselves and in exchange did not bring Chen ko to appear in court. Ch'ao Yüan and the others were called for testimony and were fined unevenly. The fines were collected. Ms. Chi's father and brother could not accept her victimization and death, and, on the date on the document, petitioned Circuit Intendant Li to look into this murder case.

Intendant Li's notation on their petition reads, 'The criminal court judge of Tung Ch'ang will look into the disposition of this case and correct ambiguities.' The said judge, Judge Ch'u, called Chen ko and all the other people implicated to be present in court and questioned each separately and stringently, thereby coming to a clear understanding of what actually happened.

Judge Ch'u finds Chen ko guilty of misleading Ch'ao Yüan more treacherously than a nine-tailed fox, and with more deadly effect than a two-headed snake. He let the new dislodge the old, and let the evil of jealously enter his household. He desired the shoddy charmer and despised his worthy wife. Chen ko slyly plotted to make Ch'ao Yüan repudiate his wife improperly. Seeing that Ms. Chi was vulnerable, and Ch'ao Yüan easily goaded into ill-judged action, Chen ko called a deer a horse, insisting that nuns were priests and slanderously calling Ms. Chi a loose woman. Having vilely insulted the mother of the household, Chen ko incited her master with filthy female machinations. Hers was the hand that drove the sword home. She evaded the warrant and covered her wily treachery from the eyes of the court.

If we do not prosecute her by her heart's intent, but merely for her material actions, we would be guilty of the same sort of error as it would be to say thay the death of Chou Po-jen was no-one's responsibility, the same as saying that Wu Po-pi's teachery was excusable. If judgement is passed by the strict letter of the law, it is possible for her to squirm out of her punishment, but if her true role in the death of an innocent woman is considered, her guilt is overwhelming. Ch'ao Yüan disregarded all of his solemn wedding vows to run after this worthless woman and discarded all that was of value in his marriage for her tawdry charms. Then he lent an ear to her slanders and planned to divorce his wife. Ms. Ch'i's situation was untenable, and she could not be expected to bear the humiliation of formal rejection by her husband. Although it was the concubine who caused the wife's death, the concubine was not prosecuted. We must pass sentence that this was a miscarriage of justice.

The messengers Wu and Shao were as useless as a cat that lies down companionably with rats, and asks the rats' permission to catch them. So the wolves let their fellow-vermin go, and abandoned their responsibilities for money. They substantially admit they did, as accused, accept two hundred taels as a bribe, and are hereby leniently granted only five years of light penal servitude as punishment.

Hai-hui is guilty of violating her vows to occupy herself exclusively with spiritual matters. Instead, she socialized incessantly. The Nun Kuo left the precincts of her temple to interfere with the domestic affairs of others. From this came the offense that fermented into tragedy. As the ultimate cause can be traced to the two nuns, they will be flogged.

Chi Ch'i-tzu, thirty-five years of age, Mrs. Kao, fifty-eight years of age, Liu-ch'ing, seventeen years of age, and Hsia-ching, thirteen years of age, have each testified as above. Ch'ao Yüan, thirty years of age, and the messengers Wu Hsiao-ch'üan, aged sixty-two, and Shao Ch'iang-jen, aged thirty-two, Hai-hui, aged twenty-four and the Nun Kuo aged forty-two, are each committed to trial as per the above.

It is hereby judged that Shih Chen ko and the other accused shall be dealt with as follows: Chen ko will be executed in the autumn for the offense of persecuting her better in the household to death. Ch'ao Yüan, for the offense of allowing his wife's persecution, will be beaten one hundred strokes, stripped of status, and exiled thirty li. The covetous and unscrupulous messengers Wu and Shao will be spared further investigation of their thievery but will be beaten one hundred strokes and exiled thirty li, as is standard when amounts over one-hundred and twenty strings of cash are involved. As the Nuns Hai-hui and Kuo have committed the weighty crime of conducting themselves in a way not fitting their station in life, they will be beaten one hundred strokes. Other than Shih Chen ko, whose sentence will not be reduced, all others are granted the court's leniency. Ch'ao Yüan and the messengers Wu and Shao will each be beaten eighty strokes and serve five years of their sentences. Hai-hui and the Nun Kuo will each be beaten seventy strokes. In consideration of the fact that Ch'ao Yüan is an academician and that the two nuns are women, they may commute their sentences into fines. The messengers Wu and Shao, being government employees, are not eligible for commutation of their sentences into fines.

This court hearing is adjourned and the sentences pronounced. Court fees will be duly paid as follows: Chi Ch'i-tz'u will pay 2.5 cash for filing the complaint, Mrs. Kao, Liu-ch'ing and Hsia-ching, Wu and Shao will each pay a commoner's paper fee of two cash, Ch'ao Yüan will pay an offical's paper fee of four cash.

As fees in commutation of sentences, Ch'ao Yüan may pay twenty-five taels to commute the exile portion of his sentence, and the two nuns may pay 2.5 cash to commute each stroke of their sentenced beatings. These moneys will be sent sealed to the treasury for deposit there. The two hundred taels which Wu and Shao swindled out of Ch'ao Yüan will be legally confiscated as government property. Academician Ch'ao will be stripped of his status. The messengers Wu and Shao will be stripped of office. The land that was to be ceded to Chi Ch'i-tz'u will be and he will also own all harvest on that land. The recipt will be tendered to this court. Here ends our committal.

It was written out in all its explicitness, and then Judge Ch'u endorsed it, stamped it, and had the court servant call the roll of the accused. Chen ko, Ch'ao Yüan, Wu and Shao had their hands fettered and were given over to a court servant to be taken to the court of Circuit Intendant Li for him to retry them and validate the committal. Now that Ch'ao Yüan and Chen ko had reached this stage, they were thoroughly dejected and went along with no complaint.

Ch'ao Yüan asked the court servant to loosen their fetters, but the court servant said, "Master, you just aren't used to these fetters, and I'm sure the lady is even less so, so of course they must be loosened. Having been treated with such consideration by you, I wouldn't think of letting you travel out on the road with these on. But let's just leave them on while we're still in the city, Judge Ch'u often sends people out to check up, and if he found out I'd taken these off, we'd be in real trouble. We'd better not take them off until we're twenty or thirty li out."

The luggage, animals, and conveyances were readied. Ch'ao Yüan was unable to ride a horse with his hands fettered, so he rented a little sedan chair. The women rode in carts. The messengers Wu and Shao were loaded on planks that were carried.

After they had gone another twenty-odd li, Ch'ao Yüan again asked the court servant to remove his fetters.

The court servant said, "We're not over a hundred li from Lin-ch'ing, why not just keep them on until we get there? If I take them off now, I'll just have to put them back on once we get to Lin-ch'ing. It seems like an awful lot of bother."

This servant was hoping to get a fat bribe out of Ch'ao Yüan for loosening the fetters. When Ch'ao Yüan heard his derisive tone, he knew this was man who wouldn't raise his little finger to help another for free. He slowly drew the man out and found his price, and then he gave an additional twenty taels to all the escorts. Only then, and with alternate pleading and bullying, did he get the fetters taken off. The messenger Shao had been pressed so hard he had been internally injured. He was only intermittantly conscious and kept crying out. After he was given a cup of cold water to drink, he quieted down, and they thought he'd gotten more comfortable, but what had happened was that he'd died.

Finally the whole party had to stop and rest. The court servant found the local law-enforcement outpost where he got a tattered mat to wrap the corpse in, and then tied the mat around the corpse with a grass rope. He had a couple of low-level servants dig a grave and put Shao's corpse in it, with barely enough dirt to cover the corpse.

After burying Shao, the party started off again. Gradually evening fell, and they found a place to stop for the night. Ch'ao Yüan and Cllen ko were as glum as if ten thousand despairs had been dumped on their heads. The court messenger Wu was in such pain he would rather have been dead. Only the court servants were enjoying themsleves. They ate and drank merrily and called for a couple of girls to amuse them. Ch'ao Yüan was paying.

When they all got up the next morning, the court servants indulged some more, Ch'ao Yüan paid, and they all set off again.

As soon as they entered the gate of the city of Lin-ch'ing, they found a place to stay. Everyone took refreshment, and the court servants, as before, had all the wine and women they wanted. Not one of those court servants heeded the examples of Wu and Shao. Each one of them was solely intent on perpetrating his crimes and swindling money.

The next morning, they rushed through their morning toilettes and had breakfast. The court servants took the accused to present the committal at the circuit court. The circuit intendant noted the presence of each and the court servant in charge of the group gave his report of Shao's death and disposal. They were ordered to be present at the morning session of the court. The whole party went back to their lodgings, where, of course, the servants continued their revelries, but the servants were the only ones who were having a good time.

Chen ko and Ch'ao Yüan sobbed desperately, "This is it for us! Tomorrow morning's the end for us!"

Ch'ao Yüan didn't say anything blaming Chen ko, but, "The day our case is over, if I'm alive, I'll get revenge in my own good time. If I'm going to die, I'll pull my wife out of her coffin and burn her corpse so her bones are scattered to the four winds, and then I'm going to take that coffin I bought for two hundred and twenty taels and give it to a beggar."

He sat there gnashing his teeth. It was Chen ko who was too downhearted to talk wildly now. Ever since that day when Ms. Chi had possessed her and beaten her, her nerve had been broken. The two of them cried for a while, and then managed to force down some wine. They wheedled the servants into letting them sleep together.

The day after that, after breakfast, they all went to the circuit court for the morning session, sent in the committal, and took the retrial papers in return. The court servant led them all inside. Ch'ao Yüan, Chen ko and Wu were all fettered as before, and roped together. They knelt before the judge's forecourt. The magnificent solemnity of the circuit intendant's yamen was was of altogether a different order than Judge Ch'u's criminal court.

> A great hall five chien wide
> With there in the middle
> a boney-faced, meager-cheeked, melancholy-miened
> King Yen Lo of Hell
> In two little three-chien rooms
> Swarmed like gnats many bright-eyed and bushy-tailed
> beaky-faced and ready to go little scourge of the world
> demon kings.
> The drum sounding the opening of the court
> Roared thrice leoninely
> Twenty staves lined up like dog's legs
>
> The seeds of winter blight were placed in the sixth month
> Now let the traitor stand on thin ice
> Let us all act as we would in the clear light of the full moon
> All grasses bend to the wind
> All people follow the morals of their officials

Circuit Intendant Li called each of the accused and questioned them separately. Since everything in Judge Ch'u's committal was firmly grounded in the truth, how could Intendant Li find any points on which to differ?

He pulled out his bamboo tallies to allot punishments, which were: twenty strokes of the flat bamboo for Ch'ao Yüan, twenty-five on her legs for Chen ko, a session with the finger presses and two hundred strokes with a baton for Wu and a session with the finger presses each for the two nuns.

Usually, if a woman knows she is likely to be beaten in court on her legs, she makes a little short panty to wear so people don't see that part they are not supposed to see, when her gown is pulled up, just her legs. Chen ko hadn't made any such preparations, and she was quite a sight that day. A bribe slipped to the man beating her did ensure the strokes were lightened.

After those beatings were over, a court employee issued the record. The record of the re-trial was to be opened in Tung-ch'ang and was annotated saying that all of the accused would be taken to Tung-ch'ang prefecture for their final trial. Ch'ao Yüan knew the location, but not the details. He folded up two taels in a piece of paper, for the court servant and asked him to find out more by going to the clerical offices and asking around.

Ch'ao Yüan and Chen ko could hardly move after their beatings, and they requested to be allowed to stay in Lin-ch'ing long enough to be treated by a surgeon. The escorts were glad to oblige, since they were having a fine time in the bustling city of Lin-ch'ing with money on tap for gambling and girls. They would have been happy to stay another year if asked.

Ch'ao Yüan and Chen ko lay in bed screaming in pain and Wu lay on a k'ang in a side room howling, making such a racket the hostel lost all its other busines and was as desolate as a Hell of wronged ghosts.

Mrs. Kao had expected to go home once she ahd answered Intendant Li's questions, but now the case was to go to Tung-ch'ang and she heard it might have to be retried three or four times, who knows where next. If she'd been gifted with good judgement, Mrs. Kao could have seen that Ch'ao Yüan and Chen ko, having been beaten until their mouths were sore with screaming, weren't much use at all at present, and, considering all the presents Ch'ao Yüan had given her in the past, she might have kept quiet, but she yammered and muttered and complained continually.

Ch'ao Yüan was at his wits' end and finally lost his temper with her, "Like my cock you have a right to be going on! Did I ask you to coming sticking yourself into the picture and giving evidence? You blame me because you got pulled into court just for being my neighbour, but when that happened, didn't I beg you to be on my side and give you thirty absolutely best quality taels, ten lengths of plain cloth and two of flossy pongee, and six strings of cash, too? Nobody's squeezing you dry on my account, but you're ready to go biting a person's cock off. After I spent about fifty taels on you so you'd say something nice to the judge you did your best to say all you could to put me in a position where I'm as good as dead! Now here I am being convicted of murder, and beaten, and never mind that you're my neighbour, just the fact you took those presents from me should make you good and ashamed for the way you're behaving. I really want to know, do you have the tiniest bit of kindness in your heart? If you want to leave, take your stinking mouth and leave. Don't expect me to beg you any more. See this money? Take it to pay your way home and from here on whether you stay or not has nothing to do with me. If you do stay, don't expect me to take care of your food or pack animals."

Mrs. Kao said, "And doesn't a stupid, soft old woman deserve to be insulted for coming along and testifying willynilly when he came begging her that day? It isn't as if I could change one word of the truth with the magistrate in front of me, is it? You heartless, ungrateful, gallowsbait. You murderer! I'm not waiting around for the next retrial in Tung-ch'ang, no more beatings for me and you'll be sorry not to have me around, but this is good-bye from Mrs. Kao to you!"

She was gathering her luggage as she scolded him, and she pulled a string of cash out from under his bed. She picked up her things and walked out. There was a court servant outside the door, resting his feet, but he didn't bother to finish his rest when he saw Mrs. Kao walk by with her quilts in her arms and dangling a string of cash. He slipped on his shoes and caught hold of her.

He asked, "What do you think you're doing?"

Then he pulled her back inside and fired a few questions at her.

She put her quilts back down.

Ch'ao Yüan said, "I already gave you your travelling money, and you already left. It was a court servant who brought you back and from now he can be the one to look after you. You might rather sleep with him too, instead of being here with me dark nights."

"You stupid fart, tell your wife to go sleep with him, " she replied

"Do you have any other suggestions? Because I don't think she'd be free to even if she wanted to," he said.

At that, he and Chen ko began to moan and scream about their hard lot, and Mrs. Kao's talents as a calm advisor would have been useful. While they were going on, Liu-ch'ing came in with a piece of paper for Ch'ao Yüan. The court servant who had been finding out what Intendant Li had written had copied some of the intendant's annotation. Ch'ao Yüan called for a candle to be brought to his bedside and read:

"Had Ms. Chi been conducting an adulterous affair, even her death would not atone for it. It has been ascertained that her visitors were nuns, not priests, yet Ms. Shih Chen ko created a disturbance and incited her master to join her in it, thus killing with a borrowed sword by forcing the legal mistress of the house to hang herself. In consideration of her heart's intent, she must be considered guilty of premeditated murder. She is sentenced to death by strangulation. Ch'ao Yüan allowed himself to be manipulated by his seductive concubine into oppressing his wife to death. Wu Sheng-tao took advantage of his official status to amass bribes, and accepted payment for helping criminals escape the net of justice. Hai-hui and the Nun Kuo did not keep to the precepts of their religions but interfered in people's households, so their accusations are judged to be in keeping with the truth.

Ms. Shih's crime in particular so blatantly calls for capital punishment that we request the court of Tung-ch'ang prefecture to ratify our sentences without further detailed investigation.

Ch'ao Yüan was happy when he read this.

"This is great," he said, "our sentences are as good as overturned already!"

Chen ko was happy, too, when she heard him say that, and asked him to read her the annotation.

He read, "'Had Ms. Chi been conducting an adulterous affair, even her death would not atone for it.' In other words, if she was having an affair, even though she did hang herself, she's the one in the wrong."

He read on, "'It has been ascertained that her visitors were nuns and priests.' Doesn't that mean she deserved to die? Our case is closed."

He was so elated he called out excitedly for a maid to warm up some wine, and he drank some in bed with Chen ko, feeling rid of the greater part of his worries.

The court servant said, "But Master Ch'ao, what are you so happy about? You don't mean to say you like that annotation, do you? From what I heard, it is very severe! I don't understand."

Ch'ao Yüan and Chen ko drank for about one watch, then blew out the light and went to sleep. The next morning, their wounds from the beatings felt worse than before, so bad that the two of them bellowed like stuck pigs. A surgeon was called in to look at them. He said that wounds like these, from a court beating, would take a month or two to heal.

Wu Sheng-tao had been finger-pressed so severely he lost consciousness two or three times a day. They all stayed in the hostel another five or six days. Whenever Wu fainted, he saw Shao's ghost in front of him. After the first couple of days, Shao's ghost was joined by all the people whose deaths he had caused, coming now to take his life. Some kicked him where he was wounded from beatings or hit him with bricks, others took huge sticks and bashed him where his bones were already crushed, or else they pierced his mangled hands with needles. They thought up a hundred, a thousand ways to inflict such unspeakable suffering on him that he just wished for a speedy death. After another five or six days, when Ch'ao Yüan and Chen ko felt a little better, the court servant began urging them to start out for Tung-ch'ang.

Chen ko and Ch'ao Yüan were afraid of the pain jolts on the road would give them, and they couldn't sit up in sedan chairs, so Ch'ao Yüan bought a reclining sedan chair. He hired sixteen men to carry it. The others travelled as they had before, in carts or on horseback. Wu's legs, feet, and hands were putrefying so the white bones glinted through and he had to be carried on a plank again, so six men were hired to carry him. Ch'ao Yüan paid for their lodgings and food, and they all said goodbye to their sad lodgings in Lin-ch'ing and started out for Tung-ch'ang.

Wu knew clearly that his death was imminent. He just hoped he could last until Tung-ch'ang. For one thing, Tung-ch'ang wasn't far from his home, and for another, the prefectural capital was a good place to buy a coffin and be buried. He didn't want to be buried the same way Shao had, wrapped in a mat and shoved into a shallow roadside grave. On their first night on the road, they stayed at the same house they had stayed in on their journey to Linch'ing. Athough Wu was in such pain he couldn't say so, he thought that Shao and those other ghosts wouldn't follow him this far.

The next morning, everyone got up and had breakfast. They started out as before. When they got to the place where Shao had died, they all heard Wu scream.

"Stop hitting me, all of you! Brother Shao, hold them back. I'll go with you! I'll go!"

After a few brief spasms he was dead.

The whole party went back to the house they had stayed at, and let their animals rest. The court servant found the same minor governnment employee who had arranged Shao's disposal. This time he only parted with three or four fragments of tattered mats, in which Wu was wrapped and hastily buried beside Shao.

Then they were ready to leave, but the minor government employee asked for a few coins as a tip. Ch'ao Yüan wouldn't give him a thing. The others urged him to give the man a tip, since he'd already laid out so much money on other things, and they had troubled this man for his old mats and the writing of two death certificates.

Ch'ao Yüan was the kind of man who had a bottomless pocket when he wanted you to stick your neck out for him, but if it was you who needed help, he wouldn't give you one cash.

The local official saw he was determined not to pay and said, "You don't have to pay me if you don't want to, but I want you to understand that if you come this way again and somebody else dies you can forget about asking me for any old mats!" and he turned to go, full of insult.

Ch'ao Chu pulled up his horse and was going after the minor official to beat him up, but the man picked up a rock as big as a chicken with which he smashed the horse's nose. the horse was in so much pain it rolled around on the ground. All for the sake of a few cash!

The next day, around sunset, they entered Tung-ch'ang and stayed at a place they knew. The day after they went to the yamen to present their papers and be counted present. The day after that they received the yamen's directives, and that was when they learned that the case had been referred to the subprefecture Liao-ch'eng for judging, and was to be returned to Tung-ch'ang after that for detailed deliberations, and then heard again at Kuan sub-prefecture. After they reached Kuan sub-prefecture, the party waited there for about ten days, were again sent to Tung-ch'ang for deliberations, and then re-referred to Jen-p'ing sub-prefecture. They all went to Jen-p'ing and waited there about half a month before being hauled back to Tung-ch'ang. No matter how many times the case was retried, it was always the same old story they went over pro forma the required three times before sentence could be confirmed as passed. Once the sentences had been formulated by a criminal court judge and a circuit intendant, there wasn't much likelihood of wriggling out of their punishments.

At last orders came from Tung-ch'ang to bring in the accused and imprison them separately while security money was sought and deliberations completed. The papers went up through all the layers of officialdom and came back endorsed, all with the sentences pronounced by Judge Ch'u and Intendant Li.

Chen ko was imprisoned in Wu-ch'eng. Ch'ao Yüan was released on bail and commuted his sentence to a fine. The families of the court messengers Wu and Shao paid back money the two had taken as bribes, and Hai-hui and the Nun Kuo were authorized to leave the area under escort. All the others—Chi Pa-la, Mrs. Kao, Hsia-ching and Liu-ch'ing—were allowed to go home.

Ch'ao Yüan took Chen ko's hand in his and wept so unrestrainedly when they reached the door of the jail that all who passed cried too at the sight of a man whose whole world had gone dark. The court servant at the jail wanted to get the paperwork wrapped up and hurried them through their parting so he could commit Chen ko. Ch'ao Yüan wanted to send in a couple of maids to attend to her needs, but the jailer wouldn't allow it.

The court servant said, "Do you think Master Chao's the sort of man who doesn't know how to show his gratitude? He's depending on you, so let those two maids in."

Then the jailer was happy to do as Ch'ao Yüan wished, and, having abruptly changed his attidtude 180 degrees said, "Master, you can relax and go home now. We'll take good care of your lady and we wouldn't dare let her suffer the smallest insult. Anything you want to have taken in to her will be—just let us know."

Ch'ao Yüan couldn't thank him enough and said, "I'll be back later with a token of my appreciation and some clothes for her."

Ch'ao Yüan said good-bye and went home, very dejected at the miserable state of things. What was he going to do now? Someone made this verse about his situation:

> Money scattered and lovers parted
> Now what's to be done?
> He lost his rank, she lost her freedom
> Today's calamity was clearly foreshadowed from afar
> Why didn't they take heed?

Chapter Fourteen

An idyll in jail
A birthday party on death row

A stupid man can't hold his wealth
Any better than too much wine
Like a baboon in an official's hat
What a fool he makes of himself

Rushing gleefully to embrace disaster
Covetous of what he sees ahead
ignorant of what lies behind
Hard to see your back, easy to point at others
—to the tune "The fortune-teller"

After Ch'ao Yüan had seen Chen ko off to jail, and taken care of his bail, he went home full of dejection and told his sister some of what had happened. Food was served, and he forced himself to eat a little. Then he went into his room. Dust was everywhere, spiderwebs veiled the bed, and it was such a sorry sight that even a man of iron would have felt sad. He couldn't help bawling, and when he'd done with that his sister insisted on going home. He couldn't persuade her to stay, so he just saw her to the door.

He had some servants send food and wine over to the jail for Chen ko, and also bedding and clothes for her. He sent Ch'ao Chu with a fair sum to bribe the officials at the jail, five taels for the criminal office of the yamen, ten taels for each of the prison administrators, twenty for the head jailor, five taels for each of the female jailors and five cash for each of the inmates other than Chen ko. The whole crew were bursting with gratitude. They swept Chen ko's floor, fixed her bed, hung up her drapes and hopped to it until there didn't remain the slightest taint of hardship in her room.

The next day, Ch'ao Yüan sent many more household things and furniture, and from then on there was a ceaseless round of meals, tea and snacks.

The local administration had been regularized, with the new magistrate instead of the treasurer temporarily acting as magistrate in charge, and also a new warden. This warden was from Hsia-hsi. His name was Che Chih-t'u. He heard that this nice piece of meat was sitting in his jail, and that nobody dared take a bite. He decided to treat himself to a feast.

One day, after the jail was closed, the warden took the keys and personally visited the women's jail. Most of the rooms were dark caves, like pits in Hell, but one was a blaze of splendor and light, with the sound of female chatter and laughter spilling out. The warden pushed open the door and strode in. He was greeted by the sight of Chen ko, wearing a dark green silk-tissue short padded jacket, a brown small-figured bodice, a pair of heavy green silk trousers, and sky-blue hemp thread shoes. She sat on a square scholar-style chair on a wool pillow that was covered in dark satin. A glowing brazier sat at her feet, with a steaming pot of tea on it. Two maids sat at the foot of the bed, and three or four female convicts on low benches or piles of straw.

The warden said, "Where am I? How lovely it is! And who is this beautiful lady?"

The jailors were busy kowtowing. Chen ko backed up against the wall, and the other female convicts knelt down.

The jailors said, "This is the junior wife of an Important Person, Ch'ao Yüan. We're following his orders in giving her special treatment."

The warden said, "So she's a convict! I thought she must certainly not be. This is no jail—it's a bower of heavenly bliss! If this is a jail, I'm one warden who'd like to give up his job and get convicted here! But don't worry, I won't beat you so badly you'll be crippled. That would look bad in court. Just fifteen strokes each."

He had Chen ko tied to the bamboo rack. The other convicts were sent back to their rooms, and only Liu-ch'ing and Hsia-ching remained.

"Who's this little one," the warden asked, "another convict?"

Liu-ch'ing said, "I'm here to serve Aunty Chen."

The warden said, "I never heard of such a thing!"

He had the two maids locked in Chen ko's room, and sealed the door. He also put a seal on Chen ko's bindings to the rack. Now he had her where no call of hers to heaven would be heard. Then he left the jail, mounted his horse, rode out of the main gate and went on a nightly inspection round. One of the jailors sent a man who could be trusted to Ch'ao Yüan, with the news of the warden's visit to Chen ko, and begging that Ch'ao Yüan come up with some money for bribes before the warden got as far as actually prosecuting the jailors for their negligence.

Ch'ao Yüan, oppressed by the long autumn night and the forlorness of his empty bed, was still up drinking alone when the man arrived. The man knocked until the door was opened, and told Ch'ao Yüan the news, which scared Ch'ao Yüan so badly, he had to cross his legs to keep his heart from falling out of his behind. Ch'ao Yüan began to calculate how much of a bribe would be necessary.

How could he get in there at this late hour? By tomorrow morning, he might be too late to prevent the filing of the warden's report.

The man said, "If you want to take care of things, now's your chance. The door is still open, because the warden's out on a nightly tour of inspection. You can make it if you hurry."

When Ch'ao Yüan heard that the warden had gone out, he was almost as relieved as he would have been to hear that Chen ko was pardoned. Knowing that the warden would have to pass his house on the way back to the jail, he saw more and more clearly what had to be done. He called his servants to lay out some wine and delciacies, sealed up sixty taels of first quality silver, and put another hundred and ten aside. Then he told his servants to light up the main hall with candles, heat some wine up piping hot, arrange the delicacies and set them out on a table. He had similar preparations made in the servants's quarters, to treat the warden's servants. Although he had been stripped of his status as an academician, he was still a privileged young man who looked well in his scholar's robe and hat.

Dressed so, he stood at his door waiting for the warden. It wasn't long before he saw a pair of lanterns, a pair of clappers, and a gendarme with a willow pole, leading the way for the warden. The warden had on his gauze hat and an old blue heavy silk straight robe, and he rode on horseback.

Ch'ao Yüan had three or four of his servants go forward to the warden. Two of them took hold of the reins of the warden's horse and held it while another knelt and said, "Our master Ch'ao Yüan heard that Your Honour was patrolling in this cold weather. He felt so worried on your behalf that he warmed some wine for you. He's waiting now to serve you some wine and let you warm yourself. This is his house, please come in."

The warden said, "Night inspection is official business, and it's too late for all this talk. He can see me in the daytime."

He was about to turn his horse to go, when Ch'ao Yüan came out on the street, bowed deeply, and said, "But I've been waiting all this time for you! I hope Your Benevolence can spare just a moment; I wouldn't dare keep you too long."

Seeing how hard Ch'ao Yüan was working at being obsequious, how could the warden help wanting to play along with him?

The warden said, "But I had no idea! I never dreamed you were here yourself, Master Ch'ao!"

As he spoke, he dismounted, and then he and Ch'ao Yüan spent some time pretending to yield to each other at the door until the warden finally strode in first. They entered the main hall. It was already the tenth month, and it was the third watch (midnight). The warden had been sorely abused by the cold wind, and now suddenly found himself surrounded by light, heat, and wine. It was a very comfortable room and he found his situation pleasant. His servants were all taken care of in the servant's quarters, warmed and regaled with wine. Ch'ao Yüan served the warden's wine with his own hands. Then he called for hot food, complete with soup and rice.

Ch'ao Yüan kept saying Your Benevolence this and Your Benevolence that, who doesn't know and respect you, what superior doesn't know of your merciful administration, and my, now that the court is relaxing the rules on promotion and issuing second and third degrees right and left, isn't it wonderful how what really counts in getting ahead is your moral qualities, and would I dare say one word of flattery? No, flattery is the lowest one can stoop . . . . Ch'ao Yüan had the warden writhing with gratification as he listened to this spate of unconscionable flattery. It looked like Ch'ao Yüan only had to say the word and the warden would name his price. But Ch'ao Yüan didn't bring it up.

Finally the warden had to say, "They didn't have a regular warden here for quite a while, and things have gotten very lax. It's to the point where I myself have to go down into the jail and on night patrols. I've seen more strange things than I can tell you. Just now, at the north gate, a man with a great big beard came out of the nuns'. I asked how there could be a man with a beard there where there should only be nuns or priests, and had my men arrest him. If he'd come along quietly, I wouldn't have prosecuted, but he ran off for all he was worth. They caught up with him and grabbed hold of his beard. It came right off in their hands! Well, I thought that was a little too much—I'd just told them to hold him, not to pull off his beard. But it was a fake beard, like actors use. He didn't have a hair on his head, either, under his hat. Whan I started to question him, it turned out that he was the priest in charge of the temple to Kuan-kung [of the beautiful beard].

If you want to talk about the jail, there are even stranger goings-on there! There's one female convict, not more than twenty years old and not bad-looking. Her rooms are set up like a corner of heaven. She wears heavy silk and has two maids to wait on her. I can't imagine how all those things and maids got in—can you? I just had all the jailors beaten fifteen strokes each and locked her up tight on the rack. I guess I'll have her beaten tomorrow, and bring this to the authorities' attention."

Ch'ao Yüan said, with manufactured surprise, "I'm afraid you must be talking about my concubine! She's been wrongly accused and sentenced to death by strangling. Now she's fallen into prison, I sent two maids to keep her company. She must be the one Your Benevolence is talking about. I was meaning to come beg Your Benevolence to look after her, but I hadn't yet prepared a suitable token of my great filial respect, so I still didn't dare make my request. Please let me wait on you tomorrow with a small expression of my sincere regard. If the person you just mentioned is my concubine, may I beg Your Benevolence to condescend to show her kindness?"

The warden rushed to reply expansively, "I'll look into it the moment I get back. If she is your dear one, I'll take care of everything."

Then the magistrate got up to go and wouldn't stay even though Ch'ao Yüan tried to pour him another drink.

"Good wine, " the magistrate said, "I got drunk before I knew what was happening."

Ch'ao Yüan said, "Then I hope Your Benevolence will allow me to pay a call in the morning, as we said, and with some wine I hope you will open yourself. Don't let any servants go ruining it by opening it incorrectly!"

The warden understood him perfectly, and took his leave. As soon as the warden entered his own gate, he called the jailor on duty.

"Let that prisoner off the rack and put her back in her room. A pretty woman like that can't take being roughed up, and if you hurt her, there'll be trouble."

Then he turned his horse to the yamen residence.

The yamen servants muttered resentfully, "You shouldn't have done that! You had a good thing there, but that Ch'ao Yüan's the meanest man in town! He breaks every bridge he crosses."

The warden said, "Don't worry about it. When I tell him to cross a bridge, not only will he go without breaking it, he'll turn around and fix the bridge with his own hand and then I'll have him build another little bridge just for you. Why else would I have put her on the rack?"

They all withdrew, but kept nattering away behind his back.

"This is some pretty sight! All he got was a few drinks and some talk he could have heard anywhere, and he's ready to let her go. She's a nice juicy one, too," some said.

Others said, "Never mind that, haven't you ever seen that little devil lying his way right out of King Yen Lo's palm?"

The next morning, not giving the warden any time for second thoughts, Ch'ao Yüan got up very early, and picked two big, round wine jugs, labelled as holding the best wine. Thinking that the sixty taels he'd prepared the night before might not be enough to satisfy the warden, he opened the seals on the jugs and added another twenty taels, so that each jug held forty taels. Then, considering that when you want to get on the good side of a man it's always wise to consider his woman, Ch'ao Yüan added to each jug a bracelet worth five taels and ten gold rings, each weighing as much as 1.5 cash. He wrapped the jugs in soft red cloth. He also packed up two stones of husked rice and wrote a note begging the warden to accept his humble salutations. He gave Ch'ao Chu ten taels to treat the warden's servants, and sent him off with the rice and the wine jugs for the warden.

The warden's servants were all pleased, and when the warden saw the jugs he ordered a servant to pour the wine out. Then all the things on the bottom of the jugs tumbled out. The warden's wife didn't care about the silver, but when she saw the bracelets, which were of fine Hui-chou craftsmanship, she was so full of smiles thay almost came out of her behind as well as her mouth. She urged the warden to have Ch'ao Chu taken back to the servant's quarters for a good meal, and to give him a tael of first-quality silver.

The warden repeatedly assured Ch'ao Chu, "About last night, I never had the slightest idea who she was or I would never have dared harm her the tiniest bit. As soon as I got home, I had her untied from the rack and let rest in her room. Please tell your master that I thank him, and that from now on, any little thing he wants, he only has to let me know and I'll see to it."

With a thousand thanks, he saw Ch'ao Chu out, but then the yamen servants went after Ch'ao Chu, and insisted he let them wine and dine him. They all said they would do their best for him from now on. And from then on, the warden and Ch'ao Yüan got along very well. Whenever the warden went down into the jail, he would stop by Chen ko's room and greet her from the doorway. Then he'd say a few reassuring words to her. He ordered the other female convicts to wait on her respectfully, and "not get out of line". He let them know that out of respect for her position, they would all be treated with more lenience, but they'd land on the rack if they forget their place. When the other convicts saw the warm blaze of Chen ko's rooms, and the abundance of tea and rice she and her maids couldn't finish, they gathered round, and soon the skinny sallow lot of them grew plump and glossy. Even the warden's wife frequently sent in special snacks.

The clerk of the yamen's criminal office, Chang Jui-feng, saw how pretty Chen ko was, and every spare moment he had, he was offering her every service she might want. It was only because there were too many eyes and ears around that he didn't make his move.

After New Year's, the weather began to get warmer. Chen ko's room, no matter how well-appointed, was after all a small room full of people, and infested with fleas and bedbugs that proliferated with each day's passing. There was some land standing vacant within the yamen precincts where she wanted to have new accomodations built. Ch'ao Yüan discussed it with the warden, who said it was no problem. Then the warden called a jailor in, whom he instructed to do so-and-so and this-and-that. The jailor said he would, and left.

When the magistrate opened court, the warden handed him a petition, and said, "The women's jail is about to fall to the ground. I request permission to have an estimate made on the necessary repairs."

Then the warden took a builder to look at the women's jail and note the cost of everything to be repaired, with the result that the builder determined all the walls would need complete rebuilding. The warden took this opportunity to have a good-sized house with a southern exposure built for Chen ko. One full-sized room became her living quarters, and the smaller room at the back, cross-ventilated by doors on either side, was her porch. Behind that a tiny kitchen was built. The roofing was finished, clever little windows set in the walls, and a brick k'ang built against the northern wall. All of her furniture and bedding was new, to avoid bedbug infestation. She divided her old things between the inmates.

A wall was built around her new house, so she had her own courtyard. Her maids came in and out freely, and she lived more as if she were in a garden than a jail. Meanwhile Ch'ao Yüan was improving his friendship with the warden, and two days out of any three he visited Chen ko. When he did, he generally stayed half the day. He had heavily bribed all the jailors, and at New Year's he gave them a fat pig, a big jug of wine, three tou of grain and also five hundred cash each. The clerks in the criminal office of the yamen also received his holiday greetings. Anyone on the yamen staff who met Ch'ao Yüan on his way in or out treated him with more respect than a director of the post would have gotten. The other inmates crowded into Chen ko's new house, too, drawn by its pretty decor and comfortable courtyard. Sometimes Ch'ao Yüan stayed for several days at a time, completely neglecting the affairs of his own household.

On the seventh day of the fourth month, Ch'ao Yüan brought two jugs of wine, steamed cakes, and many other delicacies into the jail in order to celebrate Chen ko's birthday. As evening fell, the warden came back to the yamen, from a visit to the office of the bureau of grain transport. The warden heard a gale of laughter and song coming out of the jail. He took his keys and went to open the door. Inside, he found jailors and prisoners lying down, drunk to the point they didn't even notice he had come in. Ch'ao Yüan hid inside the house.

The warden called Chen ko and counselled her, "It's all right for you to treat the others to a little wine, but think how terrible it would be if we had a fire when everyone was drunk."

He called his servants to clear up the remnants of the feast, sent the inmates to their own rooms and had the jailors shaken awake. You can imagine that if the new magistrate of Wu-ch'eng had been in to see his jail, he would have been quite surprised. However, the magistrate was always busy with guests, or settling into his chair in court, or closing court, so he never had time for things like visiting the jail. Not only did the jailors and other employees take bribes, they tormented the inmates a hundred different ways in order to extract bribes out of them. If the subprefecture of Wu-ch'eng had been governed by a proper official who regularly walked through his jails and kept his eye on everything, nobody would have dared rebuild a women's prison that had been perfectly good to start with. Nobody would have dared build a walled house on vacant ground there, or let outsiders come in and out as they pleased. But the magistrate of Wu-ch'eng cared only for fining people silver, fining them great papers, fining grain and fining bricks. So what was the jail to him?

Under this magistrate's administration, a man named Meng, who became the acting subprefect was up all night, every night, conducting hearings and he still couldn't keep up with the work, so naturally he never got around to inspecting the jail, either. There must have been guardian spirits watching over that jail the day of Chen ko's birthday party, because it all just blew over. Subprefect Meng had gone home early, so the warden was able to cover it up. Ch'ao Yüan stayed over at Chen ko's house, and the next morning he saw Ch'ao Feng led in by Chü Chiu-chou.

Ch'ao Feng kowtowed and said, "Your parents haven't heard from you in such a long time, they decided to send me to see how you're doing. They told me to say that since the lawsuit is finished, you should go to your father immediately. He has something urgent to discuss with you."

Ch'ao Yüan said, "Show me their letter."

Ch'ao Feng said, "It's at your house; I didn't think it was a good idea to bring the letter here."

"Are my parents well?" asked Ch'ao Yüan.

Ch'ao Feng said, "You're father's been so worried by your lawsuit that he couldn't sleep. His hair and beard have turned as white as white jade, so he began to dye it, and now it looks awful, all greeny. You mother's so thin she's a sight and she cries all the time. People are looking hard for Liang and Hu, and your parents are afraid they can't hide those two much longer. That's what they wanted to talk to you about."

Ch'ao Yüan said, "If that father of mine can't even take care of a little thing like that, I don't know how he ever managed to become an official. He should know better than to worry about me letting any lawsuit get in my way, so what's he upset about? What good does that do? As far as Liang and Hu go, all he has to decide is whether or not he can help them out. If he can, fine; if not, we can take care of ourselves without them."

Ch'ao Feng said, "But that's just what your father can't decide. After all, they did do us some favors, so he can't just abandon them."

Ch'ao Yüan said, "That's the stupidest thing I ever heard. Do you think they would have done us any favours if we hadn't paid them thousands of taels? I think we should get our money back."

Ch'ao Feng didn't say anything more. He walked back to the kitchen, where he got himself a drink and some food. Ch'ao Yüan dressed and was ready to go with Ch'ao Feng.

Chen ko pulled at Ch'ao Yüan's sleeve and pouted coquettishly, "I won't let you go. You'd better stay with me when I say so, or I'll go hang myself the minute your gone and haunt you the rest of your days, cursing you with your baby name."

Ch'ao Yüan said, "Just let me go have a look at this letter. I'll talk to you later."

"When are you coming back?" she asked.

"I'll see how it looks. If I can't come back today, I will tomorrow."

Ch'ao Yüan went home. All of his servants and maids listened while he read his parent's letter aloud. The letter was written very simply and plainly, since Ch'ao Ssu-hsiao knew his son couldn't read very well. Ch'ao Yüan managed to stumble through the letter, and all the servants were in tears by the time they finished hearing how his father couldn't sleep nights and his mother's eyes were always swollen and red with weeping.

Ch'ao Yüan ignored the servants' sentimentality and said, "They ought to be able to figure out that I need money after a lawsuit. What good does this thousand they sent do me? I don't think they really care at all about me."

Despite his words, he was turning over in his heart plans to leave for his parents', and he was considering what to do about Chen ko.

The next day, he went to the jail with a lot of food for the yamen staff, and then went back to see Chen ko. She couldn't bear to have him leave, but she finally let him after he said that one of things he would be doing in the capital was looking after her interests. They discussed who would stay behind to take care of her.

Ch'ao Yüan wanted to leave Li Ch'eng-ming and Ch'eng-ming's wife, but Chen ko said, "I don't know what it is about Li Ch'eng-ming, but I just can't get used to him. Why not leave Ch'ao Chu and his wife?"

"That would be the best thing," he said, "except that I can't do without them myself."

That night, Ch'ao Yüan stayed over in jail. Ch'ao Feng went to get Ch'ao Yuan's sister from the Yin household, and wasn't back until two days had passed.

Ch'ao Yüan set the thirteenth day of the fourth month as the date of his departure. Fearing that the land route would be hot, he rented a barge, along with a troupe of musicians to play on board, altogether twenty-eight taels and two taels' gratuity. He had his luggage readied and reserved a prostitute named Hsiao Pan-chiu for company on board, at the rate of five silver cash daily. Her clothes were to be extra, and she would be paid even for the days she spent coming back alone. Everything was agreed and they were ready to go. Several more days passed with preparations in the days and nights with Chen ko. On the twelfth, he went to the yamen to say good-bye to the warden, and give the warden ten taels along with the request that the warden take good care of Chen ko. He also gave two taels each to the yamen servants, for drinking money, and, to the warden's wife, a pair of jade flowers, a jade clip, a jade vase, and a length of Nanking satin with a design of plum branches on it.

The warden cheerfully accepted all of Ch'ao Yüan's gifts. Next, Ch'ao Yüan sent Ch'ao Shu and Ch'ao Shu's wife, to take care of Chen ko. He instructed them to look after Chen ko in the day, and the house at night.

On the morning of the thirteenth, Ch'ao Yüan bid a lingering farewell to Chen ko. She saw him to the jail gate. He called all the jailors over to receive their instructions, asked them again to look after her, and once more produced silver out of his sleeve.

"I'm afraid I may not be back before Tuan-wu, and there won't be anyone here to reward you for all your hard work so you can enjoy the festival. Take these five taels for a few drinks on Tuan-wu."

They all thanked him over and over, and said, "Master Ch'ao, you can relax with us here. We take responsibility for your lady. When you're here, we leave her to you, but when you're gone, we'll treat her just as we do our wives. We won't ever mind work, if it's for her. If she's not every bit as fine when you get back as she is now, then we're all sons-of-bitches, not men!"

Next Ch'ao Yüan called Ch'ao Chu and his wife over and said to them,

"Go in with her now."

He walked out then, his eyes full of tears.

Then he supervised the loading of his barge, locked up his house and sealed the door with paper, left instructions for the caretaker, and got into his sedan chair. He rode to the barge, where he burnt paper offerings and treated all on board to food and drink. Everyone who had come to see him off stood on the shore, watching the barge get underway. They beat drums and let off firecrackers.

The wind was favorable that day, so he had the sail let out, and the boat glided forward. Ch'ao Yüan stood with one hand on Pan-chiu's shoulder, outside the cabin door, but screened by a bamboo curtain. He watched the scenery pass. It was early summer. They passed groves of tenderbudded willows, a few thatched huts, and the blue cloth sign of a tavern. There were women by the river, washing vegetables or clothes or rice. Some were beautiful and some were ugly, but they all had a certain rustic charm. The boat went about three or four li. A temple came into sight, with two young women standing on the riverbank in front of it. One wore a sky-blue long-sleeved robe, and the other was in white from head to toe. They stood there watching as his boat approached. Slowly, they raised their hands in greeting and faced him.

"We two won't see you on your way, but we'll be waiting for you when you come back," they said.

Ch'ao Yüan peered at them, and they were Ms. Chi, in blue, and the fox-spirit, in white. He was so scared every hair on his head stood on end and he was covered with gooseflesh.

He asked Pan-chiu if she had seen anyone.

"Nobody at all," she said.

Ch'ao Yüan knew he had seen a couple of ghosts, and he wasn't happy about it. But there was nothing he could do but try not to think about it too much and forge ahead.

Indeed,

> The blue dragon and the white tiger travel together
> good and bad fortune, calamity and blessings, cannot be
> foreseen

Read on to see what happened.

Chapter Fifteen

A cruel man scorches the earth around his victims
A heartless fellow turns his face away from those in need

How deep the black of the world's situation
How profound its cruelty
Kindness paid out repaid in resentment
The wolf of Chung-shan that turned on
his protector
Looms everywhere

They say they're your friends
But a needle is hidden in the tangled floss
More dangerous than any long trip or precipitous cliff
Spears ranged like a forest
In the small space of their hearts
—to the tune "waves and sand"

Earlier we said how Wang Chen's crimes were huge enough to block the sky, how he wronged his country and cheated his sovereign, humiliated officials and brought calamity on the world. Nobody would deny that he deserved to have his enemies eat his flesh and sleep on his hide. But what I think is that if everyone had put his whole self into standing up and doing the right thing, even Wang Chen would have been shown to be a mere old man with no balls. If all six censors, thirteen circuit intendants, the presidents of all six boards under the cabinet and within the cabinet all the ministers, all the distinguished servitors of the emperor and all of his relatives had joined with upright men and loyal officials throughout the land, terrible in their united seriousness of purpose, to offer their faithful hearts to the emperor, they might well have succeeded and been rewarded with comfortable pensions for life. Even if they failed, I guess they'd all have some meager family resources to fall back on, and wouldn't have starved to death.

So why did everyone bury his tender conscience, put on a wily face and use every scheme he could come up with to curry favor with Wang Chen? If they had all worked together and stood firmly in concert, I can't believe that Wang Chen's net was woven so tightly he could have caught them all and wiped them all out! But somehow, unaccountably, all the men in charge of the country seemed to have gone crazy. Even the members of the cabinet, board presidents and provincial magistrates couldn't seem to stop kowtowing the moment Wang Chen appeared. They competed to call him their father, their ancestor. In my uninformed opinion, there was no need for them to make up to him like that.

The result was that Wang Chen was able to push the emperor into personally leading men into combat at T'u-mu, where the emperor was taken prisoner. With his own two eyes, the emperor saw Essen kill Wang Chen bloodily, and then slice in two Wang Chen's colluders, commanders Su and Liu. In my opinion, they just got what they had coming to them. All Wang Chen's close male relatives, and all who had been enfeoffed through Wang Chen's connivance, were hunted down and killed off with no exceptions, and I say that was the power of the law in action.

Meanwhile, all his adopted "sons" and "grandsons", who had been only to happy to lick his asshole before, now turned away from him, and with their tattered arrows proceeded to attack what was left of his reputation. Some said he hadn't died and was now Essen's follower, and others said that even if he had died, that wasn't enough punishment, and all his relatives no matter how distant, along with all his hangers on must be hunted down and killed, too. They went on and on senselessly. In my uninformed opinion, now he had fallen down the well, it didn't do any good to throw rocks in after him.

Thanks to Wang Chen, Commanders Su and Liu did indeed enjoy a few years of prosperity and prestige, the fragrance of which reached up to heaven, but a man of penetration will readily perceive that this was but a momentary illusion, no more than a dream of Nan k'o or Hantan. Soon enough they fell, lost all they had amassed, and brought grief to their wives. The actor Liang was Commander Liu's nephew, and the actor Hu was Commander Su's grandson. They two had not directly assisted the commanders in wickedness, and they hadn't really taken undue advantage of the connection. All they had done was to earn a thousand taels by helping along the meteoric rise of Ch'ao Ssu-hsiao. They hadn't even gotten offical posts for themselves. They were just small fry, and there was no need for anyone to bother with them, but those worthless turncoats who were now crying in every street with their spiel of 'unclean, traitorous remnants . . . imminent danger . . . lurking bandits" etc. included Hu and Liang among those to be found and arrested. Orders for their arrest, and a hundred taels' reward, were posted. It was generally felt to be vital that all evil co-conspirators be extirpated. Slowly, almost all were taken, but Hu and Liang were well hidden. Nobody in Magistrate Ch'ao's household dared inform on them, and nobody outside dared enter to search for them. It was as good as a refuge of seamless bronze or iron, except that Ch'ao Ssu-hsiao and Ch'ao Yüan both suffered from a small character defect. That is, they were like the Emperor Kao, who liked to kill off all those who had helped him to power.

Despite the cruelty lurking in his heart, Ch'ao Ssu-hsiao didn't quite dare show his true colors. Even after he had thought they had lost all influence, they had helped him by the letter to Hanlin scholar Hsü. But now he was only concerned with saving his own skin, and couldn't see why he should care about them. He tossed and turned nights trying to figure out whether or not he should inform on them. It didn't help to hear the tutor Hsing Kao-men's incessant preachings about the kingly way and famous anecdotes of friends in need, like Lu Chu-chia and Chi Pu, or K'ung Pao and Chang Lien. Ch'ao Ssu-hsiao didn't want to hear Hsing Kao-men's opinion of what he wanted to do, so he hesitated to do it.

Ch'ao Ssu-hsiao was lucky in that he had a virtuous wife who was determined her husband do the right thing. She was not willing to be like the wife of Ch'in Kuei, who abetted her husband in his assassination attempt on Yüeh Fei.

At night, she often said things to him, like, "It's a good thing we left Hua-t'ing when we did. If we'd stayed think what would have happened to us when Chiang Yüan arrived on his special inspection, and all the commoners set with their complaints. We were so fortunate to have Hu and Liang urging us to leave quickly, and then helping you get this fine place. Even though it wasn't for free, it was cheap at the price. It was a good investment, when you consider that this job can't be worth less than two million taels in two years. And it's all thanks to Hu and Liang. Now here we are enjoying this position and all our money, and we should remember the source of the water! Besides, I've heard that Hu and Liang have a lot of other friends and relatives, and yet it's us they've turned to. That shows that they think we're as solid as mount T'ai in their hour of need, and we should live up to their expectations. Push them out on the street to their deaths? By Amitabha Buddha, I can't do that."

Ch'ao Ssu-hsiao listened to her, and each time the flames in his heart were quenched by the cool water of her counsel. He felt he had no choice but to let the two actors continue to take refuge with him.

Nevertheless, Madame Ch'ao's good advice couldn't stand up to the influence of her own son, who was even worse than his father.

Other people feared Ch'ao Yüan as a treacherous and cruel narrow-minded man, but Ch'ao Ssu-hsiao treasured his son's words as if they were the divine utterances of Confucious or Chu Ko-liang.

On the twelfth day of the fifth month, when Ch'ao Yuan's barge reached Chang-chia wan and moored there, the misfortunes of Hu and Liang began in earnest.

Ch'ao Yüan didn't send any messenger to announce his arrival. First he wanted to take his leave of Pan Chiu. Besides all the money he had agreed before to pay her, he now sealed up twenty-five taels. She had also accumulated a pile of clothes on the way. Now he gave her two bracelets weighing four taels worth each, four gold rings, and two gold earrings too, as well as some other miscellanea. He also gave four silver taels to the boat's captain, for food on the return journey. He let Pan Chiu keep everything she wanted from the boat, and gave her attendant two taels of first quality silver. Only then did he send a messenger to the yamen, while the boat began to be prepared to cast off. When it was time for him to disembark, he was still in the cabin with Pan Chiu, up to who knows what. He came out panting.

On the bank, a number of horses and his father's great sedan-chair awaited him. Ch'ao Yüan said goodbye to Pan Chiu, and, a noisy procession clearing the way, went to the yamen.

He went into the back to see his parents and talk about family things. After that, he had his luggage brought in, and went to the library to greet Hsing Kao-men. A while after that he saw Hu and Liang, and said hello to them. Hu and Liang thought he was their sworn brother, so when they saw him, they imagined everything was fine.

After three days passed, Ch'ao Yüan brought up the subject of Hu and Liang to his father. What he had to say was cruel and lacking in all attempt at even concealing his own cold inhumanity. Even with a few more mouths I couldn't repeat it all. Just like the stone listening to the famous Ch'an master expounding, Ch'ao Ssu-hsiao could only listen and nod in assent.

Madam Ch'ao said, "A young man should always remember loyalty and friendship. Don't let a word to the contrary cross your lips, or you'll destroy all your good fortune. I finally had gotten through to your father, and now you start! You knew from the beginning they were no more than actors. Who told you to make up to them, and even swear brotherhood with them, as you did? Listen to me when I tell you, you can't depend on people and then discard them behind you. Stop this talk right now. Please don't blight your fortunes."

But what effect did her advice have have when it went in his donkey's ears? His father egged him on so that he grew even more stiff-necked.

"What do you know, mom? Can you show me anyone who isn't out for himself first? If you start looking out for others, you get your own behind burned. We're officials now, and harboring criminals in our home! Do you know what kind of crime that is? If we turn our backs on imperial orders for the sake of those two, we're talking about total destruction of our clan. That's no joking matter!"

Madam Ch'ao said, "What nonsense. Even if it does come out, never mind 'imperial orders' and 'destruction of our clan'. You just leave it to me."

Ch'ao Ssu-hsiao said, "What does a woman know! Our son, the fine official know best."

Madam Ch'ao said, "All right! But you two don't look ahead."

They had lunch and saw Ch'ao Ssu-hsiao off for the evening session. Ch'ao Yüan went into his father's East Study. He called Ch'ao Feng and Ch'ao Shu.

"Now," he said, "none of your damned tricks. And don't listen to anything my mother says. Those two actors are wanted for crimes against the imperial court and their pictures are everywhere. How dare you let them hide in this house? If it gets out, the loss of my father's job will be the least of our troubles. I'm afraid we'll be left starving and without even a chair to sit in. I was thinking, those two have had our silver, and there's no excuse for their hanging around now. No matter how they dig in, if we really get tough, they have to go. It makes me so mad I can't stand it, they way they won't budge, but now there's a price on their heads, one hundred taels. You two go look at the posters and get the details and I'll write up the surrender. Then I'll have you go take it to the secret police's yamen, and bring back the police to arrest Hu and Liang. This is only between you and me. Don't say a word to my mother, or anyone else. A hundred taels' award! Won't you like that? Fifty taels each!"

Ch'ao Shu looked at Ch'ao Feng and said, "You go. You can have the whole reward. I don't know about it . . . I'm not used to walking around here . . . ."

Ch'ao Feng said, "No, you'd better go. I can't get my heart into it, so I wouldn't be able to do it."

Ch'ao Yüan spit at Ch'ao Feng, "Then you deserve what you get! A pretty tune you two sing! I guess you think a hundred taels would be an awful inconvenience."

They said, "Sir, you had better discuss again with the old master. Don't jump into anything. In our lowly opinions, you shouldn't do this. Hu and Liang have done a lot for us all. Without their help, your father would never have been able to get this job, not even for four or five thousand taels. Even we two stayed four or five days in Commander Su's house, and not a day passed without the best of everything served to us. What did Commander Su care about us for? He did it all for Hu. When they came this time to stay with us, they were just expecting a return of the hospitality they showed us. And what happened in Hua-t'ing, with Chiang Yüan, is another thing to be grateful for. If it wasn't for Hu, how would we ever have found Hanlin scholar Hsü to help us out of that? If it wasn't for Hu's letter, that would have been a fiasco! So what if he is living here now? What if he is down and out? Those southerners have bottom."

Ch'ao Yüan said, "You sound just like that old woman. The minute you open your mouths, it's heavenly principle this, conscience that, and goodness all over. But in today's world, sons hardly even care for their fathers, and brothers sure don't care for each other! And you with your heavenly principles, conscience! Tomorrow I don't want you to eat a thing, unless you eat those words. Don't worry, I can take care of myself if anyone has anything to say about this, and I'll tell them off, too. I know enough to light incense when it's time to pray to Buddha. You just take your behinds out of this and stay out of my way. Watch, and keep your mouths shut. If you let out even a whisper about this, I'll have your legs smashed to bits."

When he had finished covering their heads in ashes this way, he chased them out. Then he put his hands behind his back, hung his head, and paced back and forth in the courtyard. He was thinking up a good plan. Early the next day, he got up, fixed his hair, and went to Hu and Liang's apartment.

He asked, "Did you two bring any money?"

They said, "A little, not much. Why?"

He said, "The prefecture sent a man here asking for a thousand taels to pay for army fodder. They don't care about the quality of the silver. They just want it fast. Right at the moment, we don't have any money in our storehouse, but this requisition is very important, so we're trying to raise the money and plnning to repay everyone once taxes come in."

Liang and Hu said, "You're welcome to what we have, but we won't be able to help to you get any more, being afraid to even look outside. If we put together all we've got, it might come to six hundred."

As they spoke, they took an assortment of coins out of a leather box. It came to six hundred and thirty taels. They gave all but thirty to Ch'ao Yüan.

He said, "Throw in the thirty, too."

He had the bundle tied up in cloth and secured with one of Hu's sky-blue phoenix sashes, then called for a man to take the bundle into his own room. He also told the man not to let Hsing Kao-men, Ch'ao Shu or Ch'ao Feng know about it.

After another day passed, Ch'ao Yüan took a blank paper from the back of one of the notices and wrote a fake report to the secret police. It said that

Hu and Liang were hiding in the home of the District Magistrate of T'ung-chou, Ch'ao Ssu-hsiao, and requested their arrest. He took this report and ran, with feigned panic, into Liang's room, made of show of making sure there were no servants around and then showed the report to Liang.

"It's out!" Ch'ao Yüan said, "Now we're in trouble. There's already been an order sent to the yamen of the secret police, and they're on their way here. We can still get out of it if they don't find you here, but if you are here, it won't just be you, our entire family will be dead thanks to you."

Liang and Hu collapsed into miserable jelly, completely unable to come up with any idea. All they could do was shake in terror.

Ch'ao Yüan said, "There's only one thing to be done. Pack up fast as fire and I'll have someone see you as far as the Hsiang-yen temple, hand you over to the person in charge there and have you hidden inside the double wall behind the Buddha. I've seen the place, and you could hide a year there without a chance of anyone ever finding you. The priest there owes us a favor, because my father helped him out once when he was captured by some bandits. When our servant tells him what to do, he'll be sure to do it. There isn't a minute to be spared, hurry up!"

The two rushed to pack their things, but all they took was a roll of bedding. They abandoned all the clothes they weren't actually wearing.

Liang said, "Give us a few coins, if you can spare any. What if something happens and we need money?"

Ch'ao Yüan said, What good is money now? Anyway, I'll have the servants keep an eye on you, and there will be plenty of time later for me to have one of them bring you money."

Hu and Liang didn't have time to say goodbye to Hsing Kao-men, but they did say, "We should say good-bye to the master and mistress."

Ch'ao Yüan said, "If you're one minute too long here, that's the end of you. They'll be searching in here, so you'd better do without good-byes to my parents."

Ch'ao Yüan said, "You have my detailed instructions. Take them there, and don't make any mistakes."

The two yamen servants said yes, yes, and shouldered the bedding. Then they were off.

The Hsiang-yen temple as about five li out of the western gate of T'ung-chou. The two yamen servants carried the bedding, and they all walked along until they reached the Han-shih bridge, where they stopped a while to rest. One of the servants said he had to urinate, and went down a little road that led under the bridge.

The other servant said, "We still have a good five or six li to go. Let me go get some horses, so that you young gentlemen can ride. That way the trip will be much nicer."

Hu and Liang said, "It isn't so far. We'll be fine if we walk slowly."

The second yamen servant said, "But there are horses for the taking. All I need to do is go get them."

He piled the bedding on the bridge railing, and was gone, just like the first servant.

Hu and Liang waited and paced and fretted, but from morninng until lunchtime, and from lunchtime through the afternoon, they didn't see a trace of either one of the yamen servants.

It was the middle of the sixth month, when the days are long. Hu and Liang were so hungry their stomachs rumbled loudly. It was very hot on the bridge. Fruit sellers and gruel sellers passed by often, but neither Hu nor Liang had even half a piece of paper money. They were so hungry they felt like crying out to heaven, but that wouldn't buy them anything to eat.

Liang and Hu grumbled unhappily, "Those two yamen servants don't respect us, because we're dressed in these old rags. Little they know we're Ch'ao Yuan's sworn brothers. Wait until we see Ch'ao Yüan next and tell him about this. They'll get a beating!"

Then they began to think about how they were wanted criminals, and that what they were doing out there was evading arrest. How could they sit out there in the open on a bridge? It was a good thing they were wearing old rags, and carrying nothing but a couple of thin old quilts, looking unworthy of anyone's attention. They talked it over and decided that the best thing would be to take their bedding and slowly make their way to the Hsiang-yen temple.

"Ch'ao Yüan will have already sent someone ahead with instructions, so if we turn up now and say who we are, of course the priests will put us up."

Each with a quilt piled on his head, they began asking the way. They walked five or six li, and came to the Hsiang-yen temple, a very fine temple. They entered the temple precinct, and then the temple proper, kowtowed to Buddha, and asked for the priest's residence. They found their way into a reception room.

A little acolyte came out and asked, "What are you doing here?"

They said, "We're relatives of the District Magistrate, and he has sent us here, to pay our respects and ask hospitality."

The boy went out, and was gone for a while. Then the abbot came in. He was:

Not under fifty years old
Maybe weighing four hundred catties
Snorting like the Ox of Wu
Fiery-eyed as the tiger of Shu
Pot-bellied as An Lu-shan
Outside he looked the image of Buddha
Inside he had the treacherous innards of Tung Cho
So if you want to talk about his character
It was slimy as a sea urchin

He greeted them at the inner door, and invited them in. After he saw them seated, he asked the purpose of their visit. They were both barely twenty years old, and the abbot noticed that Liang, while pretty, still had some resemblance to a man, whereas Hu was as coquettishly lovely as a girl. Hu's complexion was lustrously tender, not what you would expect to see in a man fallen on hard times. What was he doing in those old clothes? The priest looked a little harder and found that while the clothes they wore were not fancy, they were of good cloth and cut. But if they were really relatives of Ch'ao Ssu-hsiao, why hadn't he sent a yamen servant with them? Even if they were on their way somewhere, it didn't make sense. Why didn't they stay at the yamen? Why should the magistrate send them off to a temple? If they really were relatives, they must have done something awful, and now maybe they were running away from the consequences? But then they would have kept going, not stopped here. The abbot decided to wait and see what shape events would take. He called to have food brought in, and they ate. This temple was very prosperous, having enjoyed the patronage of an empress and being surrounded by large fields which provided sustenance. The abbot was imperially commissioned. He was very rich and lived very well. Although he did observe Buddhist dietary taboos, he was fat and glossy.

After Hu and Liang had eaten, the abbot had a room readied for them, and invited them to rest. He waited until evening, and the lighting of the lamps, but still no messenger with information abou the two came. He treated them to supper and waited a while longer, but still nobody came.

Hu and Liang still hadn't realized that Ch'ao Yüan had tricked them. They thought they had barely escaped the clutches of the secret police, who had probably gone to the yamen and searched it as soon as they left. But, not knowing for sure, how could they relax? They stayed at the temple three or four days, and finally the abbot, who still hadn't heard anything from the yamen about them, began to get suspicious. He asked them to leave.

They said, "All our things and our money are at the yamen. Originally, they said they'd send a man with all that in a few days. How can we leave without them? Let us write a letter. Then you can send somebody with it to the yamen to find out about us." They asked for letter paper and an envelope, and wrote the letter right in front of the abbot, so that he could see what they were writing.

Their letter said:

The other day we bid farewell to our benevolent elder brother, but did not get a chance to say good-bye to the elder master and mistress. We are sorry to inconvenience you with this intrusive notice of our difficulties now. The two men who were sent to accompany us both went off and left us. One said to wash his hands, and the other said to find horses. We waited until late afternoon, when we had no choice but to take our bedding and beg the temple's hospitality. Fortunately, the priest here has treated us most kindly, thanks to his regard for our elder brother. For several days, we have heard nothing from you and we are in a dilemma. Shall we stay or go? We beg our elder brother for instructions. We are penniless and beg for some assistance in this also.
—yours.

After they finished writing, they sealed the envelope with a rice-paste glue. The abbot called a servant who was familiar with the district capital, and told him to take the letter to the yamen and say that 'three days ago two young gentlemen from the yamen came to stay at the temple, and since then they had been waiting for someone to come from the yamen. Since nobody came, they asked us to bring this letter.'

The servant did so, and the letter was taken into the yamen.

Ch'ao Yüan walked over to the message box, and said in reply, "If they were a couple of young gentlemen from the yamen, of course we'd have them stay here. Why would we send them off to a temple? They must be tramps. Send them off with a beating. If you don't, you can be sure they will involve you in punishment for their crimes."

He scared the temple servant so badly the servant ran back hell for leather to the temple, handed the letter back, and repeated what Ch'ao Yüan had said.

Hu and Liang were shocked when they heard it. They paled and were absolutely speechless with anger.

The abbot didn't want them to stay, but Hu was so pretty that the abbot couldn't restrain his illicit thoughts. Some local gendarmes did come with questions, but since the abbot was imperially commissioned, they didn't dare force their way in. They just talked a while, and then left.

Hu and Liang said, "We don't dare take one step out of here. We don't have money, so how can we travel? We may as well die here. Anyway, we'll die no matter what we do."

They told the abbot the whole story, including how they had lent all their money to Ch'ao Yüan before he turned them out, and everything else.

The abbot said, "So that's how it was! It was all Ch'ao Yüan's plot. But you can relax and stay here. I guess we can afford to feed you! You two do as I say: shave off your hair and become priests. Very soon the heir apparent will be changed, and then there will be a general amnesty. Then you'll have plenty of time to let your hair grow and return to the laity. But stay here for now. I suppose that no matter how big the man after you may be, he won't dare come into my temple searching for you.

Hu and Liang said, "If you'll do that for us, we want to be your disciples for life. Never mind returning to the laity! Besides, although we're both engaged, neither of us is married. And if it all turns out well, we'll make sure you haven't lost anything by helping us out."

Later, you'll hear some more about Hu and Liang after they became priests.

Meanwhile, Ch'ao Ssu-hsiao was bedazzled at his son's skillful strategy in forcing Hu and Liang out. He thought his son was Chu Ko-liang incarnate, another Sun P'ang! When he heard the report of the "escorts" that Hu and Liang were sent on their way, Ch'ao Ssu-hsiao felt a great weight and aggravation lifted from him. But when Madam Ch'ao heard her son had chased Liang and Hu away, she was very disturbed in her heart. She was so disturbed she couldn't eat for two days.

She blamed Hu and Liang, also, "Those two are very strange! They were always welcome to come and see me, so why didn't they come to say good-bye? But they just went their merry way. I suppose they were angry at me, too. Why didn't they just put him off a little while? Once they're outside and arrested, who will help them?"

The old woman closed her door and wept miserably and ceaselessly. When she finally stopped crying, there was utter silence.

A maid went to look in her window and screamed, Oh, no! The old mistress is hanging!"

Everyone rushed into her room in a confused flurry of hands and feet, banging the door, breaking the windows, calling Ch'ao Ssu-hsiao, calling Ch'ao Yüan, and reviving the old lady.

Ch'ao Ssu-hsiao interrogated the maids and serving women, who all said, "We don't know why she did it. But she hadn't eaten for two days, and then she closed her door and cried and cried. Then it suddenly got quiet, so we took a peek, and there she was, hanging on the bedframe!"

Ch'ao Ssu-hsiao questioned his wife narrowly on why she had tried to kill herself.

She said, "No reason at all. Just that I thought I might as well while I still have a son to put on mourning for me and give me a funeral. If I wait too long, people will say I have nobody and throw me in a hole in the ground."

Ch'ao Ssu-hsiao said, "I don't know what you're talking about. We have a wonderful son, and I intend to live a long time in order to enjoy all the happiness he brings us. Why are you saying such unlucky things?"

She said, "I may be just a woman, and I haven't had a formal education, but such totally unrepentant cruelty and ingratitude I never saw! If he's going to cut his life short with his foolish behaviour, how can we enjoy a long life? We'd be better off closing our eyes and dying while the dying's good. Who told you to revive me!"

Ch'ao Yüan, though even worse than his father, couldn't help feeling a chill at heart when he heard her condemnation. And she didn't know how he had despoiled Hu and Liang of all their clothes and money before he threw them out.

They all worked hard at talking her around and calming her down. Of course, Hsing Kao-men heard about it.

It is true, as they say, that fortunate winds blow on the virtuous and gales on the cruel. What qualifications did these people have to be vessels of good fortune? And indeed, from here on in, unpleasant things began to happen.

Chapter Sixteen

An Honorable Man must finish what he has begun
A wise mother can see where it will all end

There is goodness in creation
That settles alike in male and female
Turning to firm honor in the craggy-browed
To gentle humanity in the powdered and carmined
Both the tablet and the brush are its vehicles
Men like Mu Sheng early see the state of things
Mothers like Han Yen's foresee their sons' fates
Let a man care for goodness
and then for the boudoir
And the ladies will follow suit

What good is it to hanker after beauties?
To be a prisoner of love
Like a stallion or a bull?
Alas, the fool will not be awakened
He will not hear good counsel
He turns a deaf ear to his mother's pleas
For a man in love spurns all help
and blunders on his way
——to the tune "The elegant sophisticate"

The abbot picked an auspicious day for Hu and Liang to have their heads shaved, and it was done. Liang's name in religion was P'ien-yün, and Hu's name was Wu-yi. They both became the abbot's disciples and were given duties. They and the abbot were amply satisfied with the arrangement.

But now we shall talk about Hsing Kao-men. He was a man of Che-ch'uan in Hopei. Ever since childhood, he had been studious. In his first exams, he was passed as an extra-quota student, and in the second round he was awarded a stipend 'for food'. He didn't particularly bother with mastering the intricacies of the 'eight-legged essay' used in examinations, just wrote what was called for. Instead of concentrating on empty formalities, he applied himself to the study of great books in every discipline, and became a thoroughly informed man thereby. He was not one of those men who go through life ignorant of all books except the *Four Classics* and a few pieces of contemporary writing that enjoyed transient fame.

Even though Hsing Kao-men was the child of an official, his father had been very scrupulous, and was long dead, so the family had barely enough to get by on. But Hsing Kao-men's erudition and generosity of spirit enabled him to be free of the slightest envy towards even the holders of the highest degrees.

The year he went to the provincial capital for his higher exams, when he was waiting to cross the river and enter the city of K'ai-feng, he saw that the boat was already full. There was a man who looked like a Taoist priest who had boarded with a holder of the lower degree. The Taoist priest said aside to the degree-holder that there were too many people on the boat, and they had better get back on land to wait for the next boat.

The degree-holder asked him why, and he replied, "I saw a black aura under people's noses in that boat. It's destined for a calamity!"

But just as he was saying that, Hsing Kao-men, along with a boy carrying his luggage, stepped on the boat.

The priest took one look at Hsing Kao-men, pulled his companion aside again and said, "With a great men like that on board, we'll be safe."

It was just at the time of the autumn floods, when the air was crisp and clear. Before they had gotten halfway across the river, a black tornado blotted out the sky and bore down on the boat. The oarsmen produced a flurry of activity.

A voice from the air said, "We have a Board President here! Don't bother him!"

Immediately the tornado dissolved, and a moment later the boat was across the river. Most of the people in the boat were students on their way to exams, and each was ready to believe that he was the one destined to be board president. It was just like when Emperor Kao of the Han dynasty built a tower to welcome his general, and there were plenty of men who thought he meant them, when it was only Han Hsin he had in mind.

After they had all disembarked, the Taoist priest introduced himself to Hsing Kao-men, and asked about Hsing's background.

When they parted, the priest said, "You must be very careful of yourself. It was your future glory the spirit in the air was talking about. You'll have a minor set-back at first, and be constrained to the narrow confines of mediocrity for a few years, but then your future will be bright and you will live to be one of the Eight."

Hsing took his leave with modest demurs, but he did in fact later become the Intendant of the Hu Kuang circuit, was stripped of his position for a trifle, and before long after that was promoted to a Board Secretary, eventually becoming the President of the Board of Civil Employment. But that all happened later, so there's no need to go into it here.

At the moment, he was only hoping to pass his exam. He did well in the first session, and in the second, too. But in the third round he stumbled over a question and his name was not among those to be interviewed. He was so frustrated he was almost dancing with rage. All he got was a special pass, along with a few others who otherwise wouldn't quite have made the grade. But then he remembered what the Taoist priest had said about a few years of set-back before great success, and he didn't worry anymore, though other people were indignant on his behalf. He relaxed and was a serene and good-tempered as usual.

Hsing's father had a friend named Lu. Lu had studied under the same teacher as Hsing's father, and had taken exams the same year as he. Lu's son, Lu Chieh-t'ui, had gone to the capital and there passed the exam and become a supervising Censor in the Military Board. Because of his father's friendship with Hsing's father, and knowing the current poverty of the Hsing houshold, Lu Chieh-t'ui invited Hsing Kao-men to come live with him in the capital. Lu Chieh-t'ui meant to let Hsing Kao-men have enough money to keep the midnight oil burning, so that Hsing could study without being assailed by money problems.

Lu Chieh-t'ui sent a man to Che-ch'uan to invite Hsing, and to give him the message that one had to see the capital, or be forever a country bumpkin. Hsing got his luggage ready, and returned with the messenger, arriving in less than a month. Both Lu Chieh-t'ui and Hsing Kao-men were happy to see each other again. Hsing stayed at Lu Chieh-t'ui's yamen for three months straight, and during his time there, met many scholars of the day, enjoyed the famous scenery around, and heard many strange things of the sort that never do get written down.

In his heart, Hsing thought, "This trip has been very worthwhile."

Under the administration of Censor Lu, the military headquarters of the capital were full of interesting activity. Still, eventually, Hsing wanted to go home.

When Lu Chieh-t'ui saw that Hsing was discontented and wanted to leave, he said, "The reason I asked you here is that I know how careful my father's old classmate was not to line his pockets at the public expense, so that now you barely have enough to eat. I'm worried that poverty will interfere with the achievements that should be yours, and I thought if I invited you here I put my arm into the fray for you, and at least keep you in lamp-oil. Besides, you can see what a lot is going on here at the military headquarters. You could learn a lot here, and I'd like to help you by showing you what there is to learn."

Hsing Kao-men told him, "I know you always do what you can—so I won't bother to say any more about that. And I know you would never do anything that deviated in the slightest from moral principles, nor would I ask you to. That would hurt your official standing, and also my image of you. Money, after all, is the lot of some but not of others. What's the good of running after it if it isn't meant to be mine? I already owe you a heavy debt of gratitude for these three months, and I am afraid that staying any longer would be inappropriate."

Censor Lu said, "I really do admire your scrupulosity, but you're going to have a hard life if you are always so unbending."

Hsing Kao-men said, "Oh, I expect I'll always have enough to live hand-to-mouth."

He stayed a few more days, and was in the capital at the time when Ch'ao Ssu-hsiao got his appointment to be the magistrate of Hua-t'ing. Censor Lu and Magistrate Ch'ao, out of mutual respect for their positions, frequently paid courtesy calls on each other and were always very polite.

One day, Censor Lu asked Ch'ao Ssu-hsiao into the yamen for a drink. Hsing Kao-men was one of the party. Hsing Kao-men was like a subtle wine that can't be appreciated by a beggar who only knows raw alcohol and onions, but the qualities of which are intoxicating to the connoisseur. Even though Ch'ao Ssu-hsiao was an ignorant man who couldn't make distinctions in most things, now that he had his silver belt he didn't want to associate with the stink of rotgut and onions, so he felt some respectful interest in Hsing Kao-men. One day, Ch'ao Ssu-hsiao was telling Censor Lu of his need for a tutor as part of his establishment.

Censor Lu said, "It's very hard to find a good tutor. If you don't care about quality, they're all over, but if you want a talented, well-behaved tutor, that's altogether a different matter. If you find one like that, he'll probably be so arrogant you can't stand him. But I have the perfect tutor for you, right here—Hsing Kao-men, who you met the other day. Not only is he talented and well-behaved—he knows what it means to be grateful. He's very easy to get along with, no pretences at all. You'll be very lucky if you can get him."

Ch'ao Ssu-hsiao said, "But I wonder if you can do without him?"

Censor Lu said, "Let me sound him out. I'll get back to you."

He saw Ch'ao Ssu-hsiao out, and then went to Hsing's study. Hsing was looking through looking through the Dynastic Histories while eating some light dishes, dried bamboo shoots and shrimp rice, and drinking a cup of wine.

Censor Lu sat down and began to outline the proposal that Hsing be Ch'ao Ssu-hsiao's household tutor.

Hsing mumbled a little to himself, then said, "Yes, it'll do. Coming here, I have had a chance to know such cultured men and to see such sights that I think if I had remained at home I would indeed have been like the frog in a well who thinks the patch of sky he sees is the whole world. Now I might as well broaden myself some more, by seeing the south as well, and, if I can make a living by teaching, that's what a scholar should do. The giver isn't cheated, nor the receiver humiliated when money is paid for learning. This is really very good for me, and it solves the problem of my living expenses too! Does he truly want me, though? If not, you musn't use your position to make him take me."

"He's only afraid to ask you himself, " said Censor Lu, "He hardly dares expect you'll do him the favor of accepting. Why should I use my position?"

Close to evening, Ch'ao Ssu-hsiao sent a letter asking how it had gone. Censor Lu took the letter and showed it to Hsing. They talked over the details and Lu wrote back to Ch'ao Ssu-hsiao.

Hsing Kao-men said, "It isn't like investing in a business. How can I set a price? Let's leave my salary up to him. Don't put it in the letter."

In the end, Censor Lu just wrote stating Hsing's acceptance.

The next morning, Ch'ao Ssu-hsiao came calling, with his card, which he presented. They were served food and drink, and exchanged the phrases appropriate to the occasion. Ch'ao Ssu-hsiao gave Hsing six taels to help him wind up things where he was, and twenty-four more in earnest of his invitation. Then they were all in agreement about conditions. Hsing K'ang-men said good-bye to Censor Lu, and planned to go home to relax a little before going to Hua-t'ing. He rented a mule, and Ch'ao Ssu-hsiao gave him eight taels for travelling expenses. With the eight taels, Hsing hired two men to attend him home, and thence to Hua-t'ing. Censor Lu gave Hsing one hundred taels, then twenty more as a parting gift, and also sent another man to accompany Hsing home.

On the evening of the day that Ch'ao Ssu-hsiao took office in Hua-t'ing, Hsing Kao-men arrived there, and entered the yamen, dressed in his offical robe.

Ch'ao Ssu-hsiao got his job by being a tribute student, and before that he had only been a backwater schoolmaster. All he knew were the rudiments of what every child studies. Now he was to put a gauze hat on his head, a round-collared robe on his shoulders, and black officials' shoes on his feet. He had to take his seat facing all the yamen servants from the six offices of his yamen, and also innumerable farmers and soldiers, all of whom he had to impress with suitable address, while carrying out his official duties fittingly.

And, as they say, you can't expect an old villager to read funeral odes. He could thank his lucky stars he had Hsing Kao-men there. Hsing's family had long experience in the official arena, and he had seen official life up close. Moreover, he himself was destined to be a board president. His talents and knowledge were on a completely different plane from most people's. Thanks to him, the only affairs that Ch'ao Ssu-hsiao had to see to personally were actually sitting in the daily two sessions of court, visits to superiors, and putting in an appearance at exam time. Except for these few pro forma duties, every role in the yamen was played by Hsing Kao-men, and in fine style. He never got too familiar with the servants, or hung around the message box to gossip with outsiders, so nobody outside the yamen even knew that there was any Master Hsing in there at all. In recognition of how well Hsing was carrying it all off, Ch'ao Ssu-hsiao was always very respectful to him, even though Ch'ao Ssu-hsiao was too ignorant to recognize Hsing's true worth.

Oddly enough, even Madam Ch'ao somehow knew how to treat a man like Hsing, despite the fact that her upbringing had been rustic, and her father, though formerly wealthy, nothing more than a villager after all. When her father picked a holder of the lower degree to tutor Chi Pa-la, he didn't call the tutor "elder" or "professor" as would have been proper. He called him the "Book-worker", just like the wood-worker, the brickworker and all the other laborers. One day, a lot of wheat was spread out to dry in the sun, when suddenly rain began to pelt down. The house was under renovation, so there were many workmen around—bricklayers, carpenters, mortarers, and bronze and iron workers, and they all laid down their specialized implements to pick up brooms and help sweep up the grain, working along side of the common laboreres and villagers to save the grain. Fortunately, they did get the grain in just before the rain became torrential.

Old Mr. Chi said, "We're so grateful all you specialists pitched in and kept our grain from being soaked."

He ran down the list of who had helped, and noted that the book-worker had not.

Another day, Old Mr. Chi was drinking with a couple of relatives, and he sent a servant boy to get the tutor.

"Tell that book-worker to come out here and have a drink. Why should we bother serving him in there?"

The servant boy went into the library and told the tutor, "Book-worker, you're wanted out front. You'd better get out there, so we don't have the trouble of serving you here."

The tutor was so mad he wore himself out with cursing filthily. Then he packed up his books and left.

So it was quite surprising that Madame Ch'ao, coming from such a family, was always very careful of Hsing, making sure he had his three meals a day, his clothing for the four seasons, and all the other little things he needed. If it been up to Ch'ao Ssu-hsiao, he would certainly have blundered offensively. Hsing Kao-men was only mildly grateful to Ch'ao Ssu-hsiao. The bulk of his gratitude went to Madam Ch'ao, and it was for her sake that he exerted all his energy in serving his employer in every matter that came up.

Later, when Ch'ao Yüan came to Hua-t'ing, he didn't dare to act openly insolent to Hsing Kao-men, but his arrogant swaggering was very hard to bear, and Hsing couldn't help wondering when the obnoxious young man would leave.

If Ch'ao Yüan claimed that something was east and west, Hsing, in his heart, knew it was north and south. Hsing never meant to offend Ch'ao Yüan the tiniest bit, but it wasn't surprising that a young man like Ch'ao Yüan, who was always ready to rudely criticize his parents, was hardly likely to be prostrate with respect for a mere tutor. And then, Ch'ao Yüan didn't think Hsing was obsequious enough, had no idea how to treat a man! Hsing Kao-men didn't appear to notice Ch'ao Yüan's expectations, and maintained his usual calm and equitable manner. Ch'ao Yüan felt he could easily show up Hsing if it came to a showdown, but it never did, since Hsing was always correct though relaxed, and never gave any grounds for plausible offense.

Ch'ao Yüan felt a spite in his heart which began to overflow into his speech, but out of consideration for his parents he did not quarrel with Hsing. Later, Hsing went with Ch'ao Ssu-hsiao to T'ung-chou, and learned that Ch'ao Yüan had abandoned his legal wife and brought instead his whore of a concubine to his father's official post. Then Hsing knew that Ch'ao Yüan was not merely undisciplined but utterly lacking in principles. Then when Hsing observed Ch'ao Yüan had sworn brotherhood with the actors Hu and Liang, he understood that Ch'ao Yüan was shameless and had no idea of people occupying their correct places in society. He thought it was even more abominable that Ch'ao Yüan had pushed his wife into suicide, by listening to the slanders of his concubine. When Hsing found out how Ch'ao Yüan had squeezed every item of worth out of Hu and Liang before chasing them out, Hsing decided Ch'ao Yüan was even worse than the wolf that ate Tung Kuo. Now, Ch'ao Yüan's sweet old mother was so ashamed of her son that she had tried to kill herself, and Hsing felt it was no longer enough to stand aside and silently sympathize with her. This vicious behaviour would certainly bring disaster down on them, and wouldn't Hsing be implicated in any disaster that came, for being on good terms with Ch'ao Yüan? He had better leave now, he thought. What was he waiting for?

Hsing made the excuse that he wanted to go home and prepare for an examination. When he told Ch'ao Ssu-hsiao so, Ch'ao Ssu-hsiao knew quite well the next examination was a long time away, but didn't argue with Hsing. He figured that since he had his marvellous son by his side, he didn't need Hsing Kao-men anymore. Ch'ao Yüan was eager to see the last of Hsing, and eagerly encouraged his father to let Hsing go.

Ch'ao Ssu-hsiao arranged a good horse for Hsing, and men to accompany him, picked an auspicious day, and sent him off with a banquet. It was all in all a very proper farewell.

After Hsing was gone, Ch'ao Yüan moved into Hsing's rooms and began to take over Hsing's duties. He should have asked himself what qualifications he had to do so, as in fact he had none. In no time, he had managed to tangle up all the affairs of the yamen. So Chang's complaint was attached to the report on Li's case, and regulations on penal servitude were filed under capital punishment. The highest position on the circuit was held by a man who should have been addressed as "government counsel" but Ch'ao Yüan sent him correspondance addressed to the "administrative assistant". When that same offical's wife died, Ch'ao Yüan sent a letter with an allusion to the official's lamented father, by means of an incorrect locution which he in his ignorance thought meant 'lamented wife'. The official replied with a fulmination at the idiotic and disrespectful wording of Ch'ao Yüan's letter.

Ch'ao Yüan just stuck his nose in the air and told his father, "He doesn't even know the reference, and he has the nerve to say I don't write well."

Ch'ao Ssu-hsiao commiserated with his son about the man's unreasonable touchiness, and never told his son to look it up and see if he had in fact used the reference correctly. All of this happened less than a month after Hsing Kao-men left.

Madam Ch'ao frequently saw her later father-in-law, Ch'ao Yüan's grandfather, in her dreams. The grandfather would cry and cry, hanging onto her, saying that Ms. Chi still had that red sash-around her throat and was still fighting with Ch'ao Yüan. Grandfather Ch'ao told Madam Ch'ao that he had seen Ch'ao Yüan kneeling in a tribunal of the spirits in the yamen, In the judge's seat, there had been a spirit wearing a red robe and a golden head-dress, while a crowd of demonic court servants lined the sides of the room. Grandfather Ch'ao had not been able to hear what was said, but he had seen

Ch'ao Yüan kowtow a few times, and the judge write a few lines in the register. This had happened several times. When the ghostly judge left the room, he gave a tiny red banner to one of his underlings, who stuck the banner on Ch'ao Yüan's head, and a tiny yellow banner, which was stuck in front of Madam Ch'ao's window. Madam Ch'ao was continually troubled by unlucky dreams, ever since her suicide attempt, and she couldn't find a moment's peace. She was also very distressed at her son's wilfulness, now that the restraining influence of Hsing Kao-men was gone, and Ch'ao Ssu-hsiao completely indulgent towards his son.

One day, she called Ch'ao Shu and said, "There must be a good priest at the Hsiang-yen temple. It enjoyed the patronage of an empress, after all. Take these twenty taels to the abbot there and ask him to have two monks fast and chant the Kuan-yin sutra. Then give them more of this money, for expounding the sutra, and come back and tell me about it."

Ch'ao Shu did as he was told. First he changed into new clothes, put three taels in his sleeve, and then he went with a yamen servant to the Hsiang-yen temple. When he arrived at the abbot's residence, he ran into Hu, coming out.

Hu was wearing a gauze, tasselled "calabash" hat, a straight robe of chestnut colored sheer Hu-chou silk, priest's shoes and sparkling white socks, and he was on his way to place a lotus, held in his hand, on the altar.

At first Ch'ao didn't recognize this bald man, but Hu recognized Ch'ao Shu well enough. They were happy and surprised to see each other. They told each other what they were doing there. The abbot had gone out that day, to attend the birthday party of a palace Eunuch. Liang came out to see Ch'ao Shu. They prepared a vegetarian meal, and treated Ch'ao Shu. Then they told him the whole story of how Ch'ao Yüan had borrowed all their money and them cursed them out without one coin or change of clothing.

"And he wouldn't even let us say good-bye to the old mistress. He sent two yamen servants to see us to the temple, but they only took us as far as the bridge before they ran off, one pretending he had to urinate and the other that he was going for a horse. We had to make our own way here. We were very fortunate that the abbot was kind enough to let us stay. Ch'ao Yüan said he was going to send somebody with our things, but after three or four days with nobody coming, we sent a letter. The abbot had a man take our letter to the yamen but Ch'ao Yüan wouldn't accept it. He went to the message box himself and was swearing bastard this and bastard that. He wanted to arrest the man! Then he sent a couple of petty officials to chase us out of here, too, and if we had had even five taels, we'd have used them to go home, in the south. But there we were without one coin to our names, so how could we go anywhere?

We told the abbot how it was, and he said that since we had no money and were
wanted, we'd be running into a trap if we left the temple, so we'd be better off
shaving our heads and staying here until the next general amnesty.

That's why we're here for now. It was bad enough of Ch'ao Yüan to make
up that dirty plot against us, but we feel even worse about Madam Ch'ao letting
him do it. Then there's you and Ch'ao Feng. Remember how well we always
used to get along? But after we left, we never heard from you, and you weren't
anywhere to be seen when he chased us out."

At first, Ch'ao Shu was struck dumb by their story, but then he said, "If
it weren't for your telling me this, even we servants wouldn't know a thing
about it, let alone the old lady. It was all done by Ch'u Chiu-chou, Li Ch'eng-
ming and the rest. Two days before you left, Ch'ao Yüan called me and Ch'ao
Feng, wrote a surrender, and wanted us to take it to the yamen and give you
up. He wanted the reward. We wouldn't do it, so he yelled at us for a while
and then started pacing back and forth, thinking up that dirty plot of his. You
say you feel bad that Madam Ch'ao let him do it, but she didn't know a thing
about it. Ch'ao Yüan just told her you were wanted, and that he was afraid the
whole clan would be wiped out for sheltering you. He told her that he wanted
to get rid of you, but no matter how many times he asked, she wouldn't give
her permission. She was trying so hard to talk him out of it, that he decided
to do what he wanted behind her back. The day he did, we didn't know what
was going on until we found out at breakfast that you'd gone. Later, the old
mistress found out, and she was so upset she didn't eat for two days. She cried
and cried and tried to hang herself, too, but she was saved."

Shocked, Hu and Liang said, "She was going to hang herself for us?"

"No, not for you, exactly. She said that if her son was going to behave like
that, he wasn't long for this world, so she had better die while she still had a
son to bury her properly. Otherwise, when her time came, she'd be treated like
a woman with no family. She doesn't know about Ch'ao Yüan taking your
money and clothes. How much did you give him?"

Hu said, "Together we scraped up six hundred and thirty taels. We tried
to keep the odd thirty taels, but he wouldn't let us. He tied it up in a blue cloth,
and fastened that with a sky-blue phoenix sash. Li Ch'eng-ming carried it off.
We also gave him four leather cases which contain quite a few things made
of gold and pearls, and also clothes, worth money. All together, it must be
worth seven or eight hundred taels. Can we ask you to speak to the mistress
about this for us? He can keep the cases, but we wish that he'd give us back
the money."

Ch'ao Shu said, "I wouldn't dare say a word about you to the old master. If Ch'ao Yüan farts, the old master acts like he's smelling flowers! But I will tell the old mistress, in secret. I'm sure she'll think of a way."

Ch'ao Shu finished eating, got back on his horse, and returned to the yamen. He saw that there was nobody around to overhear, so he told Madam Ch'ao all that he had heard at the Hsiang-yen temple. It was like a bowl of ice water dumped on her head.

She thought, "Who but an ogre, or some animal like a tiger or wolf, or some person totally lost to all sense of humanity could be cold-blooded enough to do something like this? How can this be? I can't believe it! Maybe he threw them out, and they're so mad they're making up the rest? It doesn't matter so much about their things, but the money! They say that Li Ch'eng-ming took it, so I'd better call him and ask him about it, without anyone else knowing. Or, no, he's one of the ones who plotted against Hu and Liang, so he wouldn't tell me the truth anyway. If I let on that I've heard about this, my son may track down how I learned it, and then Hu and Liang will be in even worse trouble. Ch'ao Shu's life wouldn't be worth much, either."

She couldn't decide what to do and was full of doubt. By chance, Ch'ao Yüan didn't eat lunch that day. He said that he didn't feel well and stayed in bed. Madam Ch'ao, with a belly full of worry, went to see him. He had the cold shakes.

She saw that, and said, "Let me get something to cover you. There was a padded quilt on the leather case at the foot of the bed. She pulled at it, and found it was weighed down by a blue cloth bundle, so heavily that she couldn't move it. The bundle was tied with a sky-blue phoenix sash, in a criss-cross. That was when she knew that what Hu and Liang had told Ch'ao Shu was true. Now that she knew her son had really done such a terrible thing, and seeing him sick, she feared he was suffering the swift and just reward for his bad behaviour. She was so terrified she didn't know what to do. She wanted to tell her husband about it, and restore the money and clothes to Hu and Liang, but when she stopped to think she realized that her husband would never listen to all her good advice, and would certainly side with his son, no matter what awful thing his son had done. He'd never thwart Ch'ao Yüan.

If she didn't make up the loss of the money and clothes to Hu and Liang, it would amount to the same thing as is she had sent the servants to abandon them or surrender them to the authorities! No, she couldn't do that. She had a little secret money put aside. It might not be enough, but what good would it do her? She'd better use it to pay this debt. It would be better to be sure there was nobody cursing her family.

The next day, she sent Ch'ao Shu to the Hsiang-yen temple again, this time with two hundred taels in his sleeve.

The abbot still hadn't returned.

In accordance with Madam Ch'ao's instructions, Ch'ao Shu said, "The mistress never dreamt such a thing had happened, but she does have a little of her own money put aside, which you are very welcome to if it can even partially repay you. Here are two hundred taels to start with. Please take it! I'll bring the rest little by little. If it's possible, I'll bring your cases, too, but if not, we may have to forget about them. She's afraid that if she asks Ch'ao Yüan for the cases, he'll start plotting your murders. She begs you to please not curse the family, out of consideration for her."

Hu and Liang said, "Amitabha Buddha! We wouldn't do that! We hate him, but we wouldn't stoop to cursing his whole family behind their backs! In fact, we'll pray to her health and long life. There's no reason for us to curse her."

They kept Ch'ao Shu to a vegetarian meal, after which he returned to the yamen and told Madam Ch'ao how it had gone.

After another day passed, the abbot returned to the temple.

He told Hu and Liang, "You two are really lucky. You don't even have to wait for an amnesty. I've already met with the grandson of one of the secret police, and he's had the orders for your arrest recalled. They'll never be seen again. If you want to go outside the temple now, there won't be anyone searching for you."

Hu and Liang thanked him profusely. They told him about Madam Ch'ao's commissions to read the Kuan-yin sutra, and also about their conversations with Ch'ao Shu. From root to twig they told the abbot exactly how Madam Ch'ao wanted to make up all their losses, and had begun with two hundred taels.

The abbot said, "Now, that's a strange story! How could such a virtuous mother have a verminous son like Ch'ao Yüan?"

He sighed in amazement and pondered the question.

Hu and Liang raised a small altar to Madam Ch'ao, which they placed in their room. Morning and evening they burnt incense to her, and prayed for her good fortune and longevity.

The abbot had the inner precincts swept and had four Ch'an priests who had never touched wine or violated their religious vows set an auspicious day to read the sutra for Madam Ch'ao.

A couple of days later, Madam Ch'ao sent Ch'ao Shu with four boxes of cakes, four of snacks, and two catties of "heavenly pool" tea for the enjoyment of the four Ch'an priests. The abbot met Ch'ao Shu, and treated him to a vegetarian meal, just as Hu and Liang had done before. Ch'ao Shu took two hundred and thirty taels out of his sleeve, which he took to Hu and Liang's room and openly handed them. They set a day for the exposition of the sutra. Ch'ao Shu brought a lot of other things as offerings and for the priests, but there's no need to go into detail about them.

After Ch'ao Shu had paid back every last bit of the six hundred and thirty taels, Hu and Liang gave him a key.

"This opens our cases. Please let the old mistress open them and see if she wants anything in them. She'll see that we've been telling the truth, but also we want her to take this key as a receipt acknowledging we received all the money from you. Please tell her, too, that the abbot has spoken to the grandson of one of the secret police about our problem, and the orders for our arrest have been recalled, so she shouldn't worry any more about us."

Full of thanks and blessings, they saw Ch'ao Shu out.

Indeed,

> Every water-plant flows out to the sea
> Every life is in encounter with others

Read on to see how it ended.

Chapter Seventeen

A fevered man grows empty-hearted and sees a ghost
A venal official gives up his position and goes home

There are thieves because of hunger
There are bandits because men are pushed to the limit
If all can eat their fill and all are clothed
Why should they chase around robbing each other?

Shameless abandon is what ghosts cannot bear
Injustice and gratitude is what brings them crowding
If they have come to attack the son with illness
and the father with loss of position
What wounded conscience that shows!
—to the tune "Mu-lan hua"

As we were saying, Ch'ao Yüan didn't feel well that morning, and he lay down without eating lunch. He felt as though he were lying on ice. After he endured chills for a while, he grew fevered, and he came down with malaria. From then on, he had two attacks a day. As the sun set, he felt the fever's onset, and the fever wouldn't break until after breakfast the next day. Then he slowly came to himself, but still haunted with visions of ghosts. All night he called for people to come and protect him from ghosts, worrying and panicking his mother until her eyes were as black as cooking pots and her hair like a tangled skein. Eventually, Ch'ao Yüan began to see the fox spirit he had shot dead the year before. She was still beautiful, and dressed in white. She came to him holding Ms. Chi's hand. Sometimes she fanned him cold, heated him with fire, or poured boiling water over him. All the game he had killed followed her, and they all bit and clawed him, as he told people.

He had been babbling about those ghosts a day or two when he saw Hu and Liang come in with a cangue and accompanied by yamen servants in dark clothes. They had a warrant from the secret police, and they had come to Ch'ao Yüan's room to get their silver and clothes, and to take him to the military police yamen to give testimony. This vision scared Ch'ao Yüan so badly he leaped naked under his bed and huddled there under a mat. There he howled all night, while Madam Ch'ao worked hard appealing to heaven and praying to the spirit of the great dipper, sacrificing meat and making vows.

Madam Ch'ao asked Dr. Cheng, who was government doctor, to try and cure her son. However, Dr. Cheng himself was incapacitated with malaria and couldn't come. One of the doormen said that he'd heard of a Taoist priest named Lang at the temple to the city god. This Lang was said to have a magic potion that was an infallible cure for malaria. Madam Ch'ao asked Lang to come.

As it happened, the Taoist priest Lang came at the same time as Dr. Cheng, and they were invited together to come into Ch'ao Yüan's room, Before they'd even settled into their seats, Dr. Cheng's teeth began to clatter and his whole body to shake in a violent attack of malaria. Everyone knew already that he had malaria, so they didn't think much of it. But then the priest too, began to behave very strangely. Just after he wrote up his charm, put on his ceremonial robe, and had taken his thunder formula in his left hand and sword in his right, he began to hop around, mumbling incomprehensibly. Somehow the sword got stuck at an angle in the floor, and Lang collapsed in a shuddering mound. He was assisted out of the room, along with Dr. Cheng, to recuperate in the next room, being too incapacitated even to go home.

The opinion of a Buddhist priest was, "If you clean the room, and place a Diamond Sutra in the place of honor, all these problems will clear up."

He was answered, "But there already is a Diamond Sutra which Ch'ao Yüan always keeps near him."

Then the Buddhist priest said, "Have a Lotus Sutra placed on top of the Diamond Sutra. Then things will certainly quiet down."

The Ch'aos sent a man to the temple of the Amitabha Buddha to get a Lotus Sutra. They had the room swept clean and placed the two sutras on an altar. However, Ch'ao Yüan continued seeing ghosts, just as he had before. It didn't do any good. Why do you think that was? If there had been any real spirits floating around there, or wild ghosts, no doubt one look at the sutras would have sent them off. No law-abiding spirit will enter a room where there are sutras. The ghosts that Ch'ao Yüan saw were born out of his own guilty heart. They were not real ghosts that came to beat him.

Take, for example, the ghosts of Hu and Liang. Hu and Liang were at that time alive and going happily about their priestly business. Besides, Madam Ch'ao had returned their money to them, so what would they be doing as spectral visitors with a cangue and demanding their money and things back? Their apparition was entirely due to Ch'ao Yüan's own unease of spirit, which expanded demonically in his fevered imagination. That was why the sutras did not help.

Ch'ao Yüan called out, "Hu and Liang have come with court servants to put me in a cangue and drag me away!"

"Well, *did* you take all their money and silver?" asked Madam Ch'ao.

Ch'ao Yüan told her the whole story, head to tail, with nothing left out, and it matched exactly what Hu and Liang had told her.

Madam Ch'ao said, "So that's what happened! No wonder they're after you. Hurry up and take their things out, so I can return them. That should satisfy them."

Ch'ao Yüan jumped out of bed, and, with his own hands, got out the package of silver. He took that out in front of his mother, along with the four leather cases. Madam Ch'ao had a servant take them all to her room. Later, Ch'ao Yüan told his mother that the ghosts of Hu and Liang had left with the yamen servants. He was never again troubled by visions of them. Only the fox spirit and Ms. Chi continued to plague him, so conditions had improved.

Madam Ch'ao wanted to have a religious service and sacrifice to the fox spirit and Ms. Chi, but she was afraid that would get the neighbors talking, so instead she decided to recite a thousand Kuan-yin sutras to the two spirits. She also directed Ch'ao Shu to take ten taels in his sleeve to the abbot of the Hsiang-yen temple. These were to pay the priests who had read sutras for her before, to pray for her family now, and to pray the spirits of the fox and Ms. Chi would speedily move on to their next incarnations. She also sent Liang and Hu the keys to their cases, and the message that they could come to pick their cases up. She had them told not to worry about the contents of the cases, and that she hadn't even opened them once to look inside.

Ch'ao Shu went off and prepared to do as she said.

Hu and Liang, or Wu-yi and P'ien-yün as they were now known, were visited that night by a spirit general in golden armor and helmet. He held an iron staff in his hand.

When the general arrived, he bowed and said, "I have taken care of your things, and left them in the keeping of a good woman. In the morning, a man will come to notify you, so get some food ready before he comes."

P'ien-yün and Wu-yi woke up, and realized they had been dreaming identical dreams. Then they realized that it was the temple's Veda door guardian who had manifested himself to them in their dreams. Early the next morning, they got up and told the abbot about it.

The abbot said, "Since it's our own Veda who said so, let's get food ready and see who will come."

They hadn't waited long before Ch'ao Shu came to the temple. The abbot and his two disciples looked at each other, surprised and pleased. Ch'ao Shu told them the message about having sutras read for the family's health, and then, in P'ien-yün's room, the whole story of their cases. "P'ien-yün and Wu-yi told him about their dreams.

After that, Ch'ao Shu was going to leave, and said, "I have to be going. With the young master unwell, we're busy at the yamen."

The abbot said, "But our Veda has had food prepared for you—it's waiting now. He's the one who wants you to stay a little longer, not I."

P'ien-yün and Wu-yi then told the abbot about the cases, and everyone agreed it was amazing.

They all went to the Veda's statue and thanked him with prayers. Ch'ao Shu went home after eating, and told Madam Ch'ao what had happened. She was very pleased, and didn't worry anymore about Hu and Liang.

Still, Ch'ao Yüan's illness continued for months with no improvement. He was so thin he looked like a ghost himself, and his mother was so tired she hardly looked human. Ever since Hsing Kao-men had left, Ch'ao Ssu-hsiao had depended on his son as absolutely as a blind man on his stick. Now even the stick was gone, and the paperwork coming out of the six offices of the yamen was in chaos. Out of any ten documents issued, nine were returned by his superiors to be redone, and the one they didn't return was not accepted by them with any great satisfaction. All his superiors were as revolted as if they had smelt piss when they read his documents. It was in this state of disorder that the yamen had to deal with an order to provision troops.

Essen's forces had been violating the borders again. A million taels were raised from the imperial treasury and distributed around the Northern Metropolitan District, to buy the fodder needed by the troops so they could exterminate the enemy. This was so that the provisioning of the troops would occasion no hardship for the farmers. This information, along with ten thousand taels were sent to T'ung-chou. Ch'ao Ssu-hsiao heard the instructions of the clerk of the revenue office, and then packed the ten thousand taels up in his yamen, for his own use. Then he had double assessments of fodder collected at every village, a small collection once in three days, and a large one once in five. The harvest was good that year, and peasants then weren't as miserably poor as they are now, so he was able to gather the whole amount once over again, not short by one kernal or stalk of fodder.

In fact, Magistrate Ch'ao assessed so much that he had three or four thousand taels left over. That, too, went into his private pocket once the extra grain he'd gathered was sold. He divided one thousand taels between the yamen staff, and sent a hundred taels to each major of the troops.

He also got a lot of money from the keeper of the storehouse, pretending it was a collection for charity. Ch'ao Ssu-hsiao took all the paperwork along with the money, so that later the storehouse keeper was accused of embezzling the money he had handed over to Magistrate Ch'ao, and had to sell his own land and houses to reimburse the official treasury.

In those days, farmers were good people. The farmers under Magistrate Ch'ao didn't even fart below the heavy yoke he placed on their shoulders. These days, they are determined to drag their persecutors down to Hell to be heard in front of King Yen Lo if they can't get a hearing in court.

Ch'ao Ssu-hsiao went on in his wicked way until one day a cabinet member, named Hsin, arrived. When this member of the cabinet had been a Hanlin scholar he had been sent to the fief of the Prince of Chiang-hsi, and he had passed through Hua-t'ing. In Hua-t'ing, his travelling documents were pigeon-holed a few days and his routine request for grooms denied. Ch'ao Ssu-hsiao. then magistrate of Hua-t'ing didn't treat Hsin to any farewell banquet, as would have been appropriate, and, in fact, was responsible for the loss of the prince's tally. Ch'ao Ssu-hsiao had mentioned Hsin at the military office. The Military office was full of drifters and worthless toughs, some of whom got together to rough up Hsin . In the scuffle which ensued, the prince's tally was lost in the river. When Hsin finally got underway, he meant to make a formal complaint, but he made the mistake of talking about it. Fortunately for Ch'ao Ssu-hsiao, Cheng Po-lung heard about it and hushed it up with eight hundred taels.

Now Hsin had been imperially summoned from Nanking to join the cabinet, and he was passing through T'ung-chou on his way. We say that enemies' eyes start out of their heads at the sight of their adversaries, and that's exactly what happened now. This time, Ch'ao Ssu-hsiao was all courtesy, but it was too late. Cabinet member Hsin had his mind made up and wouldn't accept even the smallest present, or grant a single meeting. Nor would he accept any of the T'ung-chou yamen men as escorts. Instead, he hired transient laborers and left early in the morning for Peking. Before he left, though, he told a censor from his home town to look very carefully into Magistrate Ch'ao's conduct. A report was sent up and an interrogation by the legal commission decreed. One busy scribe got off a letter to Ch'ao Ssu-hsiao and told him he had better start bribing fast.

He wrote, "I haven't yet copied out the impeachment, so nobody else knows yet exactly what it says."

Ch'ao Ssu-hsiao was so terrified he was pissing black vinegar-stinking piss non-stop.

Madam Ch'ao had a son lying sick, his life dangling by a thread, and a

husband about to be dragged off to an imperial jail. She wished a great gust
of wind would pick up Hsing Kao-men in Che-chiang and blow him back to
T'ung-chou, like Liang Ying's wife. Now there wasn't one relative or other
trustworthy person in whom she could confide.

She thought, "If he hadn't driven out Hu and Liang, I could talk to them,
and they would help us out. Now they've shaven their heads, they can't leave
that temple. My hands are tied!"

She sent Ch'ao Shu to the reporting office in the city, to see exactly what
had been written. Unaccountably, nobody could find a copy of the impeachment, so Ch'ao Shu had to trace the original document to the home of the
censor who had had it written. Ch'ao Shu had a copy of that made. When he
saw what it said, he couldn't imagine where the accusers had dug up their
information, but it was all the truest he had ever laid eyes on. With the copy
in hand, he flew as fast as a falling star shoots across the sky, and handed it
to Ch'ao Ssu-hsiao to read.

From: The Imperial Censor of the Hu-kuang Circuit, Ou-yang Ming-
feng, written to uproot a lowly and corrupt district offical and so purify the
imperial realm.

Reporting: The common people are the foundation of the state. If the
foundation is solid, the state will be safe. A wise official, to safeguard the
common people, will keep ambition in check, obey the dictates of natural
indications and ritual, and always keep the common people first in his
considerations. In so doing, he will ensure that the people under his
jurisdiction are content, and only then may he feel pride in fulfilling his
obligations. But now we see noisome officials exceeding their privileges, we
see incursions by bandits, and great distress among the defenseless subjects.
Despite their innumerable afflictions, the common people fear death will be
their retribution for speaking out, and they do not dare rise up. Officials suck
the common people's marrow and strip the riches of the earth itself. Even here
so close to the imperial capital, there is flagrant impropriety.

One of these officials, Ch'ao Ssu-hsiao, despite his outward carapace of
splendour, has only total lack of shame at heart. Formerly, he enjoyed the post
of magistrate in an important subprefecture, and his administration there was
most remiss. When he was promoted to be the magistrate of a district, men
became aware of the stink of bought office. His behaviour became yet more
furtive. We shall not delve laboriously into his myriad offenses. Only those
offenses which cry for attention in their blatancy, or which have left deep scars
on the hearts of the common people will be detailed here for the emperor's
benefit.

It is forbidden to associate with the emperor's personal servitors, and yet Ch'ao Ssu-hsiao recognized the eunuch Wang Chen as his "father". Thus he easily received a post from Wang Chen's hands, governing a great jurisdiction. This relation was a repugnant violation of the natural order. Ssu-hsiao became friendly with one actor Liang and they called each other familial nicknames. Using the yamen servant Ts'ao Ming, Ssu-hsiao bribed numberless higher officials by filling wine jugs with valuables, including eight hundred taels to P'ing Ch'i-heng, three thousand to Wu Chao-sheng, and gold and pearls to Lo Ching-hung.

Ch'ao Ssu-hsiao also fatuously depended on his ignorant son, Ch'ao Yüan, and let him pass judgement in all matters. Together, they extorted payment from Feng Chu-ling, exiled T'ai Ch'i-wei for five years and wrongfully appropriated Huan Tzu-wei's fields. They found numberless ways to line their pockets. No official document was not an instrument of monetary gain. Plaintiff and accused, witness and co-defendant in every case were all required to pay bribes. Taxes were collected at thrice the normal rate, despite the fall in the price of commodities.

The emperor graciously issued monies from his private treasury, so that the military might be provisioned without hardship for the common people. All officials except Ssu-hsiao rigorously followed the emperor's orders that this money be so used. Ssu-hsiao dared pocket this money from the imperial treasury, while also requisitioning fodder so extortionately from the farmers under his control that he made a profit of three thousand taels, out of which he used one thousand to bribe yamen officials to ensure their complaisance. One thousand more he declared as a surplus in order to make himself appear a fine administrator.

A magistrate who does not flinch at robbing the emperor can hardly be expected to care for the common people of the empire with benevolent disinterest. This official, having little native wisdom to begin with, has been entirely stupified by his greed. His covetousness has deranged his government. He relies improperly on his son. We beg the emperor to order a thorough investigation in his justified and magnificent wrath. If it is then ascertained that our words are not baseless, may Ssu-hsiao be punished to the full extent of the law and let the wrongs of those thousands he has caused to hate him be thus redressed in a demonstration of the power of the imperial sword. This will be a great benefit to governed and governors alike.

When Ch'ao Ssu-hsiao saw this draft, he just sat there a while with his mouth hanging open.

His wife asked, "What does it say, anyway?"

He just shook his head, sunk in thought. He decided he should distribute that money from the imperial treasury to the farmers, so they wouldn't testify against him. Maybe he could cover up that particular big problem, which was his first priority. Everything else could be gotten around one way or another. He had another messenger send for Ts'ao Ming, and then discussed with Ts'ao Ming what he should do.

Ts'ao Ming said, "Like they say, 'fight back when you see enemy soldiers coming, build dams when you see a flood'-if you pay them now, those farmers will take the money all right, but they won't cover up for you. It's like giving up drink when you're already drunk—doesn't do any good. And then you'll have lost all the money, too."

"What do you think I should do, then?" asked Ch'ao Ssu-hsiao.

Ts'ao Ming said, "What I think is that you should go to the source. Take your money and plaster bribes all over, up and down the line. You'll still have enough money left over to clear up those other little things. But if you give the money to the farmers, it still won't keep this quiet, and then you'll have to use your own money for bribes. That's just what I think, of course. What about you?"

Ch'ao Ssu-hsiao said, "That makes a lot of sense. Even your uncle, back in the good old days in Hua-t'ing dldn't think up better ideas than you do."

He did as Ts'ao suggested. The next day, servants from the legal commission case came to round up the accused. Two or three were Ch'ao Ssu-hsiao's escorts, and they didn't take their eyes off of him for a moment. They summoned the others named in the draft, and it looked as if Ch'ao Yüan would have to go testify, too. Every time the commission servants opened their mouths they were asked for bribes of hundreds or thousands of taels, but even after he gave them five hundred taels, they weren't willing to treat him as a man should be, but put him in manacles and tied him up. Ch'ao Ssu-hsiao was lucky to find a guardian angel in the form of Lord Chin Ying.

Lord Chin Ying, Imperial Inspector of Rites, was the most famously virtuous servitor of our court. Chin Ying had come to T'ung-chou to investigate the matter of the requisitioned fodder. When Chin Ying arrived, Ch'ao Ssu-hsiao was totally helpless before the abuse of his captors. One of Chin Ying's household servants heard that Ch'ao Ssu-hsiao had paid five hundred taels, but was still being mistreated.

Chin Ying had the order transmitted, "While magistrate Ch'ao has been accused, he has not yet been ordered relieved of his position. Nor has he been arrested by the imperial secret police. What call can there be for putting him in fetters and tying him in ropes? If his guards are found to be maltreating him again, I shall have them punished."

Thanks to that word from Chin Ying, Ch'ao Ssu-hsiao's treatment changed with the speed and éclat of a thunderclap. None of the commission servants understood that Chin Ying couldn't bear injustice. They assumed he was friends with Ch'ao Ssu-hsiao. From then on, they didn't dare give Ch'ao Ssu-hsiao any trouble. They stayed with him, resting, a couple of days, and then took him to the legal commisslon, where he was committed to the jail of the Board of Punishments. Then his interrogation began, first by the Shantung commissioner, the administrator of the commission, and then the Director and the Deputy director of jails.

Ts'ao Ming, though just a yamen runner, knew everyone who mattered and was nicknamed "Ts'ao Sky-high". While Ch'ao Yüan was too ill to even wreak havoc with the yamen paperwork, there had been no-one to cramp Ts'ao's style, and he had amassed five or six hundred taels on his own account in bribes. Now he was condemned to banishment. The Ch'aos were just charged with negligence of official duties, and relieved of official duties.

Among the farmers who had supplied the fodder, there were some kind men who said, "Even though he did swindle us by ten thousand or so taels' worth, we've already shared the burden, and if we testify against him now, the money will just go back to the government. You can be sure we won't get any of it. And we'll have to report to the yamen and stay the whole trial, and who knows how long that will be. We're the ones who will suffer, losing all that time from work. Then the officials will call us malcontents. Let's all go together and submit a statement saying he paid us for the fodder with that imperial treasury money all along, that he never requisitioned it on his own authority. This is our busiest season now, and at least that way we can get out of having to go testify."

The circuit court took their statement and it was ratified. Ch'ao Ssu-hsiao was acquitted of some charges, and Ts'ao Ming also benefitted. The original impeachment was questioned and overturned, and the revised opinion was sent up and approved. Commissioner Ou-yang had been acting on Hsin's allegation, but he had no particular grudge against magistrate Ch'ao. Everything was in order, the case was closed, and there didn't seem to be any reason to go any further into it, or seek to incriminate Ch'ao Ssu-hsiao any further, now that he had been relieved of office. Ts'ao Ming's banishment took him into service among the troops of the Tsun-hua yamen. Ch'ao Ssu-hsiao had spent five thousand taels on the affair, so he still had half the money he had made on the fodder.

When Ch'ao Ssu-hsiao went home, his wife was very happy. Ch'ao Yüan had been slowly recovering from his illness. He was conscious most of the time now, and he asked about the leather cases and money belonging to Hu and Liang. Other people then told him how he had seen ghosts and spirits and jumped under the bed to get the cases and money out. They also told him Madam Ch'ao had had the things returned to Hu and Liang and how she had made vows, prayed, and had services performed at Hsiang-yen temple.

Ch'ao Yüan said, "Ghosts? What ghosts! I was delirious. What did she have to go giving those things back to them for? I went through a lot of trouble to get those things. How could she just give them back like that! Don't tell me those two still have connections? Otherwise why should I care about them? If I inform on them, they're going to lose a lot more than those things. That was their payment to me to keep their secret, and a low payment, too. What was to keep me from asking them for ten thousand?"

He fought with Madam Ch'ao about that every day.

She said, "We have plenty here. It isn't as if you had any brothers you'd have to share your inheritance with. Even though you do have a sister, she's already married. I might leave her some little things, but since you're the only son, if you would just settle down and live reasonably, we'd have enough to last you two or three lives' worth. Why bother with stealing their little bit? If you keep insisting, I'll pay you the value of their things just to keep you from nagging me about it. You don't know what shape you were in during your illness. I was scared almost to death!"

Ch'ao Yüan said, "Well, all that's yours is going to be mine, of course, so it doesn't make any sense for you to 'pay' me the value of their things. I just want those things."

She said, "I've already had them sent,"

Would Ch'ao Yüan listen? He rolled around in a tantrum on his bed. She just nodded. She sat there a while longer, and while she did, he began to feel the effects of his malaria again. This time was worse than it had ever been before. He saw ghosts and spirits, as he had before, and Hu and Liang appearing with fetters claiming they were missing a gold pin and a set of ruby circlets, two 'burma bell' wood curios, and four large pearls. Ch'ao Yüan carried out both parts of the whole dialogue, pulled the pin out of his hair, and brought out a box which contained the other items. He gave them all to Madam Ch'ao.

She said, "Never mind the rest, but how much is this pin worth? We'd better return it, at least."

As she spoke, the burma bells began rolling around her hands as if independently, scaring her so badly she paled and dropped them. Ch'ao Ssu-hsiao had a servant pick them up and hid them in his sleeve.

The strange thing was was that there was no way that anyone except Ch'ao Yüan could have known where those objects were. Liang and Hu had never even mentioned them to Ch'ao Shu. So maybe it was the Veda of Hsiang-yen temple manifesting himself in those visions Ch'ao Yüan saw? Before he saw this, Ch'ao Ssu-hsiao hadn't believed any of what his wife had told him about his son's illness being retribution for his sins, but now he had seen it with his own eyes. Madam Ch'ao prayed and prayed for her son, and on the next day, at the fifth watch, his fever broke and he slowly came around. His father told him what had happened during his attack. He had four or five more severe attacks before the malaria finally ebbed.

Ch'ao Ssu-hsiao waited for his son to recover before leaving for home, as he had to do now that he had lost his official position. Once Ch'ao Yüan was feeling well, though, he put all of his energy into trying to convince his father to find a connection and get a petition sent up asking to have his official status reinstated. With this in mind, Ch'ao Yüan had a brush and paper set by his pillow, but he frittered away a whole day without being able to write anything. He was flushing and paling by turns at the effort of even thinking of writing when a maid came to ask if he would like something to eat.

He lashed out at her, "Here I'm all set to compose a document and this stupid maid won't let me alone!"

He tried to hit the maid, but she was too far away, and he ended up hitting himself.

His son's rantings made Ch'ao Ssu-hsiao think maybe he really should write a petition asking to be reinstated. Ts'ao Ming was busy these days, out selling his ill-gotten gains and getting what profit was to be got before he had to leave for Tsun-hua. When he came back this day, Ch'ao Ssu-hsiao asked his opinion of a petition for reinstatement.

Ts'ao Ming listened to him, then said, "My good master! What are you thinking? We should thank our lucky stars that my sacrifice helped save you from that terrible trouble we just finished with! Now you want to remind them about yourself? If you really do send up a petition for reinstatement, you'll have both yamens coming down on you, and I can tell you that even Han Chung-li's magic potion won't help cure what'll be ailing you then. Now, listen to me and start home. Take water or land, but go. Once I'm gone, there won't be anyone here to take care of things for you here."

Ts'ao managed to totally dampen any enthusiasm Ch'ao Ssu-hsiao had had for that idea, and later Ch'ao Ssu-hsiao told his son all Ts'ao had said. Ch'ao

Yüan wasn't about to give up that easily, though. He just said people should do as he said and if only he were feeling better they would. Too bad that he wasn't well enough to write the petition himself, and that there wasn't anyone dependable in the capital to look after their interests. If only he'd brought along Ch'ao Chu, Ch'ao Chu would have been a help, but as it was they were all alone!

"I guess it's just bad luck," he said bitterly.

Madam Ch'ao said, "If you two plan to go home, let's start. If you insist on sending up a petition and waiting for the answer, I'll go home for a year or two and then rejoin you here."

Ch'ao Ssu-hsiao had no choice but to start. Their lugggage was massive and heavy, and Cn'ao Yüan was still bedridden, so they decided to take the water route. They ordered two barges to be reserved and picked the twenty-eighth of the eleventh month as the day of their departure. On that day, Ts'ao Ming got some of his scruffy friends together to perform the ceremony of presenting a beloved official with shoes to send him along the road of his future. They got a pair of shoes and a box of snacks, and decorated a platform.

Ch'ao Ssu-hsiao sat on the platform with his face puffed up and stuck his feet out to have the new shoes put on. Someone made up a verse about that day:

> The ways of the world are such a laugh
> Ten thousand in his pocket for three years
> Which cheered his superiors so they impeached him
> And here we send him off with love

Madame Ch'ao had given Ch'ao Shu ten taels a couple of days before and told him to buy two lengths of coarse-woven silk and two of white capital pongee for Hu and Liang's winter outfits. She also told him to tell them to come and pick up their things once the Ch'aos were ten li on the barge route home. Hu and Liang couldn't thank Ch'ao Shu enough, and they prayed at the altar for the living they had put up for Madam Ch'ao.

The day that the Ch'aos took sail; when they reached Ch'ang Chia wan, Madam Ch'ao saw a big pile of boxes on the shore and two neat little priests standing there. When they saw the boats, they called out.

"Halt the boats!"

The minute she saw them, she knew they were Hu and Liang in their new guises as Wu-yi and P'ien-yün. Ch'ao Ssu-hsiao was in the dark, though, since he had never heard about them going to the Hsiang-yen temple and becoming priests. If he had known, he would probably have had them chased out of there long before.

The Chaos had the two priests shown on board. When they came close enough to be recognizable, Ch'ao Ssu-hsiao and Ch'ao Yüan got a nasty surprise, but couldn't do anything but invite the two on board. Ch'ao Ssu-hsiao was so embarrassed that he wished the earth would open to swallow him up. Fortunately, the two just kowtowed, said thank you for all your solicitude and didn't bring up anything unpleasant. Then they asked to see Madam Ch'ao and thanked her, too. Father and son were a comic sight as they squirmed in embarrassment and were living examples of how "guilt clouds the eye".

The boxes on the shore were carried on board, and they were full of delicacies: one of snacks and buns, two of steamed flakey cakes, two of wafers, two of Ku-p'ien cake, one of smoked bean-curd, one of sweet preserved eggplant, two of spiced bean-curd, one of Fukien pears, two of Nan-hua hams, and four bundles of sea-food. Despite their growing discomfort, Ch'ao Ssu-hsiao and Ch'ao Yüan accepted everything.

Hu and Liang told them how they had received a license from Lord Chin Ying, and become priests at the Hsiang-yen temple.

Startled, Ch'ao Ssu-hsiao said, "But Hsiang-yen temple is right in T'ung-chou! How come we never heard from you? Why didn't you ever visit? Did you forget your old friends?"

Hu and Liang rejoined, "Of course not. But what could we do? We often tried to see you and Madam Ch'ao, but the servants wouldn't let us in."

Their words made Ch'ao Yüan blush redder than a baboon's behind.

The Ch'aos kept Hu and Liang to eat, and nobody mentioned their things that Ch'ao Yüan had confiscated.

Finally, Ch'ao Ssu-hsiao said, "We didn't know where to send those boxes you left behind, so we have them with us. Why don't you take them?"

He ordered a servant to get the four leather cases and the bundle of money still tied in the sky-blue phoenix scarf, and the pin, circlets, and burma bells in a paper packet which he himself handed to Hu and Liang. Madam Ch'ao came out of the cabin for this. Hu and Liang didn't know what to do about the money. With Ch'ao Yüan and Ch'ao Ssu-hsiao there, they didn't want to say that Madam Ch'ao had already refunded them, but neither did they want to accept it.

So they said, "We'll just take the cases. We left the money as a token of our gratitude for the way you took care of us, like sons. We wouldn't dream of taking it back."

The Ch'aos and the priests deferred back and forth over the money, until finally Madam Ch'ao said, "Since you don't want to accept it as a return of your own money, let's say that it's our money, and we want you to take it to use for good works, like repairing bridges or fixing temples. If you use it in our name, it's the same thing as giving us the money."

Only then would Hu and Liang accept the money. Madam Ch'ao also asked them to open the cases so that they could check and be sure nothing was missing. However, they said they hadn't brought the key, so the cases weren't opened. In any case, it looked as if they had all their belongings, and if some little item were missing, it wouldn't be enough to occasion another visit from the Veda.

Hu and Liang didn't use that money for themselves. They used it all to buy grain that they stored in a vacant room, and which they lent poor, starving people in the lean spring and summer months. When the fall harvest came in, they were repaid with a three percent interest on the amount of grain, which they returned to the store-room, so they could lend it to more needy people. Everyone who borrowed knew they were dealing with priests' property and didn't dare renege on the loan. In the end, the two had a store of grain worth several tens of thousands of taels. All the poor of T'ung-chou turned to them in times of drought or calamity, and all concerned benefitted.

Even later, Hu and Liang rose to Buddhahood and frequently manifested themselves, but we won't talk about that now.

> A butcher can put down his knife and become a
> boddhisattva
> A hermit can have a change of heart and don armor
> But see the example of the monkey king
> unable to evade Kuan-yin's power

Chapter Eighteen

A Rich and Influential Man makes a topsy-turvy marriage proposal
A young gentleman buries two at once in a double funeral

Everyone in the world hates a heartless betrayer
Who treats his lawful wife like dirt
And has eyes only for the wild bird
He never thinks of the pity of abandoning his true mate
How could he let his taste in faces
Deepen into flaunting disdain for the proper way?

A woman can only bend with the wind
So all she can do is go home to her parents

After Ch'ao Ssu-hsiao left the scenes of his splendor, he thought nostalgically, "Never again! I remember how I used to go out in my fine sedan chair, and then take my seat in the yamen, all the pomp and ceremony centered on me. If I said 'beat him!' they all prostrated themselves. If I said 'execute him!' they dragged him on out. But look at me now. It's really too bad."

Ch'ao Yüan, too, was filled with regret that his father couldn't have lived ten thousand years, nine thousand nine hundred and ninety-nine of them as an official. He wished T'ai mountain could be turned into silver and moved into his own room.

Madam Ch'ao, however, was as content as could be. She reflected that her husband had gotten away with a light punishment and her son (thank heavens!) was almost entirely recovered. They had plenty of money to live on, too.

The weather of the tenth month wasn't terribly cold, as they still had over twenty days before the winter solstice, so they didn't have to worry about the river freezing over. Besides, times were peaceful, and there was no fear of bandits threatening their journey. She thought happily that in ten or twenty days they'd be home. What if she had more white hairs now than she used to, and more wrinkles? Eating well, and sleeping peacefully, they journeyed uneventfully for about a month before they arrived in Wu-ch'eng.

You can imagine what a grand welcome they got, not having been home in six or seven years, and now returning with all the trappings of their (former) success. Of course all their relatives turned out to greet them and to give them welcome home presents. When the local matchmakers heard that Chen ko had not come with them, they were in and out of the house every day with prospecttive matches for Ch'ao Yüan.

All that Madam Ch'ao had to go on was the matchmakers' assertions as to whether the women came from suitable families, whether divination on the number of brushstrokes in their names would prove favorable, or if they were of marriagable age. Madam Ch'ao would have been well able to look into the proposals and make a good choice if there hadn't been several hundreds of proposals, some of them from outside the subprefecture. She was groping in the dark.

Ch'ao Ssu-hsiao had no opinion in the matter. All he said was to let Yüan do as he likes, anyway we can't decide for him.

One day, two matchmakers came. They both said they had come all the way from Lin-ch'ing, one from the household of Board Vice-president T'ang, and the other from Gevernment Advisor Ch'in. They asked to come in to discuss their proposals, and it just happened that both Madam Ch'ao and Ch'ao Ssu-hsiao were in to hear them.

The two matchmakers were let in. This is what they looked like:

One palsied old lady would have been a beauty but for her
sallow face and grey hair
The other would have been a pretty young thing but that
she was all shrivelled up and hardly able to draw
her breath.
One had a dark rag on her head,
The other a faded blue skirt dragging on the ground
One said " My most humble respects to the master and may
I please have the honor of waiting on him"
The other said "My most earnest wishes for the mistress' health
and it does my eyes good to see such magnificence"
One pulled forth from her dark cloth bundle the astrological
record of her candidate's birth
The other drew out from her sleeve a divination on her candidates
name.
One squinted and burbled with all the strength of a river's
flow
The other's neat teeth and swift tongue clattered on like
the clash of spears.
One said, "This young lady I'm telling you of puts the
moon and flowers to shame. Her family's rich as
Shih Sui's."

The other said, "This ruler of the inner rooms I'm bringing
you is so beautiful birds drop dead at her sight.
Her family's as influential as Liang Yi's.
One said, "Miss Ch'in is the only daughter and her dowry
will be no mere thousand taels."
The other said, "Miss T'ang has only herself and one
nephew inheriting."
One talked till you could see holy effigies raining from
heaven and see black as white
The other until you could believe gold lotuses were springing
from the earth and horses growing horns

Ch'ao Ssu-hsiao listened to what the two matchmakers had to say. Then
he whispered to his wife that they had had a lot of proposals, but he liked these
the best yet. The question, though, was what Ch'ao Yüan would think.

The matchmaker sent by the Ch'in family said, "When I was leaving, the
master and mistress told me, 'don't take no for an answer. If our daughter
marries into their family today, old Ch'ao will be a cabinet secretary
tomorrow."

The matchmaker sent by the T'angs chimed in, "When I came, master and
mistress T'ang said that, given the appropriateness of the match, Master
Ch'ao should consent gladly. Besides, if his son son marries our daughter in
the morning, Ch'ao Ssu-hsiao will be a prefectural magistrate by evening."

Ch'ao Ssu-hsiao exclaimed, "Nonsense! Since when are prefectural
magistracies for sale?"

The matchmaker said, "Oh, pardon me, I meant a district magistrate."

"That's even less likely!" he said.

She told him, "It may not be possible to get a prefectural magistracy by
paying, but the district magistracies have always been for sale. If you don't
believe me, wait and see if you aren't the magistrate of a district within two
days of the marriage."

"Haven't I already been one? Don't try to tell me magistracies like that
are for sale."

"Master Ch'ao, didn't you buy that position?"

"You're talking a lot of nonsense, old woman. I got that job by studying
hard. Tell me any district or prefectural magistrate you know who bought his
position!"

"I wouldn't know about any others," she said, "only that you paid two
thousand."

"Don't listen to people's nonsense," he said.

He ordered a housekeeper to invite the two matchmakers into the east room for a meal.

Then he said, "It's getting late, so why don't you two stay over? Let me discuss this with the young master and we'll decide tomorrow."

He had Ch'ao Yüan summoned, but Ch'ao Yüan was not at home.

Actually, the day the Ch'aos had arrived home, Ch'ao Yüan didn't even wait for the luggage to be set down before he was off to see Chen ko. From then on, he saw his parents every morning and then went straight to the jail. Every night, he pretended to go to sleep in his own room, and then sneaked out to be with Chen ko. That was why Ch'ao Yüan was not home until the following morning.

When he came in, Ch'ao Chu said, 'Yesterday, two matchmakers came with Lin-ch'ing with proposals, and talked to the old master. He wanted to talk to you about the proposals, so I said you'd gone out to see some friends. The two matchmakers are still here now."

Ch'ao Yüan went back to greet his parents, and to hear all about the proposals. The told him how one girl was the daughter of advisor Ch'in, and seventeen years old. She was born on the tenth day of the twelfth month in the year of the wood ox. The other, as they told him, was the daughter of Board vice-president T'ang, and sixteen years old. She was born at the hour of the dragon on the sixteenth day of the second month of the year of the fire tiger.

Ch'ao Yüan looked over the astrological information, silent.

Madam Ch'ao said, "They're both fine families, and they both say that the girls are very pretty. What do you think? Both of the matchmakers are waiting."

Ch'ao Yüan said, "I can't decide just like that! I have to think it over."

Up to now, Ch'ao Yüan had been totally consumed by plans to go to the capital to find someone who could help him get Chen ko out of jail. He figured they could wait for the annual leniency review and get her penalty reduced. Then he was planning to bring her home and set her up as his wife. Chen ko had agreed to help him find another beautiful concubine. They had it all arranged. They were going to have a good time. Ch'ao Yüan had sworn on his life that that was how it was going to be, and he couldn't back out now. But here were marriage proposals from two very important people. All the girls in Lin-ch'ing were beautiful, and the daughters of great houses were sure to be exceptionally so. They were young, too. He would have liked to abandon Chen ko, but he was still afraid she'd come after him somehow, demanding satisfaction.

He told himself, "Why be faithful to a woman condemned to death? I can't let an opportunity like this go! If I marry one of these two girls, I can forget getting Chen ko out of jail. I can go there and sleep with her a few times a month. If it turns out the new girl isn't as good as Chen ko, there'll be plenty of time then to get Chen ko out. But how can I get hold of both these girls? The best way would be to marry them both, one as a wife and the other as a concubine. Except I don't think such Important People would let their daughters be concubines. I have to pick one of the two, and I need someone I can trust go look them over for me."

Decided, he turned to his parents and said, "They both sound good, but we have to have someone see them before we can pick one of the two. It isn't as if I could have both."

The matchmakers said, "These two young ladies have no call to hide their faces. It'd be hard to say if even the goddess of the moon, or the singing girls of Lin-ch'ing, are as beautiful. It isn't proper for you to see them yourself, but if you did, we're willing to bet your heart would no longer be your own from the instant you did."

Their talk had Ch'ao Yüan squirming in excitement like a monkey. He was ready to demand either girl in marriage, and to shut Chen ko up and forget all about her. Even so, he was able to think about who he should send to see the girls. He couldn't think of anyone he could trust to go. At first he wanted to send Mrs. Ch'ao Shu, since she was mature enough, but he didn't trust their taste, so after all maybe she wouldn't be such a good choice. He racked his brains until he thought of Hsia Wei-jen, Yü ming-wu's old nurse. She was sharp, down to earth and straight-forward. He asked for her to go with Mrs. Ch'ao Shu and the two matchmakers. It was agreed, and all left with four horses and a travelling servant. Ch'ao Shu brought up the rear on a donkey.

When they arrived in Lin-ch'ing, the two matchmakers went to the Ch'in and T'ang households to relate the progress so far of the proposals. Ch'ao Shu found a place for the others to stay.

The next day, Old Lady Hsia and Mrs. Ch'ao Shu joined the matchmakers. Together, they all went to the T'angs' house. There, they met the lady of the house and announced their business there. They requested to see the young lady.

> Short of stature
> Dark of face
> Crooked of brow
> Yellowish haired
> Her nose a little stubby

> Her eyes a mite sunken
> But withal the manner of a well-raised girl
> The mien of peaceful and demure bride

Madam T'ang had the girl serve them food and drink, and give them a hundred copper cash each. Then she saw them out.

Next, they went to the Ch'ins' house, where they saw the lady of the house, and asked for the young lady. She:

> Was surprised in her everyday clothes
> No airs and graces at all
> A cloud of raven locks on her head
> Her body the crystallized snow of three winters
> Not too fat and not too thin
> Lovely as Madam Wang below the trees
> Bridally beautifully as Miss Ku

At the sight of Miss Ch'in, they all ruminated, "How can anything this beautiful be real?"

They made some social conversation. Madam Ch'in did not offer any refreshments, and then came the announcement that Madam Ch'in's brother had arrived. He was shown in. He was about thirty years old, wearing a short, fine woven Khitai jacket and wool trousers. He had passed the lower exams and was an academician at the Lin-ch'ing academy, but he made his living in an inn.

He came in and greeted Madam Ch'in, who said, "There's some Important Person in Wu-ch'eng who used to be magistrate of T'ung-chou district. Ch'ao. Do you know him? He has a son, an academician. Have you heard about him? How old is he?"

Her brother said, "I don't know Ch'ao himself, just his son. He's about thirty."

"What's he like? Have you met them?"

He said, "Oh, very good-looking. Everybody in T'ung-chou knew him as a nice fellow. Yes, I'm sure I know him, there can't be two men by the same name there. Why do you ask?"

"A marriage proposal," she told him.

"What do you mean, a marriage proposal?"

"He wants to marry your niece, now that he's widowed."

"Well, yes, he's been widowed a year, now."

"How did you get to know him?" Madam Ch'in asked.

"It's a long story," he said, "But he had a wife, Ms. Chi, and then he bought a concubine, Chen ko, for eight hundred taels."

Madam Ch'in exclaimed, "So that's who Chen ko married!"

Her brother continued, "Ever since he got Chen ko, he made his wife live alone in a bare room. A couple of nuns used to visit her, and one day Chen ko saw them coming out of the back. Chen ko said Ms. Chi was having an affair with a couple of priests, and she egged Ch'ao Yüan on into divorcing Ms. Chi. In the middle of the night, Ms. Chi hung herself on Chen ko's door. Ms. Chi's brother, Chi Pa-la made a complaint, and it was ratified in the circuit court here. Later, they were reinterrogated and beaten until they could hardly move. They stayed at my inn about forty days, healing up."

Madam Ch'in said, "Who? Healing what?"

"Ch'ao Yüan and Chen ko! Healing from their beatings in court!"

"You mean they beat him, too?"

"Twenty strokes, and twenty-five for her. The nuns were pressed. He was stripped of his status as an academician and bought commutation of the rest of his sentence. She was condemned to death by strangling. Between their rent and food while all that was going on, I made a good hundred and ten taels out of them."

"Do you think we should accept the proposal?" she asked.

"I wouldn't say," he said, "That's for you and your husband to decide. His family's rich, but he's a real bastard."

Ch'ao Shu and his wife were in a side room, eating, and they heard everything Madam Ch'in's brother told her.

In their hearts, they thought, "it's all over now. With an enemy like him around, the marriage will never happen."

They finished eating, and saw Madam Ch'in again. She was cool, and told them her husband was out. She could not answer them until he had returned and she had had a chance to discuss the proposal with him.

"You may come back in a few days for our answer."

She gave them each a hundred copper cash. After they said good-bye, and left, the three began to talk it over.

"Miss T'ang's nothing special, no better than Ms. Chi was. No need to even talk about her. But Miss Ch'in! What a beauty! If only it weren't for that uncle of hers blocking the way."

They talked their way back to the stable, got their animals ready, paid for their stay and went back to tell the Ch'aos about it. After they had described the two households and the two girls, Ch'ao Yüan had relegated Miss T'ang to the farthest reaches of the universe, while Miss Ch'in found a secure nest in his heart.

When Advisor Ch'in came home, his wife told him about the delegation from the Ch'aos, and that she had been thinking of consenting to the match until she heard that Ch'ao Yüan wasn't a proper type at all, and had in fact been so over partial to his concubine that his wife had been pushed to suicide.

Now she was disposed towards a refusal, but they were so rich she could hardly give up the idea of the Ch'aos as in-laws, so she didn't know what to do.

Advisor Ch'in said, "We can't believe everything your brother says. Maybe when they stayed at his inn they had a quarrel with him, or something like that. Lin-ch'ing isn't far from Wu-ch'eng. We'll send Ch'in Fu to go and find out about them before we make a final decision."

Ch'in Fu went to Wu-ch'eng, were he dug into every nook and cranny. He talked to Chi Pa-la, Mrs. Kao, old Ho who ran the needle shop across the way, and Tailor Chen next door. They all agreed that Ch'ao Yüan had very little to reccommend him. Ch'in Fu went home and told his master what he had found out. Advisior Ch'in's interest in the match was cooling rapidly, but he still had not decided irrevocably against it. After all, Ch'ao Yüan was on good terms with a lot of money, and money was to be respected. Ch'in couldn't quite give up the idea of the marriage.

Meanwhile, Ch'ao Yüan was keeping Chen ko in the dark about the marriage negotiations on the one hand, while with the other he sent emissaries to Madam Ch'in's brother. Ch'ao Yüan sent the brother a request that he represent Ch'ao Yüan favorably in front of her. In return, Ch'ao Yüan would pay the brother two hundred taels. While this was going on, Ch'ao Yüan was in such a state of turmoil he could neither eat nor sleep and almost wasted away from lovesickness. Mrs. Ch'ao Shu was largely to blame for his lovelorn mopings, since whenever she noticed his interest flagging she was sure to come to him with glowing descriptions of Miss Ch'in's manifold charms. She talked until he could have stood death better than his longing.

As if this weren't enough, Ch'ao Ssu-hsiao, at the age of sixty-three, and long after he had shelved all that sort of thing with his wife, decided he wanted his wife's maid, Ch'un-ying, as a concubine. She was sixteen years old, and had grown into a pretty girl with a nice figure.

Madam Ch'ao said, "They say that before you invite guests for a wedding banquet, you should consider the bride's suitability—but it's up to you. I have nothing to say in the matter."

Ch'ao Ssu-hsiao said, "When I used to be busy working all the time, back when I was a lower-degree holder, that passed the time, and once I became an official the days slipped away, but now, sitting around the house, with no young children around, it's so boring that I need something to cheer me up, someone to take care of me and keep me occupied."

Sorrowfully, Madam Ch'ao gave her consent.

They picked an auspicious hour on the second day of the second month. Madam Ch'ao had bridal clothes made for the girl and set her head-dress on her head. That evening, Ch'un-ying and Ch'ao Ssu-hsiao began married life. It was the first time Ch'ao Ssu-hsiao had ever done such a shameless thing, and he didn't live to enjoy it long. On the first of the thirds month, the crabapples were in full bloom, and Ch'ao Ssu-hsiao invited some friends over for a drinking and flower-viewing party. Flushed with the enthusiasm of a bridegroom, he didn't bother to put on warm clothes, even when the evening grew chill. That night, after his guests left, he began to get a little headache and to run a fever. If he had called a reputable doctor, maybe his lucky stars would have come to his aid, but the only doctor he thought to call was Dr. Yang Ku-yüeh.

Dr. Yang came, and, right off, asked, "Does Old Ch'ao have any concubines?"

The household servants told Dr. Yang about Ch'un-ying. That was enough for Dr. Yang. He was positive what was called for was a dose of restorative soup, with an extra dose of medicine, and he ordered Ch'ao Ssu-hsiao to drink it down. This wasn't just a case of "a donkey's lips don't fit a horse's mouth"; the prescription was much worse than useless. It worsened the illness.

On the eleventh day of the third month, Ch'ao Ssu-hsiao went to his final rest, and Madame Ch'ao collapsed in tears. She cried so hard she almost died and came back alive herself. She prayed for a while in front of Ms. Chi's tablet, before moving it into a smaller room and giving Ch'ao Ssu-hsiao's the place of honor. The whole household put on white mourning, and the business of the funeral enveloped the house.

Ch'ao Yüan was the sort of a person who never did what he should in substance, but was always ready to make a show. He had the portrait painter creating Old Ch'ao's likeness while the Yin-yang functionary wrote the funerary signs. Ch'ao Yüan didn't find the stock phrase "upright official" sufficiently elegant and he forced the functionary to write "Lord Ch'ao, first in erudition and most glorious minister" instead. The functionary couldn't argue him out of it, so it was written as he wished.

All those who came to pay funerary calls found food for gossip in that phrase. Towards the end, one Chen Fang-po came to pay his respects. When he saw the sign, he was angered by Ch'ao Yüan's flouting of the accepted forms of society.

"How could you all let him carry out such a travesty of a funeral?"

After Chen Fang-po had prayed to the dead, Ch'ao Yüan came out to kowtow in thanks.

Chen Fang-po ordered Ch'ao Yüan to stand, and asked him, "When exactly did your father receive the title 'most glorious minister'?"

Ch'ao Yüan answered, "Last year, in a special dispensation."

"That title is reserved for officials of the first rank. How could a district magistrate possibly have been granted it? Change that sign this very minute! It won't be comfortable for you, not at all, if a district official comes to pay his respects and he sees that.'

Ch'ao Yüan exchanged it for the original, less boastful sign. Meanwhile, he had ordered the portrait-painter to paint his father in a dragon robe, jade belt, and gold bonnet. The painter wouldn't paint the first brushstroke, claiming that the spirit could not be a higher official than the deceased had been, and had the deceased been granted a dragon robe and jade belt in life? Moreover, he had to say he had never seen an official high enough to wear a gold bonnet, so he wasn't qualified to paint one.

"With my own eyes, I saw my father in his. Are you calling me a liar?" said Ch'ao Yüan

"How strange," the painter said, "What are you talking about?"

"If you don't believe me, I'll just have to show you. I'll make a bet with anyone here that I'm telling the truth, too."

"What will you bet?" asked the painter.

"If I can't show you his gold bonnet, I'll give you one of the pigs sent for the funeral, and if you lose, you paint the portrait for free."

They agreed on that. Ch'ao Yüan brought out a court head-dress.

"Well," he said, "Would I fool you?"

Everyone laughed, "That's a court head-dress. How can you call it a gold bonnet?"

He couldn't hold out against their combined positive derision, so he said, "If you won't paint him in this, paint him in a black prime-minister's cap. Anway, I don't want a portrait like anyone else's. This has to be something special."

"I can do that," the painter said, "I can make three, one in court audience dress, one in official robes, and one in regular dress. You'll have to pay me twenty-five taels for all three."

Before long, the painter had done a sketch that was generally agreed to resemble Old Ch'ao.

"Well," said the painter, "you can't turn day into night. It's a good thing I'd met Old Ch'ao. Now, any other painter couldn't have gotten him right."

"Nevermind making them look exactly like him," said Ch'ao Yüan, "Just make him handsome and fair with a nice, long black beard. I want it to look good, not realistic."

The painter said, "Now, that's another one of your strange ideas! I won't have any trouble with that at all, but I'm afraid Chen Fang-po will be around to see you with his complaints. That's your problem, though, and if you ask me to re-do the portraits, you'll have to pay me again."

Ch'ao Yüan said, "Just do as I say and never mind Chen Fang-po. Except for him, nobody will say anything about it."

In the end, the portrait painter produced three pictures that were the very image of the deity Wen-ch'ang Ti-chün. Ch'ao Yüan said the beard wasn't luxuriant enough and had the painter add on a few inches. When the portraits were ready, Ch'ao Yüan had them mounted and put up. He placed the one depicting his father in dragon robe and gold bonnet on the alter and opened thirteen days of clamorous funeral festivities. They had ten or so sutras read, and then closed down the festivities while the grave and coffin were readied. Ch'ao Yüan said that this would be a good time to rid the house of Ms. Chi's remains, too, so the house would be fit to welcome Miss Ch'in as his bride.

During those thirteen days, Ch'ao Yüan only stayed three days in the jail with Chen ko. The rest of the time, he left Ch'ao Chu to take care of things there.

He called the Yin-yang functionary, and they set the eighth day of the fourth month as the date the grave would be dug and the sixth day of the fourth intercalary month for the burial. Ch'ao Yüan was kept busy every day arranging the details. He prepared gifts and put aside thirty taels for "writing gratuities". He asked Hanlin scholar Hu to write the epitaph, Governor Chen Fang-po to write the inscription, and Assistant Governor Chiang to make the heading for the gravestone. They all accepted his gifts and agreed to write as asked. Ch'ao Yüan also issued invitations all over for people to come to the burial, and asked his friends to come help out. He called a mason to polish the gravestone, and sent a man to Lin-ch'ing to buy all the funeral paraphernalia, like dried vegetables, paper streamers, porcelain vessals, white mourning cloth and refreshments. He had a draft of the inscription written and then printed up, had paper offerings made for burning, and stuck them all over the grave. He had a troupe of female performers from Lin-ch'ing engaged, and invited twelve guests to the consecration.

He asked Assistant Governor Chiang to consecrate the ancestral tablet by painting in the final dot. Liu Yu-hsi performed the sacrifice to the earth. All the ceremonies were performed duly, thanks to Ch'ao Yüan's neighbour, Yü

Ming-wu, who came over and took charge. Fortunately, Ch'ao Yüan didn't bother to disagree with any of Yü's arrangements. He had the painter make two inscribed scarlet pennons. On the twenty-fourth of the fourth month, they opened to all, and people from all over came to pay their respects to the bereaved and to burn offerings to the deceased.

Ch'ao Yüan also used three taels to bribe the office of rites at the Wu-ch'eng yamen to have an official service for his father, and that went off very nicely. On the twenty-fifth, the warden, Che Chih-t'u, brought sacrifices and came to condole with Ch'ao Yüan on the loss of his father. The warden also dispatched an honor guard of four men to stand at Ch'ao Yüan's door. Just in case their official rations weren't enough, Ch'ao Yüan paid each one of the four two hundred cash a day, and he paid it ahead. He also entrusted them with two lengths of white mourning cloth for the warden.

On the twenty-sixth, all the local Important People came and filed in front of the portrait of the deceased. When it was Chen Fang-po's turn, he was about to offer incense, but, confronted by the portrait of Ch'ao Ssu-hsiao in scarlet robe, golden bonnet, fair complexion and ebony beard, he stood stock still, his hands arrested in the motion of offering incense.

Chen Fang-po asked, "To what god is this altar?"

"Why, that's Old Master Ch'ao," asserted a household servant.

"Nonsense!" said Chen Fang-po, and proceeded to berate his own servant, "I told you to take me to the Ch'aos'. Why did you bring me to the temple of the city god instead?"

He put the incense in his hand back down on the table, turned around, went out, and got back in his sedan chair, without looking back once. He did however, send a servant back with a message for the assembled Important People.

"Master Chen felt indisposed at the sudden apparition of the city god. He regrets the discourtesy, but must return home. Incidentally, Master Chen cannot take credit for the inscription as he wants you all to know that he never learned to write."

Ch'ao Yüan said, "Thank you very much! We're doing just fine here without Master Chen lowering himself to visit. I'm afraid the woodblock and stone printings of the inscription he wrote have already been made, though, so I can't change that."

After that, everyone went listlessly through the motions of offering incense, but Chen's departure had robbed the occasion of much of its luster.

Back in Lin-ch'ing, Madame Ch'in's brother had changed his tune on the subject of Ch'ao Yüan, thanks to Ch'ao Yüan's hefty promised gifts. Now, her brother tirelessly urged the match on her, but she wasn't listening. She believed what he had said before, not what he said now. Advisor Ch'in was as attracted as ever by the word "rich", though, and when he heard that Ch'ao Ssu-hsiao had died, he thought this would be a good opportunity to go in the guise of a mourner to see what kind of family the Ch'aos were, and in particular what Ch'ao Yüan looked like.

Ch'ao Yüan knew ahead of time that Advisor Ch'in was coming, so he set out a lavish banquet and invited a couple of Important People, Hanlin Scholar Hu and Assistant Commissioner Chiang. Then he had a new set of mourning clothes made, so he could look his best for Advisor Ch'in. After Advisor Ch'in had offered his incense, Ch'ao Yüan came out to thank him. Advisor Chin stood still and stared hard at Ch'ao, to see if his face had an auspicious physiognomy. Advisor Ch'in also listened carefully to the sound of Ch'ao Yüan's voice, to tell his age. Ch'ao Yüan, in his impeccable mourning, presented a most satisfactory picture to Advisor Ch'in, who then proceeded inside to eat and pick what play he would like to see performed. When Advisor Ch'in went home, he talked it over with his wife, and they were eighty percent in favor of the match.

Miss Ch'in saw that this marriage looked like it was really going to happen, and that she had better say what she thought now.

She told her mother, "His wife hung himself, and his concubine's in jail for the murder. How can he be any good? And you are ready to marry your daughter to him? If you bring up this marriage proposal again, I'm going to cut off all my hair, become a nun and leave home!"

Madam Ch'in told her husband what their daughter had said, and he finally had to give up his cherished hopes of the alliance.

Ch'ao Yüan still thought that the marriage was likely. On the sixth day of the fourth intercalary month, Ms. Chi's remains were laid in the earth to clear the house for Miss Ch'in along with the remains of Ch'ao Ssu-hsiao. Old Chi and Chi Pa-la could hardly refuse to attend Ms. Chi's burial. They came and were present at the final sacrifice to the earth and lowering of the coffins. They took her tablet home.

It was time for the wheat harvest, so Ch'ao Yüan hurried through his responses to the condolers, wanting to rush to his villa to oversee the harvest. He could hardly wait to follow up on his marriage negotiations with the Ch'ins, but he was too busy. It had been a good while since he had visited Chen ko, too.

On the eighth of the month, they had performed the ritual of the three calls to the spirit of the deceased, had had the yin-yang functionary sprinkle the main hall to lift the stain of death from the house, and Ch'ao Yüan got ready to go to Yung-shan.

Little did he know he was but a lamb going off to slaughter, every step bringing him closer to his death. Read on to see how his road ended.

Chapter Nineteen

Ch'ao Yüan plots his way to another man's wife
Little Ya splits a pair of heads

You had your own wife once
But wanted someone prettier
Scorned the partner in adversity
Bought a new mate
And the two females fought to the death

There's nothing wrong with a widower remarrying
But you care only for furtive passions
Eyes only for the roadside willow
and always roving to the next
One flagpole cannot carry two flags
—to the tune "butterfly loves flower"

Ch'ao Yüan wound up the double funeral, and thanked all for their attendance. Then he went off to the Yung-shan villa with his retinue, to oversee the wheat harvest. Once the wheat was in, he planned to call on the Ch'ins, thanking them for their condolences and expediting the marriage. Another reason why he did not intend to stay long at the villa was that he had never dared repair the damage done by the fire of the fox spirit. He didn't want to stay in those spooky surroundings.

Unknown to him, a leatherworker had taken up residence in one of the buildings on the villa grounds. This leatherworker was tall, with big, round eyes, bushy eyebrows, and a big nose. He was twenty four or five, but people still called him by his childhood name of "Little Ya". Most days he went out with his leather sack, looking for business in the vicinity. He was just a common man, but honest and well-respected. Everyone around Yung-shan village, near Ch'ao Yüan's villa, knew him.

The year before, there had been several days in a row of rain, and his house was washed away. One day, while he was repairing shoes at the Ti household on the outskirts of Yung-shan village, he was talking about how his house was gone, and how he hoped to find another place to live on the mountain.

Ti said, "There are a few empty buildings in the Ch'aos' villa. I don't know if anyone's moved into them, but let's go take a look together after you've finished those shoes. If nobody has rented them, you can move in there. It would be more convenient for your work, too."

Little Ya finished the shoes and went with Ti to Ch'ao Yüan's villa. Ti spoke to the caretaker there, Chi Ch'un-chiang.

"Little Ya here is looking for a place to live, near our village."

Chi Ch'un-chiang said, "But I've seen your place, when I took my shoes to be repaired. You have your own house, and a nice little one, too, so why are you looking for a place to rent?"

Little Ya told him, "All that rain we had a little while ago washed my house away. If I hadn't put my wife on my back and climbed up a willow, we'd be living in the dragon-king's palace now."

"So that's what happened," said Li Ch'un-chiang, "We have plenty of places here. Usually when people come asking, I say no because I don't like to rent to people I don't know, but if it's you who's moving in, that's very convenient for getting my shoes done. And then, you can help me with caretaking, and we'll be counting on your wife to help out in the kitchen, when it gets busy. Go pick out a place, put a lock on the door, and move in whenever you like."

"Whenever I like?" Little Ya asked, "Then tomorrow is when I like."

That evening, Little Ya left his leather-working tools at Chi Ch'un-chiang's house, and went home feeling much lightened. The next day, he came early with a load of rickety household goods, and moved in with his wife.

His wife came from the T'ang family. She was the daughter of another leather-worker, and just twenty years old. Chi Ch'un-chiang had imagined she would be a typical, rough country woman, but she was a lovely girl, only slightly less gorgeous than the camellia, just a blt less seductive than the peony, in grace inferior only to the crabapple, in fragrance to the plum blossom, in purity to the lotus, and in virtue to the chrysanthremum. She wasn't a famous beauty, but she was a delicate wildflower.

> In her long-sleeved, dark robe
> and Pink gauze pantaloons
> Her skirt kilted up
> Hose pulled snug
> While not as fair as white jade
> No brown tousle-headed dog either
> Neck smooth and unblemished
> Eyes inviting, clear pools
> Darting glances now and then
> Going about in her little felt shoes
> Enticing in so many ways
> And able to take the lead

When Chi Ch'un-chiang saw her, his first thought was, "What's a woman like that doing on the mountain? It's a good thing she has a big, strong husband, so nobody dares try anything. If Master Ch'ao sees, her, I'm afraid he'll start up, but I've already said they could stay here, and I can't send them away now. I'll have to let them stay."

For about a year after that, Little Ya kept a close and jealous watch on his wife. She wouldn't have dare even think a disloyal thought, and the others living around the same courtyard knew better than to be seen talking and joking with her. Chi Ch'un-chiang began to think he had been worried about nothing. After Ch'ao Yüan came to the villa, Ms. T'ang hid in her room, careful not to show her face any more than she had to. However, they weren't rich and had no servants, so she did have to wash her own rice, get water, do her milling and make her bean-curd, and she couldn't hide very effectively.

Ch'ao Yüan had caught a few glimpses of her. He knew there was a beautiful girl living on the premises, and that she would have to come outside sooner or later. He then managed to happen to run into her as she was at the well drawing water, or at the millstone, and when he did, he would find some pretext for talking to her. Ms. T'ang just hung her head and wouldn't return his glances or his remarks.

If Ms. T'ang's heart had been at one with her demeanor, if there had been no discrepancy between her outer show and inner desires, not even Ch'ao Yüan, or even ten Ch'ao Yüans, could have had their way with her. But things like that are like a rock in the privy, stinking and hard and persistent. When Ms. T'ang had seen Ch'ao Yüan, she grew lax in hiding herself. When he walked by, she would would just happen to be standing in her doorway. Even then, when a man talks to you, if you stand there like a pole, he'll look elsewhere, but if you run skittishly off, it's teasing him to pursue. If she had really meant to have nothing to do with Ch'ao Yüan, she should have stayed as far from him as fire from water. Once her rice was washed and dinner done, she should have sat quietly in her room, darning shoes and sewing. There were plenty of people living around the courtyard. It wasn't as if Ch'ao Yüan would have dared push his way past all of them and pull her out of her room, was it?

Instead, Ms. T'ang swore sisterhood with the wives of Ch'ao Chu and Li Ch'eng-ming. The minute Ch'ao-Yüan even blinked, Ms. T'ang ran to the kitchen to help the other two women knead cakes, clean rice, steam buns, and cut rolls. Meanwhile, the three women talked and laughed uproariously. They made so much food, there were always more leftovers than they could use. At first, Little Ya used to come by and check what was going on, and she just told him they were giving her all those leftovers in gratitude for his leatherwork, and her helping out in the kitchen.

Little Ya asked, "Does Master Ch'ao know about all that food they're giving you? I may be poor, but I won't take any leftovers, especially not stolen ones."

Ms. T'ang said, "In a big household, nobody counts every mouthful of food. The master has better things to do than investigating the pantry. He leaves the kitchen to the cooks."

One day, a feast for all the farmers was planned. The women would be making wheatcakes and cooking all day. Little Ya was busy at home, fixing shoes a customer had brought. Ms. T'ang sat by his side, making hemp thread. She didn't go to the kitchen.

Ch'ao Chu's wife burst in on Little Ya and Ms. T'ang. Her sleeves were hitched up, and she carried a willow basket heaped high with snowy steamed buns and rich sliced meat.

"Is your back out or something? Making me come all the way over here with this, instead of coming and getting it yourself," she cried.

Then she saw Little Ya sitting there, working on the shoes, and Ms. T'ang, one fair leg peeking out, twisting hemp thread.

"Oh, I see now why you didn't come help out! You were keeping brother-in-law company."

They talked for a little while about nothing in particular. Then Little Ya thanked her for the food and saw her out.

Back inside he asked his wife, "Who's she calling her brother-in-law?"

"You, who else?"

"How am I her brother-in-law? How are you related to her?"

"She and Ch'eng-ming's wife and I all swore sisterhood."

Little Ya snorted, "What do you want to go sistering and auntying with those old women for?"

"What's wrong with it? What did she ever do to you?"

They fell to gobbling up the buns with such noisy gusto that the old ladies in the courtyeard could hardly keep their mouths from watering.

Little Ya called out, "Old woman! You can call her your sister, if you want, and have her help out in the kitchen, but you listen to me, and don't help where you aren't wanted. No buns are going to keep me quiet, and if I hear the tiniest whisper of a rumor that you're up to anything, it's a white knife in and red out!"

Ms. T'ang flushed bright red, right down to her neck, and glared at him.

"Why do you have to go saying a rotten thing like that? Dumping insults on people! You'd better find a place tomorrow where there aren't any neighbours, so you can stop worrying someone's after your wife!"

Little Ya said, "It's a woman's heart that counts. I don't care if there are neighbours around. A right-hearted woman could live in the middle of an army camp, and then no matter how man men and horses crowd around, they'd be like nothing to her. But a pack of goods who's busy thinking what she shouldn't will mount a stone if there's no man around."

"Anyhow, a man gets the wife he deserves," she said

"I just wish I had life as easy as a woman. I could be a better wife than most, " he said.

Having eaten, Little Ya shouldered his bundle and went out. Ms. T'ang locked the door and scurried out to the kitchen.

Mrs. Li Ch'eng-ming said, "You already ate your fill, sitting there with your legs crossed! What are you doing here now? Well, there's some nice gruel in the pot, so serve yourself."

Ms. T'ang turned her attention to some squash with garlic, sesame oil and laver, which she chased with three bowls of rice gruel.

Ch'ao Yüan had seen Ms. T'ang going to the kitchen, and he tiptoed after her, his hands clasped behind his back.

"Who have we here?" he asked.

Mrs. Ch'ao Chu said, "Little Ya's wife, they live out front."

Ms. T'ang put her bowl down.

"Is that what you serve a guest?" Ch'ao Yüan asked,

"Salted squash? Couldn't you do a little better than that?"

"Some guest! She is a member of the household, after all, and over here every day helping out. Why should we treat her as a guest?"

Ch'ao Yüan left, and Ms. T'ang exclaimed, "I was always sure the master must be such a mean man, but he's really nice."

Mrs. Li Ch'eng-ming said, "Don't believe it. Usually he's impossible to please, but now, with the mistress dead and Aunty Chen in jail, he's trying to get along with the rest of us, that's all."

Ms. T'ang asked, "I heard he paid eight hundred taels for Aunty Chen. She must be something, to be worth so much money! With eight hundred taels, you could make a whole woman out of silver, couldn't you?"

Mrs. Li Ch'eng-ming said, "Listen to her? And what would he do with a lump of silver shaped like a woman? That Aunty Chen is a living treasure, she is."

Ms. T'ang said, "She must be prettier than I can imagine, for so much money."

"Dogs', " said Mrs. Ch'ao Chu, "She's just a human being, with one head and one mouth, one you-know down there, and two breasts. Well, if you want to know what she looks like, she's about the same height as you, and a little fairer but not as pretty around the mouth and nose. She even has great big eyes like yours. I bet you could fit right into her little shoes, too. "

"But this girl can't sing like she did," added Mrs. Li Ch'eng-ming.

"So that's why she cost so much," said Ms. T'ang, "I didn't know she could sing, too. "

Ch'ao Yüan came back to the kitchen and said, "Don't spend all your time yattering away here. Get started on cooking the dinner. The laborers may finish up and go home early. "

"Don't worry, anyway we have a helper now, " said Mrs. Ch'ao Chu.

"You don't need to make her work too hard on a hot day like this," he said.

"We were planning to have her scour the well!" said Mrs. Ch'ao Chu.

"You might not mind that, but I would, " he said.

From that day on, Ch'ao Yüan and Ms. T'ang gradually warmed up to each other. She went back and forth without bothering to evade his glances the way she had before. Whenever he said anything to her, she had an answer on the tip of her tongue. He was all set to make her his own, but those two villainous old ladies, Mrs. Ch'ao Chu and Mrs. Li Ch'eng-ming, were ablaze with jealousy, and they kept their eyes on Ms. T'ang. He would have to wait a long time before they would relax their vigilance.

By now, Ch'ao Yüan was so totally absorbed in trying to lick this sugar off his nose that he had forgotten all about Ms. Ch'in in Lin-ch'ing. He never thought of Chen ko, either. He let Ch'ao Chu take care of Chen ko. For some strange reason, Ch'ao Chu never came to visit his own wife at the villa, and Chen ko never sent any urgent message to Ch'ao Yüan, either. She assumed he was busy with the harvest and so forth. Ch'ao Chu's wife, likewise, didn't feel particularly suspicious about the fact that her husband hadn't been to see her for a long time. Nobody in that household was over-nice.

One day, as the fifth month neared, Ch'ao Yüan said to Mrs. Li Ch'eng-ming and Mrs. Ch'ao Chu, "Here we are at the Tuan-wu festival. Little Ya's wife is over here every day helping out, so let's give her a couple of bolts of summer cloth so she can put together two summer outfits and work here comfortably. "

Ch'ao Chu's wife said, "Why not give us the cloth, and let us each have a new outfit? You don't have to give her anything. I'd advise you to put her out of your mind. I don't care if you want to get married again, but I won't have what you're thinking about going on here. To tell you the truth, I think

Li Ch'eng-ming's wife is an extra pair of hands around here, and she feels the same way about me. Now you want to have little Ya's wife crowded in here with us, too. Just remember there can only be one hero at a time. You can't fool me! Get a hold of yourself. It's only a couple of days until it's time to go back to the city."

Ch'ao Yüan threw his head back and grinned widely.

He tried to gloss over what she'd said by muttering, "Listen to these old women! You're the household patrol, I guess? Keeping your eye on everything?"

With a whole crowd of people living around that courtyard, and the rest of the villa burnt into desolation all around it, thre wasn't any good place for him to have a rendezvous with Ms. T'ang. It looked as if only his eyes would dine, while his belly went hungry.

One day, it was discovered that twenty bundles of the harvested grain was missing. Chi Ch'un-chiang investigated energetically. He took one of the regular laborers with him door to door,and found some of the stolen grain at each house, with the exception of Little Ya's. Little Ya was out all day every day, all day, working, and he was not interested in petty thievery. Ms. T'ang was stuffed so full of Ch'ao Yüan's kitchen leftovers that she felt no interest in stealing grain. When Ch'ao Yüan heard how Little Ya's was the only innocent house, he was thrilled.

"Now I know we're a match made in heaven, " he told himself, "I couldn't have invented a better excuse myself!"

He took the theft as a pretext to evict all the tenants except for Little Ya. First he had them all indicted, but then he relented and said he wouldn't press charges if they would all leave, so they did. Now that he had chased them away, he could see his way clear to Ms. T'ang's door, and only had to make sure little Ya wasn't home. He picked up a pair of shoes, as his excuse and went to their door.

"Little Ya," he said, "Fix the heels on these shoes for me, will you?"

Ms. T'ang answered, "He isn't home. He went out early this morning."

"But I want to wear them today. When's he going to be back?"

"Today's the market. He won't be back at all. Why not take the shoes and go find him at the market?"

"How will I ever find him there? I'll leave the shoes here for him when he gets back."

Ch'ao Yüan, holding his shoes, went inside. He looked and saw that Little Ya was really gone. Then he got up to this and that, and when Ms. T'ang didn't protest was soon up to that and this. No longer mere neighbours, now they were bedmates, and their only worry was that people might find out.

From then on, whenever anyone came to inquire about renting a place, Ch'ao Yüan pretended he didn't like renting to anyone he didn't know personally, and kept them out. When Ch'ao Yüan knew that Little Ya was home, he was sure to stay as far away as possible, and if he did happen to bump into the Yas wouldn't even look Ms. T'ang full in the face. When Ms. T'ang came to help in the kitchen, she no longer joked and chattered the way she used to.

Mrs. Li Ch'eng-ming said to Mrs. Ch'ao Chu, 'It's a good thing you talked to him the other day the way you did. He's given up on her."

Mrs. Ch'ao Chu said, "With him, unless you say everything straight out he'll never give up sniffing around like a dog after shit. He's as bad as a whole temple full of priests. But we know what's what, so it's up to us to keep him from getting up to his tricks."

On the sixteenth day of the fifth month, there was a market fair at Liu market street. It was all of fifty li away.

Little Ya always stayed over and went on to the Liu-hung market on the seventeenth, telling his wife not to expect him until the next day.

This time, Ms. T'ang went right to the kitchen , and gave Ch'ao Yüan the signal. When evening fell, Mrs. Li Ch'eng-ming went home to sleep with her husband, Ch'ao Chu's wife went to her bed, and all settled down for the night. Ch'ao Yüan waited until he thought everyone would be asleep, then ran his fingers threw his hair, threw a heavy cloak over his shoulders, and slipped on his shoes. Then he crept quietly to Ms. T'ang's door. She rushed to the door and pulled him inside. It didn't take a moment before they were up to no good.

It happened that Little Ya did not stay over at the market that night. He got only halfway to the market when he was delayed by work on shoes for a bride's trousseau. That took him the better part of the afternoon. They wanted him to stay so he could finish the shoes the next day.

He said, "Since l live pretty close by, and it's a clear night, I'll just walk back on home. I'll be back tomorrow in plenty of time to finish your shoes."

He strolled back home, and by the time he got there it was past the first watch. The gates were closed. Little Ya called Chi Ch'un-chiang to come open the gate, but Chi was sound sleep, and Little Ya didn't want to keep making a racket. When Ch'ao Yüan heard that Little Ya was back, he wanted to run away, but if he charged out the door, he would probably run straight into Little Ya.

"Don't panic," said Ms. T'ang, "Calm down, and get behind the door. Don't come out. I have a plan."

She put on her trousers but left her upper body nude, and closed the front door. When Little Ya came to his door, he pushed in.

"Who's that?" she called out.

"Me."

"Thank goodness you're home! There's a scorpion crawling around here, and I was so scared. I didn't dare go out for a light. Put your things down and get one, so we can find that scorpion. Otherwise I'll never be able to get to sleep."

She gave him half a stick of incense with which to get a light, and he went. The room was brightly lit by the moon, and nobody would have suspected there was a man hiding behind the door. Ms. T'ang cleaned up the evidence before her husband came back, and Ch'ao Yüan was able to escape undetected.

Little Ya came back with the light, and they inspected the room thoroughly. There wasn't any scorpion, though there were bedbugs, and, fortuitously, a gecko on the wall, caught in the flame's light.

"That's the little bastard," said her husband.

He took off a shoe to smash to Gecko, but she grabbed he hand, "Don't kill it!"

"Why not?' he said, "You made me go out in the middle of the night to get a light and catch him!"

"It isn't as if it was a cold night out, and I just wanted to have a good look and make sure it wasn't a scorpion. Otherwise, I'd be up all night, jumping at every little noise. If you hadn't come back, I wouldn't have been able to close my eyes once. These days, the courtyard is so deserted, and I really get scared. I won't let you come home so late any more."

"The sixteenth is the Liu market, and the seventeenth is the market at Liu-hung. They're only eight li apart. It isn't worth my while to come home between the two."

She asked him, "Are you going to Liu-hung tomorrow?"

"No, I don't think I can finish that trousseau work in two days," he said.

They talked a little more, and did something else, too.

Early the next morning, Little Ya ate some cold cakes, washed down with hot water. Then he took up his bundle, as always, and set out.

Ms. T'ang told him, "Be sure to come home earlier tonight. Don't let a girl die of fear!"

After she had sent him off, she didn't even wash the breakfast dishes before she fixed her hair and face and went back to see Ch'ao Yüan.

"Taste anything bitter?" she asked.

"No, why?" he said.

"I just thought you were so scared your gall was running out of your mouth."

It is true that if you don't want people to know you are doing something, the best way is not to do it in the first place. Every since Ms. T'ang had begun her secret conversations with Ch'ao Yüan, she had become radiantly beautiful. Her hair was that much more carefully done than before, her feet wrapped more tightly and daintily, and her clothes, while coarse, suddenly became dazzlingly clean. Ch'ao Yüan felt sorry she didn't have some better clothes, but was afraid that if he gave her any he would make her husband suspicious, so he gave up the idea.

What Ch'ao Yüan did was to give Ms. T'ang seven or eight taels, which he then pretended he had lost near the main gate. He made a big fuss about it, beating the servants and investigating all the tenant farmers and any other renters left on his property. He made sure everybody heard about his "lost" silver.

"I found the master's silver," whispered Ms. T'ang to her husband.

She showed Little Ya a bundle wrapped in a not-too-new flowered kerchief. Inside there were two blackened silver money cases, and a perfume sac.

"How could you take something that isn't yours?" cried Little Ya, "What would a poor leather-worker like me be doing with that much money? If this comes out, we'll lose everything!"

He wouldn't listen to a word she said. He took the whole package, kerchief and all, and returned it to Ch'ao Yüan, saying that his wife had found it.

Duplicitously, Ch'ao Yüan said, "I'm sure I must have lost it by the main gate when I went out to see about an ox. When I came back, the silver was gone. So it was your wife that picked it up? Well, well. I beat the servants for nothing, then. How amazing that a poor man like yourself returned it, too. I never imagined there were such honest people left in the world! Let me give you half the silver as a reward.

Little Ya said, "I didn't want the whole amount, and I don't want half, either. Yes, I am a poor leather-worker, but I don't have any use for money like this."

He turned abruptly to go. Ch'ao Yüan kept his money, and the next day bought a bolt of pure white summer cloth, four bolts of blue hempen cloth, and two more of Mao-ch'ing cloth, all of which he had Li Ch'eng-ming take to Little Ya.

Li Ch'eng-ming's wife and Ch'ao Chu's wife felt utterly outdone by Ms.

T'ang. These two married ladies were not above making eyes at men and carrying on flirtations, but they were nothing compared to her. Now she had a gown of the summer cloth Ch'ao Yüan had given her, and walked around flaunting it.

Little Ya didn't see any reason to find the gift strange, Ch'ao Yüan didn't have to go to the trouble of hiding it, and Ms. T'ang could enjoy it in public. But it didn't escape the sharp eyes of Mrs. Li Ch'eng-ming and Mrs. Ch'ao Chu, and their increased vigilance forced the lovers to be more careful than ever they weren't caught.

One day, a fine rain was falling softly. Ms. T'ang saw her husband off and went back into the courtyard. Finding it empty of the two older women, she slithered into Ch'ao Yüan's room.

Mrs. Li Ch'eng-ming came out of the mill-house and saw Ms. T'ang's footprint in the mud outside Ch'ao Yüan's door. Mrs. Li pushed the screen aside and there in front of her were Ch'ao Yüan and Ms. T'ang having fun. They couldn't fool her any more. This time it was Ms. T'ang's turn to be terrorized, while Ch'ao Yüan was calmly possessed. A moment later, Ch'ao Chu's wife came in, too.

She said, "When we asked you to come over and help out, we didn't exactly have this type of help in mind, you know. You watch—the minute Little Ya comes back, I'm telling him."

"If you tell him about me, I'll tell your husbands on you, too. Then we'll all be in trouble."

Mrs. Li Ch'eng-ming said, "Our men don't care what we do, so you can tell them all you want as far as we're concerned, but it really is a crime the way you're carrying on with your husband's landlord. We never did anything that bad."

Ms. T'ang said, "Maybe you don't care what I tell your men, but when I tell mine you were the go-betweens and led me right into the young master's bed, I can bet you you won't live long afterwards. My husband holds grudges, and you're starting a quarrel that will cost someone's life."

Mrs. Ch'ao Chu said, "If that isn't the thief accusing the patrol for being out late!"

Ch'ao Yüan said, "The three of you listen to me. We have to decide what we're going to do."

Mrs. Li Ch'eng-ming was ready to walk out, but Ch'ao Yüan had Ms. T'ang hold her back. She sat down beside Mrs. Ch'ao Chu.

The two women said to Ms. T'ang, "We aren't going to stand for this. You're going to get what you have coming."

They grabbed hold of her and stripped her absolutely bare, in front of Ch'ao Yüan, and then gave her the scolding of her life. He sometimes spoke roughly to her, but he'd never spoken to her the way these two did.

But from that day on, the four of them were one happy family. They kept nothing from each other. Ch'ao Yüan finished overseeing the harvest, but he didn't say anything about how long he had been at the villa and how it was about time for him to be getting back to the city to see his mother. He didn't give a thought to Chen ko in jail, either. The three lewd women at his villa had him so entranced he never mentioned leaving. Whenever Little Ya was staying overnight at a market again, Ms. T'ang stayed in the house with Ch'ao Yüan and Mrs. Ch'ao Chu. Li Ch'eng-ming's wife went home every night, so they didn't have to take her into account.

Eventually, Little Ya began to feel an inkling of a suspicion, and when he felt that, he began spying on them by doing things like coming home unexpectedly early to catch them at it. But everything happens when it is meant to, not before. He never could catch them. When he came home, he found his wife sitting calmly in her room, and Ch'ao Yüan hurrying away outside. This went on until the thirteenth day of the sixth month. On that day, Little Ya went to celebrate his sister's birthday. She had married a man from the mountain, only thirty li distant from Yung-shan. Little Ya brought four dried, salted fish, a large lotus root, and some liquor. At the crack of dawn he got up. He told his wife he wouldn't be back that day, and not until the evening cool of the following day.

She saw him out, and then told Ch'ao Yüan and Mrs. Ch'ao Chu what he said. The three of them planned planned to "fight Lü Pu at Po-kou river" that night. Li Ch'eng-ming's wife wanted to stay with them and join in, but, luckily for her, her husband had been stung by a scorpion and was in such pain his bellows shook the ground. She had to go home and take care of him. That left only Mrs. Ch'ao Chu and Ms. T'ang with Ch'ao Yüan. The three of them ate and drank, and then enjoyed the starry night sky, beneath which they gave themselves to wild pleasure, undisturbed by the smallest compunction. Ch'ao Chu's wife became aware of a dampness between her legs, and found, by the light of the moon, she had begun her menses. She went into another room to clean herself, and then she felt so tired and sated she fell asleep where she was.

Ch'ao Yüan put a brazier in front of himself, heated some wine, and drank when he and Ms. T'ang were resting between bouts. They were busy like that until the second watch. Then he went to urinate, and then they drank some more. Then, unfortunately for them, they fell comfortably asleep without the slightest apprehension anyone would see them.

That day, Little Ya did go to his sister's to celebrate her birthday, but when the sun was setting, he turned home. His brother-in-law and his niece all tried to make him stay but he was firm. He picked up a big stick and struck out for home. When he got there, the main gate was locked.

He stood there thinking, "If I start yelling in the middle of the night for somebody to come open the door, it will be a lot of bother for old Chi Ch'un-chiang, and it'll give my wife a chance to cover up what she's been doing. I knew there was something wrong ever since that night she sent me out to get a light. I'll jump up on the wall, and walk along it. I can do that, so I don't need to go in the main gate."

He stuck the stick in the ground, and swung himself up on the wall. The dog barked a couple of times, but quieted down when it heard his familiar voice.

Little Ya hopped off the wall on the inside, and walked to his own house. He felt the door, found it locked, and knew she must be at Ch'ao Yüan's.

He decided he would go inside and have a good look, to be sure his supicions weren't unfounded. He knew Mrs. Li Ch'eng-ming usually went home for the nights, but if she and Mrs. Ch'ao Chu were around, he'd have to be careful of them. He slipped open his own door, put his bundle down inside, and took out of it a curved leather-cutting knife. He put that in his belt. Then he swung himself up on the wall again, and ran along it to Ch'ao Yüan's quarters.

The moonlight was as bright as day. He went into the main east room, where Mrs. Ch'ao Chu lay naked and white as a sheep, a little piece of cloth stuck in her crotch. She was as fast asleep as a dead dog. He turned his head and saw his wife standing there. She didn't make a sound, but turned and led him to the north room.

He thought it was certainly strange, that she was up, and that she didn't say anything when she saw him. He followed her, but she disappeared, and instead he saw the two of them lying in front of him, gleaming in their nakedness, asleep. He looked carefully at them, noting every detail. One of them was Ch'ao Yüan, and the other was without a doubt his wife. Still he thought he had to be absolutely sure. What if he killed an innocent person? That wouldn't do. He lit a lamp from the brazier, and brought it close to the sleeping couple. By its light, he made out his wife's hand on that thing of Ch'ao Yüan's.

He took the knife from his belt, and said, "I'll kill the whore first, but I'll wake him up before I kill him. He's going to know why he's dying."

He split his wife's head on the pillow. Then he ran his fingers through Ch'ao Yüan's hair, pulled it back snugly and wrapped it around his fist.

"Wake up, Ch'ao Yüan! And give me your head!

Ch'ao Yüan opened his eyes, and saw Little Ya. "Don't kill me! Ten thousand's all yours!"

"Who wants your stinking money? It's your dog's head I want."

Ch'ao Yüan screamed for help a few times, and then Little Ya sliced off his head. Little Ya tied the two heads together by their hair. He swing them over his shoulder, put the knife in his belt as before, picked up his stick and jumped up on the wall. He walked all night to reach the city.

Isn't it romantic to die for love?

Chapter Twenty

Ch'ao Yüan comes home in a dream
Magistrate Hsü uproots evil on the road

You played with life and met disaster
It's your mother now who is left grieving and alone
Every one of the five cardinal relations
thrown aside by you
Your wife abandoned
A whore your joy
And in brief, wild pursuit of pleasure
yourself stained

While happiness is waxing full
Tragedy is quickly taking shape
So you were killed in the dark
Your mother left bereaved
Cheated by her grasping in-laws

If it weren't for the good magistrate
and the birth of her late husband's child
She too would have met a bad end
—to the tune "The river all red"

Little Ya had taken the heads of Ch'ao Yüan and Ms. T'ang, tied their hair together, swung them up on his shoulder, and left by way of the wall. As before, he didn't bother with the gate. We won't go into how he got to the city.

Instead, let's hear what was happening to Ch'ao Chu's wife. She slept right until daybreak, when she opened her eyes and remembered how she had gotten her menses the night before. She thought how awful the bloodstain on the floor would look by daylight. She slid on her trousers but left her torso nude, got a basket and put some ash in the basket. She went to scrub the spot out of the floor, but she had only got one foot in the door when she noticed the extreme soundness of Ch'ao Yüan and Ms. T'ang's sleep.

She took a closer look, and her wits flew to the four corners of the earth. She dashed to throw a cloak over herself and ran out in her trousers, calling for Li Ch'eng-ming.

"Help! Someone's killed Ch'ao Yüan and Little Ya's wife!"

Li Ch'eng-ming was struck in a heap at that. He came out to see the two corpses lying there, naked and headless. He and Mrs. Ch'ao Chu looked all over for the heads, but couldn't find them. The pillows were drenched in blood. Li Ch'eng-ming rushed to call the village headman and local watchman, who arrived to see the very dead couple. It was perfectly obvious that they had been caught in the act, but since Little Ya had been at his sister's, and since the main gate and the inner doors were all shut tight and untampered with, who could have gotten in to murder the two? People looked, wide-eyed at each other, and then they all turned their eyes to Mrs. Ch'ao Chu.

They said, "Li Ch'eng-ming's wife always sleeps outside. You're the only one who stays in here. How could they possibly have been murdered without your hearing it? It looks like you did it."

She said, "Oh, no, I went to sleep very early in the east room. How could I have heard anything that was going on in here?"

Chi Ch'un-chiang said, "Then how did you know the female corpse was Little Ya's wife? Since she doesn't have a head?"

Mrs. Ch'ao Chu said, "She may not have a head, but I'd know her feet anywhere. Who else had such little feet?"

The others said, "Never mind all this. Send someone to the city to report it, and someone else to meet Little Ya on his way back and tell him about it."

There was an Important Person present, who wrote out a report of the murder to the subprefectural government. Ch'ao Chu's wife left Chi Ch'un-chiang to stand vigil over the bodies. They covered the bodies with a reed mat off of the floor, and then everyone began to drift away.

At that same moment, Ch'ao Yüan, naked, his hair flying and one hand covering that place, came bloodied and howling into his mother's room.

He grabbed hold of her and cried, "That fox-spirit brought Little Ya to kill me! Oh, it hurts so much!"

Madam Ch'ao began to cry unrestrainedly and her little maid shook her awake.

It was just a dream, after all. Madam Ch'ao was so frightened she broke out in a cold sweat, her heart fluttered, and she shook and shook. She could tell it would be dawn any minute now, so she called a servant to light lamps, got up, and fixed her hair. Then she called Ch'ao Feng, and told him to ride a donkey to the villa and give Ch'ao Yüan the following message:

"The mistress saw an evil dream last night. Young Master, pack your things and come back to the city right now."

Her maids all said, "A fox's revenge? You just had that on your mind because he was always talking about it, and that's why you had that dream. Anyhow, they say 'a bad dream means good luck', so you shouldn't worry about it."

In a few minutes, Ch'ao Feng had the donkey saddled, and he rode under Madam Ch'ao's window to say, "I'm going now, to the city gate, and as soon as it opens, I'll go to the villa."

He rode to the city gate, and waited there a while. The sky lightened, the gate opened, and he was just about to go out of it when what should he see but a fellow with two heads slung over his shoulder, coming into the city! The gate-keeper barred the way and asked what it was all about. The answer was that this fellow had come from the Yung-shan villa, where he had caught a couple of adulterers, see, here are their heads.

The gate-keeper asked, "Who's the man?"

"It's Ch'ao Yüan," said Little Ya.

Ch'ao Feng took a look, and saw that it was indeed.

He said, "Wait a minute! Where was our master sleeping with your wife? How did you catch them at it and get both their heads?"

"In his own room," said Little Ya, "And they're still there, as naked as anyone ever was."

There was no reason now for Ch'ao Feng to go to the villa.

He rushed back to tell Madam Ch'ao, "The young master's been killed."

"Who—who—who told you?" she asked.

"The one who did it. He came walking right into the city, with the two heads over his shoulder."

"Two heads? What do you mean?" she asked.

"The other was the man's wife."

Madam Ch'ao screamed and collapsed, almost dead from the shock, but, thanks to her attendants' ministrations, she came around after a long time.

Crying, she said, "My son! You never would do the right thing, always busy shortening your life with foolish bad behaviour. I always knew you'd come to a bad end, but, even so, I hoped I'd die first, so that at least my son could send me off. Who would ever have guessed that I would live to see you running into your own death! I always knew you were no good, and that's why I tried to hang myself in T'ung-chou. I was all ready to die when those busybodies let me down and revived me. I'm shattered, and no son to hold my funeral. Oh, my bad-hearted son!"

She cried so hard even a stone statue would have shed tears in empathy, even an iron effigy would have lowered its head in sympathetic sorrow.

While she cried, a messenger came from the villa to report the death. At the villa, everyone still thought Ch'ao Chu's wife had killed the two, out of jealousy. They still didn't know that Little Ya had brought the heads to the subprefectural yamen, where he was waiting for the magistrate to open court.

Madam Ch'ao had an urgent message sent to her married daughter, Mrs. Yin, to come look after the house. Then she got ready to go to the villa and take care of the funeral arrangements. She took Ch'ao Shu and the other servants with her, except for Ch'ao Feng, whom she left in the house. She went as fast as she could to the villa, which, luckily, was near a market where fir planks for coffins were stocked. By the time Madam Ch'ao arrived at the villa, it was already the hour of the dragon (8.00 p.m.), Upon arriving, she gave way to tears for a while. Then she ordered the servants to get the coffin and begin preparations for the funeral.

Chi Ch'un-chiang said, "Why should we bother to take care of that woman's corpse? Let her husband do it."

Madam Ch'ao said, "Her own husband's already killed her. If you wait for him to give her a decent burial, she'll be dumped on the roadside for dog-meat. That would be inhuman, and she and my son died for each other's sakes, so let's send them off together."

The servants began running around, making the preparations she had ordered. It was the second half of the sixth month, just when the the beat down at its most fiery. The corpses began to putrefy, and, by the time their funerary clothes were ready, had swelled up so they could hardly be stuffed into the clothes. Eventually they were, and the two headless bodies were laid aside waiting for Ch'ao Feng to retrieve their heads, but Ch'ao Feng still didn't come back. Madam Ch'ao was very worried.

What had happened to the heads was that Little Ya took them to the subprefectural yamen, and laid them on the ground while he waited for the magistrate to open court. A seamless crowd welled around him, and once the word was out that he had killed Ch'ao Yüan, there wasn't one person in the whole crowd who said what a pity that was, or what a shame or that he shouldn't have killed Ch'ao Yüan. There were plenty of people saying how cruel Ch'ao Yüan had been, how sneaky and how all-around bad. With one person giving his example of Ch'ao Yüan's viciousness, and another chiming in with his own example, in no time they had enough to fill an indictment three inches thick, cataloging Ch'ao Yüan's faults.

They said, "Little Ya's a hero and a great man. Anyone else would have squeezed a thousand taels out of a rich guy like that."

Little Ya said, "He tried to give me ten thousand, but I didn't want anything from him."

Soon Magistrate Hsü opened court. Little Ya picked up the heads and followed the paperwork in. The report which the village headman had written stated that Ch'ao Chu's wife had killed the sinful couple out of jealousy, When the headman and watchman reached the city, they heard that it was Little Ya who had killed the two, and they rewrote their report and handed it in. Little Ya had told the headman his full account.

The magistrate asked, Little Ya, "When did the two begin this adulterous affair?"

"I don't know when it started, but there were suspicious things going on for a long time. I was watching them, and I almost caught them a few times, but until last night never could. Last night I finally saw wlth my own eyes what was going on."

The magistrate asked, "Where did the village headman see the bodies?"

"On a summer bed in a large north-facing room. There was a red rug on the bed, with a sky-blue quilt and a bamboo mat over it. A pure-white, light quilt and a bamboo head-rest had fallen to the floor. The female corpse lay on the bed, but the male corpse had fallen half off of it. They looked as if they had been facing north. There was an awful lot of blood on the bed, and a small pool, not so much, in front of the bed."

The magistrate asked Little Ya, "How did you kill them?"

"They were sound asleep when I went in the room. I looked them over and made sure it really was them. I didn't want to kill anyone innocent. There was a brazier by the doorway, and I lit a lantern from it. That's when I saw her hand on his thing. I cut her head off while she was dreaming, and he still didn't wake up. I didn't think he deserved to die without knowing why, so I grabbed him hard by the hair and called out loud, 'Give me your dog's head!' He recognized me, in the light from the lantern and said, 'Don't kill me! Ten thousand's all yours!' and I chopped off his head."

Magistrate Hsü said, "How did you get in?"

"I jumped up on the wall."

"Was there anyone else in the house?"

"A household woman, asleep."

"How did you know she was there?"

"I went to the east room first, and saw they weren't there before I went to the north room."

The magistrate asked, "Who is that kneeling over there?"

Ch'ao Feng, kneeling, petitioned, "I am a member of the deceased Ch'ao Yüan's family, and have here the two heads."

The magistrate said, "Let him have the heads, have coffins bought for the dead, and ten taels to Little Ya so he can buy a new wife."

"I don't want your money," said Little Ya, I have no use for anything that doesn't have my name on it."

The magistrate said, "You could use the money as capital, for your business. Go ahead and take them. Let's have a receipt."

Little Ya said, "Even if you force those ten taels on me, I'll just throw them away. You can keep your dirty money."

The magistrate said, "Who wanted to give it to you? I was just testing you, to see what you'd say. Go sit in custody a while."

Next, the magistrate asked the village headman, "Who was the other woman sleeping in the house."

"It was the wife of Ch'ao Chu."

The magistrate pulled out a bamboo tally and had a mounted messenger get Ch'ao Chu's wife for questioning in the court's evening session. The messenger took the tally, Ch'ao Feng wrapped up the heads, and they all rode back to the villa. Then the messenger got on a donkey, with Mrs. Ch'ao Chu, and with a servant they went back to the yamen.

Madam Ch'ao couldn't stop crying once she had seen the heads. The heads were sewn onto the bodies with needle and thread, the two coffins were nailed shut, and Ms. T'ang's coffin was taken to a temple. Every day, Madam Ch'ao had paper offerings burnt to the dead woman's spirit. She also had services for both of the dead performed, to speed their spirits onto their next abodes.

Ch'ao Yüan's coffin was left in the room where he had died. We won't describe the mourning and condolences.

The messenger had taken Mrs. Ch'ao Chu to the subprefectural yamen, where Ch'ao Chu joined her.

The magistrate opened court, summoned Mrs. Ch'ao Chu and said, "You are going to tell me every detail of the whole affair, from start to finish. I want to understand exactly what happened, and that is all. I have no interest in prosecuting you, but if you are not forthcoming, I shall have a statement beaten out of you."

He had the presses brought out ready for use. She had been present at the trial over Ms. Chi's suicide, and she had witnessed the horror of the torture undergone by Wu and Shao. She was afraid the magistrate really would press her, so she told him everything, exactly as it had happened. Everything you read in chapter nineteen came out of her mouth in court. Otherwise, how would anyone know about it?

The magistrate menaced her, "You should be beaten thirty strokes for your shameless behaviour! On the other hand, you have spoken the truth, so we'll set aside the beating."

Then he asked, "Is there anyone to take charge of her?"

"Her husband, Ch'ao Chu," is here, he was answered.

"Call him forward. You shameless creature—you've taught your wife well, haven't you," the magistrate said, as he pulled out tallies allotting her twenty strokes, after which she was led away by her husband.

Then the magistrate called for Little Ya, had him beaten twenty strokes, and let him go, his back bloody.

Little Ya went back to the villa, picked up his bundle of leather-working tools, and left gladly and for good, not sparing one thought for the disposal of his wife's body. Later, he was seen working in the T'ai-an chou area.

Now the Ch'aos had no close relatives. Those distant relatives they had had made a habit of staying as far away as they possibly could, thanks to the Ch'aos' habit of acting as if those relatives weren't good enough to touch their shoes. There were two unredeemable rascals among those relatives, Ch'ao Money-lover, who was a younger third cousin on Ch'ao Ssu-hsiao's father's side, and Ch'ao Insatiable, Ch'ao Ssu-hsiao's nephew thrice removed. Everybody knew about them. There were a few other flabby no-goods who usually went along with these two. When they heard that both Ch'ao Ssu-hsiao and Ch'ao Yüan were dead, they naturally assumed that Madam Ch'ao had no heirs. They didn't know there was a five-month old baby in Ch'un-ying's womb. Even given the baby's existence, nobody knew yet if it were male or female, so there was no telling whether it could inherit or not.

These relatives descended on Madam Ch'ao, figuring that now she was without heirs all the riches of the Ch'ao household belonged to themselves. Money-lover and Insatiable laid out some money to buy a boar's head, a chicken, smoked fish, and paper offerings, which they carried between them to Madam Ch'ao's. They led the rest of their degraded clan to Madam Ch'ao, with the pretext that they had come to offer condolences. They did manage a few dry-eyed sobs, and then they began to take her to task.

"Everyone knows that while a woman's husband is alive, she should follow him, and then she must follow her son. Now that both your husband and son are dead, we other men of the clan are who you'll have to follow. Why didn't you notify us at once? You're not going to tell us, we hope, that we're still beneath your consideration like that magistrate husband and academician son of yours always implied."

She said, "It must be forty-four or five years since I came into this family, and in all that time, I never once saw any of you pay us a call; not even at New Year's did you come to make obeisance at the alter to your ancestors. Why are you so suddenly eager to claim the connection? What business is it of yours? I don't even know exactly what your relationship is to my late husband. Regardless of that, if you have come on a condolence call, you are of course welcome to my hospitality. If you've come here to accuse me of anything, then I must beg your pardon, as I really have made no preparations for accusers and therefore can offer you nothing to eat in reciprocation of your fine offerings."

Ch'ao Insatiable said, "Forgive me for not greeting you right away as my great-aunt. This here is my grand-dad, and he should have spoken up with a greeting to you as his elder sister in-law. But he never does think before he speaks. We're here to mourn great-uncle's death, and we should all be nice to each other. I'm amazed that he could have insulted you like that, since if people heard we blamed you for not letting us know, they would only laugh at us."

Madam Ch'ao said, "My husband died not too long ago, and my daughter-in-law a year ago. Up until this funeral you didn't seem to be at all worried anyone would be laughing at you. You didn't put in even the ghost of an appearance. Why are you suddenly so worried about what people think?

Ch'ao Money-lover retorted, "What do you mean by that? You never let us know about them dying. We heard of it from perfect strangers, who thought it was pretty funny we didn't know about it! You don't expect us to sit still and let people make fun of us, do you? You sent plenty of mourning cloth to other people, but we never saw even half a length, did we? I think it's too much, and I'm here to tell you so."

Madam Ch'ao said, "If you are here to mourn for the dead, you are welcome. Sit down and have something to eat."

The two sat in the place of honor, and ordered a servant to bring them white mourning clothes.

Madam Ch'ao said, "Since you didn't wear mourning for my husband, you needn't bother for my son."

They said, "Of course you didn't expect us, so you had no preparations made for us. We'll come back on the day of the funeral service, so could you have some mourning clothes made for us? It would look so much better if we could offer incense in our mourning dress. Our wives would like to come and pay their respects, too. It'd be a good idea for you to get everything ready, so you won't have to rush around at the last minute."

Madam Ch'ao said to herself, "I don't mind the cost of a few mourning clothes, but once I let these two in to prey on me, I'll be lost. Oh, Lord in Heaven, have pity on me. Who knows if that baby in her womb is a boy or girl?

How dare they assume I'm all by myself in the world? It looks like I'm feeding wolves here, not dogs."

She had engaged twelve priests to read sutras on the fifteenth and had taken her seat that day in charge of the proceedings, despite the relative's pretensions. The priests began to sound their drums and cymbals, when a black cloud suddenly whirled overhead and began dumping torrents of rain down. The road became a waterscape, and none of those relatives came.

The nineteenth marked the seventh day after Ch'ao Yüan's death. The relatives weren't going to take the chance that it might rain again, so they wanted to go one day ahead of time. Just then Ch'ao Money-lover's wife came down with a pain in heart so bad she was half-dead. Now, a snake without a head won't go anywhere, and even though Ch'ao Insatiable was bad enough on his own account, without his partner he wasn't going to lead the rest. The nineteenth came and went and neither of them visited the villa. Madam Ch'ao took charge of the ceremonies again, closed the funeral, and had the place cleaned and locked up. She left the rest up to Chi Ch'un-chiang and went back to the city. The relatives hadn't counted on her coming back to the city so fast. Ch'ao Money-lover's wife's pains stopped as suddenly as they'd begun, and once more the whole crew of grasping clan members, Money-lover at their head, stood ready like some scurrying army of crabs and shrimps, some halt and some blind and all dragging themselves up the mountain on a few scraggy mounts. The horde of hyenas was surprised and disappointed to hear Madam Ch'ao had already gone back to the city, but while they were there, they went to give a few howls in front of the altar to the dead. Chi Ch'un-chiang rushed to prepare a meal for the crowd of guests, and to have their animals fed. The women found a thousand, no, ten thousand things wrong with Ch'un-chiang's management. They ate up and told him to hand over the key to the harvested wheat,

Chi Ch'un-chiang said, "Yes, we do have some wheat, but I wouldn't dare part with one grain of it unless the mistress told me to."

Ch'ao Money-lover didn't say anything.

Ch'ao Insatiable began cursing Chi Ch'un-chiang, "What kind of dog-faced talk is that? Does your mistress have any children to carry on the family? All this is ours, and there's nothing you can do about it. If we want to be nice, we might let her stay in one of our rooms and give her a few stones of grain every year to live on. If we don't feel like being nice, we'll take a stick and beat her out of here and tell her not to come back."

Chi Ch'un-chiang said, "The way you talk doesn't sound like what I'd expect to hear in Wu-ch'eng. Sounds like a lot of foreign gabble. Besides the fact that she has a daughter, and that one of the women in the household is pregnant, even if she was a lone old woman, she'd have the right to enjoy all the riches her husband worked for! You think you're going to take a stick and beat her out onto the street, do you? Well, I don't agree. You make me so mad I'm practically having a heart attack, and if I didn't have the family's reputation in mind, believe me, I wouldn't be half as polite as I am."

Ch'ao Money-lover stepped forward and slapped Chi Ch'un-chiang in the face, yelling, "You thieving, drivelling slavey! Go ahead and get as mad as you like. See if we care!"

Chi Ch'un-chiang took him by surprise by charging headfirst at his chest. Ch'ao Money-lover landed spread-eagled on his back. Insatiable wrestled with Chi Ch'un-chiang and the rest all crowded around, pretending to counsel the contestants but actually just getting in Chi Ch'un-chiang's way. He was a pretty good fighter, but outnumbered.

Chi Ch'un-chiang's wife saw that her husband was getting the worst of it, and she ran out to get the village headman and to cry, "Help! Robbers in broad day-light!"

She had a couple of bronze cymbals and she created a real racket.

The neighbours and the local watchman gathered around the fighting realtives and Chi Ch'un-chiang. He had a bloody nose, now, and his mouth was bleeding. The wives of the relatives had torn the covers off some quilts, which they made into bags they were stuffing full of wheat. Some were even looting the altar to the deceased, squirreling away incense burners in their trousers and trampling the altar into the ground. Others pulled down the mourning drapes and secreted that cloth around their persons. The headman saw this with his own eyes.

"These are times of peace!" he protested, "how dare you attack people and rob them in broad daylight?"

He threatened to surround the villa and arrest them all, so finally Money-lover and Insatiable released Chi Ch'un-chiang.

They said, "we're here to divide the family property. What are you doing here?"

The headman said, "Madam Ch'ao is still living. She can divide her goods with you if she likes, but you have no business looting like this. Our magistrate now is very strict and fair, not one of the usual bastards, so how dare you carry on like this?"

He was ready to write a report to the subprefectural yamen. They cajoled and threatened him until he relented and only drew up an indemnity for Chi Ch'un-chiang, and ejected the whole crowd from the villa. They made their way back to the city, with their booty of wheat and other things.

Chi Ch'un-chiang wanted to be carried on a plank to the city so that he could file his complaint, despite his wounds.

Everyone counselled him that since his master was dead, and he only one man, he could hardly stand up to all of them. Even if everybody got up to testify to those relative's crimes, it wouldn't root out the problem, and would in fact make them even worse enemies than they were now.

"Listen to us," people said, "Let them be. We say they won't stop now. Back in the city they'll try for more plunder, so let's sit quiet and wait for them to write their own death warrants. Then you'll get your satisfaction."

They commiserated with Chi Ch'un-chiang a while, and then went home.

He had in fact been beaten very badly, so badly he couldn't even get out of bed. He sent a man Into the city to tell Madam Ch'ao what had happened. She too was powerless despite her indignation.

Meanwhile, Money-lover and Insatiable, those two evil men, had been calculating, "We have to strike now, before she steals everything and gives it all to her daughter. If she does that, all we'll have left won't be worth a fart. We'll all move in or her, and watch her every move to make sure not one thing leaves that house for her daughter's. Then we'll make her take out the money and divide it between us, and after that we two will take what we want out of the house. Then you can divide up the rest."

The other relatives agreed. They got together their wives and children and descended on Madam Ch'ao's house. They were all over the place, grabbing tables and chairs, riffling boxes and chests, and stealing food. They ordered the maids and servants around, beat them and persecuted them until the servant's laments shook the earth. On top of that, the relatives were screaming all day long in their own quarrels.

Madam Ch'ao was afraid they would try some dirty trick to make Ch'un-ying lose the baby. She had Ch'un-ying hide in the caretaker's tower, lock the door and keep a folding ladder she only let down for trustworthy people.

Thousands of people crowded around the front gate to watch the plundering of the Ch'ao household. If Heaven were to let those bastards go unpunished after what they did, there wouldn't be any justice in the world, would there?

What these relatives hadn't counted on was the coincidental presence of Magistrate Hsü, who was travelling on an imperial commission. He was just leaving the city when he passed the Ch'aos'. He heard a noise like thousands of troops and horses milling around raucously, and saw a crowd of tens of thousands of people. His sedan chair was immobilized by the crowd.

Magistrate Hsü was quite surprised.

He asked what was going on, and was told, "These are Magistrate Ch'ao's relatives. They're pillaging his house now he and his son are both dead."

Magistrate Hsü asked, "Aren't any members of the family stlll living?"

"Yes, the magistrate's wife."

Hsü called for the crowd to be parted, and had his sedan chair carried in the door. Then he got out of the sedanchair and walked into the main hall. In there, people were having great fun breaking up the place. They weren't aware that there was a magistrate present.

He asked someone if there was a back door, and was assured there was. He ordered the back door blocked and all the plunderers beaten fifty strokes. Two men struggled out of the crowd and ran towards the magistrate. Their hair had come loose, and their faces were bloody. Their bodies were green, red, purple and black, just like dyers', and their trousers were torn to bits. They knelt, kowtowed, and begged for mercy.

The magistrate looked at Ch'ao Feng and said, "This is the man who took the heads back the other day! What are you doing here plundering the house?"

Ch'ao Feng said, "I'm not, I'm a member of the household, and they've been beating me up."

The magistrate asked, "If you belong to this household, will you tell me where your mistress is?"

"She's almost persecuted to death," Ch'ao Feng said.

"Has she received a title?"

"Yes, twice."

"Then bring me the Lady Ch'ao."

"She's surrounded by a bunch of women who are holding her prisoner," Ch'ao Feng told him.

Magistrate Hsü had one of his yamen servants go with Ch'ao Feng to request Madam Ch'ao's presence out front. There were, as Ch'ao Feng had said, a number of fierce-looking women surrounding her and securing her as firmly as if she had been glued to the spot. They weren't about to let her go, either.

The yamen servant asked, "Which is Mistress Ch'ao?"

She answered tearfully, identifying herself. The yamen servant drove the other women away in ignominious defeat. Madam Ch'ao ordered fresh mourning robes, which she put on. Then two wounded maids supported her out to the magistrate. She prostrated herself before him.

Magistrate Hsü knelt correctly at the lintel, returning her courtesy.

Then he stood, and said, "Please calm yourself, Lady Ch'ao. Tell me what has happened, from start to finish."

She told him, "We don't have any close relatives. These people are distantly related to us. In the over forty years I've been married into this family, not one of them so much as showed his face to me. None of them came to burn incense or paper offerings at my daughter-in-law's funeral last year, or my husband's funeral recently. Now that my poor, worthless son is dead, they have all come running claiming that everything in the house belongs to them and ready to chase me out. Yesterday they were at our villa, which they stripped bare of everything of value. They even stole the incense burners and funeral drapes from my son's memorial, and beat the caretaker almost to death! Now they have brought their wives and daughters here, and they've chosen what rooms they'll have after they throw me on the street without one rag to call my own. I'm afraid the women are going to give me a body search to make sure I haven't concealed any valuables. Even with your honor here, they won't let me be. Your man can testify to that, because he saw it with his own eyes."

The magistrate asked, "How many people are there in all?"

"Eight men and fourteen or fifteen women."

"They must have a leader. What is his name?"

"Two. One is Ch'ao Money-lover, and the other is Ch'ao Insatiable."

"And where are those two now?"

"Inside."

The magistrate said, "Have the eight men manacled and brought out here."

A bunch of yamen servants ran in and manacled six men. They were short by two. The magistrate asked where those two could have escaped to.

Madam Ch'ao said, "The wall is too high for them to jump over. They must be hiding inside."

The magistrate told his men, "Search again—carefully."

One of the yamen servants told him, "But we did, everywhere. The only place we haven't searched is the caretaker's tower, and there isn't any ladder. Maybe they hid up there."

Madam Ch'ao said, "There's nobody up there except for a pregnant concubine. I was afraid they'd bring on a miscarriage with their violence, so I locked her up there with a folding ladder."

"What is this about a pregnant concubine?" asked Magistrate Hsü.

"She's my husband's concubine."

"How many months pregnant?"

"Five months now."

"But if he left a pregnant concubine, how can anyone be sure she won't have a son?"

The magistrate ordered his yamen servants to search inside again and bring out the two ringleaders. The yamen servants went in, turned the place upside down and found Money-lover hiding by the Buddhist altar. Now they only had to find Insatiable.

A maid said, "I saw a man running into the mistress' room."

The magistrate sent a man in there to get Insatiable, but there wasn't a sign of him in the room. The man pulled a pile of quilts and clothes off of the bed and there was Insatiable, who had been huddled up under the quilt. The servant clapped a chain on Insatiable's neck. Insatiable knelt and began pulling stotlen goods out of his clothes, trying to bribe the servant.

"Oh, please, I'm begging you, spare my life," he kept repeating.

Insatiable's wife, Ms. Sun, too, came to kneel beside her husband and beg for clemency.

"Just let him go and I'll do whatever you say, " she said.

The yamen servant said, "If I let you go, I can tell you that the magistrate won't let me go! What could I possibly want that you could give me?"

He led Insatiable, chained, back to the magistrate.

The magistrate asked, "Where was he hiding? You took quite a while finding him."

The yamen servant told him, I was looking all over, and then a maid told me she had seen him run into the mistress' room. I went in there, but I still couldn't find him. Then I found him, hiding under her quilt. He had a big bundle of things under his clothes that he took out and tried to bribe me with."

"Now, that's detestable," said the magistrate, "Where are those things now?"

"I gave them to his wife."

The magistrate ordered the women called forward and chained. A yamen serant took the fetters back. When those women saw what was happening, they suddenly became very friendly to Madam Ch'ao's women, calling them "dear elder sister" and "good little sis." They crawled into the oven and under tables, and tried to act like cooks or maids on their way to clean the outhouse, bucket in hand. After the way they had pushed around everyone in the Ch'ao household, it wasn't as if any of Madam Ch'ao's women would feel affectionate enough to cover up for these women. On the contrary, Madam Ch'ao's women led the yamen servants straight to the intruders, who were fettered and led away one after the other. The serving women were much more efficient than the manservants had been in running down their quarry. All fourteen were taken, not one short.

Reader! Just imagine how they looked:

> Some with features so lumpy
> Their ogreish expression could not be read
> Some chimerical as raksha demons
> Others sleek and seductive as fox-spirits
> Others still wriggling around apeishly as the monkeys
> Sun Wu-k'ung the Monkey King threw out of
> the Jade palace.
> At the same time resembling the crowd of vengeful
> ghosts who drove Mulien through Hell,

The magistrate asked Madam Ch'ao, "Are these all of the women?"

"Yes, all fourteen.

The magistrate called all of Madam Ch'ao's women to come out. They did, cringing reluctantly. He told them to search the female relatives. They did, and found rings, clasps, bracelets, hairpins, and pearl circlets. The magistrate had this inventoried and returned to Madame Ch'ao. He called for a midwife.

Now the clanswomen worried, "He'll probably want to have her stick her hands up us to be sure we haven't hidden anything there," and they looked back and forth at each other, scared into quivering jelly.

The midwife came, and the magistrate asked her, "Are you an obstetrician?"

She didn't know what that meant.

The other women told her, "His Honor's asking if you're a midwife."

"Yes, Sir!" she replied.

The magistrate turned to Madam Ch'ao and said, "Have that pregnant girl brought here."

Madam Ch'ao took out the key to the tower, gave it to Mrs. Ch'ao Shu and ordered the ladder to be brought. She called Ch'un-ying to be brought in front of the magistrate. Before long, Mrs. Ch'ao Shu came back, with Ch'un-ying.

> Not a ravishing seductress
> But dressed in the shy beauty of household virtues
> Her little feet hidden by the white mourning skirt
> Elegant jade fingers secreted beneath long sleeves
> Her age sixteen or seventeen
> Her baby due in the eleventh or twelfth month

Madam Ch'ao said, "Kneel and greet the magistrate."

The magistrate stood to receive Ch'un-ying's four bows of greeting, then said, "Midwife, take this lady to a quiet place and examine her to ascertain whether she is in fact pregnant."

Madam Ch'ao suggested the room used to receive guests.

The midwife took Ch'un-ying in there, and felt around a while before taking Ch'un-ying's pulse. Then the magistrate told Ch'un-ying to retire.

The midwife said, "A very healthy pregnancy, about five months along. Her pulse indicates a boy."

"And have you examined the other women?"

"Yes, I have."

The magistrate turned to Madam Ch'ao and said to her, "Congratulations, Lady Ch'ao. I always say a good person won't be left the last of his family. When is the baby due?"

Madam Ch'ao said, "In the eleventh month, or the beginning of the twelfth month."

"When did your husband pass away?" he asked.

"He took her as his concubine on the twelfth day of the second month, and died on the eleventh day of the third month," she said.

The magistrate calculated that to himself, and saw that it fit perfectly.

He said, "Those rascals are detestable. Here they were rushing in stirring up all kinds of rumours before your family's succession was even settled! When the baby is being born, notify the yamen. This midwife will oversee the birth."

Having finished, he told Madam Ch'ao she could retire to her rooms. She bowed deeply in gratitude. He bowed back, walked out the door, called for his sedan-chair, and had Money-lover and Insatiable taken away to the yamen. The other relatives were still standing there. He had them beaten thirty strokes each, and released. Next he had the clanswomen lined up in groups of four or five, to get ready for their beatings.

Madam Ch'ao told Ch'ao Feng to petition the magistrate, "My mistress begs your honor to consider that if their husbands had not led them into this, they would never have dared behave as they did. Since Your Honor has already beaten the men, she hopes you will extend your clemency to the women, and apologizes for not coming out to say this herself."

The magistrate said, "But it was these women who led the men in to search and plunder your house. How can Lady Ch'ao speak up for them? If it were a small offense, I would let them off with a light punishment, but this sort of brazen robbery deserves a public beating to show people we won't have it."

Madam Ch'ao sent Ch'ao Shu out with another message saying she begged clemency for the women. If the magistrate had ever meant to beat those women, they would have been a bloody pulp by this time. He wanted the clanswomen to feel indebted to Madam Ch'ao for his clemency, so he pretended to let Madam Ch'ao argue him out of the beatings.

He sent in the reply, "We will be kind to the sluts this time, but if they come thieving again, I will be here on this street, seeing them beaten."

He asked why the neighborhood headman and local watchman had not come forward.

The headman walked forward, leading the watchman, "Here we are, Sir."

The magistrate, "Aren't you in charge of this street?"

"Yes, it's our's," they answered.

"You're certainly doing a fine job of policing it, aren't you? Very fine headman and watchman you are! You didn't restrain these hooligans or report them to the yamen. Twenty strokes each."

He got back into his sedan chair and had Money-lover and Insatiable taken back to the yamen. There, they were each beaten forty heavy strokes, and pressed. In addition, Money-lover got a hundred strokes with a pole and Insatiable got an extra hundred for having the nerve to hide in Madam Ch'ao's bed, two hundred in all. The jailers were told to take the two back to jail and let them recuperate a month, but not allowed to die.

Here was a clear example of Heaven not allowing heinous behaviour. It must surely have been spirits that took the magistrate on the road the day he did, spirits who urged the plunderers to make a racket like demons in Hell, and spirits that gathered the crowd around the Ch'aos' house that day.

Magistrate Hsü was there that day to hear it all with his own ears and see it with his own eyes. He didn't need to ask for anyone's testimony in order to take care of it promptly, neatly and with not one loose end. Indeed, it must have been spirits that drew his eyes to Madam Ch'ao's plight. How many hundreds of Madam Ch'aos never do draw a magistrate's eye? Without divine intervention, she would never have won a court case, not even if they dug her eyes out.

All the people on the street coalesced into a great crowd and cried aloud, "His wisdom is divine!"

"He is our father and mother!"

They said he had taken care of it all just as he would have overseen his own descendents' affairs, decisively eliminating the immediate threat and wisely taking precautions for future stormy weather.

They all agreed one had to stop and think once in a while, divine wisdom was right there to see if we only looked.

They all hoped Ch'un-ying would have a son, so that the magistrate's tender solicitude would not be in vain. If you want to find out whether she did, you will have to read on.

Selected Bibliography

Editions of *Hsing-shih Yin-yüan chuan* 醒世姻緣傳

Hsing-shih Yin-yüan chuan 醒世姻緣傳. Beijing: Wen-hsüeh Ku-chi Kan-hsing she, 1988. Facsimile edition of 1768 edition found in Tientsin.

Hsing-shih Yin-yüan chuan 醒世姻緣傳. Shanghai: Shanghai Ku-chi ch'u-ban she, 1981. This edition is in three volumes and is part of *Chung-kuo Hsiao-shuo Yen-chiu Tzu-liao Ts'ung-shu* 中国小説研究資料叢書. It contains notes by Huang Hsiao-ch'iu 黄萧秋.

Hsing-shih Yin-yüan chuan 醒世姻緣傳. Taipei: Shih-chieh Shuchü, 1979. This edition is in two volumes. It contains a preface by Li Hung-ch'iu 李鴻球 part of Hu Shih's article cited below, the articles by Ch'ao T'iao-kuang and Wang Su-ts'un listed below and some quotations relating to attribution of authorship to P'u Sung-ling. Proper names are underlined.

Hsing-shih Yin-yüan chuan 醒世姻緣傳. Taipei: Wen-yüan Shu-chü, 1980. This edition is in one volume. Its main virtue is large print

Research

Chao T'iao-kuang 趙苕狂. "*Hsing-shih Yin-yüan chuan k'ao*" 醒世姻緣傳考. Reprint in Shih-chieh edition of the novel above.

Chu Yen-ching 朱燕靜 *Hsing-shih Yin-yüan chuan yen-chiu* 醒世姻緣傳研究. Taipei: Master's essay for Kuo-li Ta-hsüeh chung-kuo wen-hsüeh yen-chiu so. 1978.

Hu Shih 湖適. "*Hsing-shih Yin-yüan chuan* k'ao" 醒世姻緣傳考. In *Hu Shih Wen-lsun* 湖適文存. Taipei: Yuan-t'ung, (rpt) 1953, 4: 319-84.

Hsu Shuo-fang 徐朔方. "Lun *Hsing-shih Yin-yüan chuan* yi chi t'a he *Chin P'ing Mei* ti kuan-hsi"
論醒世姻緣傳以及它和金瓶梅的關係
In *She-hui k'o-hsüeh chan-hsien* 社会科学戰綫. 1986, 2: 278-97.

Liu Chieh-p'ing 劉階平. *"Hsing-shih Yin-yüan Chuan* ti tso-che i-wen" 醒世姻緣傳的作者疑問 . In *Chung-kuo i-chou* 中國一週 , 1953, 141: 22.

Liu Chieh-p'ing 劉階平. *"Hsing-shih Yin-yüan chuan* ti tso-che Hsi Chou Sheng K'ao-yi" 醒世姻緣傳的作者西周生考異 . In *Shu-mu Chi-kan* 書目季刊 , 1966, 10: 3-11.

Lu Ta-huang 路大荒. "Liao Chai ch'uan Chi chung-ti *Hsing-shih Yin-yüan chuan yü ku-tzu chi ti tso-che wen-ti"* 聊齋全集中的醒世姻緣傳与鼓詞集的作者問題 . In Wen *Hsüeh Yi-ch'an Hsüan-chi*(2)文学遺产選集,一輯.Beijing: Wen-hsüeh Yi-chan Pien-chi bu, ed., Tso-che Chu-ban she, 1957 (303-309).

Matsueda Shigeo 松枝 茂夫. "Sei-sei In-en den no Hanashi"醒世姻緣傳の話. In Matsueda, *Chugoku no Shosetsu* 中國の小說. Hakujitsu Shoin, 1948 (42-96).

Min Yu民猶. "P'ing *Hsing-shih Yin-yüan chuan"*評醒世姻緣傳.In *Wen-hsüeh Fu-kan* 文學副刊 , December 4, 1933, 309: 11.

Plaks, Andrew. "After the Fall: *Hsing-shih Yin-yüan chuan* and the Seventeenth-Century Chinese Novel". In *Harvard Journal of Asiatic Studies,* December 1985, Vol. 45 no. 2: 543-580.

Ts'ao Ta-wei 曹大為. "Hsing-shih *Yin-yüan chuan-ti* pan-ben yüan-liu he ch'eng-shu nien-dai"世姻緣傳的版本源流和成書年代.In *Wen Shih,* 文史, 1985, 23: 217-38.

Wang Chi-chen, *"Marriage as Retribution."Renditions,* 1982, 17-18: 41-94.

Wang Shou-yi 王守義. *"Hsing-shih Yin-yüan chuan-ti ch'eng-shu nien-tai"* 世姻緣傳的成書年代 . In *Kuang-ming Jih-pao* 光明日報, May 28, 1961: 4.

Wang Su-ts'un 王素存. *"Hsing-shih Yin-yüan* tso-che Hsi Chou Sheng K'ao" 醒世姻緣作者西周生考. In *Ta-lu Tsa-chih* 大陸雜誌, 1958, 16-1: 73-75. (Also reprinted in Shih-chieh edition of the novel above).